Philosophical Essays

D1082400

G. W. Leibniz

Philosophical Essays

Edited and Translated by
Roger Ariew
and
Daniel Garber

Hackett Publishing Company
Indianapolis & Cambridge

For the next generation,
David, Elisabeth, Hannah, and Daniel

The authors are grateful to Richard Arthur, David Blumenfeld, Stuart Brown, Daniel Cook, Alan Gabbey, Nicholas Jolley, Harlan Miller and M. A. Stewart, for their thoughtful suggestions for the changes that appear in this printing. We especially appreciate the care with which Jonathan Bennett worked through our text and suggested many changes, greatly improving the text.

Copyright © 1989 by Roger Ariew and Daniel Garber

All rights reserved
Printed in the United States of America

25 24 23 22   9 10 11

Cover design by Listenberger Design & Associates
Interior design by Dan Kirklin

For further information, please address
Hackett Publishing Company, Inc.
P.O. Box 44937
Indianapolis, Indiana 46244-0937

www.hackettpublishing.com

Library of Congress Cataloging-in-Publication Data
Leibniz, Gottfried Wilhelm, Freiherr von, 1646–1716.
    Philosophical essays / edited and translated by Roger Ariew and Daniel Garber
       p.   cm.
    Bibliography: p.
    Includes index.
     ISBN 0-87220-063-9—ISBN 0-87220-062-0 (pbk.)
     1. Philosophy—Early works to 1800. I. Ariew, Roger.
II. Garber, Daniel, 1949– . III. Title.
B2558   1989   88-38259
193—dc19   CIP

ISBN-13: 978-0-87220-063-0 (cloth)
ISBN-13: 978-0-87220-062-3 (pbk)

The paper used in this publication meets the minimum requirements of American National Standard for Information Sciences—Permanence of Paper for Printed Library Materials, ANSI Z39.48-1984.

Contents

Part II. Leibniz on His Contemporaries

Introduction

GOTTFRIED WILHELM LEIBNIZ was born on July 1, 1646, in Leipzig. His father, Friedrich, a scholar and a Professor of Moral Philosophy at the University of Leipzig, died in September 1652, when Leibniz was only six years old. But despite his father's early death, the younger Leibniz was later to recall how his father had instilled in him a love of learning. Learning was, indeed, to become an important part of his life. Leibniz began school when he was seven years old. Even so, he later describes himself as self-taught.[1] Leibniz seems to have taught himself Latin at age seven or eight, in order to read editions of Livy and Calvisius that fell into his hands; as a result, he was allowed admission into his late father's extensive library. There he read widely, but concentrated especially in the Church Fathers and in the Latin classics. Leibniz attended university from age fourteen to age twenty-one, first at the University of Leipzig (1661–1666) and then at the University of Altdorf (1666–1667), graduating with degrees in law and in philosophy. He was quickly recognized as a young man of great promise and talent and was invited to join the faculty at the University of Altdorf. He chose instead to go into public service. Under the patronage of Baron Johann Christian von Boineburg, Leibniz entered the service of the Elector of Mainz and occupied a number of positions in Mainz and nearby Nuremburg. There he stayed until he was sent to Paris in spring 1672 on diplomatic business, a trip that deeply affected his intellectual development.

The intellectual world of the late seventeenth century was very exciting indeed. The century began still very much under the influence of the Aristotelian philosophy that had dominated European thought since the 13th century, when the bulk of the Aristotelian corpus was rediscovered and translated from Greek and Arabic into Latin. But much had happened by the time Leibniz went to school. A new philosophy had emerged from figures like Galileo and his students, Torricelli and Cavalieri, from Descartes and his numerous camp, from Gassendi, Pascal, Hobbes, and from countless others. Not without a fight and not without hesitations, the substantial forms and primary matter of the schoolmen had given away to a new world, the mechanist world of geometrical bodies or atoms in motion. Together with this new world had come new mathematical tools for dealing with the new geometrical bodies. But this new world view raised new problems as well, including, among others, problems of necessity, contingency, and freedom in a world governed by laws of motion, problems connected with the place of the soul and its

---

1. See below, p. 6.

immortality, and problems concerning God and his creation, sustenance, and ends.

Leibniz knew little of the new philosophy before 1672. He was originally brought up in an older tradition of Aristotelian Scholasticism, supplemented with liberal doses of Renaissance humanism. He reports much later in life that he was converted to the new mechanism at age fifteen, in 1661 or 1662, presumably, and reports having given up Aristotle for the new philosophy.[2] But even so, he later confesses that the knowledge he had of the moderns was quite slim at that time, and despite his enthusiasm, the considerable amount of work he did in what he took to be the new philosophy was the work of an amateur.[3]

When in Paris from 1672 to 1676, Leibniz made his entrance into the learned world and did his best to seek out the intellectual luminaries that made Paris an important center of learning. Most important, he came to know Christiaan Huygens, under whose tutelage Leibniz was introduced to the moderns. Leibniz quickly progressed, and in those years he laid the foundations for his calculus, his physics, and the central core of what was to become his philosophy.

Before Leibniz returned to Germany in December 1676, he stopped in England and in Holland, where he met Spinoza. Both Boineburg and the Elector of Mainz had died while he was in Paris. Leibniz returned to the court of Hanover as a counselor. Though he often traveled and took on responsibilities elsewhere, Hanover was to be his main home for the rest of his life. Leibniz took on a wide variety of tasks, both for the court at Hanover and for his numerous other employers. He served as a mining engineer, unsuccessfully supervising the draining of the silver mines in the Harz mountains, as the head librarian over a vast collection of books and manuscripts, as an advisor and diplomat, and as a court historian. In this later capacity, Leibniz wrote a geological history of the region of Lower Saxony, the *Protogaea*, that proved to be an important work in the history of geology when it was finally published in 1749, many years after his death. In this connection he also published a number of volumes of the historical documents he found in the archives he combed, looking for material for his history, and he undertook some of the earliest research into European languages, their origins, and their evolution.

But all the while, through a succession of employers at Hanover and elsewhere, Leibniz continued to develop the philosophical system he had started in Paris and before, in a series of essays, letters, and two books. In metaphysics, the unpublished "Discourse on Metaphysics", composed in 1686 but anticipated in earlier writings, developed themes discussed in the letters to Arnauld written in that and the following years. Themes from the "Discourse" also appear, somewhat transformed, in the "New System of Nature," which Leibniz published in 1695—the first public exposition of his metaphysical

---

2. See Leibniz to Nicolas Remond, 10 January 1714, G III 606, translated in L 655.
3. See the letter to Foucher, below pp. 1–5. Some of his early physics is discussed in the "Specimen of Dynamics"; see below pp. 117–38.

system—and again in the unpublished essay "On the Ultimate Origination of Things" of 1697 and again in the important essay "On Nature Itself," published in 1698. These themes appear further transformed in the late summaries of his doctrines, the unpublished "Principles of Nature and Grace" and "Monadology." Behind the metaphysics of these essays is Leibniz's program for logic and a universal language, developed most conspicuously in a remarkable series of papers from the late 1670s and 1680s, in which he explicates the concept of truth which he draws upon in the celebrated characterization of the individual he gives in section 8 of the "Discourse." Leibniz was also deeply involved with the study of physics. The most extensive account of his physics is found in his *Dynamics* (1689–91), in which he sets out the basic laws of motion and force. This work was never published, but Leibniz was persuaded to publish an essay based on it. The essay "A Specimen of Dynamics" appeared in 1695; it contained a discussion of the metaphysical foundations of his physics. In the course of articulating and defending his own view, Leibniz differentiated his conception of physics from that of the Cartesians and the Newtonians and related his view to that of the schoolmen; to those ends he maintained an extensive circle of correspondents, including Huygens, De Volder, Des Bosses, and Clarke. Theology was a constant theme; it became central in the *Theodicy* of 1710, one of two philosophical books Leibniz wrote. His other philosophical book was the *New Essays on Human Understanding*, finished in 1704 but never published. The *New Essays* were meant as a response to Locke's *Essay Concerning Human Understanding*, but Locke's death in 1704 caused Leibniz to withhold publication. In general, Leibniz was an avid reader, reading and reacting to the thought of his contemporaries. In addition to the *New Essays* and other writings on Locke, Leibniz left detailed essays and notes on Hobbes and Spinoza, Descartes and Malebranche, Newton and even the very young George Berkeley, to name but a select few of those who caught Leibniz's attention.

It is natural enough to try to find order in this apparent chaos, to try to identify *the* Leibnizian doctrine of one thing or another, or to try to find the single key to Leibniz's thought, the premise from which everything follows neatly. No doubt this can be done, to some extent, and an orderly Leibnizian philosophy can be reconstructed from the somewhat disorderly notes Leibniz left. But it is also important to be sensitive to the sometimes subtle, sometimes not so subtle changes as Leibniz develops a doctrine, first trying one thing, then another, looking at the world of his philosophy from different points of view.[4] It is also important to appreciate not only the philosophical premises Leibniz uses, but also the different historical strands he attempts to weave together. Late in life Leibniz told one correspondent, Nicolas Remond, that he had always tried "to uncover and re-unite the truth buried and scattered through the opinions of the different sects of philosophers." Leibniz continued: "I have found that most sects

---

4. For an elegant example of a study of Leibniz from this point of view, see Robert M. Adams, "Leibniz's Theories of Contingency," in Hooker, ed., *Leibniz*.

are correct in the better part of what they put forward, though not so much in what they deny. . . ."⁵ In this way Leibniz hoped to unite Catholicism and Protestantism, Hobbesian materialism with Cartesian dualism, and the mechanism of the moderns with the substantial forms of the schoolmen.

Leibniz died in his bed in Hanover on November 14, 1716. The last of his many employers, Georg Ludwig, had been in London since succeeding to the throne of England as George I some two years earlier. But Leibniz was not welcome there. The official reason was that Leibniz was to stay in Hanover until the history of the House of Hanover was close to complete. But there was also great hostility at court to the then elderly counselor. Important too must have been the protracted debate between Leibniz and Newton over the priority of the discovery of the calculus, which had been going on for some years and had taken on decidedly nationalistic overtones. When Leibniz died in Hanover, what was left of the court failed to attend his otherwise proper funeral. But though his immediate fellows may not have appreciated him, he had already become extremely well known and respected by the time of his death. He never founded a school of thought, as Descartes before him had, but even after his death, his works continued to be published and his views discussed.⁶

Principle of Selection and Rationale for the Volume

PREPARING AN EDITION of Leibniz's writings in English translation is a delicate business. There is nothing in Leibniz's enormous corpus that corresponds to Descartes's *Meditations*, Spinoza's *Ethics*, or Locke's *Essay*, no single work that stands as a canonical expression of its author's whole philosophy. Although works like the "Discourse on Metaphysics" and the "Monadology" are obviously essential to any good collection of Leibniz's writings, neither of these nor any other single work is, by itself, an adequate exposition of Leibniz's complex thought. Unlike his more systematic contemporaries, Leibniz seems to have chosen as his form the occasional essay, the essay or letter written about a specific problem, usually against a specific antagonist, and often with a specific audience in mind. Even Leibniz's two mature philosophical books, the *New Essays* and the *Theodicy*, read this way, as collections of smaller essays and comments, only loosely bound together, almost as an afterthought. The problem of coming to grips with Leibniz's thought is greater still when we take account of the range of his work, notes, letters, published papers, and fragments, on a variety of philosophical, theological, mathematical, and scientific questions, written over a period of

---

5. Leibniz to Remond, 10 January 1714, G III 607, translated in L 655.
6. For a fuller account of Leibniz's life and works, see E. J. Aiton, *Leibniz, A Biography* (Bristol, 1985), and Kurt Müller and Gisela Krönert, *Leben und Werk von Gottfried Wilhelm Leibniz: eine Chronik* (Frankfurt, 1969).

more than fifty years. In addition, there is the problem of the original-language texts. While there are some good editions of individual works, there is no critical edition of the Leibnizian corpus available even now; the scholars at work on the so-called Academy Edition, in progress for over sixty years, are still in the process of completing the definitive edition of what most scholars consider Leibniz's juvenilia. The problems facing editors of a selection of Leibniz's works are immense, and the choices are difficult; the editors must be aware of the needs of students and scholars and, most of all, the need to present a fair and balanced view of Leibniz's philosophy, all within a very limited volume.

Our goals in this book are to collect, translate, and annotate a selection of Leibniz's philosophical works that, as a whole, will give an accurate picture of Leibniz's mature philosophical thought. Part I of the collection consists of a selection of essays, papers, and letters that together provide materials for the study of Leibniz's main doctrines. We have sought to include the "standard" texts, the "Discourse on Metaphysics," "Monadology," "New System of Nature," etc., which are essential to an understanding of Leibniz. But we have also included a selection of lesser-known pieces from Leibniz's mature thought—the late 1670s on—that deal with Leibniz's program for logic, his various accounts of contingency and freedom, and his account of body. In this part of the collection, we arrange the pieces in the order of their composition (as much as possible—dating is sometimes problematic) to remind the reader that chronological considerations can sometimes be helpful in sorting out a philosopher's thought.

However, it is difficult to understand and appreciate Leibniz's thought when it is detached from its historical context. Hence, in Part II of the collection, we present a selection of Leibniz's writings about other philosophers. The figures we have chosen to emphasize are the ones most often discussed in connection with Leibniz: Hobbes, Descartes, Spinoza, Malebranche, Locke, and Berkeley. In addition, we have included some of Leibniz's philosophical writings on Newton, both for the light they shed on Leibniz's own philosophy and to emphasize the extent to which Leibniz was involved in the scientific debates of his day. We hope that the writings in this section will allow the reader to see how Leibniz saw his contemporaries. The case can be made, we think, that Leibniz's thought can *only* be understood fully in the context of the contrasts he draws between his thought and that of others.

Many of the pieces included are new (and, we hope, better) translations of familiar material already available in English. In addition, we are including as much important but currently neglected material as we can, translations of never-before-translated essays and letters that deserve to be known better, and translations of significant pieces that are either currently unavailable in English or available only in unsatisfactory translations. Our main source of original language texts is C.I. Gerhardt's nineteenth-century editions of Leibniz's writings; with all their shortcomings, they are, unfortunately, the best and most comprehensive collections of Leibniz's writings currently available. We have supplemented Gerhardt's texts with other editions, including the earlier collections of Dutens, Erdmann, and Foucher de Careil, more recent collections of manuscripts omitted by Gerhardt, such as the editions of Couturat and Grua, and recent editions based on manuscripts unavailable to Gerhardt, such as Lestienne's edition of the *Discourse* and Rodis-Lewis's edition of the *Correspondence with Arnauld*. We have also consulted the previews of Academy Edition volumes yet to come out—what they call the *Vorausedition*—for the best current information concerning texts and dating, when available.

In translating the texts, we have aimed for a balance between accuracy and literal translation, keeping in mind the needs of the student reader. Our translations are supplemented by (i) brief headnotes, setting the context for individual selections; (ii) explanatory historical and philosophical footnotes (including cross-references to Leibniz's other essays and to the work of his contemporaries and predecessors necessary to understand specific portions of text); and (iii) textual and linguistic endnotes (indicated by asterisks in the text). We include bibliographies of editions and translations of Leibniz's writings, secondary sources on Leibniz, and principal secondary sources, as well as brief biographies of Leibniz's contemporaries.

We would both like to acknowledge the anonymous readers who reviewed our translations at various stages in the preparation of this book. While it was not always easy to face up to the inaccuracies in our translations or the infelicities in our style, their careful work improved the volume immeasurably. (Any imperfections that remain are, of course, their responsibility.) We would also like to recognize the numerous scholars who made helpful suggestions about the selections we chose for the volume, and the many students and colleagues who used earlier versions of the translations and shared their comments with us. And finally, we would like to thank our families for all their support; they put up with a great deal.

Selected Bibliography of the Works of Leibniz[7]

Raspe, R.E. *Oeuvres philosophiques* (Amsterdam and Leipzig, 1765).

Dutens, L. *Leibnitii opera omnia* (Geneva, 1768).

Erdmann, J.E. *Leibnitii opera philosophica* (Berlin, 1840).

[GM]: Gerhardt, C.I. *G.W. Leibniz: Mathematische Schriften*, 7 vols. (Berlin, 1849–55).

[FB]: Foucher de Careil, A. *Réfutation Inédite de Spinoza* (Paris, 1854).

[F de C]: Foucher de Careil, A. *Nouvelles lettres et opuscules inédits de Leibniz* (Paris, 1857).

---

7. Original language texts consulted in the preparation of this translation.

[GLW]: Gerhardt, C.I. *Briefwechsel zwischen Leibniz und Christian Wolf* (Halle, 1860).

[G]: Gerhardt, C.I. *G.W. Leibniz: Die philosophischen Schriften*, 7 vols. (Berlin, 1875–90).

[GD]: Gerhardt, C.I. "Zu Leibniz' Dynamik," *Archiv für Geschichte der Philosophie I* (1888): 566–81.

[S]: Stein, Ludwig. *Leibniz und Spinoza* (Berlin, 1890).

[C]: Couturat, Louis. *Opuscules et fragments inédits de Leibniz* (Paris, 1903).

[A]: *G.W. Leibniz: Sämtliche Schriften und Briefe* (Darmstadt and Leipzig, 1923-).

[W]: Kabitz, Willy. "Leibniz und Berkeley," *Sitzungsberichte der Preussischen Akademie der Wissenschaften*, Philosophisch-historische Klasse XXIV, 28 Juli 1932, pp. 623–36.

[Gr]: Grua, G. *G.W. Leibniz: Textes inédits d'après les manuscrits de la Bibliothèque provinciale de Hanovre* (Paris, 1948).

[RPM]: Leibniz, G.W. (ed. A. Robinet). *Principes de la nature et de la grace fondés en raison, et, Principes de la philosophie ou monadologie* (Paris, 1954).

[RML]: Robinet, A. *Malebranche et Leibniz, Relations personelles* (Paris, 1955).

[ALC]: Alexander, H.G. *The Leibniz-Clarke Correspondence* (New York and Manchester, 1956).

[RLC]: Robinet, André. *Correspondance Leibniz-Clarke* (Paris, 1957).

[LD]: Leibniz, G.W. (ed. H. Lestienne). *Discours de Métaphysique* (Paris, 1975).

[Dosch et al.]: Leibniz, G.W. (ed. H.G. Dosch, G.W. Most, and E. Rudolph). *Specimen Dynamicum* (Hamburg, 1982).

[VE]: *Vorausedition zur Reihe VI—Philosophische Schriften—in der Ausgabe der Akademie der DDR* (Münster, 1982-).

For more detailed bibliographical information concerning Leibniz's works, please consult E. Ravier, *Bibliographie des Oeuvres de Leibniz* (reprinted Hildesheim: Olms, 1966), along with Paul Schrecker's corrections and additions in his review, "Une bibliographie de Leibniz," *Revue philosophique de la France et de l'étranger* 63 (1938): 324–46.

Selected Bibliography of Secondary Works

Belaval, Yvon. *Leibniz critique de Descartes* (Paris, 1960).
———. *Leibniz: Initiation à sa philosophie* (Paris, 1962).
Broad, C.D. *Leibniz: an Introduction* (Cambridge, 1975).

Brown, Stuart. *Leibniz* (Minneapolis, 1984).

Cassirer, Ernst. *Leibniz' System in seinen wissenschaftlichen Grundlagen* (Marburg, 1902).

Costabel, Pierre. *Leibniz and Dynamics* (Ithaca, N.Y., 1973).

Couturat, Louis. *La logique de Leibniz* (Paris, 1901).

Frankfurt, Harry (ed.). *Leibniz* (Garden City, N.Y., 1972).

Gueroult, Martial. *Leibniz: Dynamique et métaphysique* (Paris, 1967).

Hooker, Michael (ed.). *Leibniz: Critical and Interpretative Essays* (Minneapolis, 1982).

Ishiguro, Hidé. *Leibniz's Philosophy of Logic and Language* (Ithaca, N.Y., 1972).

Jalabert, Jacques. *Le dieu de Leibniz* (Paris, 1960).

———. *La théorie leibnizienne de la substance* (Paris, 1947).

Jolley, Nicholas. *Leibniz and Locke* (Oxford, 1984).

Loemker, Leroy. *Struggle for Synthesis: the Seventeenth Century Background of Leibniz's Synthesis of Order and Freedom* (Cambridge, Mass., 1972).

MacDonald Ross, George. *Leibniz* (Oxford, 1984).

McRae, Robert. *Leibniz: Perception, Apperception, and Thought* (Toronto, 1976).

Mates, Benson. *The Philosophy of Leibniz: Metaphysics and Language* (Oxford, 1986).

Okruhlik, K., and J.R. Brown (eds.). *The Natural Philosophy of Leibniz* (Dordrecht, 1985).

Parkinson, G.H.R. *Logic and Reality in Leibniz's Metaphysics* (Oxford, 1965).

Rescher, Nicholas. *Leibniz's Metaphysics of Nature* (Dordrecht, 1981).

———. *The Philosophy of Leibniz* (Englewood Cliffs, N.J., 1967).

Robinet, André. *Architectonique disjonctive automates systématiques et idealité transcendentale dans l'oeuvre de G.W. Leibniz* (Paris, 1986).

Russell, Bertrand. *A Critical Exposition of the Philosophy of Leibniz* (London, 1900).

Woolhouse, R.S. (ed.). *Leibniz: Metaphysics and Philosophy of Science* (Oxford, 1981).

Translations and Other Texts Referred to in the Notes

[AT]:   Adam, C., and P. Tannery (eds.). *Oeuvres de Descartes* (Paris, 1897–1909; new ed., Paris, 1964–1974), 11 vols.

Arnauld, Antoine (trans J. Dickoff and P. James). *The Art of Thinking* (Indianapolis, 1964).

Bacon, Francis (ed. F.H. Anderson). *The New Organon* (Indianapolis, 1960).

Bayle, Pierre (ed. and trans. R.H. Popkin). *Historical and Critical Dictionary: Selections* (Indianapolis, 1965).

Boyle, Robert. *A Free Inquiry into the Vulgarly Received Notion of Nature*, in Boyle (ed. Thomas Birch), *Works*, vol. 5 (London, 1772), pp. 158–254.

Brush, Craig B. (ed. and trans.). *The Selected Works of Gassendi* (New York, 1972).

Cordemoy, Gerauld de (ed. P. Clair and F. Girbal). *Oeuvres philosophiques* (Paris, 1968).

[Ols]: Descartes, René (trans. Paul J. Olscamp). *Discourse on Method, Optics, Geometry, and Meteorology* (Indianapolis, 1965).

———. (trans. Thomas S. Hall). *Treatise on Man* (Cambridge, Mass., 1972).

———. (trans. Michael S. Mahoney). *The World* (New York, 1979).

[K]: ———. (ed. and trans. Anthony Kenny). *Philosophical Letters* (Minneapolis, 1981).

———. (trans. V.R. Miller and R.P. Miller). *Principles of Philosophy* (Dordrecht, 1983).

Digby, Kenelm. *Two treatises. In the one of which, the nature of bodies; in the other, the nature of mans soule . . .* (Paris, 1644).

———. *A late Discourse Made in a Solemne Assembly . . . touching the Cure of Wounds by the Powder of Sympathy* (London, 1658).

Diogenes Laertius (trans. R.D. Hicks). *Lives of the Eminent Philosophers*, 2 vols. Loeb Classical Library (New York, 1925).

Drake, Stillman (ed. and trans.). *Discoveries and Opinions of Galileo* (Garden City, N.Y., 1957).

Galilei, Galileo (trans. Stillman Drake). *Two New Sciences* (Madison, Wis., 1974).

[Geb]: Gebhardt, Carl (ed.). *Spinoza Opera* (Heidelberg, 1925), 4 vols.

Heath, T.L. *The Works of Archimedes* (Cambridge, 1897 and 1912).

Hippocrates (attr.). *The Regimen*, in W.H.S. Jones (ed. and trans.). *Hippocrates vol. IV and Heracleitus, On the Universe*, Loeb Classical Library (New York, 1931).

Hobbes, Thomas (ed. R.S. Peters). *Body, Man, and Citizen* (New York, 1962).

Huygens, Christiaan. *Horologium Oscillatorium, sive de motu pendulorum ad horologia adapto* (Paris, 1673).

———. *Discours de la cause de la pésanteur* (Leiden, 1690).

———. *Oeuvres Complètes* (La Haye, 1888–1950), 22 vols.

[L]:   Leibniz, G.W. (trans. L. Loemker). *Philosophical Papers and Letters* (Dordrecht, 1969).
————. (trans. E.M. Huggard). *Theodicy* (La Salle, Ill., 1985).
————. (trans. P. Remnant and J. Bennett). *New Essays on Human Understanding* (Cambridge, 1981).
————. (ed. and trans. G.H.R. Parkinson). *Logical Papers* (Oxford, 1966).
————. (ed. and trans. P. Riley). *The Political Writings of Leibniz* (Cambridge, 1972).
Linus, Franciscus. *Tractatus de corporum inseparabilitate . . .* (1661).
Locke, John. *Works* (London, 1824).
————. (ed. Nidditch). *An Essay Concerning Human Understanding* (Oxford, 1975).
Malebranche, Nicholas. *The Search after Truth* (trans. T.M. Lennon and P J. Olscamp) and *Elucidations of the Search after Truth* (trans. T.M. Lennon) (Columbus, Ohio, 1980).
————. *Traité de la nature et de la grâce*, vol. IV of André Robinet, ed., *Oeuvres Complètes de Malebranche* (Paris, 1958–70).
————. (trans. Willis Doney). *Dialogues on Metaphysics* (New York, 1980).
Mariotte, Edmé. *Traité de la percussion ou choc des corps* (Paris, 1673).
Newton, Isaac. *Opticks* (New York, 1952).
————. (trans. A. Motte and F. Cajori). *Mathematical Principles of Natural Philosophy* (Berkeley and Los Angeles, 1966), 2 vols.
————. (ed. I.B. Cohen). *Papers and Letters on Natural Philosophy*, 2nd ed. (Cambridge, Mass., 1978).
Packer, J.I., and O.R. Johnston. *Martin Luther on the Bondage of the Will* (London, 1957).
Pascal, Blaise (ed. Louis Lafuma). *Oeuvres Complètes* (Paris, 1963).
Schelhamer, Gunther Christopher. *Natura sibi et medicis vindicata sive de natura liber bipartitus* (1697).
Spinoza, Baruch (trans. Samuel Shirley). *The Ethics and Selected Letters* (Indianapolis, 1982).
Sturm, Johann Christopher. *Idolum naturae . . . sive de naturae agentis . . . conceptibus dissertatio* (1692).
————. *Physica electiva sive hypothetica* (1697).
————. *Physica eclectica* (1698).
Toland, John. *Christianity Not Mysterious* (London, 1696).
Vorst, C. von dem. *Tractatus theologicus de Deo* (Steinfurt, 1610).

Philosophical Essays

PART I

Basic Works

Letter to Foucher (1675)[8]

I AGREE WITH YOU that it is important once and for all to examine all of our assumptions in order to establish something solid. For I hold that it is only when we can prove everything we assert that we understand perfectly the thing under consideration. I know that such studies are not popular with the common people, but I also know that the common people do not take the trouble to understand things at their deepest level. Your aim, so far as I can see, is to examine all the truths which affirm that there is something outside of us. You seem to be quite fair in this enterprise, for you grant us all the hypothetical truths which affirm, not that there is something outside of us, but only what would happen if there were things outside of us. Thus we already save arithmetic, geometry, and a large number of propositions of metaphysics, physics, and morality, propositions whose proper expression depends on arbitrarily chosen definitions, and whose truth depends on axioms which I commonly call identities, such as, for example, that two contradictories cannot both be, that a thing is what it is at a given time—that it is, for example, as large as it is, or equal to itself, that it is similar to itself, etc. But although you quite deliberately do not enter into an examination of hypothetical propositions, I am, nevertheless, of the opinion that this should be done and that we should not admit any that have not been demonstrated completely and resolved into identities.

The principal subject of your inquiry concerns the truths that deal with what is really outside of us. Now, in the first place, we cannot deny that the very truth of hypothetical propositions is something outside of us, something that does not depend on us. For all hypothetical propositions assert what would be or what would not be if something or its contrary were posited; and consequently, they assert that the simultaneous assumption of two things in agreement with one another is possible or impossible, necessary or indifferent, or they assert that one single thing is possible or impossible, necessary or indifferent. This possibility, impossibility, or necessity (for the necessity of something is the impossibility of its contrary) is not a chimera we create, since we do nothing more than recognize it, in spite of ourselves and in a consistent manner. Thus of all things that there actually are, the very possibility or

---

8. A II, 1, 245–49; G I 369–74. French.

impossibility of being is the first. Now, this possibility or this necessity forms
or composes what we call the essences or natures and the truths we commonly
call eternal—and we are right to call them so, for there is nothing so eternal
as that which is necessary. Thus the nature of the circle with its properties is
something existent and eternal. That is, there is a constant cause outside us
which makes everyone who thinks carefully about the circle discover the same
thing. It is not merely that their thoughts agree with each other, which could
be attributed solely to the nature of the human mind, but even the phenomena
or experiences confirm these eternal truths when the appearance of a circle
strikes our senses. And these phenomena necessarily have some cause outside
of us.

But even though the existence of necessities is the first of all truths in and
of itself and in the order of nature, I agree that it is not first in the order of
our knowledge. For you see, in order to prove their existence I took it for
granted that we think and that we have sensations. Thus there are two absolute
general truths, that is, two absolute general truths which speak of the actual existence of things: the first, that we think, and the second, that there is a
great variety in our thoughts. From the former it follows that we exist, and
from the latter it follows that there is something else besides us, that is, something else besides that which thinks, something which is the cause of the variety of our appearances. Now one of these two truths is just as incontestable and as independent as the other; and Descartes, having accepted only
the former, failed to arrive at the perfection to which he had aspired in the
course of his meditations. If he had followed precisely what I call the thread
of meditating [*filum meditandi*], I believe that he would have achieved the first
philosophy. But not even the world's greatest genius can force things, and we
must necessarily enter through the entryways that nature has made, so that
we do not stray. Moreover, one person alone cannot do everything at once,
and for myself, when I think of everything Descartes has said that is beautiful
and original, I am more astonished with what he has accomplished than with
what he has failed to accomplish. I admit that I have not yet been able to read
all his writings with all the care I had intended to bring to them, and my
friends know that, as it happened, I read almost all the new philosophers before reading him. Bacon and Gassendi were the first to fall into my hands;
their familiar and easy style was better adapted to a person who wants to
read everything. It is true that I often glanced at Galileo and Descartes, but
since I became a geometer only recently, I was soon repelled by their manner of writing, which requires deep meditation. As for myself, although I always liked to meditate, I always found it difficult to read books that cannot
be understood without much meditation. For, when following one's own meditations one follows a certain natural inclination and gains profit along with
pleasure; but one is enormously cramped when having to follow the meditations of others. I always liked books that contained some fine thoughts, but
books that one could read without stopping, for they aroused ideas in me
which I could follow at my fancy and pursue as I pleased. This also prevented
me from reading geometry books with care, and I must admit that I have not

yet brought myself to read Euclid in any other way than one commonly reads novels [*histories*]. I have learned from experience that this method in general is a good one; but I have learned nevertheless that there are authors for whom one must make an exception—Plato and Aristotle among the ancient philosophers and Galileo and Descartes among ours. Yet what I know of Descartes's metaphysical and physical meditations is almost entirely derived from reading a number of books, written in a more familiar style, that report his opinions. So perhaps I have not yet understood him well. However, to the extent that I have leafed through his works myself, it seemed to me that I have glimpsed at very least what he has not accomplished and not even attempted to accomplish, that is, among other things, the analysis of all our assumptions. That is why I am inclined to applaud all those who examine the least truth to its deepest level; for I know that it is important to understand one perfectly, however small and however easy it may seem. This is the way to progress quite far and finally to establish the art of discovery which depends on a knowledge, but a most distinct and perfect knowledge of the easiest things. And for this reason I found nothing wrong in Roberval's attempt to demonstrate everything in geometry, including some axioms.[9] I admit that we should not demand such exactness from others, but I believe that it is good to demand it from ourselves.

I return to those truths, from among those asserting that there is something outside us, which are first with respect to ourselves, namely, that we think and that there is a great variety in our thoughts. Now, this variety cannot come from that which thinks, since a single thing by itself cannot be the cause of the changes in itself. For everything would remain in the state in which it is, if there is nothing that changes it; and since it did not determine itself to have these changes rather than others, one cannot begin to attribute any variety to it without saying something which, we must admit, has no reason—which is absurd. And even if we tried to say that our thoughts had no beginning, beside the fact that we would be required to assert that each of us has existed from all eternity, we would still not escape the difficulty; for we would always have to admit that there is no reason for the particular variety which would have existed in our thoughts from all eternity, since there is nothing in us that determines us to have one kind of variety rather than to another. Therefore there is some cause outside of us for the variety of our thoughts. And since we conceive that there are subordinate causes for this variety, causes which themselves still need causes, we have established particular beings or substances certain of whose actions we recognize, that is, things from whose changes we conceive certain changes in us to follow. And we quickly proceed to construct what we call matter and body. But it is at this point that you are right to stop us a bit and renew the criticisms of the ancient Academy. For, at bottom, all our experience assures us of only two things,

---

9. Roberval does attempt to demonstrate Euclid's axioms in his *Elements of Geometry*, one of Roberval's unpublished papers, which Leibniz considered publishing (A III, 1, 328). See Leibniz's *New Essays on Human Understanding*, Book IV, chap. 7, sec. 1: "Of the propositions which are named maxims or axioms."

namely, that there is a connection among our appearances which provides us the means to predict future appearances with success, and that this connection must have a constant cause. But it does not strictly follow from all this that matter or bodies exist, but only that there is something that presents well-sequenced appearances to us. For if an invisible power took pleasure in giving us dreams that are well connected with our preceding life and in conformity among themselves, could we distinguish them from realities before having been awakened? And what prevents the course of our life from being a long well-ordered dream, a dream from which we could be wakened in a moment? And I do not see that this power would be imperfect on that account, as Descartes asserts, leaving aside the fact that it does not matter if it is imperfect. For this could be a certain subordinate power, or some genie who meddles in our affairs for some unknown reason and who has as much power over someone as had the caliph who transported a drunken man into his palace and made him taste of Mohammed's paradise when he had awakened; after this he was made drunk again and was returned to the place from which he had been taken. And when the man came to himself, he did not fail to interpret what to him appeared inconsistent with the course of his life as a vision, and spread among the people maxims and revelations that he believed he had learned in his pretended paradise—this was what the caliph wished. Now, since a reality passed for a vision, what prevents a vision from passing for a reality? It is true that the more we see some connection in what happens to us, the more we are confirmed in the opinion we have about the reality of our appearances; and it is also true that the more we examine our appearances closely, the more we find them well-sequenced, as microscopes and other aids in making experiments have shown us. This constant accord engenders great assurance, but after all, it will only be moral assurance until somebody discovers the *a priori* origin of the world we see and pursues the question as to why things are the way they appear back to the ground of essence. For having done that, he will have demonstrated that what appears to us is a reality and that it is impossible that we ever be deceived about it again. But I believe that this would nearly approach the beatific vision and that it is difficult to aspire to this in our present state. However, we would learn from this how confused the knowledge we commonly have of body and matter must be, since we believe we are certain they exist but in the end we discover that we can be mistaken. And this confirms Descartes's excellent proof of the distinction between body and soul, since we can doubt the former without being able to put the latter into question. For even if there were only appearances or dreams, we would be no less certain of the existence of that which thinks, as Descartes has said quite nicely. I add that the existence of God can be demonstrated in ways other than Descartes did, ways which, I believe, bring us farther along. For we do not need to assume a being who guarantees us against being deceived, since it is in our power to undeceive ourselves about many things, at least about the most important ones. I wish, sir, that your meditations on this have all the success you desire. But to accomplish this, it is good to proceed in order and to establish propositions; that is the way to gain ground and to make sure progress. I believe that you would oblige the public by conveying to it, from time to time, selections from the Academy and especially from Plato, for I recognize that there are things in there more beautiful and solid than commonly thought.

Preface to a Universal Characteristic (1678–79)[10]

The idea of a universal language and an abstract symbolism to aid both in communication and in reasoning was one of the dreams of a number of seventeenth-century thinkers, as Leibniz notes in the following essay. This essay, written at a time when Leibniz was very busy trying to work out the details of such a universal characteristic, appears to be one of a number of introductions Leibniz wrote for a presentation of his language. Though Leibniz never completed his universal characteristic to his satisfaction and never completed the work this essay was to introduce, it is still important for the outline Leibniz gives of the project, in at least one of its forms.

THERE IS AN OLD SAYING that God made everything in accordance with weight, measure, and number. But there are things which cannot be weighed, namely, those that lack force and power [*vis ac potentia*], and there are also things that lack parts and thus cannot be measured. But there is nothing that cannot be numbered. And so number is, as it were, metaphysical shape, and arithmetic is, in a certain sense, the Statics of the Universe, that by which the powers of things are investigated.[11]

From the time of Pythagoras, people have been persuaded that enormous mysteries lie hidden in numbers. And it is plausible that Pythagoras brought this opinion into Greece from the Orient, as he did many other opinions. But since they lacked the true key to this secret, the more inquisitive slipped into futility and superstition. From this arose a certain sort of vulgar Cabbala (a Cabbala far distant from the true one), as did numerous absurdities connected to a certain falsely named magic, absurdities that fill books. Meanwhile, people have retained their inherent ability to believe that astonishing things can be discovered through numbers, characters, and through a certain new language that some people call the Adamic language, and Jacob Böhme calls the "nature language" [*die Natur-Sprache*].

But, as far as I know, no mortal until now has seen the true principle by which each thing can be assigned its own characteristic number. Indeed, the most learned persons have admitted that they did not understand what I was talking about when I casually mentioned something of this sort in their

---

10. Editors' title. VE IV, 669–75; G VII 184–89. Latin.

11. '*Figura*', shape, is also used for 'atom' in Lucretius's atomist poem, *De rerum natura*. See, e.g., book II, 11. 385, 682f, 778, etc.

presence. Not long ago, some distinguished persons devised a certain language or Universal Characteristic in which all notions and things are nicely ordered, a language with whose help different nations can communicate their thoughts, and each, in its own language, read what the other wrote. But no one has put forward a language or characteristic which embodies, at the same time, both the art of discovery and the art of judgment, that is, a language whose marks or characters perform the same task as arithmetic marks do for numbers and algebraic marks do for magnitudes considered abstractly. And yet, when God bestowed these two sciences on the human race, it seems that he wanted to suggest to us that a much greater secret lies hidden in our intellect, a secret of which these two sciences are but shadows.

However, by some chance it happened that I fell upon such thoughts when still a boy, and as usually happens with such first inclinations, these thoughts, deeply imprinted, attached themselves to my mind ever after. Two things marvelously benefited me in this (things otherwise problematic, however, and often harmful to many): first, that I was nearly self-taught and, second, that I sought out what was new in each and every branch of knowledge, as soon as I came into contact with it, even though I often had not yet sufficiently grasped things commonly known. But these two things gave me an advantage; the first prevented me from filling my mind with trifles, things that ought to be forgotten, things that are accepted on the authority of teachers rather than because of arguments, and the second prevented me from resting before I probed all the way to the depths of each subject and arrived at its very principles, from which everything I extracted could be discovered by my own efforts.

Therefore, when I was led from reading histories (which wonderfully delighted me from my youth on) and from the concern with style (which I exercised in prose and the like with such ease that my teachers feared that I would be held back by its charms) to logic and philosophy, then as soon as I began to understand something of these matters, what a blessed multitude of these fantasies that arose in my brain* did I scribble down on paper and show immediately to my amazed teachers. Among other things, I sometimes posed an objection concerning the predicaments. For, I said, just as there are predicaments or classes of simple notions,[12] so ought there to be a new genus of predicaments in which propositions themselves or complex terms might also be set out in a natural order; indeed, at that time I didn't even dream of including demonstrations, and I didn't know that geometers, who arrange propositions in accordance with which one is demonstrated from others, do what it is I sought to do. And so my objection was, indeed, empty. But since my teachers could not answer it, pursuing these thoughts on account of their novelty, I worked on constructing such predicaments for complex terms or propositions. When, through my eagerness for this project, I applied myself more intently, I inevitably stumbled onto this wonderful observation, namely, that one can devise a certain alphabet of human thoughts and that, through

12. The predicaments are the ten Aristotelian categories. They are usually given as: substance, quantity, quality, relation, place, time, situation, state, action, and passion. These are taken to be the highest genera of things, and all terms are taken to belong to one or another of them.

the combination of the letters of this alphabet and through the analysis of words produced from them, all things can both be discovered and judged. Having grasped this, I was quite overjoyed, indeed, with childlike delight, for at that time I hadn't sufficiently grasped the magnitude of the project. But afterwards, the more progress I made in understanding these matters, the more confirmed I was in my plan to follow out such a project. As it happened, when I was older, by now twenty years old, I was working on an academic exercise. And so I wrote a dissertation, *On the Art of Combinations*, published in the form of a little book in 1666, in which I presented this marvelous discovery to the public. It is, indeed, the sort of dissertation that a young man, freshly out of school, could have written, a young man not yet steeped in the real sciences, for mathematics was not cultivated in those parts, and, if I had spent my youth in Paris, as Pascal did, then perhaps I would have contributed to those sciences sooner. However, I am not sorry to have written this dissertation, for two reasons, first because it greatly pleased many very ingenious gentlemen and also because in it I already gave the world some hint of my discovery, so that now it won't seem as if I have just invented it for the first time.

Indeed, I often wondered why, as far as the recorded history of mankind extends, no mortal had approached such a project, for meditations of this kind ought to be among the first to occur to those reasoning in proper order, just as they occurred to me. I came to this discovery while still a youth, working on logic, before I had touched on morals or mathematics or physics, for the sole reason that I always searched for first principles. The real reason why people have missed the doorway [into this discovery] is, I think, because principles are, for the most part, dry and insufficiently agreeable to people, and so, barely tasted, they are dismissed. However, there are three men I am especially surprised did not approach the matter, Aristotle, Joachim Jungius, and René Descartes. For when Aristotle wrote his *Organon* and his *Metaphysics*, he examined the inner depth of notions with great skill. And while Joachim Jungius of Lübeck is a man little known even in Germany itself, he was clearly of such judiciousness and such capacity of mind that I know of no other mortal, including even Descartes himself, from whom we could better have expected a great restoration of the sciences, had Jungius been either known or assisted. Moreover, he was already of a mature age when Descartes began to flourish, so it is quite regrettable that they did not know one another.[13] As far as Descartes goes, this is certainly not the place to praise a man who, due to the magnitude of his genius, is almost beyond praise. Certainly, he prepared the path through these ideas, a path that is true and straight, a path that leads up to this very point. But since his own path was directed too much toward applause, he seems to have broken off the thread of his investigation[14] and,

13. Jungius, nine years Descartes's senior, would have been fifty-four or so when the *Meditations* were published in 1641.

14. Descartes speculated on the question of a universal language in an early letter to Mersenne, 20 November 1629, written twelve years before the *Meditations* were published; see AT I 76–82 (K 3–6). For Leibniz's comments on this letter, see C 27–28.

overly eager, gave us his Metaphysical Meditations and a piece of his geometry, by which he captured people's attention. As for other subjects, he decided to investigate the nature of matter for the sake of medicine, and rightly
so, had he but completed the task of ordering the ideas he had in mind, for
then he would have shed more light by his experiments than anyone could believe. And so, the reason why he didn't apply his mind to this task can only be
the fact that he had not sufficiently grasped the reason for pursuing such a
program and its import. For if he had seen a way of establishing a rational
philosophy as clear and unshakable as arithmetic, one can hardly believe that
he would have used any other way for creating a sect, something he dearly
wanted. For by the very nature of things, a sect using this sort of reasoning
would immediately arise as soon as it exercised control over reason, as in geometry, and would not perish or weaken until the human race lost knowledge
altogether through the invasion of some new barbarian horde.

Though distracted in so many other ways, I was absorbed in these meditations for the sole reason that I saw their great importance and saw a wonderfully easy way of attaining the goal. And indeed, by rigorous meditation
I finally discovered the very thing I sought. And so now, nothing more is
needed to construct the characteristic I am working on to the point where it
is sufficient both to provide a grammar of such a wonderful language and a
dictionary for most of the more frequent items, that is, to the point of having characteristic numbers for all ideas; I say, nothing more is needed than
for the philosophical and mathematical curriculum [cursus], as it is called, to
be set up in accordance with a certain new method that I could set out. So
conceived, the curriculum would contain nothing in itself either more difficult
than other curricula or very far from what is ordinarily used and understood,
or very foreign to common habits of writing. Nor does it require much more
work than we see already expended on several curricula or encyclopedias, as
they are called. I think that a few chosen persons could complete the task in
five years; in two years they could set forth those doctrines most often used
in daily life, that is, morals and metaphysics in an unshakable calculus.

Once the characteristic numbers of most notions are determined, the human race will have a new kind of tool, a tool that will increase the power of
the mind much more than optical lenses helped our eyes, a tool that will be
as far superior to microscopes or telescopes as reason is to vision. The compass never provided navigators with anything more useful than what this North
Star would give us for swimming the sea of experiments. What other consequences will follow from this tool are in the hands of the fates, but they can
only be great and good. For although people can be made worse off by all
other gifts, correct reasoning alone can only be for the good. Moreover, who
could doubt that reasoning will finally be correct, when it is everywhere as
clear and certain as arithmetic has been up until now. And so that troublesome
objection by which one antagonist now commonly harasses the other would
be eliminated, an objection that turns many away from wanting to reason.
What I have in mind is that, when someone offers a proof, his opponent
doesn't examine the argument as much as he responds in general terms, how

do you know that your reason is more correct than mine? What criterion of truth do you have? And even if the one antagonist appeals to his arguments, listeners lack the patience to examine them. For it is usually the case that many things must thoroughly be examined, a task taking several weeks, if we were carefully to follow the laws of reasoning accepted up until now. And so, after great agitation, emotions rather than reasons win most often, and we end the dispute by cutting the Gordian knot rather than untying it. This happens especially in deliberations pertaining to life, where something must be decided; here only a few people can weigh (as on a balance) the favorable and unfavorable factors, both of which are often numerous. And so, the better someone has learned to represent to himself more forcefully, here one, there another circumstance, following the various inclinations of his soul, or to ornament and paint them for others more eloquently and effectively, the more he will stir himself up and capture for himself the minds of men, especially if he is astute in using their emotions. There is scarcely anyone who can take account of both sides of the complete table of credits and debits, that is, who not only can enumerate the favorable and unfavorable factors, but can also weigh them correctly. And so two people who argue look to me almost like two merchants who owe money to one another from numerous transactions, but who never want to reckon up the accounts, while meanwhile each in different ways exaggerates what he himself is owed by the other and exaggerates the validity and size of certain particular claims. Thus, the controversy will never end. We should not be surprised that this happens in a large proportion of the controversies where the matter is unclear, that is, where the dispute cannot be reduced to numerical terms. But now our characteristic will reduce them all to numerical terms, so that even reasons can be weighed, just as if we had a special kind of balance. For even probabilities are subject to calculation and demonstration, since one can always judge what is more likely [*probabilius*] to happen on the basis of given circumstances. And, finally, anyone who has been persuaded of the certain truth of religion and, what follows from this, anyone who embraces others with such love that he hopes for the conversion of the human race will certainly admit, as soon as he understands these things, that nothing is more effective for the propagation of faith than this invention, except for miracles and the holiness of an Apostolic man or the victories of a great monarch. For wherever missionaries can once introduce this language, the true religion, the religion entirely in agreement with reason will be established and in the future apostasy will be feared no more than we fear that people will condemn arithmetic or geometry, once they have learned it. And so I repeat what I have often said, that a person who is neither prophet nor prince could undertake nothing better adapted to the good of the human race or to the glory of God. But we must go beyond words. Since, due to the wonderful interconnection of things, it is extremely difficult to produce the characteristic numbers of just a few things, considered apart from the others, I have contrived a device, quite elegant, if I am not mistaken, by which I can show that it is possible to corroborate reasoning through numbers. And so, I imagine that those so very wonderful characteristic numbers are already given, and, having observed a certain general property that characteristic numbers have, I meanwhile assume that these numbers I imagine, whatever they might be, have that property. By using these numbers I can immediately demonstrate through numbers, and in an amazing way, all of the logical rules and show how one can know whether certain arguments are in proper form. When we have the true characteristic numbers of things, then at last, without any mental effort or danger of error, we will be able to judge whether arguments are indeed materially sound and draw the right conclusions.

Samples of the Numerical Characteristic (1679)[15]

The notes in this section all date from April 1679, when Leibniz was trying to work out the details of his universal characteristic. The notes seem to exemplify the kind of strategy outlined in the last paragraph of the previous selection, in which Leibniz discusses using the characteristic to explicate the laws of logical reasoning. It is important to note, though, that these are just preliminary sketches, and represent only one of a number of different formalisms Leibniz explored before eventually setting the problems aside.

A. A Calculus of Consequences[16]

T HERE ARE two things that should be distinguished in every argument, namely, form and subject matter. For it can happen that sometimes an argument works with respect to a certain subject matter but cannot be applied to all other examples of the same form. For example, if we were to reason in this way:

> Every triangle is trilateral.

> Some triangle is not equilateral.

> Therefore, something equilateral is not trilateral.

The conclusion is correct, but by virtue of the subject matter, not by virtue of the form, for one can give examples of the same form which do not work, for example:

> Every metal is mineral.

> Some metal is not gold.

> Therefore something gold is not mineral.

And so, a calculus that deals with subject matter can be separated from a formal calculus. For although I discovered that one can assign a *characteristic*

---

15. Editors' title. Latin.
16. C 84–89.

number to each term or notion (with whose help to calculate and to reason will, in the future, be the same) in fact, on account of the marvelous complexity of things, I cannot yet set forth the true characteristic numbers, not before I have put in order the most general categories [*summa capita*] under which most things fall. Nevertheless, I reflected, the form of inferences can be dealt with in a calculus and demonstrated with fictitious numbers, which, for the time being, can be used in place of the true characteristic numbers. This is what I shall set out here.

In every categorical proposition (for from them I can show elsewhere that other kinds of propositions can be dealt with by changing a few things in the calculus) there are two terms, the subject and the predicate. To these are added a copula ("is"), affirmation or negation, that is, quality, and finally, the sign, that is "all" or "some," which is the quantity. For example, in this proposition, "a pious person is happy," "pious" and "happy" are the terms, of which "pious" is the subject, and "happy" the predicate; "is" is the copula. The *quality of the proposition* is affirmation or negation. And so this proposition, "a pious person is happy," affirms, but this one, "a wicked person is not happy," denies. The *quantity of the proposition* is universality or particularity. For example, when I say "every pious person is happy" or if I were to say "no wicked person is happy" the propositions are universal, the former universal affirmative, the latter negative. But if I were to say "some wicked person is wealthy," "some pious person is not wealthy," the propositions are particular, the former affirmative, the latter negative.

In every proposition, the predicate is said to be in the subject, that is, the notion of the predicate is contained [*involvitur*] in the notion of the subject.[17] For, in a universal affirmative proposition, when I say "every man is an animal" I mean "the concept of animal is contained in the concept of man" (for the concept of man is to be a rational animal). And when I say "every pious person is happy" I mean that whoever understands the nature of piety will also understand that it contains within itself true happiness. And so, in a universal affirmative proposition, it is obvious that the predicate is contained in the subject considered by itself. But if the proposition is particular affirmative, then the predicate is not contained in the notion of the subject considered by itself, but in the notion of the subject with something extra added; that is, the predicate is contained in some special case [*species*] of the subject. For the notion of a special case arises from the notion of genus with the addition of some difference.[18]

Similarly, in a negative proposition, by denying that the predicate is in the subject (in the way I indicated) we affirm by the very act that the negation of the predicate or a term contradictory to the predicate is in the subject. For example, when I say "no wicked person is happy," it is the same as if I said

---

17. Originally Leibniz limited this claim to affirmative propositions, but the word "*addirmativa*" was crossed out.

18. Leibniz's terminology here draws on the traditional idea that a genus together with a specific difference defines a species.

"every wicked person is not-happy," or "not-happiness is in the wicked." And when I say "a pious person is not-wealthy," I mean, "not-wealthiness is in a special case or instance of the pious."

Furthermore, we must consider that every composite notion is composed of other notions, sometimes positive, and sometimes negative. For example, when I say "prime number" I understand this: number nondivisible by a number greater than one.[19] And so, to proceed in a general way, we shall express each notion by means of two characteristic numbers, one with the sign "+" or "plus," the other with the sign "−" or "minus." For example:

"A prime is a number that is indivisible."
+22   −17

We must also consider the fact that all negative terms have the property that when positive terms are related as genus and species, their negations, on the other hand, are inversely related, as species and genus. For example, "body" is genus, and "animal" is species, for "body" is broader than "animal" since "body" contains animals, plants, and other things. But, on the other hand, "nonanimal" is broader than "nonbody." For all nonbodies are also nonanimals, but not conversely, for there are nonanimals which, however, are not nonbodies, for example, plants. Thus, just as there are more bodies than animals, so, on the other hand, there are more nonanimals than nonbodies.

Now that we have understood these things, we can lay down the true foundations of our calculus. Indeed, for every positive (negative) notion, we shall construct its positive (negative) characteristic number, that is, the characteristic number furnished with the "+" (or "−") sign, by multiplying all of the characteristic numbers of those positive (negative) notions from which the positive (negative) notion of that term is composed.

Thus, suppose:	animal	rational
	+13 −5	+8 −7
Then for this term:		man
The characteristic number is:		$+(13 \times 8) -(5 \times 7)$
that is:		+104 −35

In constructing these numbers, we must be careful of only one thing, that no number is contained both in the positive and negative part, that is, that the positive and negative numbers are not divisible by one and the same number, that is, that they do not have a common divisor. For if we were to have written this:

animal   rational
+13 −5   +10 −7
        man
    +130 −35

---

19. In a deleted sentence, Leibniz wrote: "And indeed, only the notion of God is purely positive, and involves no limitation or negation."

we would have written an absurdity. For the notion which is signified by "+5" is the contradictory of the one signified by "−5". And so, since 5 is contained in 10, the positive notion of "rational" (for 10 is divisible by 5, that is, 10 is the product of 5 and 2), that is, since 5 is found in "rational," while, on the other hand, 5 is denied in "animal," that is, "animal" contains the contradictory of 5, it follows that "animal" and "rational" are incompatible, and therefore "man," composed of them, implies a contradiction, since both its positive characteristic number, +130, and its negative characteristic number are divisible by 5. But since this is false, it follows that this way of expressing the notions would be absurd, and therefore we must always be careful that the positive and negative numbers do not have the same divisor.

Now that we understand the terms we have chosen, taken one by one, we might also see how they can be joined to one another, that is, how the quantity, quality, and *truth* of propositions can be distinguished, insofar as it can be done by reason, that is, by characteristic numbers. And indeed, in general, every *false* proposition that can be known through reason alone, that is, every one that involves falsity in its terms, is such that its subject and predicate contain incompatible notions. That is, in the proposition, two particular characteristic numbers from different terms (one from the subject, the other from the predicate) and with different signs (the one with the sign "+", the other with the sign "−") have a common divisor. For example, consider the proposition

A pious person is wretched

+ 10 −3   +14 −5

It is obvious that the terms "+10" (that is, "+ twice 5") and "−5" are incompatible, for they signify contradictories, and thus directly from the characteristic numbers of these terms, it is obvious that the proposition in which these numbers are found is *false* by virtue of its terms, and that its contrary is *true* by virtue of its terms.

Furthermore, before we apply characteristic numbers to the particular forms that propositions take with respect to quantity and quality, we must, in general, repeat what we said above, that the notion of the predicate is always in the subject or a special case of the subject. Let us now translate this into characteristic numbers in the following way. Consider the universal affirmative proposition:

Every wise person is pious

+70 −33   +10 −3

It is obvious that the predicate must be in the notion of the subject taken by itself, since it is in it in every case, and therefore, it is obvious that the characteristic numbers of the subject are divisible by the characteristic numbers of the predicate having the same sign, as, for example, +70 is divisible by +10, and −33 by −3. Similarly:

Every man is an animal that is rational

+ 130 −35   +13 −5   +10 −7

It is obvious that +130 is divisible by +13 and by +10, and that −35 is divisible by −5 and by −7.

Moreover, as we said above, in an affirmative particular proposition it is sufficient for the notion of the predicate to be in the notion of the subject, increased by something extra, or for the predicate to be in a special case of the subject, that is, that it be possible for the characteristic numbers of the subject, multiplied by the other numbers, to be rendered divisible by the characteristic numbers of the predicate. And since this can always be done (for any number can be rendered divisible by any other number through multiplication), it is thus obvious that an affirmative particular proposition is always in order, unless some incompatibility or contradiction of the sort mentioned above arises. For example:

Some wealthy person is wretched

+11 −9   +5 −14

It is obvious that wretchedness can be brought about in some special case of the wealthy, namely, in a wealthy person who prefers things that happen through fortune to things eternal. For, some special case of the wealthy has a notion composed of the notion of the wealthy, the genus as it were, together with the notion of the difference that distinguishes this wealthy person [i.e., one who is wretched] from another who is not wretched. Let that difference be "+15 −28."

Thus

Some wealthy person

$-(15 \times 11) - (28 \times 9)$

Now 15×11 is divisible by 5,* and 28×9 by 14. And so it is obvious that one can bring it about that the predicate is in a special case of the subject.

The same principle can also be transferred to negative propositions, *mutatis mutandis.* For example:[20]

B. A Fragment on Rules for Drawing Consequences[21]

W E CAN judge the validity [*bonitas*] of consequences through numbers by observing these rules:

(I) If a proposition is presented, then for each of its terms (namely, for both the subject and the predicate), two numbers are to be written down, one furnished with the plus sign, "+", the other with a minus sign, "−". For example, let the proposition be "every wise person is pious." Let the number corresponding to "wise" be +20 −21, and the number corresponding to "pious" be +10 −3. Be careful only that the two numbers of the same term

---

20. The manuscript breaks off here.
21. Editors' title. C 89–92.

have no common divisor. If, for example, the number for "wise" were +6 −9, both of which are divisible by 3, the number would be altogether unsuitable.[22]

(II) If any one term is found only in one premise (a premise is what I call a proposition from which another is inferred), then its numbers can be chosen arbitrarily (observing only the preceding rule I); otherwise they cannot be chosen arbitrarily, but in accordance with rules soon to be given, rules that set out the relation which the numbers of one term ought to have with respect to the numbers of the other term of the same proposition.

(III) *If the premise is universal negative* (for example, "no pious person is wretched") and if we have already chosen numbers (+5 −4) for one term (for example, "wretched"), then for the other term ("pious") we ought to choose numbers (+10 −3), in such a way that *two particular numbers of different signs* (that is, one of which has the sign + the other −) *that pertain to different terms* (that is, one of which is taken from the subject, the other from the predicate, as are, indeed, the two numbers −4 and +10) *have a common divisor,* that is, they should be chosen in such a way that they are divisible by one and the same number (namely 2). And, *on the other hand, if it is found in the conclusion that the numbers* (correctly chosen in accordance with the form of the premises) *are related in this way in subject and predicate, then this will be a sign that that universal negative conclusion is correctly deduced from the premises.*

Corollary. From this it follows directly that a universal negative is *convertible simpliciter.*[23] For example, from the fact that no pious person is wretched, it can correctly be inferred that no wretched person is pious. For it is enough that in these two numbers, +10 −3 and +5 −4, it happens that two particular numbers different in sign and from different terms (in this case +10 and −4) have the common divisor 2. For in the rule there is no distinction, nor does it matter which of the numbers is chosen from the predicate, and which from the subject. And so both the one and the other term can be either subject or predicate without violating the rule.

(IV) *If the premise is particular affirmative* (for example, "some wealthy person is wretched") and we have chosen numbers (+5 −4) for one term (for example, "wretched"), then for the other term ("wealthy") we can choose any numbers whatsoever (+10 −7) (always observing rule I, which I shall always presuppose in what follows), provided that *what we just required in a universal negative should not be found.* That is, numbers should be chosen so that two particular numbers of different signs from different terms do not have a common divisor, as neither +10 and −4 nor +5 and −7 do.[24] And, on the other hand, if it happens in the conclusion that the numbers correctly chosen for the terms in

---

22. Leibniz deleted the following: "It must be noted that, if any term is to be denied, we must change only the signs. So if the sign of 'pious' is +10 −3, the sign of not-pious will be +3 −10."

23. This is a technical term. A proposition is convertible if it remains true when the subject and predicate terms are interchanged; it is convertible *simpliciter* if it remains true without any alteration of the quality and convertible *particulariter* if we are required to change a conversion to a particular in order to maintain truth, as below in corollary 2 of rule V.

24. Leibniz seems to have made an elementary blunder here, since +10 and −4 have the common divisor 2.

the premises are not related in this way (that is, as we said they are in the universal negative proposition), this is a sign that the particular affirmative conclusion is correctly deduced from the premises.

Corollary 1. From this it follows direcdy that *a particular affirmative is opposed to a universal negative as a contradictory,* that is, they can be neither true nor false at the same time. For what we said in rule III is required for the universal negative, namely a common divisor of the sort specified there, cannot be found in a particular affirmative, as we said here in rule IV.

Corollary 2. From this it also follows directly that a particular affirmative is convertible *simpliciter,* just as we said of the universal negative, to which it is opposed. For in both cases, the conditions do not distinguish the subject from the predicate, and it is sufficient that their numbers different in sign either have (in the universal negative) or lack (in the particular affirmative) a common divisor.

(V) *If the premise is universal affirmative, it is required that each number of the subject be divisible by the number of the same sign in the predicate.* And, on the other hand, if these two conditions are found in the terms of a conclusion, terms correctly chosen in accordance with the premises, then that conclusion is correctly deduced universally and affirmatively from the premises. And so, for example, in the proposition "every wise person is pious," let the number of "wise" be $+20$ -21 and the number of "pious" be $+10$ -3, and then a universal affirmative results. This is because in the proposition, the two numbers different in sign, namely, the numbers different in sign from different terms, $+20$ and -3, $+10$ and -21 (for the matter is always obvious with respect to those numbers which belong to the same term, by rule I), have no common divisor, nor do $+10$ and -3 (in accordance with rule I), nor $+20$ and -3, nor -21 and $+10$ have a common divisor (otherwise by rule III one would have a universal negative).[25] But the number of the subject, $+20$, is divisible by the number of the predicate, $+10$, and the number of the subject, -21, is divisible by the number of the predicate, -3. This property belongs to those terms which can be affirmed universally of one another.

Corollary 1. Thus from a universal affirmative follows a particular affirmative. Every wise person is pious. Therefore some wise person is pious. How this is true is obvious from what is said immediately below the sign$\odot$.[26]

Corollary 2. The universal affirmative is convertible *particulariter.* Every wise person is pious, therefore, some pious person is wise. For, if every wise person is pious, then some wise person is pious, by the preceding corollary. But if some wise person is pious, then by rule IV corollary 2, some pious person is wise.

Corollary 3. A universal affirmative proposition is universally convertible through

---

25. The repetition can be explained by a hasty addition Leibniz made in the manuscript.
26. Leibniz's footnote: "$\odot$ since every* universal affirmative has that which is common to any particular affirmative, it follows that the universal affirmative has whatever belongs to the particular affirmative."

contraposition, as they say. Every wise person is pious, therefore, nobody who is not pious is wise. For let the proposition be:

Every wise person is pious

prior arrangement: +20 –21   +10 –3

   Written differently:

Nobody not-pious is wise

reversed arrangement: +3 –10   +20 –21

by rule I[27]

From this it is obvious that +3 and –21 (also –10 and +20), numbers different in sign from the different terms, are always divisible by the same number, namely 3, for 3 divided by 3 is 1, and 21 divided by 3 is 7 (in the same way –10 and +20 are divisible by 10). This is because, in the universal affirmative proposition, the number that stands in the position of 21 in the prior arrangement is always divisible by the number that stands in the position of 3, by rule V. Now, if in the later arrangement, that is, in the converse, the number that stands in the position of 3 and the number that stands in the position of 21 have a common divisor, then by rule III the proposition is a universal negative proposition. And so we have what we sought, that is, "wise" can universally be denied of "nonpious."

(VI) If the premise is particular negative, then something we said is required for the truth of a universal affirmative must be lacking. And so either the numbers of different sign in the different terms have a common divisor (in which case one also has a universal negative, from which ⦅[28] it is obvious that the particular negative follows from the universal negative) or the numbers in the subject are not divisible by the numbers in the predicate of the same sign.[29]

C. On Characteristic Numbers[30]

I N EVERY categorical proposition let there be a characteristic number

of the subject: +s –σ

of the predicate: +p –π

   Let there be two equations, namely

1s = mp

and λσ = μπ

observing this one [constraint], that the numbers expressed in corresponding Latin and Greek letters (namely s and σ, p and π, also 1 and λ, and finally m and μ) be relatively prime, that is, have no common divisor except the number one.

---

27. The appeal to rule I is to the passage Leibniz deleted; see above, note 22.
28. The ⦅ probably indicates a note missing in the manuscript.
29. The manuscript breaks off here.
30. Editors' title. C 245–47.

From this it follows that:

$$s = mp/l \qquad \sigma = \mu\pi/\lambda$$
$$p = ls/m \qquad \pi = \lambda\sigma/\mu^{31}$$

In a universal affirmative proposition l will equal one and λ will equal one.[32]

In a particular negative proposition either l or λ will be greater than one.

In a universal negative proposition either s and π or σ and p will be nonprime with respect to one another; that is, they will have a common divisor.

In a particular affirmative proposition both s and π and σ and p will be prime with respect to one another, that is, they will have no common divisor.

Let it be proposed that we examine the syllogism:

Every wise person is pious	(wise +70 −33)
Some wise person is wealthy	(pious +10 −3)
Therefore, some wealthy person is pious.	(wealthy +8 −11)
+8−11 +10−3	

The conclusion follows, since neither 8 is divisible by 3, nor is 11 divisible by 10. . . .[33]

From this calculus one can derive every mode and figure [of the syllogism] through numerical rules alone. If we want to know whether some figure works by virtue of its form, we see whether the contradictory of the conclusion is compatible with the premises, that is, whether numbers can be found that satisfy the premises and the contradictory of the conclusion at the same time. But if none can be found, the argument draws its conclusion by virtue of its form.[34]

---

31. In a marginal note Leibniz added:

as = mp   aσ = $\mu\pi$

es = mp/l   eσ = $\mu\pi/\lambda$

es/π or eπ/s are reducible.

32. In a marginal note Leibniz added: "badly."

33. At this point Leibniz sketched part of another example that was deleted. The deleted text is as follows:

Also:

Every pious person is happy

Some pious person is not wealthy

Therefore, some wealthy person is not happy.   (happy +5 −1)

+8 −11   +5 −1

This does not follow because

The deleted fragment ends here, perhaps because, given the assignment of characteristic numbers, the conclusion of this invalid syllogism turns out to be true.

The sketch continues at this point with further attempts to represent syllogistic reasoning through this scheme, fragmentary notes that are omitted here.

34. This paragraph concludes the sketch and follows the examples we have omitted.

On Freedom and Possibility (1680–82?)[35]

ALL THINGS in God are spontaneous.[36]

It can scarcely be doubted that every person has the freedom of doing what he wills.[37]

A volition [*voluntas*] is an endeavor [*conatus*] for acting of which we are conscious.

A deed necessarily follows from a volition and the ability [to do it] [*facultas*].

There is no volition where all of the conditions requisite for both willing and being unwilling [to do something] are equal. Rather there is indifference, that is, even if all of the conditions requisite for acting are assumed, an action can be prevented if contrary conditions obtain. A person resists reasons through forgetfulness alone, that is, by turning his mind away from them. And so it is indeed possible to resist reasons.

Unless we admit this proposition, *that there is nothing without reason, that is, that there is no proposition in which there is no connection between the subject and the predicate, that is, no proposition which cannot be proved a priori.*[38]

There are two primary propositions: one, the principle of necessary things, *that whatever implies a contradiction is false*, and the other, the principle of contingent things, *that whatever is more perfect or has more reason is true.* All truths of metaphysics, or all truths that are absolutely necessary, such as those of logic, arithmetic, geometry, and the like, rest on the former principle, for someone who denies them can always be shown that the contrary implies a contradiction. All truths contingent by their nature, which are necessary only on the hypothesis of the volition of God or of some other being, rest on the latter principle.

And so all truths that concern possibles or essences and the impossibility of a thing or its necessity (that is, the impossibility of its contrary) rest on the principle of contradiction; all truths concerning contingent things or the existence of things, rest on the principle of perfection. Except for the existence of God alone, all existences are contingent. Moreover, the reason [*causa*] why some particular contingent thing exists, rather than others, should not be sought in its definition alone,[39] but in a comparison with other things. For, since there are an infinity of possible things which, nevertheless, do not exist, the reason [*ratio*] why these exist rather than those should not be sought in their definition (for then nonexistence would imply a contradiction, and those others would not be possible, contrary to our hypothesis), but from an extrinsic source, namely, from the fact that the ones that do exist are more perfect than the others.

---

35. Editors' title. VE II 275–78; Gr 287–91. Latin.

36. See marginal comment A below.

37. Leibniz deleted the following: "that is, doing what he judges best. One can ask whether people also have freedom of willing."

38. This sentence is incomplete in the ms.

39. Leibniz originally continued the sentence as follows: "but from some further reason [*ratio*]. Indeed, since there was a reason [*ratio*] for it to exist rather than not to exist." This was deleted, and the sentence finished as in the main text.

For, above all, I hold a notion of possibility and necessity according to which there are some things that are possible, but yet not necessary, and which do not really exist. From this it follows that a reason that always forces a free mind to choose one thing over another (whether that reason derives from the perfection of a thing, as it does in God, or from our imperfection) does not eliminate our freedom.

From this it is also obvious how the free actions of God are to be distinguished from his necessary actions. And so it is necessary that God love himself, for this is demonstrable from the definition of God. But it cannot be demonstrated that God makes[40] that which is most perfect, since the contrary does not imply a contradiction; otherwise the contrary would not be possible, contrary to the hypothesis. Moreover, this conclusion derives from the notion of existence, for only the most perfect exists.[41] Let there be two possible things, A and B, one of which is such that it is necessary that it exists, and let us assume that there is more perfection in A than in B. Then, at least, we can explain why A should exist rather than B and can foresee which of them will exist; indeed, this can be demonstrated, that is, rendered certain from the nature of the thing. And, if being certain were the same as being necessary, then, I admit, it would also be necessary for A to exist. But I call such necessity hypothetical, for if it were absolutely necessary that A exist, then B would imply a contradiction, contrary to the hypothesis. And so we must hold that everything having some degree of perfection is possible and, moreover, that the possible that occurs is the one more perfect than its opposite, and that this happens not because of its nature but because of God's general resolve to create that which is more perfect. Perfection, or essence, is an urge for existence [*exigentia existentiae*] from which existence indeed follows *per se*, not necessarily, but[42] from the denial that another thing more perfect prevents it from existing. All truths of physics are of this sort; for example, when we say that some body persists in the speed with which it begins, we mean it does so if nothing prevents it.

God produces the best not by necessity but because he wills it. Indeed, if anyone were to ask me whether God wills by necessity, I would request that he explain what he means by necessity by adding more detail, that is, I would request that he give a complete formulation of the question. For example, you might ask whether God wills by necessity or whether he wills freely, that is, because of his nature or because of his will. I respond that God, of course, cannot will voluntarily, otherwise there would be a will for willing on to infinity. Rather, we must say that God wills the best through his nature. "Therefore," you will say, "he wills by necessity." I will say, with St. Augustine, that such necessity is blessed. "But surely it follows from this that things exist by necessity." How so? Since the nonexistence of what God wills to exist implies a contradiction? I deny that this proposition is absolutely true, for

---

40. Leibniz originally wrote "chooses" here, but deleted it in favor of "makes."
41. See marginal comment B below.
42. Leibniz originally continued the sentence as follows: "from the hypothesis of God's production or".

otherwise that which God does not will would not be possible. For things remain possible, even if God does not choose them. Indeed, even if God does not will something to exist, it is possible for it to exist, since, by its nature, it could exist if God were to will it to exist. "But God cannot will it to exist." I concede this, yet, such a thing remains possible in its nature, even if it is not possible with respect to the divine will, since we have defined as in its nature possible anything that, in itself, implies no contradiction, even though its coexistence with God can in some way be said to imply a contradiction. But it will be necessary to use unequivocal meanings for words in order to avoid every kind of absurd locution.[43]

Therefore I say: a possible thing is something with some essence or reality, that is, something that can distinctly be understood. For example, a pentagon would remain possible even if we were to imagine that no exact pentagon ever was or would be in nature. However, one should give some reason for why no pentagon ever existed or would exist. The reason for this state of affairs is nothing but the fact that the pentagon is incompatible with other things that include more perfection, that is, with other things that include more reality, which, to be sure, exist ahead of that pentagon. But, you infer: therefore it is necessary that it does not exist. This I concede if it is understood in the sense that the proposition, "a pentagon will not exist nor has one ever existed" is necessary. But the claim is false if it is understood in the sense that the proposition, "no pentagon exists" (abstracted from time) is necessary, because I deny that this proposition can be demonstrated. For the pentagon is not absolutely impossible, nor does it imply a contradiction, even if it follows from the harmony of things that a pentagon can find no place among real things. This can best be illustrated by analogy with imaginary roots in algebra. For the square root of −1 involves some notion, though it cannot be pictured, and if anyone wanted to picture it by a circle, he would find that the straight line required for this [way of picturing roots] does not intersect the circle.[44] But there is a great difference between problems that are insoluble on account of imaginary roots and those that are insoluble because of their absurdity, as for example, if someone were to look for a number which multiplied by itself is 9 and also added to 5 makes 9. Such a number implies a contradiction, for it must, at the same time, be both 3 and 4, that is, 3 and 4 must be equal, a part equal to the whole. But if anyone were to look for a number such that its square added to nine equals that number times three, he could certainly never show, by admitting such a number that the whole is equal* to its part, but nevertheless, he could show that such a number cannot be designated.[45]

---

43. Quotation marks have been added in this paragraph to distinguish Leibniz's remarks from those made by the imaginary antagonist.

44. Leibniz has in mind here a way of determining the imaginary roots of an equation by noting where a given line intersects a particular circle. This method is discussed in an unpublished manuscript on universal mathematics, GM VII 73–74. There Leibniz also discusses why it fails when the roots are imaginary.

45. The equation in question is:

$$x^2 + 9 = 3x$$

Unlike the previous example, the number that squared is equal to 9 and that added to 5 equals

If God had decreed that there should be no real line incommensurable with other real lines (what I call a real line is one that really bounds some body), it would not therefore follow that it would imply a contradiction for any incommensurable line to exist, even if, because of the principle of perfection, God could not have made things differently.

Given these considerations, we can eliminate difficulties concerning the foreknowledge of future contingents. For God, who foresees the future reasons why some things should exist rather than others, foresees them in their causes with certain knowledge. And indeed, he has certain knowledge of them and formulates propositions that are necessary, given that the state of the world has, once and for all, been settled, that is, given the harmony of things. But the propositions are not necessary in an absolute sense, as mathematical propositions are necessary.

Only the proposition that God [exists is necessary in an absolute sense].[46]

If an [exact] pentagon exists, it follows that it is more perfect than other things; but it is not. Therefore an [exact] pentagon does not exist. But it does not follow from this that it is impossible for it to exist. This is the best answer. We must therefore say that it is possible for the imperfect rather than the more perfect to exist. But, you say: it is impossible for something to exist that God does not will to exist. I deny that what is not going to exist is, in its nature, thereby impossible. And so we must say that what God does not will to exist does not exist, but we must therefore deny its necessity.

Marginal Comments:

A. Hence, a Scholastic, cited in Bonartes, *The Harmony of Knowledge with Faith*, claimed that God is indifferent not as to acting but as to willing.

B. If complete indifference is required for freedom, then there is scarcely

---

9, there are numbers that satisfy the constraints $3/2$ $1\pm \sqrt{-3}$) But both roots of the equation are imaginary, and in that sense cannot be represented through line segments as other roots can by the construction outlined in the previous note.

This example is followed by the following two equations, added to the original text:

"xx from x equals $-b^2$"

"xx equals $bx - bb$"

That is

$x - x^2 = -b^2$

$x^2 = bx - b^2$

It is likely that these are intended to be transformations of the equation under discussion, $x^2 + 9 = 3x$, with $b = 3$. In that case, the first of the two equations should read:

bx from xx equals $-b^2$

or

$x^2 - bx = -b^2$

It is not obvious why the equations were added.

46. There is a lacuna in ms here, filled in by the editors. Leibniz's thought seems to be that "God exists" is the only existential proposition that is absolutely necessary.

ever a free act [*actus*], since I think that the case in which everything on both sides is equal scarcely ever comes up. For even if, by chance, the reasons are equal, the passions will not be, and why should we argue about circumstances that do not arise? Nor do I think that one can produce an instance in which it is the will [*voluntas*] that chooses, since there is [always] some reason for choosing one of two things.

The Thomists place freedom in the power [*potentia*] of the will, which stands over and above every finite good in such a way that the will can resist it. And so, in order to have indifference of will, they seek indifference of intellect. They think that necessity is not inconsistent with freedom in God and that the freedom God has for loving himself is such a free necessity. But with respect to creatures he does not decide with necessity. [Vincent] Baron denies that God created those things which are most perfect.

Meditations on Knowledge, Truth, and Ideas (1684)[47]

The "Meditations on Knowledge, Truth, and Ideas" was Leibniz's first mature philosophical publication; it appeared in the November 1684 issue of the Leipzig journal Acta Eruditorum, *in which many of Leibniz's most important publications in mathematics and physics are also to be found. The controversies to which Leibniz refers in the opening paragraph were the famous Arnauld-Malebranche debate, occasioned by the publication of Arnauld's* Des vraies et des fausses idées *in 1683, an attack on Malebranche's philosophy, which began a long series of exchanges. Leibniz presents himself as a mediator in this essay, which is often cited and paraphrased in his later writings. In the title and in most of the occurrences in this essay, what we have translated as* knowledge *is* cognitio, *knowledge in the weak sense, something close to understanding, acquaintance, or even cognition. It is to be distinguished from* scientia, *which is knowledge in the strict sense and which normally entails certainty and truth.*

SINCE CONTROVERSIES rage today among distinguished persons over true and false ideas and since this is an issue of great importance for recognizing truth, an issue on which Descartes himself is not altogether satisfactory, I would like to explain briefly what I think can be established about the distinctions and criteria that relate to ideas and knowledge [*cognitio*]. Thus, knowledge is either obscure or *clear*, and again, clear knowledge is either confused or *distinct*, and distinct knowledge either inadequate or *adequate*, and adequate knowledge either symbolic or intuitive: and, indeed, if knowledge were, at the same time, both adequate and *intuitive*, it would be absolutely perfect.

A notion which is not sufficient for recognizing the thing represented is *obscure*, as, for example, if whenever I remember some flower or animal I

---

47. G IV 422–26; VE V 1075–81. Latin.

once saw, I cannot do so sufficiently well for me to recognize that flower or animal when presented and to distinguish it from other nearby flowers or animals, or, for example, if I were to consider some term insufficiently explained in the schools, like Aristotle's entelechy, or his notion of a cause insofar as it is something common to material, formal, efficient and final causes, or if I were to consider other terms of that sort, for which we have no settled definition. Whence, a proposition which involves such a notion is also obscure. Therefore, knowledge is *clear* when I have the means for recognizing the thing represented. Clear knowledge, again, is either confused or distinct. It is confused when I cannot enumerate one by one marks [*nota*] sufficient for differentiating a thing from others, even though the thing does indeed have such marks and requisites into which its notion can be resolved. And so we recognize colors, smells, tastes, and other particular objects of the senses clearly enough, and we distinguish them from one another, but only through the simple testimony of the senses, not by way of explicit marks. Thus we cannot explain what red is to a blind man, nor can we make such things clear to others except by leading them into the presence of the thing and making them see, smell, or taste the same thing we do, or, at very least, by reminding them of some past perception that is similar. This is so even though it is certain that the notions of these qualities are composite and can be resolved because, of course, they do have causes. Similarly, we see that painters and other artists correctly know [*cognosco*] what is done properly and what is done poorly, though they are often unable to explain their judgments and reply to questioning by saying that the things that displease them lack an unknown something. But a *distinct notion* is like the notion an assayer has of gold, that is, a notion connected with marks and tests sufficient to distinguish a thing from all other similar bodies. Notions common to several senses, like the notions of number, magnitude, shape are usually of such a kind, as are those pertaining to many states of mind, such as hope or fear, in a word, those that pertain to everything for which we have a *nominal definition* (which is nothing but an enumeration of sufficient marks). Also, one has distinct knowledge of an indefinable notion, since it is *primitive*, or its own mark, that is, since it is irresolvable and is understood only through itself and therefore lacks requisites. But in composite notions, since, again, the individual marks composing them are sometimes understood clearly but confusedly, like heaviness, color, solubility in *aqua fortis*, and others, which are among the marks of gold, such knowledge of gold may be distinct, yet *inadequate*. When everything that enters into a distinct notion is, again, distinctly known, or when analysis has been carried to completion, then knowledge is adequate (I don't know whether humans can provide a perfect example of this, although the knowledge of numbers certainly approaches it). However, we don't usually grasp the entire nature of a thing all at once, especially in a more lengthy analysis, but in place of the things themselves we make use of signs, whose explicit explanation we usually omit for the sake of brevity, knowing or believing that we have the ability to produce it at will.[48] And so when I think about a chiliagon, that is,

---

48. Literally: "knowing or believing that we have them in our power."

a polygon with a thousand equal sides, I don't always consider the nature of a side, or of equality, or of thousandfoldedness (that is, of the cube of tenfoldedness), but in my mind I use these words (whose sense appears only obscurely and imperfectly to the mind) in place of the ideas I have of these things, since I remember that I know the meaning of those words, and I decide that explanation is not necessary at this time. I usually call such thinking, which is found both in algebra and in arithmetic and, indeed, almost everywhere, *blind* or *symbolic*. And indeed, when a notion is very complex, we cannot consider all of its component notions at the same time. When we can, or indeed insofar as we can, I call knowledge *intuitive*. There is no knowledge of a distinct primitive notion except intuitive, just as our thinking about composites is for the most part symbolic.

From this it already follows that we don't perceive ideas of even those things we know distinctly, unless we make use of intuitive thinking. And, indeed, it happens that we often mistakenly believe that we have *ideas* of things in mind when we mistakenly suppose that we have already explained some of the terms we use. Furthermore, what some maintain, that we cannot say anything about a thing and understand what we say unless we have an idea of it, is either false or at least ambiguous.[49] For, often, we do understand in one way or another the words in question individually or remember that we understood them previously. But since we are content with this blind thinking and don't pursue the resolution of notions far enough, it happens that a contradiction that might be included in a very complex notion is concealed from us. An argument for the existence of God, celebrated among the Scholastics long ago and revived by Descartes, once led me to consider this point more distinctly. The argument goes: whatever follows from the idea or definition of anything can be predicated of that thing. Since the most perfect being includes all perfections, among which is existence, existence follows from the idea of God (or the idea of the most perfect being, or the idea of that than which nothing greater can be thought).[50] Therefore existence can be predicated of God. But one must realize that from this argument we can conclude only that, if God is possible, then it follows that he exists. For we cannot safely use definitions for drawing conclusions unless we know first that they are real definitions, that is, that they include no contradictions, because we can draw contradictory conclusions from notions that include contradictions, which is absurd. To clarify this I usually use the example of the fastest motion, which entails an absurdity. For let us suppose some wheel turning with the fastest motion. Everyone can see that any spoke of the wheel extended beyond the edge would move faster than a nail on the rim of the wheel. Therefore the nail's motion is not the fastest, contrary to the hypothesis. However, at first glance we might seem to have the idea of a fastest motion, for we certainly understand what we say; but yet we certainly have no idea of impossible things. And so, in the same way, the fact that we think about a most

---

49. See, for example, Malebranche, *Search after Truth*, book III, pt. 2, chap. 1.

50. The reference here is to the ontological argument as formulated first by St. Anselm of Canterbury in his *Proslogion* and given by Descartes in Meditation V.

perfect being is not sufficient for us to assert that we have an idea of it. And so, in the demonstration given a bit earlier, either we must show or we must assume the possibility of a most perfect being in order properly to draw the conclusion. However, nothing is truer than that we have an idea of God and that a most perfect being is possible, indeed, necessary; yet the argument is not sufficient for drawing the conclusion and was long ago rejected by Aquinas.[51]

And so we also have a distinction between *nominal definitions,* which contain only marks of a thing to be distinguished from other things, and *real definitions,* from which one establishes that a thing is possible. And with this we give our due to Hobbes, who claimed that truths are arbitrary, since they depend on nominal definitions, without considering the fact that the reality of a definition is not a matter of decision and that not just any notions can be joined to one another.[52] Nominal definitions are insufficient for perfect knowledge [*scientia*] except when one establishes in another way that the thing defined is possible. It is also obvious, at last, what *true* and *false* ideas are; namely, an idea is true when its notion is possible and false when it includes a contradiction. Moreover, we can know the *possibility* of a thing either *a priori* or *a posteriori.* The possibility of a thing is known *a priori* when we resolve a notion into its requisites, that is, into other notions known to be possible, and we know that there is nothing incompatible among them. This happens, among other cases, when we understand the way in which a thing can be produced, whence *causal definitions* are more useful than others. The possibility of a thing is known *a posteriori* when we know through experience that a thing actually exists, for what actually exists or existed is at very least possible. And, indeed, whenever we have adequate knowledge, we also have *a priori* knowledge of possibility, for having carried an analysis to completion, if no contradiction appears, then certainly the notion is at least possible. I won't now venture to determine whether people can ever produce a perfect analysis of their notions or whether they can ever reduce their thoughts to *primitive possibilities* or to irresolvable notions or (what comes to the same thing) to the absolute attributes of God, indeed to the first causes and the ultimate reason for things. For the most part we are content to have learned the reality of certain notions through experience, from which we then compose others following the example of nature.

From this I think that we can finally understand that one cannot always appeal safely to an idea and that many use this splendid honorific improperly to prop up certain creatures of their imagination, for we don't always have an idea corresponding to every thing we consciously think of, as I showed a while ago with the example of the greatest speed. Nor do I see that the people of our day have abused any less the principle that they have laid down, that *whatever I clearly and distinctly perceive about a thing is true or is assertable of the thing in question.* For, often, what is obscure and confused seems clear and distinct to people careless in judgment. Therefore, this axiom is useless unless we use criteria for the clear and distinct, criteria which we have made explicit,

---

51. See St. Thomas, *Summa Theologiae* I, q. 2 art. 1 ad 2.
52. See Hobbes's *De Corpore,* pt. I, chap. 3, sec. 7–9, in *Body, Man, and Citizen,* pp. 48–50.

and unless we have established the truth of the ideas. Furthermore, the rules of *common logic*, which even the geometers use, are not to be despised as criteria for the truth of assertions, as, for example, the rule that nothing is to be admitted as certain, unless it is shown by careful testing or sound demonstration. Moreover, a sound demonstration is one that follows the form prescribed by logic. Not that we always need syllogisms ordered in the manner of the schools (in the way that Christian Herlinus and Conrad Dasypodius presented the first six books of Euclid); but at very least the argument must reach its conclusion by virtue of its form. Any correct calculation can also be considered an example of such an argument conceived in proper form. And so, one should not omit any necessary premise, and all premises should have been either previously demonstrated or at least assumed as hypotheses, in which case the conclusion is also hypothetical. Those who carefully observe these rules will easily protect themselves against deceptive ideas. Pascal, a most talented man, largely agrees with this in his excellent essay "On the Geometrical Mind" (a fragment of which appears in the admirable book of the distinguished Antoine Arnauld on the art of thinking well). The geometer, he says, must define all terms which are even a bit obscure and prove all truths which are even a bit dubious. But I wish that he had defined the limits beyond which a notion or statement is no longer even a bit obscure or dubious. Nevertheless, what belongs here can be gathered from an attentive consideration of what we have said above, for we are now trying to be brief.[53]

As to the controversy over whether we see everything in God (which is certainly an old opinion and should not be rejected completely, if it is understood properly) or whether we have our own ideas, one must understand that, even if we were to see everything in God,[54] it would nevertheless be necessary that we also have our own ideas, that is, not little copies of God's, as it were, but affections or modifications of our mind corresponding to that very thing we perceived in God. For certainly there must be some change in our mind when we have some thoughts and then others, and, in fact, the ideas of things that we are not actually thinking about are in our mind as the shape of Hercules is in rough marble. Moreover, it is necessary not only that there actually be in God an idea of absolute and infinite extension but also that there be an idea of each shape, which is nothing but a modification of absolute extension. Furthermore, when we perceive colors or smells, we certainly have no perception other than that of shapes and of motions, though so very numerous and so very small that our mind cannot distinctly consider each individual one in this, its present state, and thus does not notice that its perception is composed of perceptions of minute shapes and motions alone, just as when we perceive the color green in a mixture of yellow and blue powder, we sense only yellow and blue finely mixed, even though we do not notice this, but rather fashion some new thing for ourselves.

---

53. See Pascal, *Oeuvres complètes*, p. 350, and Arnauld, *The Art of Thinking*, p. 13. See also Leibniz's further remarks on this view of Pascal's in a fragment dated 1674, C 181–82.

54. The view Leibniz discusses here is one of Malebranche's most controversial. See his *Search after Truth*, book III, pt. 2, chap. 6.

On Contingency (1686?)[55]

EXISTENCE DOES NOT DIFFER from essence in God, or, what is the same thing, it is essential for God to exist. Whence God is a necessary being.

Creatures are contingent, that is, their existence does not follow from their essence.

Necessary truths are those that can be demonstrated through an analysis of terms, so that in the end they become identities, just as in algebra an equation expressing an identity ultimately results from the substitution of values [for variables]. That is, necessary truths depend upon the principle of contradiction.

Contingent truths cannot be reduced to the principle of contradiction; otherwise everything would be necessary and nothing would be possible other than that which actually attains existence.

Nevertheless, since we say that both God and creatures exist and we say that necessary propositions are true no less than contingent ones, it is necessary that there be some common notion, both of contingent existence and of essential truth.[56]

In my view it is common to every truth that one can always give a reason for every nonidentical proposition; in necessary propositions, that reason necessitates; in contingent propositions, it inclines.

And it seems to be common to things that exist, both necessarily and contingently, that they have more reason for existing than others would, were they put in their place.

Every true universal affirmative proposition, either necessary or contingent, has some connection between subject and predicate. In identities this connection is self-evident; in other propositions it must appear through the analysis of terms.

And with this secret the distinction between necessary and contingent truths is revealed, something not easily understood unless one has some acquaintance with mathematics. For in necessary propositions, when the analysis is continued indefinitely, it arrives at an equation that is an identity; this is what it is to demonstrate a truth with geometrical rigor. But in contingent propositions one continues the analysis to infinity through reasons for reasons, so that one never has a complete demonstration, though there is always, underneath, a reason for the truth, but the reason is understood completely only by God, who alone traverses the infinite series in one stroke of mind.

The matter can be illustrated with an appropriate example from geometry and numbers. Just as in necessary propositions, where, through a continual

---

55. Editors' title. Gr 302–6. Latin.

56. The "contingent" and "essential" were late additions to the sentence. The paragraphs that follow suggest that they are carelessly and improperly placed in this sentence, and that it should read "… it is necessary that there be a notion of existence and a notion of truth, common both to contingent and essential propositions."

analysis of the predicate and the subject, things can at last be brought to the point where it is apparent that the notion of the predicate is in the subject, so too, when dealing with numbers, one can, in the end, arrive at a common measure through a continual analysis that consists of dividing first the one, then the other. But just as there is also a proportion or relation even among incommensurables themselves, despite the fact that their resolutions proceed to infinity and never end (as Euclid has demonstrated), so too in contingent truths there is a connection between the terms, that is, there is truth, even if that truth cannot be reduced to the principle of contradiction or necessity through an analysis into identities.

One can ask whether the proposition *God chooses the best* is necessary or whether it is one of his free decrees, indeed his primary free decree.

Similarly, one can also ask whether this proposition is necessary: nothing exists without there being a greater reason for it to exist than for it not to exist.

It is certain that there is a connection between subject and predicate in every truth. Therefore, when one says "Adam who sins exists," it is necessary that there be something in this possible notion, "Adam who sins," by virtue of which he is said to exist.

It seems that we must concede that God always acts wisely, that is, in such a way that anyone who knew his reasons would know and worship his supreme justice, goodness, and wisdom. And in God there never seems to be a case of acting purely because it pleases him to act in this way, unless, at the same time, it is pleasing for good reason.

Since we cannot know the true formal reason for existence in any particular case because it involves a progression to infinity, it is therefore sufficient for us to know the truth of contingent things *a posteriori*, that is, through experience, and yet, at the same time, to hold, universally or in general, that principle divinely implanted in our mind, confirmed both by reason and experience itself (to the extent that we can penetrate things), that nothing happens without a reason, as well as the principle of opposites, that that which has the more reason always happens.

And just as God himself decreed that he would always act only in accordance with true reasons of wisdom, so too he created rational creatures in such a way that they act only in accordance with prevailing or inclining reasons, reasons that are true or, in their place, apparent.

Unless there were such a principle, there would be no principle of truth in contingent things, for the principle of contradiction certainly has no place among contingent truths.

One must certainly hold that not all possibles attain existence, otherwise one could imagine no novel that did not exist in some place and at some time.* Indeed, it does not seem possible for all possible things to exist, since they get in one another's way. There are, in fact, an infinite number of series of possible things. Moreover, one series certainly cannot be contained within another, since each and every one of them is complete.

From these two principles, the rest follows:

1. God always acts with the mark of perfection or wisdom.

2. Not every possible thing attains existence.

To these one can add:

3. In every true universal affirmative proposition the predicate is in the subject, that is, there is a connection between predicate and subject.

Assuming that the proposition "the proposition that has the greater reason for existing [i.e., being true] exists [i.e., is true]" is necessary, we must see whether it then follows that the proposition that has the greater reason for existing [i.e., being true] is necessary.[57] But it is justifiable to deny the consequence. For, if by definition a necessary proposition is one whose truth can be demonstrated with geometrical rigor, then indeed it could be the case that this proposition is demonstrable: "every truth and only a truth has greater reason," or this: "God always acts with the highest wisdom." But from this one cannot demonstrate the proposition "contingent proposition A has greater reason [for being true]" or "contingent proposition A is in conformity with divine wisdom." And therefore it does not follow that contingent proposition A is necessary. So, although one can concede that it is necessary for God to choose the best, or that the best is necessary, it does not follow that what is chosen is necessary, since there is no demonstration that it is the best. And here the distinction between necessity of the consequence [*necessitas consequentiae*] and necessity of the consequent [*necessitas consequentis*] is in some way relevant; in the end, the proposition in question is a necessity of the consequence, not of the consequent, because it is necessary once we grant the hypothesis that we take it to be the best, assuming that the best is necessarily chosen.[58]

It seems safer to attribute to God the most perfect way possible of carrying things out. In creatures one cannot be so certain that they will act in accordance with even the most obvious reason; with respect to creatures, this proposition cannot be demonstrated.

Primary Truths (1686?)[59]

T HE PRIMARY TRUTHS are those which assert the same thing of itself or deny the opposite of its opposite. For example, "A is A," "A is not not-A," or "if it is true that A is B, then it is false that A is not B or that A is not-B." Also "every thing is as it is," "every thing is similar or equal to itself,"

---

57. The question is: does □ (if p has greater reason then p is true) entail (if p has greater reason then □ p)?

58. This distinction is made somewhat clearer by appeal to the following passage, from some notes on Bellarmine that may date from 1680–82(?):

Necessity of the consequence is when something follows from something else as a necessary consequence; absolute necessity [what Leibniz calls necessity of the consequent in the text?] is when the contrary of a thing implies a contradiction. (Gr 297).

59. Editors' title. C 518–23. Latin. "Primary Truths" has been redated as 1689.

"nothing is greater or less than itself," and others of this sort. Although they themselves may have their degrees of priority, nonetheless they can all be included under the name 'identities.'

Moreover, all remaining truths are reduced to primary truths with the help of definitions, that is, through the resolution of notions; in this consists *a priori proof*, proof independent of experience. As an example, I shall give this proposition from among the axioms accepted equally by mathematicians and all others alike: "the whole is greater than its part," or "the part is less than the whole," something easily demonstrated from the definition of "less" or "greater," with the addition of the primitive axiom, that is, the axiom of identity. For the *less* is that which is equal to a part of the other (the *greater*), a definition easy to understand and in agreement with the practice of the human race, when people compare things with one another and, taking away from the greater something equal to the lesser, they find something that remains. Hence there is an argument of this sort: the part is equal to a part of the whole (it is, of course, equal to itself through the axiom of identity, that each and every thing is equal to itself), and what is equal to a part of a whole is less than the whole (from the definition of "less"). Therefore, the part is less than the whole.

Therefore, the predicate or consequent is always in the subject or antecedent, and the nature of truth in general or the connection between the terms of a statement, consists in this very thing, as Aristotle also observed. The connection and inclusion of the predicate in the subject is explicit in identities, but in all other propositions it is implicit and must be shown through the analysis of notions; *a priori* demonstration rests on this.

Moreover, this is true for every affirmative truth, universal or particular, necessary or contingent, and in both an intrinsic and extrinsic denomination. And here lies hidden a wonderful secret, a secret that contains the nature of contingency, that is, the essential difference between necessary and contingent truths, a secret that eliminates the difficulty concerning the fatal necessity of even those things that are free.

Many things of great importance follow from these considerations, considerations insufficiently attended to because of their obviousness. For the received axiom that *nothing is without reason,* or *there is no effect without a cause,* directly follows from these considerations; otherwise there would be a truth which could not be proved *a priori*, that is, a truth which could not be resolved into identities, contrary to the nature of truth, which is always an explicit or implicit identity. It also follows that, when in the givens everything on the one side is the same as it is on the other side, then everything will be the same in the unknowns, that is, in the consequents. This is because no reason can be given for any difference, a reason which certainly must derive from the givens. And a corollary of this, or better, an example, is Archimedes' postulate at the beginning of the book on statics, that, given equal weights on both sides of a balance with equal arms, everything is in equilibrium.[60] And hence

---

60. See Archimedes, *On the Equilibrium of Planes,* book I, postulate 1, in Heath, *The Works of Archimedes,* p. 189.

there is even a reason for eternal things. If we imagine that the world has been from eternity, and we imagine only little balls in it, then we would have to explain why there are little balls rather than cubes.

From these considerations it also follows that, *in nature, there cannot be two individual things that differ in number alone.* For it certainly must be possible to explain why they are different, and that explanation must derive from some difference they contain. And so what St. Thomas recognized concerning separated intelligences, which, he said, never differ by number alone,[61] must also be said of other things, for never do we find two eggs or two leaves or two blades of grass in a garden that are perfectly similar. And thus, perfect similarity is found only in incomplete and abstract notions, where things are considered [*in rationes veniunt*] only in a certain respect, but not in every way, as, for example, when we consider shapes alone, and neglect the matter that has shape. And so it is justifiable to consider two similar triangles in geometry, even though two perfectly similar material triangles are nowhere found. And although gold and other metals, also salts and many liquids might be taken to be homogeneous, this can only be admitted with regard to the senses, and it is not true that they are, in all rigor.

It also follows that *there are no purely extrinsic denominations*, denominations which have absolutely no foundation in the very thing denominated. For it is necessary that the notion of the subject denominated contain the notion of the predicate. And consequently, whenever the denomination of a thing is changed, there must be a variation in the thing itself.

The complete or perfect notion of an individual substance contains all of its predicates, past, present, and future. For certainly it is now true that a future predicate will be, and so it is contained in the notion of a thing. And thus everything that will happen to Peter or Judas, both necessary and free, is contained in the perfect individual notion of Peter or Judas, considered in the realm of possibility by withdrawing the mind from the divine decree for creating him, and is seen there by God. And from this it is obvious that God chose from an infinite number of possible individuals those he thought most in accord with the supreme and hidden ends of his wisdom. Properly speaking, he did not decide that Peter sin or that Judas be damned, but only that Peter who would sin with certainty, though not with necessity, but freely, and Judas who would suffer damnation would attain existence rather than other possible things; that is, he decreed that the possible notion become actual. And, although the future salvation of Peter is also contained in his eternal possible notion, it is, however, not without the concurrence of grace, for in the same perfect notion of that possible Peter, even the aid of divine grace to be given him is found, under the notion of possibility.

Every individual substance contains in its perfect notion the entire universe and everything that exists in it, past, present, and future. For there is no thing on which one cannot impose some true denomination from another thing, at very least a denomination of comparison and relation. Moreover, there is no

---

61. See St. Thomas, *Summa Theologiae* I, q. 50 art. 4.

purely extrinsic denomination. I have shown the same thing in many other ways, all in harmony with one another.

Indeed, *all individual created substances are different expressions of the same universe* and different expressions of the same universal cause, namely God. But the expressions vary in perfection, just as different representations or drawings of the same town from different points of view do.

Every individual created substance exerts physical action and passion on all the others. From a change made in one, some corresponding change follows in all the others, since the denomination[62] is changed. And this is in agreement with our experience of nature. For, in a vessel filled with a liquid (and the whole universe is just such a vessel) motion made in the middle is propagated to the edges, although it is rendered more and more insensible, the more it recedes from its origin.

Strictly speaking, one can say that *no created substance exerts a metaphysical action or influx on any other thing*. For, not to mention the fact that one cannot explain how something can pass from one thing into the substance of another, we have already shown that from the notion of each and every thing follows all of its future states. What we call causes are only concurrent requisites, in metaphysical rigor. This is also illustrated by our experience of nature. For bodies really rebound from others through the force of their own elasticity, and not through the force of other things, even if another body is required in order for the elasticity (which arises from something intrinsic to the body itself) to be able to act.

Also, assuming the distinction between soul and body, from this we can explain their union without the common hypothesis of an influx, which is unintelligible, and without the hypothesis of an occasional cause, which appeals to a *Deus ex machina*. For God from the beginning constituted both the soul and the body with such wisdom and such workmanship that, from the first constitution or notion of a thing, everything that happens through itself [*per se*] in the one corresponds perfectly to everything that happens in the other, just as if something passed from one to the other. This is what I call the hypothesis of concomitance. This hypothesis is true in all substances in the whole universe but cannot be sensed in all of them, unlike the case of the soul and the body.

There is no vacuum. For the different parts of empty space would then be perfectly similar and mutually congruent and could not be distinguished from one another. And so they would differ in number alone, which is absurd. One can also prove that time is not a thing in the same way as we did for space.[63]

There is no atom, indeed, there is no body so small that it is not actually subdivided. Because of that, while it is acted upon by everything else in the

---

62. Originally Leibniz wrote "extrinsic denomination."

63. The following passage was deleted here: "*There is no corporeal substance in which there is nothing but extension or size, shape and their variations,* for in this way two substances perfectly similar to one another could exist, which would be absurd. From this it follows that there is something in corporeal substances analogous to the soul which they [i.e., the Scholastics] call form."

whole universe and receives some effect from everything (an effect which must cause change in a body), it also preserves all past impressions and contains, before they happen, all future impressions. And if anyone were to say that that effect is contained in the motions impressed on the atom, which receives* the effect as a whole without being divided, one can respond that not only must there be effects produced in an atom from all the impressions of the universe, but also, in turn, the state of the whole universe must be inferred from the atom, from the effect, the cause. But since the same motion can come about through different impressions, through no regress can one infer the impressions by means of which it [i.e., the atom] had come to its present state, from the shape and motion of an atom alone—not to mention the fact that one cannot explain why bodies of a certain smallness cannot be divided further.

From this it follows that *every particle of the universe contains a world of an infinity of creatures.* However, the continuum is not divided into points, nor is it divided in all possible ways—not into points, since points are not parts but boundaries, and not in all possible ways, since not all creatures are in a given thing, but there is only a certain progression of them *ad infinitum*, just as one who assumes a straight line and any part derived by bisection sets up divisions different from someone who trisects it.

There is no determinate shape in actual things, for none can be appropriate for an infinite number of impressions. And so neither a circle, nor an ellipse, nor any other line we can define exists except in the intellect, nor do lines exist before they are drawn, nor parts before they are separated off.[64]

Extension and motion, as well as bodies themselves (insofar as only motion and extension are placed in bodies) are not substances, but true phenomena, like rainbows and parhelia. For there are no shapes in things, and if we consider their extension alone, then bodies are not substances, but many substances.

Something lacking extension is required for the substance of bodies, otherwise there would be no source [*principium*] for the reality of phenomena or for true unity. There is always a plurality of bodies, and never one, and therefore, in reality, there is not even a plurality. Cordemoy proved atoms using a similar argument.[65] But since atoms are excluded, what remains is something lacking extension, analogous to the soul, which they once called form or species.

Corporeal substance can neither arise nor perish except through creation or annihilation. For when corporeal substance once endures, it will always endure, since there is no reason for any difference, and the dissolution of parts of a body has nothing in common with its destruction. Therefore, *animate things neither arise nor perish, but are only transformed.*

---

64. Leibniz deleted the following here: "Space, time, extension, and motion are not things, but modes of contemplating things that have a foundation."
65. See Cordemoy, *Le discernement du corps et de l'ame*, premier discours, in Cordemoy, *Oeuvres philosophiques.*

Discourse on Metaphysics (1686)[66]

In February 1686, Leibniz wrote a letter to the Landgrave Ernst von Hessen-Reinfels, saying: "being somewhere having nothing to do for a few days, I have lately composed a short discourse on metaphysics about which I would be very happy to have Mr. Arnauld's opinion. For questions on grace, God's concourse with creatures, the nature of miracles, the cause of sin and the origin of evil, the immortality of the soul, ideas, etc. are touched upon in a manner which seems to provide new openings capable of illuminating some very great difficulties" (G II, 11). Leibniz does not appear to have sent out the full "Discourse," as it later came to be known, following Leibniz's own characterization, though he did append "summaries" of it to his letter (which the Landgrave transmitted to Arnauld); the summaries are also preserved as the titles of each article of the "Discourse" (in a later version of the "Discourse" than the manuscript in Leibniz's handwriting discovered by Henri Lestienne). Arnauld replied with a letter criticizing section 13, and the Leibniz-Arnauld correspondence began. See the Letters to Arnauld.

1. On Divine Perfection, and That God Does Everything in the Most Desirable Way.

THE MOST widely accepted and meaningful notion we have of God is expressed well enough in these words, that God is an absolutely perfect being; yet the consequences of these words are not sufficiently considered. And, to penetrate more deeply into this matter, it is appropriate to remark that there are several entirely different perfections in nature, that God possesses all of them together, and that each of them belongs to him in the highest degree.

We must also know what a perfection is. A fairly sure test for being a perfection is that forms or natures that are not capable of a highest degree are not perfections, as for example, the nature of number or figure. For the greatest of all numbers (or even the number of all numbers), as well as the greatest of all figures, imply a contradiction, but the greatest knowledge and omnipotence do not involve any impossibility. Consequently, power and knowledge are perfections, and, insofar as they belong to God, they do not have limits.

Whence it follows that God, possessing supreme and infinite wisdom, acts in the most perfect manner, not only metaphysically, but also morally speaking, and that, with respect to ourselves, we can say that the more enlightened and informed we are about God's works, the more we will be disposed to find them excellent and in complete conformity with what we might have desired.

---

66. G IV 427–63 and LD. French.

2. Against Those Who Claim That There Is No Goodness in God's Works, or That the Rules of Goodness and Beauty Are Arbitrary.

T HUS I AM far removed from the opinion of those who maintain that there are no rules of goodness and perfection in the nature of things or in the ideas God has of them and who say that the works of God are good solely for the formal reason that God has made them.[67] For, if this were so, God, knowing that he is their author, would not have had to consider them afterwards and find them good, as is testified by the Sacred Scriptures—which seem to have used such anthropomorphic expressions only to make us understand that the excellence of God's works can be recognized by considering them in themselves, even when we do not reflect on this empty external denomination which relates them to their cause. This is all the more true, since it is by considering his works that we can discover the creator. His works must therefore carry his mark in themselves. I confess that the contrary opinion seems to me extremely dangerous and very near to the opinion of the recent innovators[68] who hold that the beauty of the universe and the goodness we attribute to the works of God are but the chimeras of those who conceive of God in terms of themselves. Thus, in saying that things are not good by virtue of any rule of goodness but solely by virtue of the will of God, it seems to me that we unknowingly destroy all of God's love and all his glory. For why praise him for what he has done if he would be equally praiseworthy in doing the exact contrary? Where will his justice and wisdom reside if there remains only a certain despotic power, if will holds the place of reason, and if, according to the definition of tyrants, justice consists in whatever pleases the most powerful? Besides, it seems that all acts of will presuppose a reason for willing and that this reason is naturally prior to the act of will. That is why I also find completely strange the expression of some other philosophers[69] who say that the eternal truths of metaphysics and geometry and consequently also the rules of goodness, justice, and perfection are merely the effects of the will of God; instead, it seems to me, they are only the consequences of his understanding, which, assuredly, does not depend on his will, any more than does his essence.

3. Against Those Who Believe That God Might Have Made Things Better.

N OR CAN I approve of the opinion of some moderns who maintain boldly that what God has made is not of the highest perfection and that he could have done much better.[70] For it seems to me that the consequences of

---

67. This is Descartes's view. See, e.g., the *Sixth Replies*, AT VII 432, 435–36.
68. Spinoza, and by extension, Descartes. The earlier draft, as reported by Lestienne, explicitly mentions the Spinozists alone in this regard. See Spinoza, appendix to *Ethics*, part 1.
69. Descartes is mentioned in an earlier draft, but deleted.
70. See e.g., Malebranche, *Traité de la nature et de la grace*, Pr. disc., sec. xiv. Malebranche's *Traité* seems to be one of the main targets of this essay.

this opinion are wholly contrary to the glory of God: as a lesser evil is relatively good, so a lesser good is relatively evil. And to act with less perfection than one could have is to act imperfectly. To show that an architect could have done better is to find fault with his work. This opinion is also contrary to the Sacred Scripture, which assure us of the goodness of God's works. For, if their view were sufficient, then since the series of imperfections descends to infinity, God's works would always have been good in comparison with those less perfect, no matter how he created them but something is hardly praiseworthy if it can be praised only in this way. I also believe that a great many passages from Sacred Scripture and the holy fathers will be found favoring my opinion, but scarcely any will be found favoring the opinion of these moderns, an opinion which is, in my judgment, unknown to all antiquity and which is based only on the inadequate knowledge we have of the general harmony of the universe and of the hidden reasons for God's conduct. This enables us to judge audaciously that many things could have been rendered better. Besides, these moderns insist on certain dubious subtleties, for they imagine that nothing is so perfect that there is not something more perfect—this is an error.

They also believe that in this way they are able to safeguard God's freedom, as though it were not freedom of the highest sort to act in perfection following sovereign reason. For to believe that God does something without having any reason for his will—overlooking the fact that this seems impossible—is an opinion that conforms little to his glory. Let us assume, for example, that God chooses between A and B and that he takes A without having any reason to prefer it to B. I say that this action of God is at the very least not praiseworthy; for all praise must be based on some reason, and by hypothesis there is none here. Instead I hold that God does nothing for which he does not deserve to be glorified.

4. That the Love of God Requires Our Complete Satisfaction and Acquiescence with Respect to What He Has Done without Our Being Quietists as a Result.

THE GENERAL KNOWLEDGE of this great truth, that God acts always in the most perfect and desirable way possible, is, in my judgment, the foundation of the love that we owe God in all things, since he who loves seeks his satisfaction in the happiness or perfection of the object loved and in his actions. To will the same and dislike the same is true friendship. And I believe that it is difficult to love God well when we are not disposed to will what God wills, when we might have the power to change it. In fact, those who are not satisfied with what God does seem to me like dissatisfied subjects whose attitudes are not much different from those of rebels.

I hold, therefore, that, according to these principles, in order to act in accordance with the love of God, it is not sufficient to force ourselves to be patient; rather, we must truly be satisfied with everything that has come to us according to his will. I mean this acquiescence with respect to the past. As for the future, we must not be quietists[71] and stand ridiculously with arms folded, awaiting that which God will do, according to the sophism that the ancients called *logon aergon*, the lazy reason. But we must act in accordance with what we presume to be the *will of God*, insofar as we can judge it, trying with all our might to contribute to the general good and especially to the embellishment and perfection of that which affects us or that which is near us, that which is, so to speak, in our grasp. For, although the outcome might perhaps demonstrate that God did not wish our good will to have effect at present, it does not follow that he did not wish us to act as we have. On the contrary, since he is the best of all masters, he never demands more than the right intention, and it is for him to know the proper hour and place for letting the good designs succeed.

5. What the Rules of the Perfection of Divine Conduct Consist in, and That the Simplicity of the Ways Is in Balance with the Richness of the Effects.

THEREFORE IT IS sufficient to have the confidence that God does everything for the best and that nothing can harm those who love him. But to know in detail the reasons that could have moved him to choose this order of the universe—to allow sins, to dispense his saving grace in a certain way— surpasses the power of a finite mind, especially when it has not yet attained the enjoyment of the vision of God.

However, we can make some general remarks concerning the course of providence in the governance of things. We can therefore say that one who acts perfectly is similar to an excellent geometer who can find the best constructions for a problem; or to a good architect who makes use of his location and the funds set aside for a building in the most advantageous manner, allowing nothing improper or lacking in the beauty of which it is capable; or to a good householder, who makes use of his holdings in such a way that there remains nothing uncultivated and sterile; or to a skilled machinist who produces his work in the least difficult way possible; or to a learned author who includes the greatest number of truths [*realités*] in the smallest possible volume. Now, the most perfect of all beings, those that occupy the least volume, that is, those that least interfere with one another, are minds, whose perfections consist in their virtues. That is why we mustn't doubt that the happiness of minds is the principal aim of God and that he puts this into practice to the extent that general harmony permits it. We shall say more about this below.

As for the simplicity of the ways of God, this holds properly with respect to his means, as opposed to the variety, richness, and abundance, which holds with respect to his ends or effects. And the one must be in balance with the

---

71. The quietists were followers of Miguel de Molinos (ca. 1640–97), author of the *Guida spirituale* (1675), and others, who stressed passive contemplation and complete resignation to the will of God.

other, as are the costs of a building and the size and beauty one demands of it. It is true that nothing costs God anything—even less than it costs a philosopher to build the fabric of his imaginary world out of hypotheses—since God has only to make decrees in order that a real world come into being. But in matters of wisdom, decrees or hypotheses take the place of expenditures to the extent that they are more independent of one another, because reason requires that we avoid multiplying hypotheses or principles, in somewhat the same way that the simplest system is always preferred in astronomy.

6. God Does Nothing Which Is Not Orderly and It Is Not Even Possible to Imagine Events That Are Not Regular.

THE VOLITIONS or acts of God are commonly divided into ordinary or extraordinary. But it is good to consider that God does nothing which is not orderly. Thus, what passes for extraordinary is extraordinary only with some particular order established among creatures; for everything is in conformity with respect to the universal order. This is true to such an extent that not only does nothing completely irregular occur in the world, but we would not even be able to imagine such a thing. Thus, let us assume, for example, that someone jots down a number of points at random on a piece of paper, as do those who practice the ridiculous art of geomancy.[72] I maintain that it is possible to find a geometric line whose notion is constant and uniform, following a certain rule, such that this line passes through all the points in the same order in which the hand jotted them down.

And if someone traced a continuous line which is sometimes straight, sometimes circular, and sometimes of another nature, it is possible to find a notion, or rule, or equation common to all the points of this line, in virtue of which these very changes must occur. For example, there is no face whose contours are not part of a geometric line and cannot be traced in one stroke by a certain regular movement. But, when a rule is extremely complex, what is in conformity with it passes for irregular.

Thus, one can say, in whatever manner God might have created the world, it would always have been regular and in accordance with a certain general order. But God has chosen the most perfect world, that is, the one which is at the same time the simplest in hypotheses and the richest in phenomena, as might be a line in geometry whose construction is easy and whose properties and effects are extremely remarkable and widespread. I use these comparisons to sketch an imperfect likeness of divine wisdom and to point out something that can at least elevate our minds to conceive in some way what cannot be sufficiently expressed. But I do not claim to explain in this way the great mystery upon which the entire universe depends.

---

72. Geomancy is the art of divination by means of lines or figures.

7. That Miracles Conform to the General Order, Even Though They May Be Contrary to the Subordinate Maxims; and about What God Wills or Permits by a General or Particular Volition.

NOW, since nothing can happen which is not in the order, one can say that miracles are as much within the order as are natural operations, operations which are called natural because they are in conformity with certain subordinate maxims that we call the nature of things. For one can say that this nature is only God's custom, with which he can dispense for any stronger reason than the one which moved him to make use of these maxims.

As for the general or particular volitions, depending upon how the matter is understood, we can say that God does everything following his most general will, which is in conformity with the most perfect order he has chosen, but we can also say that he has particular volitions which are exceptions to these aforementioned subordinate maxims. For the most general of God's laws, the one that rules the whole course of the universe, is without exception.

We can say also that God wills everything that is an object of his particular volition. But we must make a distinction with respect to the objects of his general volition, such as the actions of other creatures, particularly the actions of those that are reasonable, actions with which God wishes to concur. For, if the action is good in itself, we can say that God wills it and sometimes commands it, even when it does not take place. But if the action is evil in itself and becomes good only by accident, because the course of things (particularly punishment and atonement) corrects its evilness and repays the evil with interest in such a way that in the end there is more perfection in the whole sequence than if the evil had not occurred, then we must say that God permits this but does not will it, even though he concurs with it because of the laws of nature he has established and because he knows how to draw a greater good from it.

8. To Distinguish the Actions of God from Those of Creatures We Explain the Notion of an Individual Substance.

IT IS RATHER DIFFICULT to distinguish the actions of God from those of creatures; for some believe that God does everything, while others imagine that he merely conserves the force he has given to creatures. What follows will let us see the extent to which we can say the one or the other. And since actions and passions properly belong to individual substances [*actiones sunt suppositorum*],[73] it will be necessary to explain what such an individual substance is.

It is indeed true that when several predicates are attributed to a single subject

---

73. Leibniz is making use of Scholastic logical terminology: a *suppositum* is an individual subsistent substance; *actiones sunt suppositorum* therefore means that actions are of individual subsistent substances.

and this subject is attributed to no other, it is called an individual substance; but this is not sufficient, and such an explanation is merely nominal. We must therefore consider what it is to be attributed truly to a certain subject.

Now it is evident that all true predication has some basis in the nature of things and that, when a proposition is not an identity, that is, when the predicate is not explicitly contained in the subject, it must be contained in it virtually. That is what the philosophers call *in-esse*, when they say that the predicate is in the subject. Thus the subject term must always contain the predicate term, so that one who understands perfectly the notion of the subject would also know that the predicate belongs to it.

Since this is so, we can say that the nature of an individual substance or of a complete being is to have a notion so complete that it is sufficient to contain and to allow us to deduce from it all the predicates of the subject to which this notion is attributed. An accident, on the other hand, is a being whose notion does not include everything that can be attributed to the subject to which the notion is attributed.[74] Thus, taken in abstraction from the subject, the quality of being a king which belongs to Alexander the Great is not determinate enough to constitute an individual and does not include the other qualities of the same subject, nor does it include everything that the notion of this prince includes. On the other hand, God, seeing Alexander's individual notion or haecceity,[75] sees in it at the same time the basis and reason for all the predicates which can be said truly of him, for example, that he vanquished Darius and Porus; he even knows *a priori* (and not by experience) whether he died a natural death or whether he was poisoned, something we can know only through history. Thus when we consider carefully the connection of things, we can say that from all time in Alexander's soul there are vestiges of everything that has happened to him and marks of everything that will happen to him and even traces of everything that happens in the universe, even though God alone could recognize them all.[76]

9. That Each Singular Substance Expresses the Whole Universe in Its Own Way, and That All Its Events, Together with All Their Circumstances and the Whole Sequence of External Things, Are Included in Its Notion.

SEVERAL notable paradoxes follow from this; among others, it follows that it is not true that two substances can resemble each other completely and

---

74. An earlier draft of the following passage read: "Thus the circular shape of the ring of [Gyges] [Polycrates] does not contain everything that the notion of this particular ring contains, unlike God [knowing] seeing the individual notion of this ring [seeing, for example, that it will be swallowed by a fish and yet returned to its owner]." (Words in brackets were deleted by Leibniz.)

75. The word *haecceitas* (or *heccëité*, what we are translating as "haecceity") was coined by John Duns Scotus (ca. 1270–1308) to refer to an individual essence or "thisness"—what *haecceitas* means literally.

76. An earlier draft added: "I speak here as if it were assumed that this ring [has consciousness] [is a substance]."

differ only in number [*solo numero*],[77] and that what Saint Thomas asserts on this point about angels or intelligences (that here every individual is a lowest species)[78] is true of all substances, provided that one takes the specific difference as the geometers do with respect to their figures. It also follows that a substance can begin only by creation and end only by annihilation; that a substance is not divisible into two; that one substance cannot be constructed from two; and that thus the number of substances does not naturally increase and decrease, though they are often transformed.

Moreover, every substance is like a complete world and like a mirror of God or of the whole universe, which each one expresses in its own way, somewhat as the same city is variously represented depending upon the different positions from which it is viewed. Thus the universe is in some way multiplied as many times as there are substances, and the glory of God is likewise multiplied by as many entirely different representations of his work. It can even be said that every substance bears in some way the character of God's infinite wisdom and omnipotence and imitates him as much as it is capable. For it expresses, however confusedly, everything that happens in the universe, whether past, present, or future—this has some resemblance to an infinite perception or knowledge. And since all other substances in turn express this substance and accommodate themselves to it, one can say that it extends its power over all the others, in imitation of the creator's omnipotence.

10. That the Belief in Substantial Forms Has Some Basis, but That These Forms Do Not Change Anything in the Phenomena and Must Not Be Used to Explain Particular Effects.

IT SEEMS that the ancients, as well as many able men accustomed to deep meditation who have taught theology and philosophy some centuries ago (some of whom are respected for their saintliness) have had some knowledge of what we have just said; this is why they introduced and maintained the substantial forms which are so decried today. But they are not so distant from the truth nor so ridiculous as the common lot of our new philosophers imagines.

I agree that the consideration of these forms serves no purpose in the details of physics and must not be used to explain particular phenomena. That is where the Scholastics failed, as did the physicians of the past who followed their example, believing that they could account for the properties of bodies by talking about forms and qualities without taking the trouble to examine their manner of operation. It is as if we were content to say that a clock has a quality of clockness derived from its form without considering in what all of this consists; that would be sufficient for the person who buys the clock, provided that he turns over its care to another.

But this misunderstanding and misuse of forms must not cause us to reject

---

77. An earlier draft added the following: "also, that if bodies are substances, it is not possible that their nature consists only in size, shape, and motion, but that something else is needed."
78. See St. Thomas, *Summa Theologiae* I, q. 50, art. 4.

something whose knowledge is so necessary in metaphysics that, I hold, without it one cannot properly know the first principles or elevate our minds sufficiently well to the knowledge of incorporeal natures and the wonders of God.

However, just as a geometer does not need to burden his mind with the famous labyrinth of the composition of the continuum, there is no need for any moral philosopher and even less need for a jurist or statesman to trouble himself with the great difficulties involved in reconciling free will and God's providence, since the geometer can achieve all his demonstrations and the statesman can complete all his deliberations without entering into these discussions, discussions that remain necessary and important in philosophy and theology. In the same way, a physicist can explain some experiments, at times using previous simpler experiments and at times using geometric and mechanical demonstrations, without needing[79] general considerations from another sphere. And if he uses God's concourse, or else a soul, animating force [archée], or something else of this nature, he is raving just as much as the person who, in the course of an important practical deliberation, enters into a lofty discussion concerning the nature of destiny and the nature of our freedom. In fact, people often commit this fault without thinking when they encumber their minds with the consideration of fatalism and sometimes are even diverted from a good resolution or a necessary duty in this way.

11. That the Thoughts of the Theologians and Philosophers Who Are Called Scholastics Are Not Entirely to Be Disdained.

I KNOW that I am advancing a great paradox by attempting to rehabilitate the old philosophy in some fashion and to restore the almost banished substantial forms to their former place.[80] But perhaps I will not be condemned so easily when it is known that I have long meditated upon the modern philosophy, that I have given much time to experiments in physics and demonstrations in geometry, and that I had long been persuaded about the futility of these beings, which I finally was required to embrace in spite of myself and, as it were, by force, after having myself carried out certain studies. These studies made me recognize that our moderns do not give enough credit to Saint Thomas and to the other great men of his time and that there is much more solidity than one imagines in the opinions of the Scholastic philosophers and theologians, provided that they are used appropriately and in their proper place. I am even convinced that, if some exact and thoughtful mind took the trouble to clarify and summarize their thoughts after the manner of the analytic geometers, he would find there a great treasure of extremely important and wholly demonstrative truths.

---

79. An earlier draft continued "[forms and other] [considerations of substantial forms]".

80. A marginal note in an earlier draft: "I do this, however, only under an hypothesis, insofar as one can say that bodies are substances."

12. That the Notions Involved in Extension Contain Something Imaginary and Cannot Constitute the Substance of Body.

B UT, to resume the thread of our discussion, I believe that anyone who will meditate about the nature of substance, as I have explained it above, will find[81] that the nature of body does not consist merely in extension, that is, in size, shape, and motion, but that we must necessarily recognize in body something related to souls, something we commonly call substantial form, even though it makes no change in the phenomena, any more than do the souls of animals, if they have any. It is even possible to demonstrate that the notions of size, shape, and motion are not as distinct as is imagined and that they contain something imaginary and relative to our perception, as do (though to a greater extent) color, heat, and other similar qualities, qualities about which one can doubt whether they are truly found in the nature of things outside ourselves. That is why qualities of this kind cannot constitute any substance. And if there were no other principle of identity in body other than the one just mentioned, a body could not subsist for more than a moment.

Yet the souls and substantial forms of other bodies are entirely different from intelligent souls, which alone know their actions. Not only don't intelligent souls perish naturally, but they also always preserve the basis for the knowledge of what they are; this is what renders them alone susceptible to punishment and reward and makes them citizens of the republic of the universe, whose monarch is God. It also follows that all other creatures must serve them—something which we will later discuss more fully.

13. Since the Individual Notion of Each Person Includes Once and for All Everything That Will Ever Happen to Him, One Sees in It the A priori Proofs of the Truth of Each Event, or, Why One Happened Rather Than Another. But These Truths, However Certain, Are Nevertheless Contingent, Being Based on the Free Will of God or of His Creatures, Whose Choice Always Has Its Reasons, Which Incline without Necessitating.

B UT before going further, we must attempt to resolve a great difficulty that can arise from the foundations we have set forth above. We have said that the notion of an individual substance includes once and for all everything that can ever happen to it and that, by considering this notion, one can see there everything that can truly be said of it, just as we can see in the nature of a circle all the properties that can be deduced from it. But it seems that this would eliminate the difference between contingent and necessary truths,

---

81. An earlier draft interpolates: "either that bodies are not substances in metaphysical rigor (which was, in fact, the view of the Platonists), or".

that there would be no place for human freedom, and that an absolute fatalism would rule all our actions as well as all the other events of the world. To this I reply that we must distinguish between what is certain and what is necessary. Everyone grants that future contingents are certain, since God foresees them, but we do not concede that they are necessary on that account. But (someone will say) if a conclusion can be deduced infallibly from a definition or notion, it is necessary. And it is true that we are maintaining that everything that must happen to a person is already contained virtually in his nature or notion, just as the properties of a circle are contained in its definition; thus the difficulty still remains. To address it firmly, I assert that connection or following [*consécution*] is of two kinds. The one whose contrary implies a contradiction is absolutely necessary; this deduction occurs in the eternal truths, for example, the truths of geometry. The other is necessary only *ex hypothesi* and, so to speak, accidentally, but it is contingent in itself, since its contrary does not imply a contradiction. And this connection is based not purely on ideas and God's simple understanding, but on his free decrees and on the sequence of the universe.

Let us take an example. Since Julius Caesar will become perpetual dictator and master of the republic and will overthrow the freedom of the Romans, this action is contained in his notion, for we assume that it is the nature of such a perfect notion of a subject to contain everything, so that the predicate is included in the subject, *ut possit inesse subjecto*.[82] It could be said that it is not in virtue of this notion or idea that he must perform this action, since it pertains to him only because God knows everything. But someone might insist that his nature or form corresponds to this notion, and, since God has imposed this personality on him, it is henceforth necessary for him to satisfy it. I could reply by citing future contingents, since they have no reality as yet, save in God's understanding and will, and, because God gave them this form in advance, they must in the same way correspond to it.

But I much prefer to overcome difficulties rather than to excuse them by giving some other similar difficulties, and what I am about to say will illuminate the one as well as the other. It is here, then, that we must apply the distinction concerning connections, and I say that whatever happens in conformity with these predeterminations [*avances*] is certain but not necessary, and if one were to do the contrary, he would not be doing something impossible in itself, even though it would be impossible [*ex hypothesi*] for this to happen. For if someone were able to carry out the whole demonstration by virtue of which he could prove this connection between the subject, Caesar, and the predicate, his successful undertaking, he would in fact be showing that Caesar's future dictatorship is grounded in his notion or nature, that there is a reason why he crossed the Rubicon rather than stopped at it and why he won rather than lost at Pharsalus and that it was reasonable, and consequently certain, that this should happen. But this would not show that it was necessary in itself nor that the contrary implies a contradiction. It is

---

82. The Latin is an approximate paraphrase of the preceding clause.

reasonable and certain in almost the same way that God will always do the best, even though what is less perfect does not imply a contradiction.

For it will be found that the demonstration of this predicate of Caesar is not as absolute as those of numbers or of geometry, but that it supposes the sequence of things that God has freely chosen, a sequence based on God's first free decree always to do what is most perfect and on God's decree with respect to human nature, following out of the first decree, that man will always do (although freely) that which appears to be best. But every truth based on these kinds of decrees is contingent, even though it is certain; for these decrees do not change the possibility of things, and, as I have already said, even though it is certain that God always chooses the best, this does not prevent something less perfect from being and remaining possible in itself, even though it will not happen, since it is not its impossibility but its imperfection which causes it to be rejected. And nothing is necessary whose contrary is possible.

We will therefore be in a position to satisfy these sorts of difficulties, however great they may appear (and in fact they are not made any the less pressing by considering the other thinkers who have ever treated this matter), as long as we recognize that all contingent propositions have reasons to be one way rather than another or else (what comes to the same thing) that they have *a priori* proofs of their truth which render them certain and which show that the connection between subject and predicate of these propositions has its basis in the natures of both. But they do not have necessary demonstrations, since these reasons are based only on the principle of contingency or the principle of the existence of things, that is, based on what is or appears to be best from among several equally possible things. On the other hand, necessary truths are based on the principle of contradiction and on the possibility or impossibility of essences themselves, without regard to the free will of God or his creatures.

14. God Produces Various Substances According to the Different Views He Has of the Universe, and through God's Intervention the Proper Nature of Each Substance Brings It about That What Happens to One Corresponds with What Happens to All the Others, without Their Acting upon One Another Directly.

AFTER having seen, in some way, what the nature of substances consists in, we must try to explain the dependence they have upon one another and their actions and passions. Now, first of all, it is very evident that created substances depend upon God, who preserves them and who even produces them continually by a kind of emanation, just as we produce our thoughts. For God, so to speak, turns on all sides and in all ways the general system of phenomena which he finds it good to produce in order to manifest his glory, and he views all the faces of the world in all ways possible, since there is no relation that escapes his omniscience. The result of each view of the universe, as seen from a certain position, is a substance which expresses the universe in conformity with this view, should God see fit to render his thought actual and to produce this substance. And since God's view is always true, our perceptions are always true; it is our judgments, which come from ourselves, that deceive us.

Now we said above, and it follows from what we have just said, that each substance is like a world apart, independent of all other things, except for God; thus all our phenomena, that is, all the things that can ever happen to us, are only consequences of our being. And since these phenomena maintain a certain order in conformity with our nature or, so to speak, in conformity with the world which is in us, an order which enables us to make useful observations to regulate our conduct, observations justified by the success of future phenomena, an order which thus allows us often to judge the future from the past without error, this would be sufficient to enable us to say that these phenomena are true without bothering with whether they are outside us and whether others also perceive them. Nevertheless, it is very true that the perceptions or expressions of all substances mutually correspond in such a way that each one, carefully following certain reasons or laws it has observed, coincides with others doing the same—in the same way that several people who have agreed to meet in some place at some specified time can really do this if they so desire. But although they all express the same phenomena, it does not follow that their expressions are perfectly similar; it is sufficient that they are proportional. In just the same way, several spectators believe that they are seeing the same thing and agree among themselves about it, even though each sees and speaks in accordance with his view.

And God alone (from whom all individuals emanate continually and who sees the universe not only as they see it but also entirely differently from all of them) is the cause of this correspondence of their phenomena and makes that which is particular to one of them public to all of them; otherwise, there would be no interconnection. We could therefore say in some way and properly speaking, though not in accordance with common usage, that one particular substance never acts upon another particular substance nor is acted upon by it, if we consider that what happens to each is solely a consequence of its complete idea or notion alone, since this idea already contains all its predicates or events and expresses the whole universe. In fact, nothing can happen to us except thoughts and perceptions, and all our future thoughts and perceptions are merely consequences, though contingent, of our preceding thoughts and perceptions, in such a way that, if I were capable of considering distinctly everything that happens or appears to me at this time, I could see in it everything that will ever happen or appear to me. This would never fail, and it would happen to me regardless, even if everything outside of me were destroyed, provided there remained only God and me. But since we attribute what we perceive in a certain way to other things as causes acting on us, we must consider the basis for this judgment and the element of truth there is in it.

15. The Action of One Finite Substance on Another Consists Only in the Increase of Degree of its Expression Together with the Diminution of the Expression of the Other, Insofar as God Requires Them to Accommodate Themselves to One Another.

BUT, without entering into a long discussion, in order to reconcile the language of metaphysics with practice, it is sufficient for now to remark that we ascribe to ourselves—and with reason—the phenomena that we express most perfectly and that we attribute to other substances the phenomena that each expresses best. Thus a substance, which is of infinite extension insofar as it expresses everything, becomes limited in proportion to its more or less perfect manner of expression. This, then, is how one can conceive that substances impede or limit each other, and consequently one can say that, in this sense, they act upon one another and are required, so to speak, to accommodate themselves to one another. For it can happen that a change that increases the expression of one diminishes that of another. Now, the efficacy [vertu] a particular substance has is to express well the glory of God, and it is by doing this that it is less limited. And whenever something exercises its efficacy or power, that is, when it acts, it improves and extends itself insofar as it acts. Therefore, when a change takes place by which several substances are affected (in fact every change affects all of them), I believe one may say that the substance which immediately passes to a greater degree of perfection or to a more perfect expression exercises its power and acts, and the substance which passes to a lesser degree shows its weakness and is acted upon [pâtit]. I also hold that every action of a substance which has perfection* involves some pleasure, and every passion some pain and vice versa. However, it can happen that a present advantage is destroyed by a greater evil in what follows, whence one can sin in acting, that is, in exercising one's power and finding pleasure.

16. God's Extraordinary Concourse Is Included in That Which Our Essence Expresses, for This Expression Extends to Everything. But This Concourse Surpasses the Powers of Our Nature or of Our Distinct Expression, Which Is Finite and Follows Certain Subordinate Maxims.

IT NOW only remains to explain how God can sometimes influence men and other substances by an extraordinary and miraculous concourse, since it seems that nothing extraordinary and supernatural can happen to them, given that all their events are only consequences of their nature. But we must remember what we have said above concerning miracles in the universe—that they are always in conformity with the universal law of the general order, even though they may be above the subordinate maxims. And to the extent that every person or substance is like a small world expressing the large world, we can say equally that the extraordinary action of God on this substance does not fail to be miraculous, despite the fact that it is included in the general order of the universe insofar as it is expressed by the essence or individual notion of this substance. That is why, if we include in our nature everything that it expresses, nothing is supernatural to it, for our nature extends everywhere, since an effect always expresses its cause and God is the true cause of substances. But what our nature expresses more perfectly belongs to it in a particular way, since it is in this that its power consists. But since it is limited, as I have just explained, there are many things that surpass the powers of our nature and even surpass the powers of all limited natures. Thus, to speak more clearly, I say that God's miracles and extraordinary concourse have the peculiarity that they cannot be foreseen by the reasoning of any created mind, no matter how enlightened, because the distinct comprehension of the general order surpasses all of them. On the other hand, everything that we call natural depends on the less general maxims that creatures can understand. Thus, in order that my words may be as irreproachable as my meaning, it would be good to connect certain ways of speaking with certain thoughts. We could call that which includes everything we express our essence or idea; since this expresses our union with God himself, it has no limits and nothing surpasses it. But that which is limited in us could be called our nature or our power; and in that sense, that which surpasses the natures of all created substances is supernatural.

17. An Example of a Subordinate Maxim or Law of Nature; in Which It Is Shown, against the Cartesians and Many Others, That God Always Conserves the Same Force but Not the Same Quantity of Motion.

I HAVE already mentioned the subordinate maxims or laws of nature often enough, and it seems appropriate to give an example of one. Our new philosophers commonly make use of the famous rule that God always conserves the same quantity of motion in the world. In fact, this rule is extremely plausible, and, in the past, I held it as indubitable. But I have since recognized what is wrong with it. It is that Descartes and many other able mathematicians have believed that the quantity of motion, that is, the speed multiplied by the size of the moving body, coincides exactly with the moving force, or, to speak geometrically, that the forces are proportional to the product of the speeds and [sizes of] bodies. Now, it is extremely reasonable that the same force is always conserved in the universe. Also, when we attend to the phenomena, we see that there is no perpetual mechanical motion, because then the force of a machine, which is always diminished somewhat by friction and which must sooner or later come to an end, would restore itself, and consequently would increase by itself without any new external impulsion. We observe also that the force of a body is diminished only in proportion to the force it imparts to some bodies contiguous to it or to its own parts, insofar as they have separate motion.

Thus they believed that what can be said about force can also be said about the quantity of motion. But to show the difference between them, I assume that a body falling from a certain height acquires the force to rise up that height, if its direction carries it that way, at least, if there are no impediments. For example, a pendulum would rise again exactly to the height from which it descended, if the resistance of the air and some other small obstacles did not diminish its acquired force a little.

I assume also that as much force is required to elevate A, a body of one pound, to CD, a height of four fathoms, as to elevate B, a body of four pounds, to EF, a height of one fathom. All this is admitted by our new philosophers.

It is therefore evident that, having fallen from height CD, body A acquired exactly as much force as did body B, which fell from height EF; for since body (B) reached F and acquired the force to rise to E (by the first assumption), it has the force to carry a body of four pounds, that is, itself, to EF, the height of one fathom; similarly, since body (A) reached D and acquired the force to rise to C, it has the force to carry a body of one pound, that is, itself, to CD, a height of four fathoms. Therefore (by the second assumption), the force of these two bodies is equal.

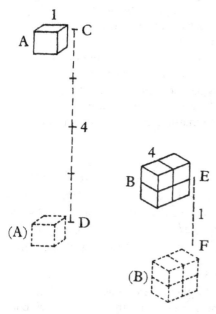

Figure 1

Let us now see whether the quantity of motion is also the same in each. But here we will be surprised to find a very great difference. For Galileo demonstrated that the speed acquired by the fall CD is twice the speed acquired by the fall EF, even though the one height is four times the other. Let us therefore multiply body A, proportional to 1, with its speed, proportional to 2; the product or quantity of motion will be proportional to 2. On the other hand, let us multiply body B, proportional to 4, by its speed, proportional to 1; the product or quantity of motion will be proportional to 4. Therefore the quantity of motion of body (A) at point D is half of the quantity of motion of body (B) at point F; yet their forces are equal. Hence, there is a great difference between quantity of motion and force—which is what needed to be proved.

Thus we see that force must be calculated from the quantity of the effect it can produce, for example, by the height to which a heavy body of a certain size and kind can be raised; this is quite different from the speed that can be imparted to it. And to give it double the speed, it must be given more than double the force.

Nothing is simpler than this proof. Descartes fell into error here only because he had too much confidence in his own thoughts, even when they were not sufficiently ripe. But I am surprised that his followers have not since then discovered this mistake; and I fear that they are beginning, little by little, to imitate some of the Peripatetics, whom they ridicule, like them gradually acquiring the habit of consulting their master's writings rather than reason and nature.[83]

18. The Distinction between Force and Quantity of Motion Is Important, among Other Reasons, for Judging That One Must Have Recourse to Metaphysical Considerations Distinct from Extension in Order to Explain the Phenomena of Bodies.

THIS consideration, the distinction between force and quantity of motion, is rather important, not only in physics and mechanics, in order to find the true laws of nature and rules of motion and even to correct the several errors of practice which have slipped into the writings of some able mathematicians, but also in metaphysics, in order to understand the principles better. For if we consider only what motion contains precisely and formally, that is, change of place, motion is not something entirely real, and when several bodies change position among themselves, it is not possible to determine, merely from a consideration of these changes, to which body we should attribute motion or rest, as I could show geometrically, if I wished to stop and do this now.

But the force or proximate cause of these changes is something more real, and there is sufficient basis to attribute it to one body more than to another. Also, it is only in this way that we can know to which body the motion belongs. Now, this force is something different from size, shape, and motion, and one can therefore judge that not everything conceived in body consists solely in extension and in its modifications, as our moderns have persuaded themselves. Thus we are once again obliged to reestablish some beings or forms they have banished. And it becomes more and more apparent that, although all the particular phenomena of nature can be explained mathematically or mechanically by those who understand them, nevertheless the general

---

83. This section is a summary of an important paper Leibniz published in the *Acta Eruditorum* on 6 January 1686, "A Brief Demonstration of a Notable Error of Descartes," translated in L 296–301, in which he argues against the conservation of quantity of motion, size times speed, a law first framed by Descartes (*Principles of Philosophy* II 36), and widely held by his followers. This essay began a long exchange in the learned journals that came to be known as the *vis viva controversy*, over the quantity, living force or *vis viva*, that Leibniz held was conserved. See below, "A Specimen of Dynamics," part I.

principles of corporeal nature and of mechanics itself are more metaphysical than geometrical, and belong to some indivisible forms or natures as the causes of appearances, rather than to corporeal mass or extension. This is a reflection capable of reconciling the mechanical philosophy of the moderns with the caution of some intelligent and well-intentioned persons who fear, with some reason, that we are withdrawing too far from immaterial beings, to the disadvantage of piety.

19. The Utility of Final Causes in Physics

SINCE I do not like to judge people wrongly, I do not accuse our new philosophers, who claim to banish final causes from physics.[84] But I am nevertheless obliged to confess that the consequences of this opinion appear dangerous to me, especially if I combine it with the one I refuted at the beginning of this discourse, which seems to go so far as to eliminate final causes altogether, as if God proposed no end or good in acting or as if the good were not the object of his will. As for myself, I hold, on the contrary, that it is here we must seek the principle of all existences and laws of nature, because God always intends the best and most perfect.

I am quite willing to admit that we are subject to deception when we wish to determine God's ends or counsels. But this is only when we try to limit them to some particular design, believing that he had only one thing in view, when instead he regards everything at the same time. For instance, it is a great mistake to believe that God made the world only for us, although it is quite true that he made it in its entirety for us and that there is nothing in the universe which does not affect us and does not also accommodate itself in accordance with his regard for us, following the principles set forth above. Thus when we see some good effect or perfection occurring or ensuing from God's works, we can say with certainty that God had proposed it. For he does nothing by chance and is not like us, who sometimes fail to do the good. That is why, far from being able to fall into error in this, as do extreme politicians who imagine too much subtlety in the designs of princes or as do commentators who look for too much erudition in their author, we cannot attribute too much reflection to this infinite wisdom, and there is no subject in which error is to be feared less, provided we limit ourselves to affirmations and avoid negative propositions that limit God's designs.

Anyone who sees the admirable structure of animals will find himself forced to recognize the wisdom of the author of things. And I advise those who have any feelings of piety and even feelings of true philosophy to keep away from the phrases of certain would-be freethinkers who say that we see because it happens that we have eyes and not that eyes

---

84. The "new philosophers" Leibniz has in mind include Descartes and Spinoza, who explain everything mechanically and reject final causes. See Descartes, *Principles of Philosophy* I 28, and the appendix to part I of Spinoza's *Ethics*. In an earlier draft, it is impiety that Leibniz is not accusing them of, but the phrase was deleted.

were made for seeing. When one seriously holds these opinions ascribing everything to the necessity of matter or to some chance (even though both must appear ridiculous to those who understand what we have explained above), it is difficult to recognize an intelligent author of nature. For the effect must correspond to its cause; indeed, the effect is best recognized through a knowledge of the cause. Moreover, it is unreasonable to introduce a supreme intelligence as orderer of things and then, instead of using his wisdom, use only the properties of matter to explain the phenomena. This is as if, in order to account for the conquest of an important place by a great prince, a historian were to claim that it occurred because the small particles of gunpowder, set off by the contact of a spark, escaped with sufficient speed to push a hard and heavy body against the walls of the place, while the little particles that make up the brass of the cannon were so firmly interlaced that this speed did not separate them, instead of showing how the foresight of the conqueror enabled him to choose the suitable means and times and how his power overcame all obstacles.

20. A Noteworthy Passage by Socrates in Plato against the Philosophers Who Are Overly Materialistic.

THIS reminds me of a beautiful passage by Socrates in Plato's *Phaedo*. This passage agrees marvelously with my opinions on this point and seems to be directed expressly against our overly materialistic philosophers. Thus I have been tempted to translate this account, even though it is a little long; perhaps this sample will give an incentive to some of us to share in many of the other beautiful and solid thoughts which can be found in the writings of this famous author.[85]

21. If Mechanical Rules Depended Only on Geometry without Metaphysics, the Phenomena Would Be Entirely Different.

NOW, since we have always recognized God's wisdom in the detail of the mechanical structure of some particular bodies, it must also be displayed in the general economy of the world and in the constitution of the laws of nature. This is true to such an extent that one can observe the counsels of this wisdom in the laws of motion in general. For if there were nothing in bodies but extended mass and nothing in motion but change of place and if everything should and could be deduced solely from these definitions by geometrical necessity, it would follow, as I have shown elsewhere, that, upon contact, the smallest body would impart its own speed to the largest body without losing any of this speed; and we would have to accept a number of such rules which

---

85. Leibniz's marginal note: "The passage from Plato's *Phaedo* where Socrates ridicules Anaxagoras, who introduces mind but does not make use of it, is to be inserted." Leibniz repeats the passage in "Two Sects of Naturalists"; see below, pp. 281–84.

are completely contrary to the formation of a system.[86] But the decree of
divine wisdom always to conserve the same total force and the same total
direction has provided for this.

I even find that several effects of nature can be demonstrated doubly, that
is, by considering first the efficient cause and then by considering the final
cause, making use, for example, of God's decree always to produce his effect by the easiest and most determinate ways, as I have shown elsewhere in
accounting for the rules of catoptrics and dioptrics;[87] I shall say more about
this soon.

22. Reconciliation of Two Ways of Explaining Things, by Final Causes and by Efficient Causes, in Order to Satisfy Both Those Who Explain Nature Mechanically and Those Who Have Recourse to Incorporeal Natures.

IT IS appropriate to make this remark in order to reconcile those who hope
to explain mechanically the formation of the first tissue of an animal and the
whole machinery of its parts, with those who account for this same structure
using final causes. Both ways are good and both can be useful, not only for
admiring the skill of the Great Worker, but also for discovering something
useful in physics and in medicine. And the authors who follow these different
routes should not malign each other.

For I see that those who apply themselves to explaining the beauty of the
divine anatomy laugh at others who imagine that a movement of certain fluids
that seems fortuitous could have produced such a beautiful variety of limbs,
and call these people rash and profane. And the latter, on the other hand, call
the former simple and superstitious, comparing them to the ancients who
regarded physicists as impious when they maintained that it is not Jupiter
that thunders, but some matter present in the clouds. It would be best to join
together both considerations, for if it is permitted to use a humble comparison, I recognize and praise the skill of a worker not only by showing his designs in making the parts of his machine, but also by explaining the instruments
he used in making each part, especially when these instruments are simple
and cleverly contrived. *And God is a skillful enough artisan* to produce a machine which is a thousand times more ingenious than that of our body,
while using only some very simple fluids explicitly concocted in such a way
that only the ordinary laws of nature are required to arrange them in the right
way to produce so admirable an effect; but it is also true that this would not
happen at all unless God were the author of nature.

However, I find that the way of efficient causes, which is in fact deeper
and in some sense more immediate and *a priori*, is, on the other hand, quite
difficult when one comes to details, and I believe that, for the most part, our

---

86. See, e.g., pp. 245-50 for the full argument.
87. The reference is to the "Unicum Opticae, Catoptricae et Dioptricae Principium, Autore G. G.
L.," from the *Acta Eruditorum* (June 1682).

philosophers are still far from it. But the way of final causes is easier, and is not infrequently of use in divining important and useful truths which one would be a long time in seeking by the other, more physical way; anatomy can provide significant examples of this. I also believe that Snell, who first discovered the rules of refraction, would have waited a long time before discovering them if he first had to find out how light is formed. But he apparently followed the method which the ancients used for catoptrics, which is in fact that of final causes. For, by seeking the easiest way to lead a ray from a given point to another point given by reflection on a given plane (assuming that this is nature's design), they discovered the equality of angles of incidence and angles of reflection, as can be seen in a little treatise by Heliodorus of Larissa, and elsewhere.[88] That is what, I believe, Snell and Fermat after him (though without knowing anything about Snell) have most ingeniously applied to refraction. For when, in the same media, rays observe the same proportion between sines (which is proportional to the resistances of the media), this happens to be the easiest or, at least, the most determinate way to pass from a given point in a medium to a given point in another. And the demonstration Descartes attempted to give of this same theorem by way of efficient causes is not nearly as good. At least there is room for suspicion that he would never have found the law in this way, if he had learned nothing in Holland of Snell's discovery.[89]

23. To Return to Immaterial Substances, We Explain How God Acts on the Understanding of Minds and Whether We Always Have the Idea of That About Which We Think.

I found it appropriate to insist a bit on these considerations of final causes, incorporeal natures, and an intelligent cause with respect to bodies, in order to show their use even in physics and mathematics: on the one hand, to purge the mechanical philosophy of the impiety with which it is charged and, on the other hand, to elevate the minds of our philosophers from material considerations alone to nobler meditations. It is now appropriate to return from bodies to immaterial natures, in particular to minds, and to say something of the means God uses to enlighten them and act on them. In this matter, too, we must not doubt that there are certain laws of nature, of which I could speak more fully elsewhere. But for now it will be sufficient to touch somewhat on ideas, whether we see all things in God and how God is our light.[90]

---

88. Heliodorus of Larissa, or Damianos, was a Greek mathematician who flourished after Ptolemy. He was probably known to Leibniz through an edition, *De opticis libri duo*, published by Erasmus Bartholinus in Paris in 1657.
89. The law of refraction was first published in the second discourse of Descartes's *Dioptrics*. Descartes does indeed attempt to derive the law from hypotheses about the nature of light (see Ols, pp. 75–83). Snell discovered the same laws at roughly the same time as Descartes, and there was (and continues to be) a lively dispute about who discovered the law first, and whether Descartes actually discovered the law or learned it from Snell. Leibniz seems to favor Snell.
90. See Malebranche, *Search after Truth*, book III, pt. 2, chap. 6.

It may be appropriate to observe that the improper use of ideas gives rise to several errors. For when we reason about something, we imagine ourselves to have the idea of that thing; and that is the foundation upon which certain ancient and new philosophers have built a certain extremely imperfect demonstration of God. For, they say, I must have an idea of God or of a perfect being since I think of him, and one cannot think without an idea. Now, the idea of this being contains all perfections, and existence is a perfection, so consequently he exists. But since we often think of impossible chimeras—for example, of the highest degree of speed, of the greatest number, of the intersection of the conchoid with its base or rule—this reasoning is insufficient. It is therefore in this sense that we can say that there are true and false ideas, depending upon whether the thing in question is possible or not. And it is only when we are certain of its possibility that we can boast of having an idea of the thing. Thus the argument above proves, at least, that God exists necessarily, if he is possible. It is indeed a prerogative of divine nature, one that surpasses all others, that divine nature needs only its possibility or essence in order actually to exist, and it is precisely this that is called *ens a se*.

24. What Is Clear or Obscure, Distinct or Confused, Adequate and Intuitive or Suppositive[91] Knowledge; Nominal, Real, Causal, and Essential Definition.

IN ORDER to understand better the nature of ideas, we must to some extent touch on the varieties of knowledge. When I can recognize a thing from among others without being able to say what its differences or properties consist in, the knowledge is *confused*. It is in this way that we sometimes know something *clearly*, without being in any doubt whether a poem or a picture is done well or badly, simply because it has a certain something, I know not what, that satisfies or offends us. But when I can explain the marks which I have, the knowledge is called *distinct*. And such is the knowledge of an assayer, who discerns the true from the false by means of certain tests or marks which make up the definition of gold.

But distinct knowledge has degrees, for ordinarily the notions that enter into the definition would themselves need definition and are known only confusedly. But when everything that enters into a distinct definition or distinct knowledge is known distinctly, down to the primitive notions, I call this knowledge *adequate*. And when my mind understands all the primitive ingredients of a notion at once and distinctly, it has *intuitive* knowledge of it; this is extremely rare, since the greater part of human knowledge is only confused or *suppositive*.[92]

It is also good to distinguish nominal and real definitions. I call a definition

---

91. Cf. "Meditations on Knowledge, Truth, and Ideas" (1684), above. Instead of 'suppositive' Leibniz there uses the term 'symbolic'.

92. In the margin: "A notion intermediate between intuitive and clear is when I have been deprived of clear knowledge of all surrounding notions."

nominal when one can still doubt whether the notion defined is possible, as, for example, if I say that an endless helix is a solid line whose parts are congruent or can be superimposed on one another; anyone who does not know from elsewhere what an endless helix is could doubt whether such a line is possible, even though having such congruent parts is in fact one of the reciprocal properties of the endless helix, for other lines whose parts are congruent (which are only the circumference of a circle and the straight line) are planar, that is, they can be inscribed on a plane. This shows that any reciprocal property can serve as a nominal definition; but when the property makes known the possibility of the thing, it constitutes a real definition. As long as we have only a nominal definition, we cannot be certain of the consequences we derive, for if it concealed some contradiction or impossibility, the opposite conclusions could be derived from it. That is why truths do not depend upon names and are not arbitrary, as some new philosophers have believed.[93]

Furthermore, there are still great differences between the kinds of real definitions. For when possibility is proved only by experience, as in the definition of quicksilver, whose possibility we know because we know that there actually is such a body which is an extremely heavy but rather volatile fluid, the definition is merely real and nothing more; but when the proof of the possibility is *a priori*, the definition is both real and *causal*, as when it contains the possible generation of the thing. And when a definition pushes the analysis back to the primitive notions without assuming anything requiring an *a priori* proof of its possibility, it is perfect or *essential*.

25. In What Case Our Knowledge Is Joined to the Contemplation of the Idea.

N OW, it is evident that we have no idea of a notion when it is impossible. And in the case where knowledge is only *suppositive*, even when we have the idea, we do not contemplate it, for such a notion is only known in the way in which we know notions involving a hidden impossibility [*occultement impossibles*]; and if a notion is possible, we do not learn its possibility in this way. For example, when I think of a thousand or of a chiliagon, I often do this without contemplating the idea—as when I say that a thousand is ten times a hundred without bothering to think of what 10 and 100 are because I *suppose* I know it and do not believe I need to stop now and conceive it. Thus, it could happen, as in fact it often happens, that I am mistaken with respect to a notion I suppose or believe that I understand, although in fact the notion is impossible, or at least incompatible with those to which I join it. And whether I am mistaken or not, this suppositive way of conceiving remains the

93. Leibniz probably has Hobbes in mind here. See the "Dialogue" (August 1677), pp. 268–72 below.

same. Therefore, only in confused notions when our knowledge is *clear* or in distinct notions when it is *intuitive* do we see the entire idea in them.[94]

26. That We Have All Ideas in Us; and of Plato's Doctrine of Reminiscence.

IN ORDER properly to conceive what an idea is, we must prevent an equivocation. For some take the idea to be the form or difference of our thoughts, and thus we have an idea in the mind only insofar as we think of it; every time we think of it again, we have other ideas of the same thing, though similar to the preceding ideas. But it seems that others take the idea as an immediate object of thought or as some permanent form that remains when we are not contemplating it. And, in fact, our soul always has in it the quality of representing to itself any nature or form whatsoever, when the occasion to think of it presents itself. And I believe that this quality of our soul, insofar as it expresses some nature, form, or essence, is properly the idea of the thing, which is in us and which is always in us, whether we think of it or not. For our soul expresses God, the universe, and all essences, as well as all existences.

This agrees with my principles, for nothing ever enters into our mind naturally from the outside; and we have a bad habit of thinking of our soul as if it received certain species as messengers and as if it has doors and windows. We have all these forms in our mind; we even have forms from all time, for the mind always expresses all its future thoughts and already thinks confusedly about everything it will ever think about distinctly. And nothing can be taught to us whose idea we do not already have in our mind, an idea which is like the matter of which that thought is formed.

This is what Plato so excellently recognized when he proposed his doctrine of reminiscence, a very solid doctrine, provided that it is taken rightly and purged of the error of preexistence and provided that we do not imagine that at some earlier time the soul must already have known and thought distinctly what it learns and thinks now. Plato also strengthened his view by way of a fine experiment, introducing a little boy, whom he leads insensibly to extremely difficult truths of geometry concerning incommensurables without teaching him anything, merely by asking appropriate questions in proper order.[95] This demonstrates that our soul knows all these things virtually and requires only *attention* to recognize truths, and that, consequently, it has, at very least, the ideas upon which these truths depend. One can even say that it already possesses these truths, if they are taken as relations of ideas.

---

94. An earlier draft continues: "However, we actually have in our mind all possible ideas, and we always think of them in a confused way."
95. This is a reference to Plato's *Meno*, 82b *et seq.*, where, in a familiar passage, Socrates leads a young slave boy through some geometrical arguments.

27. How Our Soul Can Be Compared to Empty Tablets and How Our Notions Come from the Senses.

ARISTOTLE preferred to compare our soul to tablets that are still blank, where there is room for writing,[96] and he maintained that nothing is in our understanding that does not come from the senses. That agrees better with the popular notions, as is Aristotle's way, but Plato goes deeper. However, these kinds of doxologies or practicologies may be acceptable in ordinary usage, much as we see that those who follow Copernicus do not stop saying that the sun rises and sets. I even find that they can be given a good sense, a sense according to which they have nothing false in them, just as I have already noted how one can truly say that particular substances act on one another. In this same way, one can also say that we receive knowledge from the outside by way of the senses, because some external things contain or express more particularly the reasons that determine our soul to certain thoughts. But when we are concerned with the exactness of metaphysical truths, it is important to recognize the extent and independence of our soul, which goes infinitely further than is commonly thought, though in ordinary usage in life we attribute to it only what we perceive most manifestly and what belongs to us most particularly, for it serves no purpose to go any further.

However, it would be good to choose terms proper to each conception [*sens*] in order to avoid equivocation. Thus, the expressions in our soul, whether we conceive them or not, can be called *ideas*, but those we conceive or form can be called *notions*, *concepts* [*conceptus*]. But however we take these expressions, it is always false to say that all our notions come from the external senses, for the notions I have of myself and of my thoughts, and consequently of being, substance, action, identity, and of many others, arise from an internal experience.

28. God Alone Is the Immediate Object of Our Perceptions, Which Exist Outside of Us, and He Alone Is Our Light.

NOW, in rigorous metaphysical truth, there is no external cause acting on us except God alone, and he alone communicates himself to us immediately in virtue of our continual dependence. From this it follows that there is no other external object that touches our soul and immediately excites our perception. Thus we have ideas of everything in our soul only by virtue of God's continual action on us, that is to say, because every effect expresses its cause, and thus the essence of our soul is a certain expression, imitation or image of the divine essence, thought, and will, and of all the ideas comprised in it. It can then be said that God is our immediate external object and that we see all things by him. For example, when we see the sun and the stars, it is God who has given them

---

96. Aristotle, *De Anima*, Book II, chap. 4. The doctrine that nothing is in the intellect that was not first in the senses, attributed to Aristotle by the Scholastics, does not actually occur in Aristotle; perhaps it is a rendering of *Posterior Analytics*, Book II, chap. 19, or *Nicomachean Ethics*, Book VI, chap. 3, sec. 3.

to us and who conserves the ideas of them in us, and it is God who determines us really to think of them by his ordinary concourse while our senses are disposed in a certain manner, according to the laws he has established. God is the sun and the light of souls, the light that lights every man that comes into this world,[97] and this is not an opinion new to our times. After Holy Scripture and the Church Fathers, who have always preferred Plato to Aristotle, I remember having previously noted that from the time of the Scholastics, several believed that God is the light of the soul and, in their way of speaking, the active intellect of the rational soul. The Averroists gave the sense of this a bad turn,[98] but others, among whom was, I believe, William of St. Amour, and several mystical theologians, have taken it in a manner worthy of God and capable of elevating the soul to the knowledge of its good.

29. Yet We Think Immediately through Our Own Ideas and Not through Those of God.

HOWEVER, I am not of the opinion of certain able philosophers who seem to maintain that our very ideas are in God and not at all in us.[99] In my opinion, this arises from the fact that they have not yet considered sufficiently either what we have just explained about substances or the full extent and independence of our soul, which makes it contain everything that happens to it, and makes it express God and, with him, all possible and actual beings, just as an effect expresses its cause. Also, it is inconceivable that I think through the ideas of others. The soul must actually be affected in a certain way when it thinks of something, and it must already have in itself not only the passive power of being able to be affected in this way (which is already wholly determined) but also an active power, a power by virtue of which there have always been in its nature marks of the future production of this thought and dispositions to produce it in its proper time. And all this already involves the idea included in this thought.

30. How God Inclines Our Soul without Necessitating It; That We Do Not Have the Right to Complain and That We Must Not Ask Why Judas Sins but Only Why Judas the Sinner Is Admitted to Existence in Preference to Some Other Possible Persons. On Original Imperfection before Sin and on the Degrees of Grace.

THERE ARE a number of considerations with respect to the action of God on human will which are so difficult that it would be inordinately lengthy to pursue them here. Roughly speaking, however, here is what can be said.

---

97. John 1:9.
98. Averroists were Christian followers of Averroes (or Ibn Rushd—1126–98), the great Arabic commentator on Aristotle, who held that the active intellect in each man is part of a single active intellect. The doctrine of a single world-soul was condemned as heresy.
99. Malebranche, again, is Leibniz's primary target, as above in sec. 23.

In concurring with our actions, God ordinarily does no more than follow the laws he has established, that is, he continually conserves and produces our being in such a way that thoughts come to us spontaneously or freely in the order that the notion pertaining to our individual substance contains them, a notion in which they could be foreseen from all eternity. Moreover, in virtue of his decree that the will always tend toward the apparent good, expressing or imitating his will in certain particular respects (so that this apparent good always has some truth in it), God determines our will to choose what seems better, without, however, necessitating it. For, absolutely speaking, the will is in a state of indifference, as opposed to one of necessity, and it has the power to do otherwise or even to suspend its action completely; these two alternatives are possible and remain so.

Therefore the soul must guard itself against deceptive appearances [*les surprises des apparences*] through a firm will to reflect and neither to act nor to judge in certain circumstances except after having deliberated fully. But it is true, and it is even assured from all eternity, that a certain soul will not make use of this power in such a situation. But who is to blame? Can the soul complain about anything other than itself? All these complaints after the fact are unjust, if they would have been unjust before the fact. Now, could this soul, a little before sinning, complain about God in good faith, as if God determined it to sin? Since God's determinations in these matters cannot be foreseen, how does the soul know that it is determined to sin, unless it is actually sinning already? It is only a matter of not willing, and God could not put forth an easier and more just condition; thus judges do not seek the reasons which have disposed a man to have a bad will, but only stop to consider the extent to which this particular will is bad. But perhaps it is certain from all eternity that I shall sin? Answer this question for yourself: perhaps not; and without considering what you cannot know and what can give you no light, act according to your duty, which you do know.

But someone else will say, why is it that this man will assuredly commit this sin? The reply is easy: otherwise it would not be this man. For God sees from all time that there will be a certain Judas whose notion or idea (which God has) contains this free and future action. Therefore only this question remains, why does such a Judas, the traitor, who is merely possible in God's idea, actually exist? But no reply to this question is to be expected on earth, except that, in general, one must say that, since God found it good that he should exist, despite the sin that God foresaw, it must be that this sin is paid back with interest in the universe, that God will derive a greater good from it, and that it will be found that, in sum, the sequence of things in which the existence of that sinner is included is the most perfect among all the possible sequences. But we cannot always explain the admirable economy of this choice while we are travellers in this world; it is enough to know it without understanding it. And here is the occasion to recognize the *altitudinem divitarum*, the depth and abyss of divine wisdom, without seeking a detail that involves infinite considerations.[100]

---

100. The Latin translates: "depth of riches," a reference to Romans 11:33.

Yet one sees clearly that God is not the cause of evil. For not only did original sin take possession of the soul after the innocence of men had been lost, but even before this, there was an original imperfection or limitation connatural to all creatures, which makes them liable to sin or capable of error. Thus, the supralapsarians[101] raise no more problems than the others do. And it is to this, in my view, that we must reduce the opinion of Saint Augustine and other authors, the opinion that the root of evil is in nothingness, that is to say, in the privation or limitation of creatures, which God graciously remedies by the degree of perfection it pleases him to give. This grace of God, whether ordinary or extraordinary, has its degrees and its measures; in itself, it is always efficacious in producing a certain proportionate effect, and, further, it is always sufficient, not only to secure us from sin, but even to produce salvation, assuming that man unites himself to it by what derives from him.[102] But it is not always sufficient to overcome man's inclinations, for otherwise he would have nothing more to strive for; this is reserved solely for the absolutely efficacious grace which is always victorious, whether it is so by itself or by way of appropriate circumstances.

31. On the Motives of Election, on Faith Foreseen, on Middle Knowledge, on the Absolute Decree and That It All Reduces to the Reason Why God Has Chosen for Existence Such a Possible Person Whose Notion Includes Just Such a Sequence of Graces and Free Acts; This Puts an End to All Difficulties at Once.

FINALLY, God's graces are wholly pure graces, upon which creatures have no claim. However, just as it is not sufficient to appeal to God's absolute or conditional foresight into the future actions of men in order to account for his choice in the dispensation of these graces, we also must not imagine absolute decrees that have no reasonable motive. As for God's foreknowledge of faith or good works, it is very true that he has elected only those whose faith and charity he foresaw, whom he foreknew he would endow with faith. But the same question returns, why will God give the grace of faith or of good works to some rather than to others? And as for this knowledge God has, which is the foresight not of faith and good works, but of their grounds [matière] and predisposition, that is, foresight of what a man would contribute to them on his side (for it is true that there are differences among men whenever there are differences in grace and that, in fact, although a man needs to be stimulated to the good and be converted, he must also act in that direction afterward), it seems to several people that one could say that God, seeing what a man would do without grace or extraordinary assistance, or at least seeing the sort of person he is, leaving grace aside, might resolve to give

---

101. Calvinists who held that God's decrees of election and reprobation preceded the fall. Cf. *Theodicy* I, sec. 77–84.
102. The text also contains "by his will" as a possible ending for the sentence.

grace to those whose natural dispositions were better or, at least, less imperfect or less bad. But even if that were the case, one can say that these natural dispositions, insofar as they are good, are still the effect of grace, although ordinary grace, since God has favored some more than others. And since he knows that these natural advantages he gives will serve as motives for grace or extraordinary assistance, is it not true, according to this doctrine, that in the end everything is completely reduced to his mercy?

Since we do not know how much and in what way God takes account of natural dispositions in the dispensation of grace, I believe, then, that the most exact and surest thing to say, according to our principles, as I have already noted, is that among the possible beings there must be the person of Peter or John, whose notion or idea contains this entire sequence of ordinary and extraordinary graces and all the rest of these events with their circumstances, and that it pleased God to choose him for actual existence from among an infinity of equally possible persons. After this it seems that there is nothing more to ask and that all difficulties vanish.

For, with respect to this single great question, why it pleased God to choose him from among so many other possible persons, one would have to be very unreasonable not to be content with the general reasons we have given, reasons whose details lie beyond us. Thus, instead of having recourse to an absolute decree which is unreasonable, since it is without reason, or to reasons which do not solve the difficulty completely and are in need of further reasons, it would be best to say with Saint Paul, that God here followed certain great reasons of wisdom or appropriateness, unknown to mortals and based on the general order, whose aim is the greatest perfection of the universe. It is to this that the motives of the glory of God and the manifestation of his justice are reduced, as well as of his mercy and generally of his perfections and finally the immense depth of his riches, with which the soul of Saint Paul was enraptured.

32. The Utility of These Principles in Matters of Piety and Religion.

FOR THE REST, it seems that the thoughts we have just explained, particularly the great principle of the perfection of the operations of God and the principle that the notion of a substance contains all its events with all their circumstances, far from harming, serve to confirm religion, to dispel enormous difficulties, to enflame souls with a divine love, and to elevate minds to the knowledge of incorporeal substances, much more than hypotheses we have seen until now. For one sees clearly that all other substances depend on God, in the same way as thoughts emanate from our substance, that God is all in all, and that he is intimately united with all creatures, in proportion to their perfection, that it is he alone who determines them from the outside by his influence, and, if to act is to determine immediately, it can be said in this sense, in the language of metaphysics, that God alone operates on me, and God alone can do good or evil to me; the other substances contribute only by reason of these determinations, because God, having regard for all, shares his blessings and requires them to accommodate themselves to one another. Hence God alone brings about the connection and communication among substances, and it is through him that the phenomena of any substance meet and agree with those of others and consequently, that there is reality in our perceptions. But, in practice, one ascribes an action to particular reasons[103] in the sense that I have explained above, because it is not necessary always to mention the universal cause in particular cases.

We also see that every substance has a perfect spontaneity (which becomes freedom in intelligent substances), that everything that happens to it is a consequence of its idea or of its being, and that nothing determines it, except God alone. And that is why a person of very exalted mind, revered for her saintliness, was in the habit of saying that the soul must often think as if there were nothing but God and itself in the world.[104]

Now, nothing gives us a stronger understanding of immortality than the independence and extent of the soul in question here, which shelters it absolutely from all external things, since the soul alone makes up its whole world and is sufficient to itself with God. And it is as impossible that it should perish without annihilation, as it is that the world (of which it is a perpetual living expression) should destroy itself; hence, it is impossible that the changes in this extended mass called our body should do anything to the soul or that the dissolution of this body should destroy what is indivisible.

33. Explanation of the Union of Soul and Body, a Matter Which Has Been Considered as Inexplicable or Miraculous, and on the Origin of Confused Perceptions.

W E ALSO see the unexpected illumination of this great mystery of the union of the soul and the body, that is, how it happens that the passions and actions of the one are accompanied by the actions and passions, or by the corresponding phenomena, of the other. For there is no way to conceive that the one has any influence on the other, and it is unreasonable simply to appeal to the extraordinary operation of the universal cause in an ordinary and particular thing. But here is the true reason: we have said that everything that happens to the soul and to each substance follows from its notion, and therefore the very idea or essence of the soul carries with it the fact that all its appearances or perceptions must arise spontaneously from its own nature and precisely in such a way that they correspond by themselves to what happens in the whole universe. But they correspond more particularly and more perfectly to what happens in the body assigned to it, because the soul

---

103. An earlier draft had "occasional causes" rather than "particular reasons".

104. Leibniz probably had St. Theresa in mind here. In a letter from 1696 he wrote: "In [her writings] I once found this lovely thought, that the soul should conceive of things as if there were only God and itself in the world. This even provides a considerable object to reflect upon in philosophy, which I usefully employed in one of my hypotheses" (Gr. 103).

expresses the state of the universe in some way and for some time, according to the relation other bodies have to its own body. This also allows us to know how our body belongs to us, without, however, being attached to our essence. And I believe that persons who can meditate will judge our principles favorably, because they will be able to see easily what the connection between the soul and the body consists in, a connection which seems inexplicable in any other way.

We also see that the perceptions of our senses, even when they are clear, must necessarily contain some confused feeling [*sentiment*], for our body receives the impression of all other bodies, since all the bodies of the universe are in sympathy, and, even though our senses are related to everything, it is impossible for our soul to attend to everything in particular; that is why our confused sensations are the result of a truly infinite variety of perceptions. This is almost like the confused murmur coming from the innumerable set of breaking waves heard by those who approach the seashore. Now, if from several perceptions (which do not come together to make one), there is none which stands out before the others and if they make impressions that are almost equally strong or equally capable of gaining the attention of the soul, the soul can only perceive them confusedly.

34. On the Difference between Minds and Other Substances, Souls or Substantial Forms, and That the Immortality Required Includes Memory.

ASSUMING[105] that the bodies that make up an *unum per se*, as does man, are substances, that they have substantial forms, and that animals have souls, we must admit that these souls and these substantial forms cannot entirely perish, no more than atoms or the ultimate parts of matter can, on the view of other philosophers. For no substance perishes, although it can become completely different. They also express the whole universe, although more imperfectly than minds do. But the principal difference is that they do not know what they are nor what they do, and consequently, since they do not reflect on themselves, they cannot discover necessary and universal truths. It is also because they lack reflection about themselves that they have no moral qualities. As a result, though they may pass through a thousand transformations, like those we see when a caterpillar changes into a butterfly, yet from the moral or practical point of view, the result is as if they had perished; indeed, we may even say that they have perished physically, in the sense in which we say that bodies perish through their corruption. But the intelligent soul, knowing what it is—having the ability to utter the word "I," a word so full of meaning—does not merely remain and subsist metaphysically, which it does to a greater degree than the others, but also remains the same morally

---

105. An earlier draft began with this first sentence: "I do not attempt to determine if bodies are substances in metaphysical rigor or if they are only true phenomena like the rainbow and, consequently, if there are true substances, souls, or substantial forms which are not intelligent."

and constitutes the same person. For it is memory or the knowledge of this self that renders it capable of punishment or reward. Thus the immortality required in morality and religion does not consist merely in this perpetual subsistence common to all substances, for without the memory of what one has been, there would be nothing desirable about it. Suppose that some person all of a sudden becomes the king of China, but only on the condition that he forgets what he has been, as if he were born anew; practically, or as far as the effects could be perceived, wouldn't that be the same as if he were annihilated and a king of China created at the same instant in his place? That is something this individual would have no reason to desire.

35. The Excellence of Minds and That God Considers Them Preferable to Other Creatures. That Minds Express God Rather Than the World, but That the Other Substances Express the World Rather Than God.

B UT SO THAT we may judge by natural reasons that God will always preserve not only our substance, but also our person, that is, the memory and knowledge of what we are (though distinct knowledge is sometimes suspended during sleep and fainting spells), we must join morals to metaphysics, that is, we must not only consider God as the principle and cause of all substances and all beings, but also as the leader of all persons or intelligent substances and as the absolute monarch of the most perfect city or republic, which is what the universe composed of all minds together is, God himself being the most perfect of all minds and the greatest of all beings. For certainly minds are the most perfect beings[106] and best express divinity. And since the whole nature, end, virtue, and function of substance is merely to express God and the universe, as has been sufficiently explained, there is no reason to doubt that the substances which express the universe with the knowledge of what they are doing and which are capable of knowing great truths about God and the universe, express it incomparably better than do those natures, which are either brutish and incapable of knowing truths or completely destitute of sensation and knowledge. And the difference between intelligent substances and substances that have no intelligence at all is just as great as the difference between a mirror and someone who sees.

Since God himself is the greatest and wisest of all minds, it is easy to judge that the beings with whom he can, so to speak, enter into conversation, and even into a society—by communicating to them his views and will in a particular manner and in such a way that they can know and love their benefactor—must be infinitely nearer to him than all other things, which can only pass for the instruments of minds. So we see that all wise persons value a man infinitely more than any other thing, no matter how precious it is, and

---

106. An earlier draft of this sentence began: ". . . minds are either the only substances one finds in the world, in the case in which bodies are only true phenomena, or else they are at least the most perfect . . ."

it seems that the greatest satisfaction that a soul, content in other ways, can have is to see itself loved by others. With respect to God, though, there is the difference that his glory and our worship cannot add anything to his satisfaction, since knowledge of creatures is only a consequence of his supreme and perfect happiness—far from contributing to it or being its partial cause. However, what is good and reasonable in finite minds is found preeminently in him, and, just as we would praise a king who would prefer to preserve the life of a man rather than the most precious and rarest of his animals, we should not doubt that the most enlightened and most just of all monarchs is of the same opinion.

36. God Is the Monarch of the Most Perfect Republic, Composed of All Minds, and the Happiness of This City of God Is His Principal Purpose

INDEED, minds are the most perfectible substances, and their perfections are peculiar in that they interfere with each other the least, or rather they aid one another the most, for only the most virtuous can be the most perfect friends. Whence it obviously follows that God, who always aims for the greatest perfection in general, will pay the greatest attention to minds and will give them the greatest perfection that universal harmony can allow, not only in general, but to each of them in particular.

One can even say that God, insofar as he is a mind, is the originator of existences; otherwise, if he lacked the will to choose the best, there would be no reason for a possible thing to exist in preference to others. Thus the quality that God has of being a mind himself takes precedence over all the other considerations he can have toward creatures; only minds are made in his image and are, as it were, of his race or like children of his household, since they alone can serve him freely and act with knowledge in imitation of the divine nature; a single mind is worth a whole world, since it does not merely express the world but it also knows it and it governs itself after the fashion of God. In this way we may say that, although all substances express the whole universe, nevertheless the other substances express the world rather than God, while minds express God rather than the world. And this nature of minds, so noble that it brings them as near to divinity as it is possible for simple creatures, has the result that God draws infinitely more glory from them than from all other beings, or rather the other beings only furnish minds the matter for glorifying him.

That is why this moral quality God has, which makes him the lord or monarch of minds, relates to him, so to speak, personally and in a quite singular manner. It is because of this that he humanizes himself, that he is willing to allow anthropomorphism, and that he enters into society with us, as a prince with his subjects; and this consideration is so dear to him that the happy and flourishing state of his empire, which consists in the greatest possible happiness of its inhabitants, becomes the highest of his laws. For

happiness is to people what perfection is to beings. And if the first principle of the existence of the physical world is the decree to give it the greatest perfection possible, the first intent of the moral world or the City of God,
which is the noblest part of the universe, must be to diffuse in it the greatest
possible happiness.

Therefore we must not doubt that God has ordered everything in such a
way that minds not only may live always, which is certain, but also that they
may always preserve their moral quality, so that the city does not lose a single
person, just as the world does not lose any substance. And consequently they
will always know what they are, otherwise they would not be susceptible to
reward or punishment, something, however, essential to a republic, but above
all essential to the most perfect republic, in which nothing can be neglected.

Finally, since God is at the same time the most just and most good-natured
of monarchs and since he demands only a good will, as long as it is sincere
and serious, his subjects cannot wish for a better condition, and, to make
them perfectly happy, he wants only for them to love him.

37. Jesus Christ Has Revealed to Men the Mystery and Admirable Laws of the Kingdom of Heaven and the Greatness of the Supreme Happiness That God Prepares for Those Who Love Him.

THE ANCIENT philosophers knew very little of these important truths;
Jesus Christ alone has expressed them divinely well and in a manner so clear
and familiar that the coarsest of minds have grasped them. Thus his gospel
has entirely changed the course of human affairs; he has brought us to know
the kingdom of heaven, or that perfect republic of minds which deserves the
title of City of God, whose admirable laws he has disclosed to us. He alone
has made us see how much God loves us and with what exactitude he has
provided for everything that concerns us; that, caring for sparrows, he will
not neglect the rational beings which are infinitely more dear to him; that all
the hairs on our head are numbered; that heaven and earth will perish rather
than the word of God and what pertains to the economy of our salvation; that
God has more regard for the least of the intelligent souls than for the whole
machinery of the world; that we must not fear those who can destroy bodies
but cannot harm souls, because God alone can make souls happy or unhappy; and that the souls of the just, in his hands, are safe from all the upheavals
of the universe, God alone being able to act upon them; that none of our actions are forgotten; that everything is taken account of, even idle words or a
spoonful of water well used; finally, that everything must result in the greatest
welfare of those who are good; that the just will be like suns; and that neither
our senses nor our mind has ever tasted anything approaching the happiness
that God prepares for those who love him.

From the Letters to Arnauld (1686–87)[107]

As previously indicated, Arnauld's critique of section 13 of the "Discourse"
started off a correspondence with Leibniz. Leibniz does a good job of
summarizing the debate that ensued (from February to May 1686), in the first
selection we have chosen from that correspondence. Passages in double brackets
below are not in the copies Arnauld received and may be either earlier thoughts
or later additions. Only selected variants are noted.

Remarks on Arnauld's Letter about My Proposition That the Individual Notion of Each Person Includes Once and for All Everything That Will Ever Happen to Him [May 1686].

I THOUGHT (says Arnauld) *that we might infer that God was free to create*
or not to create Adam, but assuming that he wanted to create him, everything that
has happened to humankind had to happen, or ought to happen, by a fatal necessity,
or at least, I thought that, assuming he wanted to create Adam, God is no more
free, with respect to all this, than he would be not to create a creature capable
of thought, assuming that he wanted to create me. I first replied that we must
distinguish between absolute and hypothetical necessity. To this, Arnauld replies here that *he is speaking only of hypothetical necessity.* After this assertion,
the argument takes a different turn. The terms he used, fatal necessity, are ordinarily understood only as applied to absolute necessity, so I was required
to make this distinction, which however, is no longer called for, inasmuch
as Arnauld does not insist upon this *fatal necessity,* since he uses alternative
phrases: by a fatal necessity or at least, etc. It would be useless to dispute
about the word. But, as for the thing itself, Arnauld still finds it strange that
I seem to maintain *that all human events occur* necessitate ex hypothesi, *given the*
single assumption that God wanted to create Adam. To this I have *two replies* to
make. The *first* is that my assumption is not merely that God wanted to create an Adam whose notion was vague and incomplete, but that God wanted
to create a particular Adam, sufficiently determined as an individual. And
according to me, this complete individual notion involves relations to the
whole series of things. This should appear more reasonable, given that Arnauld grants here the interconnections among God's resolutions, that is, he
grants that God, having resolved to create Adam, takes into consideration
all the resolutions he has concerning the whole series of the universe; this is
somewhat like a wise man who, making a decision about one part of his plan
and having the whole plan in view, would decide so much the better, if his
decision could settle all the parts at once.

The other reply is that the conclusion [conséquence], by virtue of which all
the events follow from the hypothesis, is indeed always certain, but it is not
always necessary with metaphysical necessity as is the one found in Arnauld's

example: that God in resolving to create me cannot fail to create a nature capable of thought. The conclusion is often only physical and assumes God's free decrees, as do conclusions which depend on the laws of motion or which depend on the moral principle that all minds will pursue what appears best to them. It is true that, when the assumption of those decrees that yield the conclusion is added to the first assumption which had constituted the antecedent, namely, God's resolution to create Adam, to make up a single antecedent out of all these assumptions or resolutions; then, I say, it is true in that case that the conclusion follows.

Since I have already touched upon these two replies in some way in the letter I sent to the Landgrave, Arnauld brings forward replies to them that must be considered. He admits in good faith that he took my view to be that all the events of an individual can be deduced from his individual notion in the same way and with the same necessity as the properties of a sphere can be deduced from its specific notion or definition; he also supposed that I considered the notion of the individual in itself, without taking account of the way in which it exists in the divine understanding or will. *For* (he says) *it seems to me that we don't usually consider the specific notion of a sphere in relation to its representation in God's understanding, but in relation to what it is in itself, and I thought that it was the same for the individual notion of each person. But, he adds, now that he knows what I think about this, that is sufficient to enable him to accept it for the purpose of asking whether it overcomes all the difficulties;* he is still doubtful of this. I see that Arnauld has not remembered, or at least did not concern himself with, the view of the Cartesians, who maintain that it is through his will that God establishes the eternal truths, like those concerning the properties of the sphere. But since I am not of their opinion any more than Arnauld is, I will only say why I think that we must philosophize differently about the notion of an individual substance than about the specific notion of the sphere. The reason is because the notion of a *species* includes only eternal or necessary truths, but the notion of an individual includes considered as possible what, in fact, is true, that is, considerations related to the existence of things and to time, and consequently it depends upon God's free decrees considered as possible; for truths of fact or existence depend upon God's decrees. Thus the notion of sphere in general is incomplete or abstract, that is, we consider in it only the essence of a sphere in general or in theory, without regard to particular circumstances, and consequently it does not in any way include what is required for the existence of a certain sphere. But the notion of the sphere Archimedes had placed on his tomb is complete and must include everything belonging to the subject of that shape. That is why, in individual or practical considerations, which are concerned with singulars, in addition to the shape of the sphere, we must consider the matter of which it is made, the place, the time, and the other circumstances, considerations which, by a continual linkage, would in the end include the whole series of the universe, if everything these notions included could be pursued. For the notion of the piece of matter of which this sphere is made involves all the changes it has undergone and will undergo one day. And according to me, each individual substance always contains traces of what has ever happened to it and marks of what will ever happen to it. But what I have just said can suffice to explain my line of thought.

Now, Arnauld states that, by taking the individual notion of a person in relation to the knowledge God had of it when he resolved to create it, what I have said about this notion is quite certain. And similarly, he even grants that the volition to create Adam was not detached from God's volition concerning what would happen to him and to his posterity. But he now asks whether the link between Adam and what happens to his posterity is dependent on or independent of God's free decrees; *that is,* as he explains, *whether God knew what would happen to Adam and his posterity only as a consequence of the free decrees by which God ordained everything that will happen, or whether there is an intrinsic and necessary connection, independent of these decrees, between Adam and the events in question.* He does not doubt that I would choose the latter alternative, and in fact I could not choose the first as he explained it, but it seems to me that there is a middle ground. However, he proves that I must choose the latter, because I consider the individual notion of Adam as possible when I maintain that, among an infinity of possible notions, God has chosen the notion of an Adam such as this, and notions possible in themselves do not depend upon God's free decrees.

But here I must explain myself a little better. Therefore, I say that the connection between Adam and human events is not independent of all of God's free decrees, but also, that it does not depend upon them so completely that each event could happen or be foreseen only in virtue of a particular primitive decree made about it. I therefore think that there are only a few free primitive decrees that regulate the course of things, decrees that can be called laws of the universe, and which, joined to the free decree to create Adam, bring about the consequence. This is a bit like needing few hypotheses to explain phenomena—something I will explain more distinctly in what follows. As for the objection that possibles are independent of God's decrees, I grant it with respect to actual decrees (even though the Cartesians do not agree with this), but I hold that possible individual notions include some possible free decrees. For example, if this world were only possible, the individual notion of some body in this world, which includes certain motions as possible, would also include our laws of motion (which are free decrees of God), but also only as possible. For, since there is an infinity of possible worlds, there is also an infinity of possible laws, some proper to one world, others proper to another, and each possible individual of a world includes the laws of its world in its notion.

The same things can be said about miracles or God's extraordinary operations. These belong to the general order and conform to God's principal plans and, consequently, are included in the notion of this universe, which is a result of these plans; just as the idea of a building results from the ends or plans of the builder, so the idea or notion of this world is a result of one of God's plans considered as possible. For everything must be explained by its cause, and God's ends are the cause of the universe. Now, in my opinion, each individual substance expresses the whole universe from a certain point of view, and consequently it also expresses the miracles in question. All this must be understood of the general order, of God's plans, of the course of this universe, of individual substance, and of miracles, whether they are taken in the actual state or whether they are considered *sub ratione possibilitatis*. For another possible world will also have all this in its own way, though the plans of our world have been preferred.

It can also be seen from what I have just said about God's plans and primitive laws that this universe has a certain principal or primitive notion, a notion of which particular events are merely the result, with the exception of what is free and contingent, to which certainty does no harm, since the certainty of events is based in part upon free acts. Now, each individual substance of this universe expresses in its notion the universe into which it enters. And not only does the assumption that God has resolved to create this Adam include resolutions for all the rest, but so does the assumption that he created any other individual substance whatsoever, because it is the nature of an individual substance to have a notion so complete that everything that can be attributed to it can be deduced from it, even the whole universe, because of the interconnection of things. Nevertheless, to proceed carefully, it must be said that it is not so much because God decided to create this Adam that he decided on all the rest. Rather, both the decision he made with regard to Adam and the one he made with regard to other particular things are the result of the decision he made with regard to the whole universe and a result of the principal plans that determine its primitive notion and establish in it this general and inviolable order. Everything is in conformity with this order, even miracles, which are, no doubt, in conformity with God's principal plans, although they do not always observe the particular maxims that are called laws of nature.

I have said that all human events can be deduced not simply by assuming the creation of a vague Adam, but by assuming the creation of an Adam determined with respect to all these circumstances, chosen from among an infinity of possible Adams. This has given Arnauld the occasion to object, not without reason, that it is as difficult to conceive of several Adams, taking Adam as a particular nature, as it is to conceive of several mes. I agree, but when speaking of several Adams, I was not taking Adam as a determinate individual. I must therefore explain myself. This is what I meant. When one considers in Adam a part of his predicates, for example, that he is the first man, set in a garden of pleasure, from whose side God fashioned a woman, and similar things conceived *sub ratione generalitatis*, in a general way (that is to say, without naming Eve, Paradise, and other circumstances that fix individuality), and when one calls Adam the person to whom these predicates are attributed, all this is not sufficient to determine the individual, for there can be an infinity of Adams, that is, an infinity of possible persons, different from one another, whom this fits. Far from disagreeing with what Arnauld says against this multiplicity of the same individual, I myself used this to make it better understood that the nature of an individual must be complete and determinate. I am even quite convinced of what Saint Thomas had already taught about intelligences, which I hold to apply generally, namely, that it is not possible for there to be two individuals entirely alike, or differing only numerically.[108] Therefore, we must not conceive of a vague Adam, that is, a person to whom certain attributes of Adam belong, when we are concerned with determining whether all human events follow from positing his existence; rather, we must attribute to him a notion so complete that everything that can be attributed to him can be deduced from it. Now, there is no room for doubting that God can form such a notion of him, or rather that he finds it already formed in the realm of possibles, that is, in his understanding.

It, therefore, also follows that he would not have been our Adam, but another Adam, had other events happened to him, for nothing prevents us from saying that he would be another. Therefore, he is another. It seems obvious to us that this block of marble brought from Genoa would have been altogether the same if it had been left there, because our senses allow us to judge only superficially. But at bottom, because of the interconnection of things, the whole universe with all its parts would be quite different and would have been different from the beginning, if the least thing in it had happened differently than it did. It does not follow from this that events are necessary, but rather that they are certain, given God's choice of this possible universe, whose notion contains this series of things. I hope that what I am going to say will enable Arnauld himself to agree with this. Let there be a straight line ABC representing a certain time. And let there be an individual substance, for example, I, enduring or subsisting during that time. Let us first take me subsisting during time AB, and then me subsisting during time BC. Then, since the assumption is that it is the same individual substance that endures throughout, or rather that it is I who subsists in time AB, being then in Paris, and that it is still I who subsists in time BC, being then in Germany, there must necessarily be a reason allowing us truly to say that we endure, that is to say that I, who was in Paris, am now in Germany. For if there were no such reason, we would have as much right to say that it is someone else. It is true that my internal experience convinces me *a posteriori* of this identity; but there must also be an *a priori* reason. Now, it is not possible to find any reason but the fact that both my attributes in the preceding time and state and my attributes in the succeeding time and state are predicates of the same subject—they are in the same subject. Now, what is it to say that the predicate is in the subject, except that the notion of the predicate is in some way included in the notion of the subject? And since, once I began existing, it was possible truly to say of me that this or that would happen to me, it must be admitted that these predicates were laws included in the subject or in my complete notion, which constitutes what is called I, which is the foundation of the connection of all my different states and which God has known perfectly from all eternity. After this, I think that all doubts should disappear, for, when I say that the individual notion of Adam includes every-

108. The reference is to St. Thomas's doctrine that, with intelligences, every individual is a lowest species; cf. the "Discourse on Metaphysics," sec. 9.

thing that will ever happen to him, I don't mean to say anything other than what all philosophers mean when they say that the predicate is included in the subject in a true proposition. It is true that the results of so evident a doctrine are paradoxical, but that is the fault of the philosophers who do not sufficiently pursue the clearest notions.

I now think that Arnauld, being as penetrating and fair-minded as he is, will no longer find my proposition so strange, even if he is not able to approve of it entirely (though I almost flatter myself that I have his approval). I agree with what he so judiciously adds about the circumspection we must use when appealing to divine knowledge [*la science divine*] in order to find out what we ought to judge concerning the notions of things. But, properly understood, what I have just said must hold, even though we should speak of God only as much as is necessary. For even if we did not say that God, when considering Adam whom he is resolving to create, sees in him everything that will happen to him, it suffices that one can always prove that there must be a complete notion of this Adam which contains them. For all the predicates of Adam either depend upon other predicates of the same Adam or they do not. Then, setting aside all of those predicates that depend upon the others, we need only gather together all the primitive predicates in order to form Adam's complete notion, a notion sufficient for deducing everything that will ever happen to him, and this is as much as we need for us to be able to explain it. It is evident that God can construct—and even actually conceive—a notion sufficient to explain all the phenomena pertaining to Adam; but it is no less evident that this notion is possible in itself. It is true that we should not enter unnecessarily into an investigation of the divine knowledge and will, because of the great difficulties involved. Nevertheless, we can explain what we have derived from such an investigation relevant to our question without entering into the difficulties Arnauld mentions—for example, the difficulty of understanding how God's simplicity is reconcilable with what we must distinguish in it. It is also very difficult to explain perfectly how God has knowledge he might not have had, namely, the knowledge by intuition [*la science de la vision*]; for, if things that exist contingently in the future didn't exist, God would not have any intuition of them. It is true that he would have simple knowledge of them, which would become intuition when it is joined to his will, so that this difficulty is perhaps reduced to a difficulty concerning his will, namely, how God is free to will. No doubt this is beyond us, but it is not necessary to understand it in order to resolve our question.[109]

As for the way in which we conceive that God acts by choosing the best among several possibles, Arnauld is right in finding some obscurity there. He seems, nevertheless, to recognize that we are led to conceive that there is an infinity of possible first men, each connected to a long sequence of persons and events, and that God has chosen from them the one who, together with

---

109. Knowledge of simple understanding [*scientia simplicis intelligentiae*] is God's knowledge of possibles; knowledge by intuition [*scientia visionis*] is God's knowledge of actuals, which differs from the former only in God's reflexive knowledge of his own decrees. Cf. G IV 440–41, C 16–17.

his sequence, pleased him. So this is not as strange as it had first appeared to him. It is true that Arnauld testifies that he is strongly led to think that these purely possible substances are only chimeras. I do not wish to dispute this, but I hope that, in spite of this, he will grant me what I need. I agree that there is no other reality in pure possibles than the reality they have in the divine understanding, and we see from this that Arnauld himself will be required to fall back on divine knowledge to explain them, whereas it seemed earlier that he thought that we should seek them in themselves. When I also grant what Arnauld is convinced of and what I do not deny—that we conceive no possibles except through the ideas actually found in the things God has created—it does no harm to me. For when speaking of possibilities, I am satisfied that we can form true propositions about them. For example, even if there were no perfect square in the world, we would still see that it does not imply a contradiction. And if we wished absolutely to reject pure possibles, contingency would be destroyed; for, if nothing were possible except what God actually created, then what God created would be necessary, in the case he resolved to create anything.

Finally, I agree that in order to determine the notion of an individual substance it is good to consult the one I have of myself, just as one must consult the specific notion of the sphere in order to determine its properties. Yet there is a considerable difference, for my notion and the notion of every other individual substance is infinitely broader and more difficult to understand than a specific notion, like that of the sphere, which is only incomplete. It is not enough that I sense myself [*je me sente*] to be a substance that thinks; I must distinctly conceive what distinguishes me from all other minds, and I have only a confused experience of this. The result is that, though it is easy to determine that the number of feet in the diameter is not included in the notion of sphere in general, it is not so easy to judge whether the trip I intend to make is included in my notion; otherwise, it would be as easy for us to be prophets as to be geometers. I am uncertain whether I will make the trip, but I am not uncertain that, whether I go or not, I will always be me. This is a presumption that must not be confused with a distinct notion or item of knowledge. These things appear undetermined to us only because the foreshadowings or marks which are in our substance are not recognizable to us. This is a bit like those who, consulting only the senses, would ridicule someone who says that the least motion is also communicated as far as matter extends, because experience alone cannot demonstrate this; but, when the nature of motion and matter are considered, one is convinced of this. It is the same here: when someone consults the confused experience he has of his individual notion in particular, he is far from perceiving this interconnection of events; but when the general and distinct notions which enter into it are considered, it is discovered. In fact, in considering the notion I have of every true proposition, I find that every predicate necessary or contingent, past, present, or future is included in the notion of subject; and I ask no more of it.

Indeed, I believe that this will open up to us a way of reconciling our views.

For I suspect that Arnauld did not want to grant me this proposition only because he took the connection I am maintaining to be both intrinsic and necessary, whereas I hold it to be intrinsic, but in no way necessary; for now, I have sufficiently explained that it is founded on free decrees and acts. I do not intend any connection between the subject and the predicate other than that which holds in the most contingent of truths, that is, that we can always conceive something in the subject which serves to provide a reason why this predicate or event belongs to it, or why this happened rather than not. But these reasons for contingent truths incline, rather than necessitate. Therefore, it is true that I could fail to go on this trip, but it is certain that I shall go. This predicate or event is not connected with certainty to my other predicates, conceived incompletely or *sub ratione generalitatis*; but it is connected with certainty to my complete individual notion, since I suppose that this notion was constructed explicitly so that everything that happens to me can be deduced from it. No doubt, this notion is found *a parte rei*, and it is properly the notion that belongs to me, who finds myself in different states, since this notion alone is capable of including all of them.

I have so much deference for Arnauld and such a good opinion of his judgment that I easily give up my opinions, or at least my way of expressing them as soon as I see that he finds something objectionable in them. That is why I precisely followed the difficulties he proposed, and having attempted to satisfy them in good faith, it seems to me that I am not far removed from his* opinions.

The proposition at issue is of great importance and deserves to be firmly established, for from this it follows that every soul is like a world apart, independent of every other thing outside of God, that it is not only immortal and, so to speak, undisturbable, but that it holds in its substance the traces of everything that happens to it. From this also follows that in which the interaction [*commerce*] of substances consists, particularly the union of soul and body. This interaction does not occur in accordance with the ordinary hypothesis of physical influence of one substance on another, since every present state of a substance happens to it spontaneously and is only a result of its preceding state. This interaction also does not occur in accordance with the hypothesis of occasional causes, according to which God ordinarily intervenes in some way other than conserving each substance in its course, and according to which God, on the occasion of something happening in the body, arouses thoughts in the soul which would change the course it would have taken without this intervention. It occurs in accordance with the hypothesis of concomitance, which appears demonstrative to me. That is, each substance expresses the whole series of the universe according to the point of view or relation proper to it, from which it happens that they agree perfectly; and when we say that one acts upon another, we mean that the distinct expression of the one acted upon is diminished, and that of the one acting is augmented, in conformity with the series of thoughts involved in its notion. For although every substance expresses everything, in common usage we correctly attribute to it only the most evident expressions in accordance to its relation to us.

Finally, I believe that after this, the propositions contained in the summary sent to Arnauld will appear not only more intelligible, but perhaps also more solid and more important than might have been thought at first.[110]

To Arnauld (28 November/8 December 1686) [excerpts][111]

AS I FOUND something extraordinary in the frankness and sincerity with which you accepted some arguments I used, I cannot avoid recognizing and admiring it. I suspected that the argument taken from the general nature of propositions would make some impression on your mind; but I also confess that there are few people able to appreciate truths so abstract, and that perhaps no one else would have been able to perceive its cogency so readily.

I should like to be informed of your meditations about the possibilities of things; they can only be profound and important since they are concerned with speaking of these possibilities in a way worthy of God. But this will be at your convenience. As for the two difficulties you found in my letter, the one concerning the hypothesis of concomitance, that is, the hypothesis of the agreement of substances among themselves, and the other concerning the nature of the forms of corporeal substances, I confess that they are considerable, and if I were able to satisfy them completely, I think that I would be able to decipher the greatest secrets of nature in its entirety. But it is something to advance to a certain point.[112] As for the first, I find that you yourself have sufficiently explained the obscurity you found in my thought concerning the hypothesis of concomitance; for when the soul has a sensation of pain at the same time that the arm is injured, I think that the situation is, in fact, as you say, Sir, that the soul itself forms this pain, which is a natural result of its state or notion. I admire Saint Augustine for having apparently recognized the same thing (as you have remarked) when he said that the pain the soul has in these encounters is nothing but a sadness that accompanies the ill disposition of the body. In fact, this great man had very solid and very profound thoughts. But (it will be asked), how does the soul know this ill disposition of the body? I reply that it is not by any impression or action of bodies on the soul, but because the nature of every substance carries a general expression of the whole universe and because the nature of the soul carries, more particularly, a more distinct expression of that which is now happening with regard to its body. That is why it is natural for the soul to mark and

110. Again, Arnauld seems not to have been sent the whole "Discourse," but only a summary which corresponds closely to the titles of successive sections.
111. Arnauld wrote to Leibniz on September 28, 1686, saying that he sees "no other difficulties except about the possibility of things, and about this way of conceiving God as having chosen the universe he created from an infinity of other possible universes he saw at the same time and did not wish to create" (G II, 64). Arnauld then asked Leibniz to explain himself further about the hypothesis of concomitance and about the nature of the form of corporeal substance; he formulated a series of seven queries on the latter problem. Leibniz's response takes up each query individually.
112. Horace, *Epistles*, I.1.32.

know the accidents of its body through accidents of its own. The situation is the same for the body when it accommodates itself to the thoughts of the soul. And when I wish to raise my arm, it is exactly at the moment when everything in the body is disposed for that effect, so that the body moves by virtue of its own laws. But through the wondrous though unfailing agreement of things among themselves, it happens that these laws work together exactly at the moment that the will is so inclined, since God took this into account in advance when he formed his resolution about this series of all the things in the universe. All these things are only consequences of the notion of an individual substance, which contains all its phenomena in such a way that nothing can happen to a substance that does not come from its own depths, though in conformity to what happens to another, despite the fact that the one acts freely and the other without choice. [[And this agreement is one of the best proofs that can be given of the necessity for there to be a substance which is the supreme cause of everything.]]

I should like to be able to explain myself as clearly and decisively about the other question, concerning the substantial forms. The first difficulty you indicated, Sir, is that our soul and our body are two really distinct substances; therefore, it seems that the one is not the substantial form of the other. I reply that, in my opinion, our body in itself or the *cadaver*, setting the soul apart, can be called a substance only in an improper sense, just as in the case of a machine or a pile of stones, which are only beings by aggregation; for regular or irregular arrangement does not constitute substantial unity. Besides, the last Lateran council declares that the soul is truly the substantial form of our body.

As for the second difficulty,[113] I grant that the substantial form of the body is indivisible, and it seems to me that this is also Saint Thomas's opinion; and I further grant that every substantial form or, indeed, every substance is indestructible and even ingenerable—which was also the opinion of Albertus Magnus and, among the ancients, the opinion of the author of the book *De diaeta*, attributed to Hippocrates.[114] Therefore, they can only come into being by an act of creation. And I am greatly inclined to believe that all reproduction among animals deprived of reason, reproduction which does not deserve a new act of creation, is only the transformation of another animal already living but sometimes imperceptible, like the changes that happen to a silkworm and other similar animals; nature is accustomed to reveal its secrets in some cases and hide them in others. Thus the souls of brutes* would have all been created from the beginning of the world, in accordance with the fruitfulness in seed

---

113. Arnauld asked: If the substantial form of the body is divisible, "we would not gain anything with respect to the unity of body [literally: to body being a *unum per se*]" (G II, 66); if it is indivisible, "it seems that body would be as *indestructible* as our soul" (ibid.).

114. The reference to St. Thomas might be to *Summa Theologica* I, q. 76, art. 8, but Leibniz is probably not representing Aquinas accurately. See below, the "New System of Nature," for a different set of attributions. The reference to Albertus Magnus is too vague to be specified. On Hippocrates, see *The Regimen* 1.4. While the text is part of the Hippocratic corpus, it is probably not by Hippocrates himself. See below, "Letter to Samuel Masson," pp. 225–26, in which Leibniz's claims about this text are modified.

mentioned in Genesis. But the rational soul is created only at the time of the formation of its body, being entirely different from the other souls we know, because it is capable of reflection and it imitates the divine nature on a small scale.

Third,[115] I think that a block of marble is, perhaps, only like a pile of stones, and thus cannot pass as a single substance, but as an assemblage of many. Suppose that there were two stones, for example, the diamond of the Great Duke and that of the Great Mogul. One could impose the same collective name for the two, and one could say that they constitute a pair of diamonds, although they are far part from one another; but one would not say that these two diamonds constitute a substance. More and less do not make a difference here. Even if they were brought nearer together and made to touch, they would not be substantially united to any greater extent. And if, after they had touched, one joined to them another body capable of preventing their separation—for example, if they had been set in the same ring—all this would make only what is called an *unum per accidens*.[116] For it is as by accident that they are required to perform the same motion. Therefore, I hold that a block of marble is not a complete single substance, any more than the water in a pond together with all the fish it contains would be, even if all the water and all the fish were frozen, or any more than a flock of sheep would be, even if these sheep were tied together so that they could only walk in step and so that one could not be touched without all the others crying out. There is as much difference between a substance and such a being as there is between a man and a community, such as a people, an army, a society, or a college; these are moral beings, beings in which there is something imaginary and dependent on the fabrication [*fiction*] of our mind. A substantial unity requires a thoroughly indivisible and naturally indestructible being, since its notion includes everything that will happen to it, something which can be found neither in shape nor in motion (both of which involve something imaginary, as I could demonstrate), but which can be found in a soul or substantial form, on the model of what is called *me*. These are the only thoroughly real beings, as was recognized by the ancients, and above all, by Plato, who clearly showed that matter alone is not sufficient to form a substance. Now, the aforementioned I, or that which corresponds to it in each individual substance, can neither be made nor destroyed by the bringing together or separation of parts, which is a thing entirely external to what constitutes a substance. I cannot say precisely whether there are true corporeal substances other than those that are animated, but souls at least serve to give us some knowledge of others by analogy.

All this can contribute to clearing up the fourth difficulty.[117] For without

---

115. Arnauld asked: "What happens to this substantial form [of a block of marble] when it stops being one, because someone has broken it in two?" (G II, 66).

116. Accidental unity.

117. Arnauld asked: "Do you give to extension a general substantial form, such as certain Scholastics admitted when they called it *forma corporeitatis*, or do you want there to be as many different substantial forms as there are different bodies, and different species when these are bodies of different species?" (G II, 66).

bothering with what the Scholastics have called the form of corporeity [*formam corporeitatis*], I assign substantial forms to all corporeal substances that are more than mechanically united. But fifth,[118] if I am asked in particular what I say about the sun, the earthly globe, the moon, trees, and other similar bodies, and even about beasts, I cannot be absolutely certain whether they are animated, or even whether they are substances, or, indeed, whether they are simply machines or aggregates of several substances. But at least I can say that if there are no corporeal substances such as I claim, it follows that bodies would only be true phenomena, like the rainbow. For the continuum is not merely divisible to infinity, but every part of matter is actually divided into other parts as different among themselves as the two aforementioned diamonds. And since we can always go on in this way, we would never reach anything about which we could say, here is truly a being, unless we found animated machines whose soul or substantial form produced a substantial unity independent of the external union arising from contact. And if there were none, it then follows that, with the exception of man, there is nothing substantial in the visible world.

Sixth,[119] since the notion of individual substance in general, which I have given, is as clear as that of truth, the notion of corporeal substance will also be clear and, consequently, so will that of substantial form. But even if this were not so, we are required to admit many things whose knowledge is not sufficiently clear and distinct. I hold that the notion of extension is much less clear and distinct—witness the strange difficulties of the composition of the continuum. And it can indeed be said that *because of the actual subdivision of parts, there is no definite and precise shape in bodies.* As a result, *bodies would doubtless be only imaginary and apparent, if there were only matter and its modifications.* However, it is useless to mention the unity, notion, or substantial form of bodies when we are concerned with explaining the particular phenomena of nature, just as it is useless for the geometers to examine the difficulties concerning the composition of the continuum when they are working on resolving some problem. These things are still important and worthy of consideration in their place. All the phenomena of bodies can be explained mechanically, that is, by the corpuscular philosophy, following certain principles of mechanics posited without troubling oneself over whether there are souls or not. But in the final analysis of the principles of physics and even of mechanics, we find that these principles cannot be explained by the modifications of extension alone, and that the nature of force already requires something else.

Finally, in the seventh place[120] I remember that Cordemoy, in his treatise,

---

118. Arnauld asked: "Where do you situate the unity we attribute to the earth, the sun, the moon ... ?" (G II, 66).

119. Arnauld asked: "Finally, it will be said that it is not worthy of a philosopher to admit entities of which we have no clear and distinct idea" (G II, 67).

120. Arnauld wrote: "There are Cartesians who, in order to find unity in bodies, have denied that matter is divisible to infinity, and [have asserted] that one must admit indivisible atoms. But I do not think that you share their opinion" (G II, 67).

On the Distinction between Body and Soul, thought he needed to admit atoms, or extended indivisible bodies, to save substantial unity in bodies, so as to find something fixed to constitute a simple being. But you rightly concluded that I am not of that opinion. It appears that Cordemoy recognized something of the truth, but he did not yet see what the true notion of substance consists in; but this is the key to the most important knowledge. The atom* which contains only a shaped mass of infinite hardness (which I hold not to be in conformity with divine wisdom, any more than the void is) cannot contain in itself all its past and future states, and even less all those of the entire universe.

To Arnauld (April 30, 1687)

SINCE your letters are of considerable benefit to me and the marks* of your genuine liberality, I have no right to ask for them, and consequently your reply is never too late. However agreeable and useful they may be to me, I take into consideration what you owe to the public good, and thus I suppress my wishes. Your reflections are always instructive for me and I will take the liberty to go through them in order.

I do not think that there is any difficulty in my saying that *the soul expresses more distinctly, other things being equal, that which belongs to its body*, since it expresses the whole universe in a certain sense, in particular in accordance with the relation other bodies have to its own, since it cannot express all things equally well; otherwise there would be no differences among souls. But it does not follow from this that it must perceive perfectly everything occurring in the parts of its body, since there are degrees of relation between these very parts, parts which are not all expressed equally, any more than external things are. The greater distance of external bodies is compensated for by the smallness, or some other hindrance, with respect to the internal parts—Thales saw the stars, though he did not see the ditch at his feet.

For us the nerves are more sensitive than the other parts of our bodies, and perhaps it is only through them that we perceive the others. This apparently happens because the motions of the nerves or of the fluids in them imitate the impressions better and confuse them less, and the most distinct expressions in the soul correspond to the most distinct impressions of the body. This is not because the nerves act on the soul, or the other bodies on the nerves, metaphysically speaking, but because the former represent the state of the latter through a spontaneous relation [*spontanea relatione*]. We must also take into account that too many things take place in our bodies for us to be able to perceive them all individually. What we sense is only a certain resultant to which we are habituated, and we are not able to distinguish the things that enter into the resultant because of their multitude, just as when one hears the noise of the sea from afar, one does not discern what each wave does, even though each wave has an effect on our ears. But when a striking change happens in our body, we soon notice it and notice it more clearly than external changes which are not accompanied by a notable change in our organs.

I do not say that the soul knows the pricking before it has the sensation of pain, except insofar as it knows or expresses confusedly all things in accordance with my previously established principles. But this expression which the soul has of the future in advance, although obscure and confused, is the true cause of what will happen to it and of the clearer perception it will have afterwards, when the obscurity is lifted, since the future state is a result of the preceding one.

I said that God created the universe in such a way that the soul and the body, each acting according to its laws, agree in their phenomena. You judge that *this is in accord with the hypothesis of occasional causes*. If this were so, I would not be sorry, and I am always glad to find others who hold my positions. But I have only a glimpse of your reason for thinking this; you suppose that I wouldn't say that a body can move by itself, and thus, since the soul is not the real cause of the motion of the arm, and neither is the body, the cause must therefore be God. But I am of another opinion. I hold that what is real in the state called motion proceeds as much from the corporeal substance as thought and will proceed from the mind. Everything happens to each substance as a consequence of the first state God gave to it in creating it, and, extraordinary concourse apart, his ordinary concourse consists only in the conservation of the same substance, in conformity with its preceding state and the changes it brings about. Yet it is rightly said that one body pushes another, that is, that it never happens that a body begins to have a certain tendency unless another body touching it has a proportionate loss, in accordance with the unvarying laws that we observe in phenomena. And in fact, since motions are real phenomena rather than beings, a motion considered as a phenomenon is the immediate result or effect of another phenomenon in my mind, and similarly in the minds of others, but the state of a substance is not the immediate result of the state of another particular substance.

I do not dare assert that plants have no soul, life, or substantial form, for although a part of a tree planted or grafted can produce a tree of the same kind, it is possible that there is a seminal part in it that already contains a new vegetative thing, as perhaps there are already some living animals, though extremely small, in the seeds of animals, which can be transformed within a similar animal. Therefore, I don't yet dare assert that only animals are living and endowed with a substantial form. Perhaps there is an infinity of degrees in the forms of corporeal substances.

You say that those who maintain the hypothesis of occasional causes, saying that *my will is the occasional cause and God is the real cause of the motion of my arm, do not claim that God does this in time by means of a new volition he has each time I wish to raise my arm, but through the unique act of eternal will, by which he willed to do everything he foresaw it would be necessary for him to do.* To this I reply that one could say, for the same reason, that even miracles are not accomplished by a new volition of God, since they are in conformity with his general plan, and I already remarked that each volition of God involves all the others, but in a certain order of priority. In fact, if I properly understand the views of the authors of occasional causes, they introduce a miracle which is no less miraculous for being continual. For it seems to me that the notion of miracle does not consist in rarity. One might say that in this matter God acts only according to a general rule, and consequently he acts without miracle. But I do not grant that consequence, and I believe that God can make general rules for himself even with respect to miracles. For example, if God had resolved to give his grace immediately or to perform some other action of this nature every time a certain condition was satisfied, this action, though ordinary, would nevertheless still be a miracle. I admit that the authors of occasional causes might give another definition of the term, but, according to common usage, it seems that a miracle differs internally and substantively from the performance of an ordinary action, and not by the external accident of frequent repetition; properly speaking, God performs a miracle when he does something that surpasses the forces he has given to creatures and conserves in them. [[For example, if God made a body, put into circular motion by means of a sling, freely go in a circular path when released from the sling, without it being pushed or retained by anything whatever, that would be a miracle, for according to the laws of nature, it should continue in a straight line along a tangent; and if God decided that this should always happen, he would be performing natural miracles, since this motion could not be explained by anything simpler.]] Thus, in the same way, we must say, in accordance with the received view, that if continuing the motion exceeds the force of bodies, then the continuation of the motion is a true miracle. But I believe that corporeal substance has the ability [force] to continue its changes in accordance with the laws God put into its nature and conserves there. To make myself better understood, I believe that the actions of minds change nothing at all in the nature of bodies, nor do bodies change anything in the nature of minds, and even that God changes nothing on their occasion, except when he performs a miracle. In my opinion, things are so interconnected that the mind never wills anything efficaciously except when the body is ready to accomplish it in virtue of its own laws and forces; [[but, according to the authors of occasional causes, God changes the laws of bodies on the occasion of the action of the soul, and *vice versa*. That is the essential difference between our opinions.]] Thus, on my view, we should not worry about how the soul can give some motion or some new determination to animal spirits, since, in fact, it never gives them any at all, insofar as there is no proportion between mind and body, and there is nothing that can determine what degree of speed a mind can give a body, nor even what degree of speed God would want to give to a body on the occasion of the action of the mind in accordance with a certain law. The same difficulty found in the hypothesis of a real influence of soul on body, and vice versa, is also found in the hypothesis of occasional causes, insofar as we can see no connection nor can we see a foundation for any rule. And if someone were to say, as, it seems, Descartes wishes to say, that the soul, or God on its occasion, changes only the direction or determination of a motion and not the force which is in bodies (since it does not seem probable to him that at every moment God would violate the general law of nature that the same force must persist, on the occasion of every volition minds have), I would reply that it would still be quite difficult to explain what connection there can be between the thoughts of the soul and the paths or angles of the direction of bodies. Furthermore, there is in nature yet another general law which Descartes did not perceive, a law no less important, namely, that the same sum of determination or direction must always persist. For I find that if one were to draw any straight line, for example, from east to west through a given point, and if one were to calculate all the directions of all the bodies in the world insofar as they advance or recede in lines parallel to this line, the difference between the sum of all the easterly directions and of all the westerly directions would always be the same. This holds both for certain particular bodies, assuming that at present they have interactions only among themselves, and for the whole universe, in which the difference is always zero, since everything is perfectly balanced, and easterly and westerly directions are perfectly equal in the universe. If God does something in violation of this rule, it is a miracle.[121]

It is therefore infinitely more reasonable and more worthy of God to suppose that, from the beginning, he created the machinery of the world in such a way that, without at every moment violating the two great laws of nature, namely, those of force and direction, but rather, by following them exactly (except in the case of miracles), it happens that the springs in bodies are ready to act of themselves, as they should, at precisely the moment the soul has a suitable volition or thought; the soul, in turn, has this volition or thought only in conformity with the preceding states of the body. Thus the union of the soul with the machinery of the body and with the parts entering into it, and the action of the one on the other, consist only in this concomitance that marks the admirable wisdom of the creator, far better than any other hypothesis. It cannot be denied that this hypothesis is at least possible and that God is a sufficiently great craftsman to be able to execute it; hence, we can easily judge that this hypothesis is the most probable, being the simplest, the most beautiful, and most intelligible, at once avoiding all difficulties—to say nothing of criminal actions, in which it seems more reasonable to have God concur only through the conservation of created forces.

To use a comparison I will say that this concomitance I maintain is like several different bands of musicians or choirs separately playing their parts, and placed in such a way that they do not see and do not even hear each other, though they nevertheless can agree perfectly, each following his own notes, so that someone hearing all of them would find a marvelous harmony there, one more surprising than if there were a connection among them. It is quite possible that someone next to one of two such choirs could judge from the one what the other was doing (particularly if we supposed that he could hear his choir without seeing it and see the other without hearing it), he would, as a result, form such a habit that, with the help of his imagination, he would no longer think of the choir where he was, but of the other, and he would mistake his own choir for an echo of the other, attributing to his own only certain interludes in which some rules of composition [*symphonie*], by which

---

121. The rule in question here is what is now called the conservation of momentum, mass times velocity, which, Leibniz claims here, holds both for the universe as a whole and for any closed system within the universe.

he distinguished the other, were not satisfied. Or, attributing to his own choir a certain beating of the tempo, performed on his side according to certain plans, he might think, because of the agreement on this he finds as the melody continues,* that the beating of the tempo is being imitated by the others, since he doesn't know that those on the other side are also acting in accordance with their own plans, though in agreement with his.

Yet I do not disapprove at all of the assertion that minds are in some way the occasional causes, and even the real causes, of the movements of bodies. For, with respect to divine resolutions, what God foresaw and pre-established with regard to minds was the occasion for his regulating bodies from the beginning so that they might fit together in accordance with the laws and forces he will give them. And since the state of the one is an unfailing, though frequently contingent, and even free, consequence of the state of the other, we can say that God brings about that there is a real connection by virtue of this general notion of substances, which entails that substances express one another perfectly. This connection is not, however, immediate, since it is founded only upon what God has done in creating substances.

If my opinion that substance requires a true unity were founded only on a definition I had formulated in opposition to common usage, *then the dispute would be only one of words*.[122] But besides the fact that most philosophers have taken the term in almost the same fashion, distinguishing between a unity in itself and an accidental unity, between substantial and accidental form, and between perfect and imperfect, natural and artificial mixtures, I take things to a much higher level, and setting aside the question of terminology, *I believe that where there are only beings by aggregation, there aren't any real beings*. For every being by aggregation presupposes beings endowed with real unity, because every being derives its reality only from the reality of those beings of which it is composed, so that it will not have any reality at all if each being of which it is composed is itself a being by aggregation, a being for which we must still seek further grounds for its reality, grounds which can never be found in this way, if we must always continue to seek for them. I agree, Sir, that there are only machines (that are often animated) in all of corporeal nature, but I do not agree that *there are only aggregates of substances*; and if there are aggregates of substances, there must also be true substances from which all the aggregates result.[123] We must, then, necessarily come down either to mathematical points, of which some authors constitute extension, or to the atoms of Epicurus and Cordemoy (which are things you reject along with me), or else we must admit that we do not find any reality in bodies; or finally, we must recognize some substances that have a true unity. I have already said in another letter that the composite made up of the diamonds of the Grand Duke and of the Great Mogul can be called a pair of diamonds,

---

122. Arnauld had written that Leibniz's arguments "amount to saying that all bodies whose parts are mechanically united are not substances, but only machines or aggregates of many substances," and that "there is only a quibble over words here; for Saint Augustine feels no difficulties about recognizing that bodies have no true unity" (G II, 86).
123. The version Arnauld received concludes: "... of which all aggregates are made."

but this is only a being of reason. And when they are brought closer to one another, it would be a being of the imagination or perception, that is to say, a phenomenon. For contact, common motion, and participation in a common plan have no effect on substantial unity. It is true that there are sometimes more, and sometimes fewer, grounds for supposing that several things constitute a single thing, in proportion to the extent to which these things are connected. But this serves only to abbreviate our thoughts and to represent the phenomena.

It also seems that what constitutes the essence of a being by aggregation is only a mode [*manière d'être*] of the things of which it is composed. For example, what constitutes the essence of an army is only a mode of the men who compose it. This mode therefore presupposes a substance whose essence is not a mode of a substance.[124] Every machine also presupposes some substance in the pieces of which it is made, and there is no plurality without true unities. To put it briefly, I hold this identical proposition, differentiated only by the emphasis, to be an axiom, namely, *that what is not truly* one *being is not truly one* being *either.* It has always been thought that one and being are mutually supporting. Being is one thing and beings are another; but the plural presupposes the singular, and where there is no being still less will there be several beings. What could be clearer? [[I therefore believed that I would be allowed to distinguish beings by aggregation from substances, since these beings have their unity in our mind only, a unity founded on the relations or modes [*modes*] of true substances. If a machine is one substance, a circle of men holding hands will also be one substance, and so will an army, and finally, so will every multitude of substances.]]

I do not say that there is nothing substantial or nothing but appearance in things that do not have a true unity, for I grant that they always have as much reality or substantiality as there is true unity in that which enters into their composition.

You object that it might be of the essence of body not to have a true unity. But it would then be of the essence of body to be a phenomenon, deprived of all reality, like an ordered dream, for phenomena themselves, like the rainbow or a pile of stones, would be completely imaginary if they were not composed of beings with a true unity.

You say that you do not see what leads me to admit these substantial forms,* or rather, these corporeal substances endowed with a true unity; but that is because I conceive no reality without a true unity. On my view, the notion of singular substance involves consequences incompatible with a being by aggregation. I conceive properties in substance that cannot be explained by extension, shape, and motion, besides the fact that there is no exact and fixed shape in bodies due to the actual subdivision of the continuum to infinity, and the fact that motion involves something imaginary insofar as it is only a modification of extension and change of location, so that we cannot determine which of the changing subjects it belongs to, unless we have recourse to the

---

124. In the draft Arnauld received Leibniz wrote: "of another substance."

force which is the cause of motion and which is in corporeal substance. I confess that we do not need to mention these substances and qualities to explain particular phenomena, but for this we also do not need to examine God's concourse, the composition of the continuum, the plenum, and a thousand other things. I confess that we can explain the particularities of nature mechanically, but that can happen only after we recognize or presuppose the very principles of mechanics, principles which can only be established *a priori* by metaphysical reasonings. And even the difficulties concerning the composition of the continuum will never be resolved as long as extension is considered as constituting the substance of the bodies, and as long as we entangle ourselves in our own chimeras.

I also think that to want to limit true unity or substance almost exclusively to man is to be as shortsighted in metaphysics as were those in physics who wanted to confine the world in a sphere. And since there are as many true substances as there are expressions of the whole universe, and as many as there are replications of divine works, it is in conformity with the greatness and beauty of the works of God for him to produce as many substances as there can be in this universe, and as many as higher considerations allow, for these substances hardly get in one another's way. By assuming mere extension we destroy all this marvelous variety, since mass [*massa*] by itself (if it is possible to conceive it), is as far beneath a substance which is perceptive and representative* of the whole universe, according to its point of view and according to the impressions (or rather the relations) its body receives mediately or immediately from all others, as a cadaver is beneath an animal, or rather, it is as far beneath a substance as a machine is beneath a man. It is also because of this that the features of the future are formed in advance, and that the features of the past are conserved forever in each thing, and that cause and effect give way to one another* exactly up to the least detail of the least circumstance, even though every effect depends on an infinity of causes, and every cause has an infinity of effects; it would not be possible for this to happen if the essence of body consisted in a certain determinate shape, motion, or modification of extension. Thus, there is nothing of the kind in nature. Everything is strictly indefinite with respect to extension, and the extensions we attribute to bodies are merely phenomena and abstractions; this enables us to see how easily we fall into error when we do not reflect in this way, something so necessary for recognizing the true principles and for having a proper idea of the universe. [[And it seems to me that there is as much prejudice in refusing such a reasonable idea as there is in not recognizing the greatness of the world, the subdivision to infinity, and mechanical explanations in nature. It is as great an error to conceive of extension as a primitive notion without conceiving the true notion of substance or action as it was to be content considering substantial forms as a whole without entering into the details of the modifications of extension.]]

The multitude of souls (to which, in any case, I do not always attribute pleasure or pain) should not trouble us, any more than does the multitude of Gassendi's atoms, which are as indestructible as these souls. On the contrary, it is a perfection of nature to have many of them, a soul or animated substance being infinitely more perfect than an atom, which is without variety or subdivision, whereas every animated thing contains a world of diversity in a true unity. Now, experience favors this multitude of animated things. We find that there is a prodigious quantity of animals in a drop of water imbued with pepper;[125] and with one blow millions of them can be killed [[neither the frogs of the Egyptians nor the quails of the Israelites, of which you spoke, Sir, approach this number.]] Now, if these animals have souls, we would have to say of their souls what we can probably say of the animals themselves, namely, that they were already alive from the creation of the world, and that they will live to its end, and that since generation is apparently only a change consisting in growth, so death will only be a change consisting in diminution, which causes this animal to reenter the recesses of a world of minute creatures* where perceptions are more limited, until the order comes, perhaps calling them to return to the stage. The ancients were mistaken in introducing the transmigration of souls instead of the transformations of the same animal which always preserves the same soul; they put *metempsychoses pro metaschematismis*.[126] But minds are not subject to these revolutions, [[or rather, the revolutions in bodies must serve the divine economy with respect to minds.]] God creates them when it is time and detaches them from the body [[(at least the coarse body)]] by death, since they must always keep their moral qualities and their memory, in order to be [[perpetual]] citizens of this universal, perfect republic, of which God is the monarch; this republic can never lose any of its members and its laws are superior to those of bodies. I confess that the body by itself, without the soul, has only a unity of aggregation, but that the reality inhering in it derives from the parts composing it, which retain their [[substantial]] unity [[through the countless living bodies included in them.]]

Nevertheless, although a soul can have a body made up of parts animated by other souls, the soul or form of the whole is not, as a consequence, composed of the souls or forms of its parts. It is not necessary for the two parts of an insect cut in half to remain animated, although there may be some movement in them. At very least, the soul of the whole insect will remain only on one side. And since, in the formation and growth of the insect, the soul was, from the beginning, in a certain part that was already living, after the destruction of the insect it will still remain in a certain part that is still alive, a part as small as is necessary for it to be protected from the action of someone tearing or destroying the body of that insect. Hence, we do not need to imagine, with the Jews, that there is a little bone of insurmountable hardness in which the soul takes refuge.

I agree that there are degrees of accidental unity,[127] that an ordered society has more unity than a confused mob, and that an organized body, or rather

---

125. Leeuwenhoek experimented with pepper water.

126. Change of souls in place of change of shape.

127. Arnauld stated that "although it is true that there is true unity only in intelligent natures, all of which can say *I* [*moi*], there are nevertheless various degrees in this improper unity suitable to the body" (G II, 88).

a machine, has more unity than a society, that is to say, it is more appropriate to conceive them as a single thing, because there are more relations among the constituents. But in the end, all these unities become realized only by thoughts and appearances, like colors and other phenomena, which, nevertheless, are called real. The tangibility of a heap of stones or a block of marble does not prove its substantial reality any more than the visibility of a rainbow proves its substantial reality; and since nothing is so solid that it does not have some degree of fluidity, perhaps this block of marble is only a heap of an infinite number of living bodies, or like a lake full of fish, even though these animals cannot ordinarily be distinguished by the eye except in partially decayed bodies. We can therefore say of these composites and similar things what Democritus said so well of them, namely, they depend for their being on opinion or custom.[128] And Plato held the same opinion about everything which is purely material. Our mind notices or conceives some true substances which have certain modes; these modes involve relations to other substances, so the mind takes the occasion to join them together in thought and to make one name account for all these things together. This is useful for reasoning, but we must not allow ourselves to be misled into making substances or true beings of them; this is suitable only for those who stop at appearances, or for those who make realities out of all abstractions of the mind, and who conceive number, time, place, motion, shape, [[and sensible qualities]] as so many separate beings. Instead I hold that philosophy cannot be better reestablished and reduced to something precise, than by recognizing only substances or complete beings endowed with a true unity, together with the different states that succeed one another; everything else is only phenomena, abstractions, or relations.

No regularity will ever be found which can make a true substance out of several beings by aggregation. For example, if parts fitting together in the same plan are more suitable for composing a true substance than those touching, then all the officers of the Dutch East India Company will make up a real substance, far better than a heap of stones. But what is a common plan other than a resemblance, or an order of actions and passions that our mind notices in different things? But if we prefer the unity of contact, we will find other difficulties. Perhaps solid bodies have nothing uniting their parts except the pressure of the surrounding bodies, and have no more union in themselves and in their substance than does a pile of sand without lime.[129] Why should several rings, interlaced so as to make a chain, compose a genuine substance any more than if they had openings so that they could be separated? It may be that no part of the chain touches another, and even that none encloses another, and that, nevertheless, they are so interlaced that, unless they are approached in a certain way, they cannot be separated, as in the enclosed figure. Are we to say, in this case, that the substance composed of these things is, as it were, in abeyance and dependent of the future skill of whoever may wish to disentangle them? These

---

128. See Diogenes Laertius, *Lives of the Eminent Philosophers*, IX 45 (Loeb ed., vol. II, pp. 454–55).
129. I.e., shifting sands with nothing to bind them.

are all fictions of the mind, and as long as we do not discern what a complete

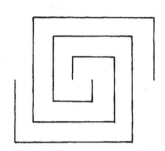

being, or rather a substance, really is, we will never have something at which we can stop; [[and this is the only way of establishing solid and real principles.]] In conclusion, nothing should be posited without good grounds. Therefore, those who imagine beings and substances without genuine unity are left to prove that there is more reality than what we have just said,[130] and I am waiting for a notion of substance or of being which can include all these things—after which mock suns* and perhaps even dreams will someday lay claim to reality, unless very precise limits are set for this *droit de bourgeoisie*[131] that is to be granted to beings formed by aggregation.

Figure 2

I have treated these matters so that you may be able to judge not only my opinions, but also, the arguments which forced me to adopt them. I submit them to your judgment, whose fairness and exactness I know. I also send something which you could have found in the *Nouvelles de la république des lettres*, to serve as a response to the Abbé Catelan.[132] I consider him an able man, given what you say of him; but what he has written against Huygens and against me makes it clear that he goes a little too fast. We will see what use he will make of this now.

I am delighted to learn of the good state of your health, and I hope for its continuation with all the zeal and all the passion which makes me what I am, etc.

P.S. I reserve for another time some other matters you have touched upon in your letter.

On Copernicanism and the Relativity of Motion (1689)[133]

Leibniz was in Italy from March 1689 to March 1690. While there, he wrote this essay, in which he confronts a particularly sensitive issue for his Italian colleagues, the Church's condemnation of Copernicanism, and offers an

---

130. Writing to Arnauld, Leibniz continued: "and to show what it consists in."

131. A kind of inferior citizenship.

132. The paper in question is probably the "Réplique de M. L. à M. l'Abbé D. C. . . . ," published in the *Nouvelles* in February 1687. It was part of the so-called *vis-viva* controversy. See the *Discourse on Metaphysics*, sec. 18.

133. Editors' title. C 590–93. Latin. On the identification of the text, see section 2 of Domenico Bertoloni Meli, "Leibniz on the Censorship of the Copernican System," *Studia Leibniziana* 20 (1988), 19–42.

interesting solution to the problem from the point of view of his system. This
essay is sometimes identified as the preface to the dialogue Leibniz entitled
"Phoranomus," which deals with related issues concerning motion and dynamics.
[See GD, pp. 575–81.] However, it is now thought to be a separate work.

SINCE we have already proved through geometrical demonstrations the equivalence of all hypotheses with respect to the motions of any bodies whatsoever, however numerous, moved only by collision with other bodies, it follows that not even an angel could determine with mathematical rigor which of the many bodies of that sort is at rest, and which is the center of motion for the others. And whether the bodies are moving freely or colliding with one another, it is a wondrous law of nature that no eye, wherever in matter it might be placed, has a sure criterion for telling from the phenomena where there is motion, how much motion there is, and of what sort it is, *or even whether God moves everything around it, or whether he moves that very eye itself,* [cf. Seneca, *Naturales Quaestiones* VII. 2.] To summarize my point, since space without matter is something imaginary, motion, in all mathematical rigor, is nothing but a change in the positions [*situs*] of bodies with respect to one another, and so, motion is not something absolute, but consists in a relation. This already follows from the Aristotelian definition of place, for motion is the change of place, and place is the surface of the surrounding body, so when this changes, motion occurs, and either the surrounding body or the thing in the place can be assumed to have moved away, leaving the other at rest.

But since, nevertheless, people do assign motion and rest to bodies, even to bodies they believe to be moved neither by a mind [*intelligentia*], nor by an internal impulse [*instinctus*], we must look into the sense in which they do this, so that we don't judge that they have spoken falsely. And on this matter we must reply that one should choose the more intelligible hypothesis, and that the truth of a hypothesis is nothing but its intelligibility. Now, from a different point of view, not with respect to people and their opinions, but with respect to the very things we need to deal with, one hypothesis might be more intelligible than another and more appropriate for a given purpose. And so, from different points of view, the one might be true and the other false. Thus, for a hypothesis to be true is just for it to be properly used. So, although a painter can present the same palace through drawings that use different perspectives, we would judge that he made the wrong choice if he brought forward the one which covers or hides parts that are important to know for a matter at hand. In just the same way, an astronomer makes no greater mistake by explaining the theory of the planets in accordance with the Tychonic hypothesis than he would make by using the Copernican hypothesis in teaching spherical astronomy and explaining day and night, thereby burdening the student with unnecessary difficulties. And the observational astronomer [*Historicus*] who insists that the Earth moves, rather than the Sun, or that the Earth rather than the Sun is in the sign of Aries, would speak improperly, even though he follows the Copernican system; nor would Joshua have spoken less falsely (that is, less absurdly) had he said "be still, Earth."

And so it is not necessary to flee, with Marin Mersenne and Honoratus Fabri, gentlemen I grant both learned and religious, to the view that the severe judgment against those who argue that Holy Scripture spoke in the words of the common man[134] should be considered only provisional (if it is permitted to speak in this way), as if once the motion of the Earth were demonstrated, the Church could declare that the words of Holy Scripture ought to be understood in the same way as we understand the words of the poet: "we are carried from port, and the lands and cities withdraw."[135] But it is correct to say that in this place Holy Scripture spoke in a way that serves both the truth and the proper meaning of the words; it is less correct to say that it accommodates itself in the beliefs people have than to say that it transmits the greatest hidden treasures of wisdom of all kinds, for this is something more worthy of its author, God.

But since, in explaining the theory of the planets, the Copernican hypothesis wonderfully illuminates the soul, and beautifully displays the harmony of things at the same time as it shows the wisdom of the creator, and since other hypotheses are burdened with innumerable perplexities and confuse everything in astonishing ways, we must say that, just as the Ptolemaic account is the truest one in spherical astronomy, on the other hand the Copernican account is the truest theory, that is, the most intelligible theory and the only one capable of an explanation sufficient for a person of sound reason. Claudius de Chales, a learned gentleman of the Jesuits, frankly confessed that one cannot hope for another hypothesis which satisfies the mind, and most distinguished astronomers have openly admitted that they are held back from presenting the Copernican system only by the fear of censure. But they would not need such caution any more and could freely follow Copernicus without damaging the authority of the censors, if only they were to recognize, with us, that the truth of a hypothesis should be taken to be nothing but its greater intelligibility, indeed, that it cannot be taken to be anything else, so that henceforth there would be no more distinction between those who prefer the Copernican system as the hypothesis more in agreement with the intellect, and those who defend it as the truth. For the nature of the matter is that the two claims are identical; nor should one look for a greater or a different truth here. And since it is permissible to present the Copernican system as the simpler hypothesis, it would also be permissible to teach it as the truth in this particular sense. This would preserve the authority of the censors, so that a retraction would never be needed in the future, no matter what new things should finally be uncovered in the heavens or on the earth, while at the same

---

134. Galileo argued that the Bible speaks in terms understandable to the common people, and should not be used as a guide for the make-up of the physical world. See his "Letter to the Grand Duchess Christina," translated in Stillman Drake, ed., *Discoveries and Opinions of Galileo*.
135. Virgil, *Aeneid* III, 72.

time, there would be no violence done to the distinguished discoveries of our age through the outward appearance of official condemnation.

Once this is understood, we can finally restore philosophical freedom to those of ability, without damaging respect for the Church, and we will free Rome and Italy from the slander that great and beautiful truths are there suppressed by censors, something that is known to be said and written widely among the English and Dutch (not to mention the French). And certainly, unless the learned gentlemen who profess religious obedience take such a consideration into account, enormous damage will be done to the great light of our age, namely, it might appear as if they had been condemned to darkness, having themselves extinguished their ability to find extraordinary truths, while others are snatching up honor, to the disgrace of Italy. No sane person believes that the great gentlemen who have the power of the censor have such an intention. Nor can we deny that Copernicus brought, as it were, a certain light to the world, and that those who do not understand his doctrine wander about in nature as they would in the darkest night. For not only do the labyrinths concerning the stations and retrogrades of the planets[136] disappear with one mental stroke, without any effort, but magnetic observations are also united in a marvelous way since the earth itself is like a magnet, not only with respect to the magnets of our everyday experience, but also with respect to the heavenly bodies themselves. Since this very magnetic law is so conspicuous in Jupiter with its moons, and similarly in the ring of Saturn with its moons, it would seem that Copernicus could hardly have hoped for any greater confirmation of his view. But nevertheless, this system has done itself one better in Kepler, who was the first to lay bare to mortals "the laws of the heavens, the regularity [fides] of things, and the laws of the Gods," observing that all of the phenomena can be derived if the earth and all of the primary planets are assumed to travel on an ellipse in whose focus is the sun, and if it is assumed that it is a law of motion for the orbiting of a planet that the areas swept out with respect to the sun are proportional to the times.

It remained for a physical explanation to be given for such an unexpected law, an explanation that has at last come to us, to our great delight. For I found that this universal motion of the planets can be explained beautifully by means of a vortex around the sun common [for all of the planets]. Indeed, it follows geometrically from Kepler's law of motion that the trajectory can be distinguished into two, a harmonic circulation of the planet around the sun (that is, one whose velocity is proportionally less when the body is more distant from the sun) and a rectilinear approach to the sun, like gravity [gravitas] or magnetism. Afterwards, I demonstrated that it is a general and reciprocal property of harmonic circulation (that is, circulation in which the velocities decrease regularly as the distance from the center

---

136. The stations of a planetary trajectory are the places where the planet appears to stop its forward or backward motions; the retrogrades are where it appears to move backward. On the Copernican system, stations and retrogrades are explained in terms of the planets moving in regular, circular paths, but viewed from an earth which is also moving in a regular, circular path.

uniformly increases, and conversely) that the areas swept out with respect to the center of circulation are proportional to the times, no matter what law governs the motion toward or away from the center. And so the matter comes directly down to this, that we have done something that the ancients seemed scarcely to have touched upon even in their prayers, that through geometrical analysis we have reduced the primary phenomena of the universe to principles that are the simplest and clearest for understanding, that is to the best, and, in our sense, truest hypothesis.[137]

On Freedom (1689?)[138]

HOW FREEDOM and contingency can coexist with the series of causes and with providence is the oldest worry of the human race. And the difficulty of the problem has only increased through the investigations Christians have made concerning God's justice in providing for the salvation of men.

When I considered that nothing happens by chance or by accident (unless we are considering certain substances taken by themselves), that fortune distinguished from fate is an empty name, and that no thing exists unless its own particular conditions [requisitis] are present (conditions from whose joint presence it follows, in turn, that the thing exists), I was very close to the view of those who think that everything is absolutely necessary,[139] who judge that it is enough for freedom that we be uncoerced, even though we might be subject to necessity, and close to the view of those who do not distinguish what is infallible or certainly known to be true, from that which is necessary.

But the consideration of possibles, which are not, were not, and will not be, brought me back from this precipice. For if there are certain possibles that never exist, then the things that exist, at any rate, are not always necessary, for otherwise it would be impossible for others to exist in their place, and thus, everything that never exists would be impossible. Nor can we really deny that many stories, especially those called novels, are thought to be possible, though they might find no place in this universal series God selected—unless one imagined that in such an expanse of space and time there are certain poetical regions, where you can see King Arthur of Great Britain, Amadis of Gaul, and the illustrious Dietrich von Bern of the German stories, all wandering through the world. This seems not too far from the view of a certain distinguished philosopher of our age, who in a certain place explicitly affirms that matter successively takes on all of the forms of which it is capable (*Principles of Philosophy*, part III, art. 47), something hardly defensible.[140] For it would

---

137. The last paragraph refers to the theory Leibniz gives in the "Tentamen de Motuum Coelestium Causis," two versions of which are given in GM VI, pp. 144–87.
138. Editors' title. F de C 178–85 & Gr 326. Latin.
139. Leibniz first wrote, then deleted: "and judged that being possible is the same as actually existing at some time."
140. The "certain distinguished philosopher" is, of course, Descartes.

eliminate all beauty from the universe and all choice among things, not to speak of other considerations by which the contrary can be proved.

Therefore, recognizing the contingency of things, I further considered what a clear notion of truth might be, for I hoped, and not absurdly, for some light from that direction on how necessary and contingent truths could be distinguished. Now, I saw that it is common to every true affirmative proposition, universal and particular, necessary or contingent, that the predicate is in the subject, that is, that the notion of the predicate is involved somehow in the notion of the subject. And this is the source [*principium*] of infallibility in every sort of truth for that being who knows everything *a priori*. But this seemed only to increase the difficulty, for if the notion of the predicate is in the notion of the subject at a given time, then how could the subject lack the predicate without contradiction and impossibility, and without changing that notion?

At last a certain new and unexpected light shined from where I least expected it, namely, from mathematical considerations on the nature of infinity. For there are two labyrinths of the human mind, one concerning the composition of the continuum, and the other concerning the nature of freedom, and they arise from the same source, infinity. That same distinguished philosopher I cited a short while ago preferred to slash through both of these knots with a sword since he either could not solve the problems, or did not want to reveal his view. For in his *Principles of Philosophy* I, art. 40 and 41, he says that we can easily become entangled* in enormous difficulties if we try to reconcile God's preordination with freedom of the will; but, he says, we must refrain from discussing these matters, since we cannot comprehend God's nature. And also, in *Principles of Philosophy* II, art. 35, he says that we should not doubt the infinite divisibility of matter even if we cannot grasp it. But this is not satisfactory, for it is one thing for us not to comprehend something, and quite something else for us to comprehend that it is contradictory. And so, we must at least be able to respond to those arguments, which seem to entail that freedom or the division of matter implies a contradiction.

Therefore, we must realize that all creatures have impressed upon them a certain mark [*character*] of divine infinity, and that this is the source of many wonderful things which amaze the human mind.

Indeed, there is no portion of matter so tiny that it does not contain a sort of world of creatures infinite in number, and there is no individual created substance so imperfect that it does not act on all others and is not acted upon by all others, no substance so imperfect that it does not contain the entire universe, and whatever it is, was, or will be, in its complete notion (as it exists in the divine mind), nor is there any truth of fact or any truth concerning individual things that does not depend upon the infinite series of reasons; whatever is in this series can be seen by God alone. This is also the reason why God alone knows contingent truths *a priori* and sees their infallibility in a way other than through experience.

After I considered these matters more attentively, a most profound distinction between necessary and contingent truths was revealed. Namely, every truth is either basic [*originaria*] or derivative. Basic truths are those for which we cannot give a reason; identities or immediate truths, which affirm the same thing of itself or deny the contradictory of its contradictory, are of this sort. Derivative truths are, in turn, of two sorts, for some can be resolved into basic truths, and others, in their resolution, give rise to a series of steps that go to infinity. The former are necessary, the latter contingent. Indeed, a necessary proposition is one whose contrary implies a contradiction. Every identical proposition and every derivative proposition resolvable into identical propositions is of such a kind, as are the truths called metaphysical or geometrical necessities. For demonstrating is nothing but displaying a certain equality or coincidence of the predicate with the subject (in the case of a reciprocal proposition) by resolving the terms of a proposition and substituting a definition or part of one for that which is defined, or in other cases at least displaying the inclusion so that what lies hidden in the proposition and was contained in it virtually is made evident and explicit through demonstration. For example, if by a ternary, senary, and duodenary number we understand one divisible by 3, 6, 12, then we can demonstrate the proposition that every duodenary number is senary. For every duodenary number is a binary-binary-ternary (which is the resolution of a duodenary into its prime factors, $12 = 2 \times 2 \times 3$, that is,* the definition of a duodenary), and every binary-binary-ternary is binary-ternary (which is an identical proposition), and every binary-ternary is senary (which is the definition of senary, $6 = 2 \times 3$). Therefore, every duodenary is senary ($12 = 2 \times 2 \times 3$, and $2 \times 2 \times 3$ is divisible by 2×3, and 2×3 is equal to 6. Therefore, 12 is divisible by 6).

But in contingent truths, even though the predicate is in the subject, this can never be demonstrated, nor can a proposition ever be reduced [*revocari*] to an equality or to an identity, but the resolution proceeds to infinity, God alone seeing, not the end of the resolution, of course, which does not exist, but the connection of the terms or the containment of the predicate in the subject, since he sees whatever is in the series. Indeed, this very truth was derived in part from his intellect, in part from his will, and it expresses his infinite perfection and the harmony of the entire series of things in its own particular way.

However, two ways remain for us to know contingent truths, one through experience, and the other through reason—by experience when we perceive a thing sufficiently distinctly through the senses, and by reason when something is known from the general principle that nothing is without a reason, or that there is always some reason why the predicate is in the subject. And so, we can take it for certain that God made everything in the most perfect way, and that he does nothing without a reason, and that nothing happens anywhere unless he who understands, understands its reason, that is, why the state of things is this way rather than that. And so, reasons can be given no less for the actions of minds than for the actions of bodies, although the choices minds make lack necessity. Sins arise from the original limitation of things. God does not choose sins as much as he chooses to admit into existence certain possible substances, which involve free sins as possible in their com-

plete notions and even contain the whole series of things in which they will
be contained.* Nor should we doubt that there are hidden reasons that completely transcend the grasp of a creature, reasons why God prefers one series of things, although it includes a sin, over another. But God chooses only
perfection, that is, what is positive. However, limitation and, arising from
that, sin is permitted, since by establishing certain positive decrees, its absolute rejection is ruled out. But none of the precepts [*rationes*] of wisdom
are of use here except the one that limitation and sin are to be compensated for
by an otherwise unobtainable good. However, these matters are not appropriate
here.

But in order better to fix the attention of the mind so that it doesn't leap
from one aimless objection to another, a certain analogy between truth
and proportions comes to mind, which seems marvelously to illuminate
the entire matter and place it in a clear light. Just as in every proportion
a smaller number is in a larger one or an equal is in an equal, so in every
truth the predicate is in the subject. And just as in every proportion between homogeneous quantities, one can undertake a certain analysis of
equals or congruents, and can subtract the lesser from the greater by sub-
tracting from the greater a part equal to the lesser, and similarly, one
can subtract a remainder from the result of that subtraction, and so on, either
as far as you like, or to infinity, so too in the analysis of truths, an equivalent can always be substituted for a term, so that the predicate is resolved
into the things contained in the subject. But in proportions, while the analysis sometimes comes to an end, and arrives at a common measure, namely, one that measures out each term of the proportion through exact rep-
etitions of itself, in other cases the analysis can be continued to infinity,
as happens in the comparison between a rational number and an irrational number, such as the comparison of the side and the diagonal of a
square. So, similarly, truths are sometimes provable, that is, necessary,
and sometimes they are free or contingent, and so cannot be reduced by
any analysis to an identity, to a common measure, as it were. And this is an
essential distinction, both for proportions and for truths.

However, just as incommensurable proportions* are treated in the science of geometry, and we even have proofs about infinite series, so to a
much greater extent, contingent or infinite truths are subordinate to God's
knowledge, and are known by him not, indeed, through demonstration (which would imply a contradiction) but through his infallible intuition [*visio*].[141] However, God's intuition should hardly be thought of as a
kind of experiential knowledge (as if he sees something in things distinct
from himself), but as *a priori* knowledge, knowledge derived from the reasons for truths, insofar as he sees things within himself [*ex se ipsâ*], possibles
through a consideration of his own nature, and existing things through the
additional* consideration of his free will and his decrees, the most important

---

141. The reference here is to the *scientia visionis*, knowledge by intuition, discussed in connection
with the Arnauld correspondence. See note 109 to p. 74.

of which is that everything happens in the best way, and for the best reason. However, what they call middle knowledge is nothing but the knowledge of contingent possibles.[142]

Moreover, once these things have properly been considered, I don't think that any difficulty on this matter can arise whose solution cannot be derived from what has been said. For having accepted the notion of necessity everyone accepts, namely that those things whose contrary implies a contradiction are precisely those that are necessary, it readily appears from a consideration of the nature of demonstration and analysis that there surely can be, indeed there must be, truths which cannot be reduced by any analysis to identical truths or to the principle of contradiction, truths endowed with an infinite series of reasons, fully known to God alone. And, it readily appears, this is the nature of everything called free and contingent, especially those which involve place and time. This has sufficiently been shown above from the very infinity of the parts of the universe and from the mutual interpenetration and connection of things.

The Source of Contingent Truths (1685–89?)[143]

THE SOURCE [*origo*] of contingent truths in an infinite progression, on analogy with the proportion between incommensurable quantities:

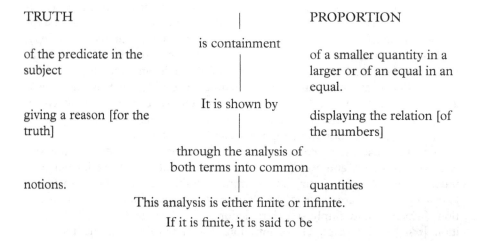

TRUTH		PROPORTION
	is containment	
of the predicate in the subject		of a smaller quantity in a larger or of an equal in an equal.
	It is shown by	
giving a reason [for the truth]		displaying the relation [of the numbers]
	through the analysis of both terms into common	
notions.		quantities

This analysis is either finite or infinite.

If it is finite, it is said to be

---

142. Middle knowledge or *scientia media* is a notion due to Louis de Molina. Molina argued that God knows propositions of the form "P will freely perform action A in circumstances C" independently of his knowledge of what he will create. This is what Molina called middle knowledge, which he distinguished from God's knowledge by intuition, that is, his knowledge of what he wills, and God's knowledge of simple understanding, that is, his knowledge of pure possibles. See also note 109 to p. 74 of the Arnauld correspondence.
143. Editors' title. C 1–3 & Gr 325–26. Latin.

a demonstration, and
the truth is necessary

the discovery of a common measure or a commensuration, and the proportion is expressible [*effabilis*],

for it is reduced to

identical truths,

congruence with respect to the same repeated measure,

that is, to the primary principle

of contradiction or identity.

of equality of those things which are congruent.

But if the analysis proceeds to infinity and never attains completion then

the truth is contingent, one which involves an infinite number of reasons,

the proportion is unexpressible, one which has an infinite number of quotients,

but in such a way that there is always something that remains,

for which we must, again, give some reason.

a new reminder that furnishes a [new] quotient.

Moreover, the analysis continued yields an infinite series

which, however, is known perfectly by God.

about which geometry knows many things.

And this is

knowledge by intuition [*scientia visionis*],

the doctrine of irrational numbers, like what is contained in book X of the *Elements* [of Euclid],

which is distinct

from knowledge of simple understanding [*scientia simplicis intelligentiae*].[144]

from common arithmetic.

However, neither is experiential but both are a priori infallibles, and known each according to its kind

through certain reasons evident to God, who alone comprehends the infinite. However, they are not necessary,

through necessary demonstrations known to geometry. However, they cannot be captured by expressible numbers,

---

144. See note 109 to p. 74.

for it is impossible	
to give demonstrations of contingent truths	for irrational proportions to be understood arithmetically, that is, they cannot be explained through the repetition of a measure.[145]

That[146] there are contingent truths, in whose explanation the progression of reasons is infinite, can also be understood from the fact that there is an actually infinite number of creatures in any part of the universe whatsoever, and each and every individual substance contains the whole series of things in its complete notion, and harmonizes with everything else, and to that extent contains something of the infinite. Because this has not been understood, the union of the soul and the body has also been taken to be inexplicable. For, in metaphysical rigor, they do not flow into one another, nor, indeed, does God move the one on the occasion of the other and divert it from its own proper course. But following its own laws from the time they were instituted with an admirable but infallible constancy [directio], each agrees with the other as exactly as they would if there were a true influx. And there is something similar in all substances, even those the most distant from one another, although in them the agreement does not appear so distinctly.

If everything that exists were necessary, then it would follow that only things which existed at some time would be possible (as Hobbes and Spinoza hold) and that matter would receive all possible forms (as Descartes held). And so, one could not imagine a novel that did not actually take place at some time and in some place, which is absurd. And so, we should say, rather, that from an infinite number of possible series, God chose one for reasons that go beyond the comprehension of his creatures.

The cause of evil derives from the original limitation of creatures, before all sin. God decrees only that which is purely positive, or which consists in perfection, and therefore, evil is only permitted by God. But things are

---

145. A few pages later in the ms Leibniz repeats this list of comparisons and adds the following two new ones:

(21) There is no middle between these two. Indeed, what they call middle knowledge [science media] is knowledge by intuition [scientia visionis] of contingent possibles.	(21) There is no middle between these two.
(22) From these things it appears that the root of contingency is infinity in reasons.	(22) From these things it appears that the root of incommensurability is infinity in the parts of matter.

On middle knowledge, see note 109 to p. 74.

146. Here begins the fragment published by Grua.

otherwise with people, who, in general, do not strive by their nature [*per se*] for the greater good.

Every truth which is not an identity admits of a proof; a necessary truth is proved by showing that the contrary implies a contradiction, a contingent truth by showing that there is more reason for that which has been done that there is for its opposite. For as with a wise person, so with God, the first decree and intention is that everything happen in accordance with the best reason. And so, if we were to imagine the case in which it is agreed that a triangle of given circumference should exist, without there being anything in the givens from which one could determine what kind of triangle to create, we must say that God would create an equilateral triangle, freely, or course, but without a doubt. There is nothing in the givens which prevents another kind of triangle from existing, and so, an equilateral triangle is not necessary. However, all that it takes for no other triangle to be chosen is the fact that in no triangle except for the equilateral triangle is there any reason for preferring it to others. Circumstances are the same if one were ordered to draw a line from one given point to another, without being given anything by which to determine what kind of line or how long a line to draw. Surely it would be a straight line, but it would be drawn freely, for just as nothing prevents a curve, nothing recommends one either.

Notes on Some Comments by Michel Angelo Fardella (1690)[147]

Venice, March 1690

In February and March of 1690, Leibniz was in Venice where he met the philosopher and theologian, Michel Angelo Fardella, beginning an association that was to last until 1714. The following document seems to be conversational notes, a record of Leibniz's positions, Fardella's objections, and responses Leibniz thought appropriate.

I COMMUNICATED several of my metaphysical thoughts to the Reverend Father Michel Angelo Fardella of the Order of Friars Minor, because I saw that he combined meditation on intellectual things with an understanding of mathematics, and because he pursued truth with great ardor. And so, after he grasped my views, he wrote out certain propositions at home to remember them in order to master what he heard from me, along with objections, which, it so happens, he sent to me for my examination.

---

147. Editors' title. S 322–25; F de C 317–23. Latin.

Proposition I

GOD foreknew and predetermined, from the beginning, not only the infinite series of things, but also the infinite number of possible combinations of actions, passions, and changes of those things; and in the same way, he also foreknew and predetermined the free effects of individual created minds.

The Objection of the Rev. Father

I DON'T understand well enough how this sort of divine foreknowledge and predetermination can be reconciled with the freedom of the human mind. For on this view, whatever a man did, he would do for some necessary, and, as it were, fated reason. If the human mind didn't have some power [virtus] to determine itself by itself, but if the mind were determined by something else, that would certainly not exhibit any freedom outside of that which God has. It is not obvious that there is this kind of predetermination, just as one can doubt whether God has this foreknowledge with respect to the futures of free things. Nor does this divine foreknowledge seem necessary. For what prevents God from having constituted human minds, free in their action and decision, in such a way that he neither determines nor foreknows their free actions?

Clarification

WE MUST distinguish between a series of possible things and a series of actual things. From an infinite number of possibilities God chose a certain universal series, composed of an infinite number of substances, each of which exhibits an infinite series of operations. But if God had not foreknown or preordained the entire series of actual things, then it would follow that he would have made a judgment for a reason [causa] insufficiently understood by him, and that he would have chosen something insufficiently clear to him. The actions of free minds cannot be excepted from this, since they make up part of the series of things and have important connections with all other things, so that the one cannot be perfectly understood without the other. And since every ordered series involves a rule for continuing, or a law of progression, God, by examining any part of the series whatsoever, sees in it everything that precedes and everything that follows. But this does not eliminate freedom in minds. For infallible certainty is different from absolute necessity, as St. Augustine, St. Thomas, and other learned men have known for a long time. Certainly, the truth or falsity of future contingents, even those that are free, is determined, even if we imagine that they are unknown. And so, God's foreknowledge, and even his preordination, does not eliminate freedom. Furthermore, we must understand that the mind is not determined by something else, but by itself, and that there is no other hypothesis which favors human freedom more than ours does. This is because (as is evident from what follows) one created substance does not influence another, and therefore, the mind derives all of its operations from within itself, even though its nature is so ordered from the beginning that its operations harmonize with the operations of all other things.

Proposition 2

THE INFINITELY many series of things and of changes so correspond to one another and are connected with such symmetry that any given one agrees perfectly with all the others, and conversely.

Hence, each thing is so connected to the whole universe, and one mode of each thing contains such order and consideration with respect to the individual modes of other things, that in any given thing, indeed in each and every mode of any given thing, God clearly and distinctly sees the universe as implied and inscribed. As a result, when I perceive one thing or one mode of a thing, I always perceive the whole universe confusedly; and the more perfectly I perceive one thing, the better I come to know many properties of other things from it.

And from this perfect consonance of things there also arises the greatest harmony and beauty of the universe, which exhibits to us the power [*vis*] and wisdom of the Highest Maker.

> No objection was made against this proposition, either because the former objection holds for this one as well, or because this proposition would seem completely in accord with reason, if the previous objection were eliminated.

Proposition 3

A BODY is not a substance but an aggregate of substances, since it is always further divisible, and any given part always has another part, to infinity.

Hence, it is contradictory to hold that a body is a single substance, since it necessarily contains in itself an infinite multitude, or an infinity of bodies, each of which, in turn, contains an infinite number of substances.

Therefore, over and above a body or bodies, there must be substances, to which true unity belongs. For indeed, if there are many substances, then it is necessary that there be one true substance. Or, to put the same thing another way, if there are many created things it is necessary that there be some created thing that is truly one. For a plurality of things can neither be understood nor can exist unless one first understands the thing that is one, that to which the multitude necessarily reduces [*referatur*].

Hence, unless there are certain indivisible substances, bodies would not be real, but would only be appearances or phenomena (like the rainbow), having eliminated every basis from which they can be composed.

However, from this, one must not infer that the indivisible substance enters into the composition of body as a part, but rather as an essential, internal requisite, just as one grants that a point is not a part that makes up a line, but rather something of a different sort which is, nevertheless, necessarily required for the line to be, and to be understood.

Hence, since I am truly a single indivisible substance, unresolvable into many others, the permanent and constant subject of my actions and passions, it is necessary that there be a persisting individual substance over and above the organic body. This persisting individual substance is completely different from the nature of body, which, assuming that it is in a state of continual flux of parts, never remains permanent, but is perpetually changed.

And so, there must be some incorporeal, immortal substance in man, over and above the body, something, indeed, incapable of being resolved into parts.

Furthermore, the union of soul and body in man consists in that most perfect agreement, in which the series of motions corresponds to the series of thoughts, so that neither the body (in a physical way), nor God (on the occasion of a body), changes the series of thoughts arising spontaneously from the nature of the mind, nor does either produce something new in the mind. Rather, the soul itself brings forth from the power [*virtus*] of its own substance ways of acting for itself which harmonize with the motions that bodies have from the basic laws of motion. As a result, it happens that one mode of a body or of a soul is indeed a consequence of another mode of a body or of a soul. And the operation of one substance on another is nothing but the action of one substance which, by virtue of the general consensus, results in an action of the other substance.

Hence, it seems probable that animals, which are indeed analogous to us, and similarly plants, which correspond to animals in many ways, are not composed of body alone, but also of soul, by which the animal or plant, the single indivisible substance, the permanent subject of its actions, is controlled. This is well understood by the mind, though the imagination cannot grasp it.[148]

Souls of this sort never perish, but when they seem to perish, they remain hidden in some inconspicuous part of a fragmented mixture.

Objection

WHEN DEALING with a multitude of stones ABC, either stone A or B or C must be understood first. But it is not the same with a soul which, with other souls, does not constitute body. And it seems that there is some difficulty in the argument that, given that there are bodies composed of substances in the world, there must necessarily be something which is a single indivisible substance. Now, this can legitimately be inferred if the unity, as a part of the same sort, intrinsically composed the aggregate. But the substantial unity in question does not intrinsically constitute the aggregate, and is not a portion of it, but is understood to be essentially altogether different from it. How, then, is it required in order for this aggregate to subsist?

---

148. Leibniz wrote in the margin here: "I judge that it is probable that plants and animals are animate, though I cannot say anything with confidence about any body in particular except the human body with which I am intimately acquainted. However, I do venture to assert that they contain animate bodies or bodies analogous to animate bodies, that is, substances."

Clarification

I DO NOT say that the body is composed of souls, nor that body is constituted by an aggregate of souls, but that it is constituted by an aggregate of substances. Moreover, the soul, properly and accurately speaking, is not a substance, but a substantial form, or the primitive form existing in substances, the first act, the first active faculty.[149] Moreover, the force of the argument consists in this, that body is not a substance, but substances or an aggregate of substances.

Therefore either there is no substance, and therefore there are no substances, or, there is something other than body. Further, although the aggregate of these substances constitutes body, they do not constitute it as parts, just as points are not parts of lines, since a part is always of the same sort as the whole. However, the organic bodies of substances included in any mass of matter are parts of that mass. So in a fish pond there are many fishes and the liquid in each fish is, in turn, a certain kind of fish pond which contains, as it were, other fishes or animals of their own kinds; and so on to infinity. And therefore there are substances everywhere in matter, just as points are everywhere in a line. And just as there is no portion of a line in which there are not an infinite number of points, there is no portion of matter which does not contain an infinite number of substances. But just as a point is not a part of a line, but a line in which there is a point is such a part, so also a soul is not a part of matter, but a body in which there is a soul is such a part of matter. We must consider whether we can say that an animal is a part of matter, as a fish is part of a fish pond, or cattle are a part of a herd. And indeed, if the animal is conceived of as a thing having parts, that is, as a body divisible and destructible, endowed with a soul, then it must be conceded that the animal is part of matter, since every part of matter has parts. But it cannot then be conceded that it is a substance or an indestructible thing. And it is the same for man. For if a man is the I [*Ego*] itself, then he cannot be divided, nor can he perish, nor is he a homogeneous part of matter. But if by the name 'man' one understands that which perishes, then a man would be part of matter, whereas that which is truly indestructible would be called 'soul,' 'mind,' or 'I,' which would not be a part of matter.[150]

Dynamics: On Power and the Laws of Corporeal Nature

Preliminary Specimen: On the law of nature relating to the power of bodies (1691?)[151]

Leibniz seems to have read Newton's great Mathematical Principles of Natural Philosophy *for the first time in Rome in 1689. [See p. 309 below].*

---

149. See Aristotle's definition of the soul in De Anima, 412a 27 ff.

150. We wish to acknowledge the assistance of Don Rutherford, who compared the printed sources with the manuscript and who supplied an unpublished marginal note.

151. GM VI 287–92. Latin.

During that same stay in Rome, Leibniz also began drafting his own systematic
physics, which he entitled the Dynamica, *the* Dynamics. *[GM III 259].*
Though the work was almost certainly intended for publication, it was never
published during Leibniz's lifetime. The main body of the work is organized
in a very formal way, with definitions, axioms, and propositions, like Euclid's
Geometry *and Newton's* Principia. *It begins, though, with a preliminary*
specimen, a very useful summary of four different ways of establishing the
refutation of Descartes's conservation law, first published in the "Brief
Demonstration" of 1686 [see "Discourse on Metaphysics," sec. 18]. The
reference Leibniz makes in the third demonstration to the problem of actually
transferring all power from one body to another suggests that the preliminary
specimen is a later addition to the original manuscript of 1689. The problem did
not seem to have concerned Leibniz until January 1691, when Denis Papin
noted it in a critique of Leibniz's anti-Cartesian arguments. [See GM VI
204f.]

I HAVE DISCOVERED that the *power* [*potentia*] of bodies does not consist in *quantity of motion*, that is, in the product of weight times velocity (as is
commonly believed), and that in transferring power from body to body,
the same quantity of motion is not conserved (as the Cartesians are greatly
persuaded). Furthermore, I have discovered that this *law of nature* holds instead, namely, that *the whole effect has the same power as its full cause*, so that
one cannot obtain perpetual motion, without violating the order of things
through an increase in the power of the effect beyond that of its cause
(something I take to be absurd for sure, and I show that the view opposed
to mine can be reduced to this absurdity). When I discovered these things, I
judged that it was worth the trouble to muster the force of my reasonings
through demonstrations of the greatest evidence, so that, little by little, I
might lay the foundations for the *true elements of the new science of power and*
action, which one might call *dynamics*. I have gathered certain preliminaries
of this science for special treatment,[152] and I wanted to select a ready specimen from these in order to excite clever minds to seek truth and to receive
the genuine laws of nature, in place of imaginary ones. It will be obvious from
this specimen how unsafe it is to affirm anything in mathematics on the basis of probable arguments, since the forces [*vires*] contained in two bodies of
equal weight, but endowed with unequal velocities, are not proportional to
their velocities, but are proportional to the heights from which they could
have derived those velocities by falling. Moreover, it is agreed that those
velocities are not proportional to the heights but to the square roots of those
heights. From this another paradox immediately arises, that it is easier to im-
print a given degree of velocity on a body at rest than it is to give the same
degree of velocity to the same body once it has already been put into motion
to that degree, so that its velocity in the same direction is doubled. The

---

152. Leibniz here is referring to the *Dynamics*, the treatise that follows this preface.

opposite of this might have seemed indubitable on the basis of the badly understood doctrine of the composition of motions. But lest anyone suspect that this is only a verbal dispute, or that we are arguing about the various meanings of 'power,' you must understand that what we seek is, for example, the velocity that a previously resting body one pound in weight, say, must acquire if the total power or action contained in a four-pound body endowed with one degree of velocity were transferred to it, so that the four-pound body was reduced to rest, leaving only the one-pound body in motion. The common opinion, and, indeed, the celebrated opinion that best agrees with that found in the writings of the Cartesians, is that such a body would receive a velocity of four degrees. My view is that it can only receive two degrees. They settle the matter in that way so as to conserve the same quantity of motion, which they confuse with power. I do so in order to conserve the same quantity of power, that is, to preserve the equality of cause and effect, to prevent perpetual motion from arising by the one exceeding the other. But it is time for us to proceed to demonstration.

Proposition

ASSUME *that the full power of a four-pound body moving horizontally with one degree of velocity is to be transferred to a one-pound body, previously at rest, so that motion remains in the one-pound body alone and the four-pound body, in turn, is at rest. Then the same quantity of motion as there was before could not be conserved and a velocity of four degrees be allotted to the one-pound body, and the one-pound body could never receive a velocity greater than two degrees.*

Lemma common to the first three of the following demonstrations, already demonstrated:

The perpendicular heights of heavy bodies are proportional to the squares of the speeds which they can acquire by falling from those heights, or to the squares of the speeds by virtue of which they can raise themselves to those very heights. This proposition is due to Galileo, demonstrated from the nature of the motion of a heavy body uniformly accelerated; it is accepted by mathematicians and confirmed by numerous experiments.

First Demonstration

AXIOM: *It takes the same power to raise four pounds one foot as it does to raise one pound four feet.*

This granted, let us assume that body A of four pounds can raise itself to a (perpendicular) height of, say, one foot by virtue of its velocity (which is one degree), if, for example, it were moved on a pendulum or on an inclined plane in such a way that it could direct its force upwards. Therefore, body A has power enough to raise four pounds (that is, the four pounds that belong to the body itself) to a height of one foot, or what comes to the same thing (by the preceding axiom), power enough to raise one pound four feet. On the other hand, if body A is raised one foot by virtue of a velocity of one degree,

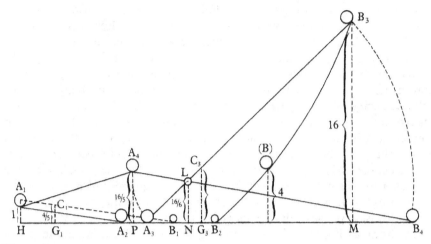

Figure 3

then certainly B, [a body of one pound], can be raised sixteen feet by virtue of a velocity of four degrees (by the previously presented lemma derived from Galileo). And so, body B has force enough to raise one pound (that is, the one pound that belongs to the body itself) sixteen feet. Therefore, B has four times as much power as A does, which, we showed, can only raise one pound four feet. This is contrary to the hypothesis, by which we postulated that the same power which was in A was to be transferred to B.

Second Demonstration

AXIOM: *There is no perpetual mechanical motion.*

This granted, let body A be four pounds, advancing on the horizontal A_2A_3 with velocity of one degree. (See Fig. 3.) Let us suppose that all of its power is transferred to body B, of one pound, resting in place B_1* so that only B then moves, through B_1B_2, while A is at rest at A3.I say that the quantity of motion in B could not become equal to the quantity of motion there was in A, that is, B could not receive a velocity of four degrees, or even anything greater than two. For let B receive four degrees of velocity, if this were possible, and let us assume something that could have happened, that body A received its velocity of one degree by descending from the perpendicular height A_1H of one foot on the inclined plane A_1A_2. Let us then assume that B, having received four degrees of velocity, ascends as high as it can on the upward slope B_2B_3; by the previously presented lemma derived from Galileo, it will ascend to the height B_3M of sixteen feet. Assume that a balance A_3LB_3 is already prepared, stretching from A_3 (the place on the horizontal where A is at rest) to B_3 (the place to which B has ascended), and divided by its fulcrum or center L in such a way that the arm LB_3 is just over four times the length of arm LA_3; for example, suppose it is five times the length of LA_3. Therefore,

B, raised to B_3 by virtue of its own impetus so that it can there fall upon the balance, will outweigh A on the balance, placed at the opposite end, A_3, because while A is four times the weight of B, the distance of B from the center L is more than four times the distance of A from L. And so B descending to B_4 on the horizontal HM will raise A from A_3 to A_4. Now, from A_4, L, and B_3 drop perpendiculars A_4P, LN and B_3M^* to the horizontal. And so, since B_3L is five times A_3L (if you please), A_3L will be one sixth of A_3B_3, and LN will thus be one sixth of B_3M. On the other hand, A_4B_4 is to B_4L as six is to five. LN has already been shown to be to B_3M as one is to six. So, A_4P is to B_3M as one is to five, that is, A_4P is $^{16}/_5$ feet. So, while in the beginning we had the four-pound body A raised only to a height of one foot, A_1H, we now have that same body raised $3^1/_5$ feet, for that is the height of A_4P. And so, by virtue of its descent alone and the descent of other things which were brought about due to the power derived from the original body, a body has raised itself almost four times higher than it had been before. This is absurd by the immediately preceding axiom, for in that way we can have perpetual motion whenever we like. For it could happen that heavy body A rolls back from A_4 to A_1, and while falling through a height of more than two feet, performs some desired mechanical tasks (like raising other bodies, or splitting a log, or some similar activity) and, nevertheless, returning then to A_1, where it had been in the beginning, is in position to repeat the same task. For B can also return again to its proper place B_1 if we assume that when it is at B_4 it has not descended directly to the horizontal HM, but stopped just a bit above it, so that it could roll back from B_4 to B_1. Thus, everything having been restored to its prior place, we have a machine capable of mechanical perpetual motion. And a similar absurdity can be shown, changing only the numbers, as long as the height B_3M, the height to which B can ascend by virtue of the velocity it has received, is greater than four feet, that is, by the lemma, as long as the velocity B receives is more than twice the velocity that A had. Q.E.D.

Third Demonstration

AXIOM: *The center of gravity of bodies cannot ascend by the force of gravity itself*

This granted, it follows in the first situation A_1B_1, assuming B_1 on the horizontal and A_1 elevated to the height A_1H of one foot above the horizontal, that the common center of gravity of A_1 and B_1, C_1, will be elevated $^4/_5$ of a foot. [See Fig. 3.] For the straight line A1B1 will be divided at C1 in such a way that B_1C_1 is four times A_1C_1, and therefore, $C_1G_1^*$ stands at $^4/_5$ of A_1H, that is, $^4/_5$ of a foot. But in the following state or situation, A_3B_3, we find that C_3, the common center of gravity, has risen to C_3G_3, $^{16}/_5$ feet. For A_3B_3 is divided at C_3 in such a way that C_3B_3 is four times $C_3A_3^*$; C_3 will be the center of gravity of A and B, and since C_3A_3 is one fifth of A_3B_3, C_3G_3 will be one fifth of B_3M, that is, one fifth of sixteen feet. Therefore, it stands at $^{16}/_5$ feet, and thus C_3, the common center of gravity, is elevated to the height C_3G_3, four times the previous height C_1G_1, which was only $^4/_5$ of a foot. By the immediately preceding axiom this is absurd, for in this way the common center of gravity of two heavy bodies will ascend by virtue of gravity itself. Nor can one avoid this absurdity unless B receives a velocity which is not greater* than two degrees, so that it cannot ascend beyond (B), a height of four feet.

Scholium.   The way in which we can actually bring it about that the power imparted to a whole given body A can be transferred to another given body B, previously at rest, was explained in a specimen of the elements of dynamics.[153] In this context it is sufficient for us to conceive of the transference as possible, so that from that hypothesis we can understand, for a given velocity in A, how much velocity B ought to receive in order for it to have the same power as does A. And certainly, two powers (the powers, for example, of a four-pound body with one degree of velocity, and a one-pound body with four degrees of velocity) cannot be equal if one substituted in place of another gives rise to perpetual motion.

F ROM considerations relating to motions, abstracted from sensible matter.   *Fourth Demonstration*

An action bringing about double the effect in a single unit of time is double the action bringing about double the effect in two units of time; an action bringing about double the effect in two units of time is double the action bringing about a single effect in a single unit of time. Therefore, an action bringing about double the effect in a single unit of time is four times the action bringing about a single effect in a single unit of time, that is, in the same amount of time.

But it is worth our while to set the matter out in a bit more detail. Let L be the action of traversing a single unit of space in a single unit of time, let M be the action of traversing two units of space in two units of time, and finally, let N be the action of traversing two units of space in one unit of time. Moreover, let these always be understood as concerning entirely unrestrained motion, as is uniform, horizontal motion in a nonresisting medium. Furthermore, let us understand that the body in motion in these three cases is the same body, or, at least, that the moving bodies are equal. Now, N is double M (the traversal of two leagues in one hour is double the traversal of two leagues in two hours), and M is double L (the traversal of two leagues in two hours is double the traversal of one league in one hour, for if two leagues are traversed in two hours, the action of traversing one league in one hour is performed twice). Therefore, N is four times L (the traversal of two leagues in one hour is four times the traversal of one league in one hour). That is, to have twice the speed in equal time is four times the action, and similarly, to have three times the speed is nine times the action, and so on. Now, uniform actions taking place in equal times are, among themselves, proportional to

---

153. See GM VI, 204ff.

their powers of acting. And so, certainly, if in equal mobile bodies, the speed of one is double that of the other, the power will be four times as great, or, if the bodies are assumed to be equal, their powers will be proportional to the square of their velocities. From this it is obvious that the powers of unequal bodies are jointly proportional to the size of the bodies and the square of the velocities. And so, if the entire power of a four-pound body A endowed with a velocity of one unit is to be given to a one-pound body B, then B ought to receive a velocity of two units. For the power of A, four times one (the square of the velocity of one unit), is equal to the power of B, one times four (the square of the velocity of two units). Q.E.D.

Scholium to the fourth demonstration.

Although this last demonstration is, perhaps, not to everyone's taste nor within everyone's power of comprehension, it should, however, especially please those who seek a clear perception of truths. Certainly, it seems to me that, although presented last, it is first in merit since it proceeds *a priori* and arises from the bare contemplation of space and time, without assuming gravity or any other hypotheses posterior in nature. Thus, we already not only have a remarkable agreement among truths, but also a new way is opened for demonstrating Galileo's propositions about the motion of heavy bodies without the hypothesis he had to use, namely, that in their uniformly accelerated motion, heavy bodies acquire equal increments of velocity in equal times. For this very fact, as well as the lemma assumed above, can be derived from our fourth demonstration, which does not depend on them as assumptions. This seemed quite remarkable, and of the greatest importance for perfecting the science of motion.

Dialogue on Human Freedom and the Origin of Evil (25 January 1695)[154]

The following document is a dialogue with Baron Dobrzensky, counselor of state and war to Brandenburg. Given what Leibniz wrote in a later letter to Dobrzensky, 26 January 1695 (Gr 369), it appears quite likely that the dialogue is a record of an actual conversation.

A.—I AM often bothered by the thought that sin appears to be necessary and inevitable.[155] Many fine things are said on this question, and I would not be able to reply well to them, but, at bottom, they do not satisfy me, and they soon fade away.

B.—These things require deep meditation, and unless one gives them the attention they require, one may not be sufficiently satisfied.

A.—Father Sperandio at Munich advised me not to apply myself at all to the

---

154. Gr 361–69. French.

155. Leibniz deleted and did not replace "by the thought that sin appears to be inevitable."

matter. One day I presented my doubts to him and he replied with much eloquence, and in such a plausible way, that it reduced me to silence. After he finished, he asked me if what he said didn't appear right to me. I said yes. And so, [he said], sir, content yourself with this for now, and so that you might have peace of mind, think no longer about this matter. It is true that I have not been able to heed his advice.

B.—It would be easy for a mediocre mind to follow the advice of this Father, but not a person of your intelligence. I admit that one does not need to bother with such subtle questions, and I do not advise anyone to interest himself in them. I only say that when someone has enough diligence to raise these difficulties for himself, then he must have enough to investigate their solutions. As for Father Sperandio's advice, I do not approve of it. Good and solid answers are of such nature that, the more one reflects on them, the more solid they appear; and it is a characteristic of evasions that, to find them satisfactory, one should consider them as little as possible.

A.—I will tell you, then, what bothers me. We are all in agreement that God knows all things and that the future is present to him just like the past. I cannot now move my arm without his having foreseen it from all eternity. He knows whether I will commit a murder, a crime, or some other sin. And since his foresight is infallible, it is infallible that I will commit the sin that he foresaw. It is therefore necessary that I will sin and it is not within my power to abstain from it. Thus, I am not free.

B.—It must be admitted, sir, that we are not completely free; only God is completely free, since he alone is independent. Our freedom is limited in many ways: I am not free to fly like an eagle nor to swim like a dolphin, because my body lacks the necessary equipment. Something similar can be said about our mind. Sometimes we admit that we do not have a free mind. And, speaking rigorously, we never have perfect freedom of mind. But that does not prevent us from having a certain degree of freedom that beasts do not have, that is, our faculty of reasoning and choosing in accordance with how things appear to us. As for divine foreknowledge, God foresees things as they are and does not change their nature. Events that are fortuitous and contingent in themselves remain so, notwithstanding the fact that God has foreseen them. Thus they are assured, but they are not necessary.

A.—Assured or infallible, isn't that almost the same thing?

B.—There is a difference: it is necessary that three times three is nine and this depends on no condition. God himself cannot prevent this. But a future sin can be prevented, if the man does his duty, even though God foresees that he will not do it. This sin is necessary because God foresaw it, and if God foresaw it only because it will be, it follows that it is as if one had said: it will necessarily happen, assuming that it will happen. This is what one calls conditional necessity.

A.—These distinctions do not resolve the difficulty.

B.—I must confess that I don't see any difficulty. Is there something wrong with granting that God foresees everything? On the contrary, since it is so, it wouldn't be of any use to be displeased by it; indeed, it would amount to not loving God.

A.—I am completely satisfied with divine foreknowledge. It only displeases me that I am not able to reply to the troublesome consequences which seem to me to arise from the certainty or necessity resulting from it, whether one takes it as conditional or as absolute. For if a sin is necessary, or at least if it is foreseen, and if it is infallible that I will sin, then regardless of my attempts to avoid it, it will nonetheless happen.

B.—These troublesome consequences have no place here. The ancient philosophers had a similar sophism, called the sloth's syllogism, because it concludes that we should do nothing. For if something is foreseen and infallible, it will happen without my effort, and if it is not foreseen, it will not happen, even though I am able to do it. I reply to this by denying something put forward without proof, that the thing foreseen will happen, whatever I do. If it is foreseen that I will do it, it is also foreseen that I will do what is needed to do it, and if it will not happen because of my laziness, my laziness itself will also have been foreseen. What a German proverb says about death, that it needs to have a cause, can also be said about eternal death or damnation, sin, or any other thing. Thus since we know nothing of what is foreseen, we should do our part without pausing over the useless question as to whether success is foreseen or not, all the more so since God is content with our good will when it is sincere and ardent.

A.—This is very good advice, and it completely accords with my view. However, the great difficulty about the origin of evil still remains. I am asking about the origin of the origins, and I am not easily satisfied with the ordinary evasions. It is said that man sins because his nature is corrupted by Adam's sin. But we return to the same question with respect to Adam himself, for how did it happen that he sinned? Or, more generally speaking, how did sin come into the world, since God, the creator of the world, is infinitely good and infinitely powerful? To account for sin there must be another infinite cause capable of counterbalancing the influence of divine goodness.

B.—I can name you such a thing.

A.—You would therefore be a Manichean, since you admit two principles, one of good and the other of evil.

B.—You yourself will acquit me of this charge of Manicheanism when I name this other principle.

A.—Then please name it now, sir.

B.—It is nothingness [le Néant.]

A.—Nothingness? But is nothingness infinite?

B.—No doubt it is; it is infinite, it is eternal, and it has many attributes in common with God. It includes an infinity of things, for all things that do not exist are included in nothingness, and all things that are no longer have returned into nothingness.

A.—You are joking, no doubt. [This is] almost like a wise man whose book about Nothing I remember having seen. (Passentius, de Nihilo.)

B.—No, I am not joking. The Platonists and Saint Augustine himself have already shown us that the cause of good is positive, but that evil is a defect, that is, a privation or negation, and consequently, it arises from nothingness or nonbeing.

A.—I do not see how nothingness, which is nothing, can enter into the composition of things.

B.—Yet you know that, in arithmetic, zeros joined to ones make up different numbers, such as 10, 100, 1000; a witty fellow, having written several zeros in a row, wrote above them: on the other hand, a "one" is needed too. But, without going so far, you would admit that all created things are limited, and that their limits, or their *non plus ultra* if you wish, constitute something negative. For example, a circle is limited on account of the fact that the separation of the compass used to inscribe that circle was not larger. Thus the boundaries or the *non plus ultra* of this separation determine the circle. It is the same for all other things, for they are bounded or imperfect by virtue of the principle of negation or of nothingness they contain, by virtue of the lack of an infinity of perfections in them, and which are only a nothingness with respect to them.

A.—Yet you would admit that everything was created good and in such a way that God had reason to be pleased with it, as the Sacred Scriptures tell us.[156] Original sin came after. And that is what I find surprising, namely, how original sin could have arisen in things wholly good.

B.—Before all sin, there was an original imperfection in all created things, an imperfection which arises from their limitation. In the same way that an infinite circle is impossible, since any circle is bounded by its circumference, an absolutely perfect created thing is also impossible; that is why it is believed that the Sacred Scriptures meant to refer even to angels when they suggested that among the ministers of God, there are none without defects. There was no positive evil in created things at the beginning, but they always lacked many perfections. Thus, because of a lack of attention, the first man was able to turn away from the supreme good and be content with some created thing, and thus, he fell into sin. That is, from an imperfection that was merely privative in the beginning, he fell into a positive evil.

A.—But where does the original imperfection antecedent to original sin come from?

B.—It can be said that it arises from the very essences or natures of created things; for the essences of things are eternal, even though things aren't. It has always been true that three times three is nine and it will always be so. These things do not depend on God's will, but on his understanding. For example, essences or properties of numbers are eternal and immutable, and nine is a perfect square, not because God wants it to be so, but because its definition entails that it is, for it is three times three, and thus it is a result of the multiplication of a number by itself. God's understanding is the source of the

---

156. Leibniz deleted the first sentence of this paragraph, which was: "But how can these boundaries cause sin to arise?"

essences of created things, such as they are in him, that is, bounded. If they are imperfect, one can only blame their limitation on their boundaries, that is to say, the extent of their participation in nothingness.

A.—I acknowledge, after what you have just said, that created things are necessarily limited, a bit like the circle we spoke of earlier. But it seems that it was up to God to create them at least perfect enough so that they don't fall.

B.—I believe that God did create things in ultimate perfection, though it does not seem so to us considering the parts of the universe. It's a bit like what happens in music and painting, for shadows and dissonances truly enhance the other parts, and the wise author of such works derives such a great benefit for the total perfection of the work from these particular imperfections that it is much better to make a place for them than to attempt to do without them. Thus, we must believe that God would not have allowed sin nor would he have created things he knows will sin, if he could not derive from them a good incomparably greater than the resulting evil.

A.—I would like to know what this great good is.

B.—I can assure you that it is, but I cannot explain it in detail. One would have to know the general harmony of the universe for that, whereas we know only a very small part. It is when speaking in rapture about the depths of divine wisdom, that is, when explaining this same matter, that Saint Paul exclaimed, "Oh, depth of riches."[157]

A.—Yet it is strange that there are creatures who have fallen and others who have been elevated. Where does this difference come from, then?

B.—The difference between created things arises originally from their essence, as I believe I have just shown, and the order of things, something from which divine wisdom did not wish to deviate, required this variety. I will give you an example from geometry, something not unknown to you.

A.—It is true that this science touches upon things, and shows what the human mind is capable of, if it is led in an orderly way. But I do not see how one can find something there relevant to our concerns. So, I will be even more pleased to hear it.

B.—Geometers draw a great distinction between commensurable and incommensurable lines. They call lines commensurable when they can be expressed* by numbers, that is, by measures or by parts of a measure. But when neither a whole number nor a fraction of a number can be found to express them, they are incommensurable. For example, if there were two lines, one nine feet and one ten feet long, they would be commensurable, for they have a common measure, the foot. And if one of them was ten feet and the other nine feet and a fifth, they would still be commensurable, for the fifth of a foot would be the common measure, being contained fifty times in the line ten feet long and 46 times in the line 9⅕ feet long.

A.—That is easy to understand, but incommensurables are a bit more difficult.

B.—Here is an example: the square root of two is incommensurable with the

_____

157. Romans 11:33.

unit. This number is called a surd [*nombre sourd*] because it cannot be expressed exactly either by whole numbers or by fractions. And you will never find a whole number, nor a fraction, nor half a whole number, nor half a fraction, which multiplied by itself produces the number two, as one can easily understand by searching for such a number.

A.—But I was expecting incommensurable lines, rather than incommensurable numbers.

B.—Here is one, corresponding to the square root of two, namely, the diagonal of the perfect square, for it was long ago noticed that this line is incommensurable with the side of the square. Let ABCD be a perfect square, whose sides are all equal and whose angles are also equal, that is, all right angles; I claim that its diagonal AC is incommensurable with its side, for example, with AB.

A.—Let's see the proof of this.

B.—It is an easy proof. Construct another perfect square whose side is the diagonal of the first square. This new square will be ACEF. It is evident that the second square is exactly twice the preceding square, ABCD, for square ABCD contains two triangles ABC and ADC, whereas square ACEF contains four of these triangles, namely, ADC, CDE, EDF, and FDA, and all these triangles are equal. And that which contains a same magnitude fourfold is no doubt twice that which contains it only twofold.

A.—That's certainly evident, but what do you conclude from it?

B.—It follows that if a side of the small square ABCD, namely, the line AB, is one foot long, the side of the large square ACEF, namely, AC, will be the square root of two. For the square on that side has the value of two square feet, and, in order to find its side, we must take the square root of the area, which is two, as all mathematicians know. But we have already shown that the square root of two is incommensurable with the unit and completely inexpressible in rational numbers [*nombres exact*].

A.—Now that is surprising. Wouldn't God be able to find a number capable of expressing exactly the square root of two or the length of the diagonal of a square?

B.—God can't find absurd things. That would be as if we asked God to teach us the way to divide three coins into two equal parts without breaking one, that is, without getting* a one and a half or the like.

A.—You are right; that would be to ask for absurdities unworthy of God, or rather, that would be to ask for nothing or not to know what it is that one is asking for. I see the necessity of what you are saying about incommensurables, although it goes beyond our imagination. This should enable us to understand, at the same time, both our inadequacy and our adequacy. For many things we know *that* they are, but we cannot claim to know perfectly *why* they are. Yet, what do you derive from this fine geometrical meditation that can be applied to our question?

B.—Here it is: isn't it true that if the order of things or divine wisdom required God to produce perfect squares, then God, having resolved to do this, couldn't fail to produce incommensurable lines, even though they have the imperfection of not being able to be expressed exactly?[158] For a square cannot fail to have a diagonal, which is the distance between its opposite angles. Let us push the comparison further, and let us compare commensurable lines with minds who sustain themselves in their purity, and incommensurables with less regulated minds who then fall into sin. It is evident that the irregularity of incommensurable lines arises from the very essence of figures, and must not be imputed to God; it is even evident that this incommensurability is not an evil that God can fail to produce. It is also true that God could have avoided it by creating, not figures and continuous quantities, but only numbers or discrete quantities. But the imperfection of incommensurables has been paid back with even greater advantages, insofar as it was better to allow them to occur so as not to deprive the universe of all figures. It is the same with minds less firm in sustaining themselves, whose original imperfection arises from their essence, which is bounded in accordance with their degree. Their sin, which is only something accidental or contingent (though it is grounded in their essence, without, however, resulting from it as a necessary consequence), arises from their will; and the incommensurably greater good that God knows how to derive from this evil comes from his infinite wisdom, and led him not to exclude them from existence, nor to prevent them from sinning. This he could have done, by using his absolute power, but it would, at the same time, have overturned the order of things that his infinite wisdom chose.

A.—These are singular meditations and they shed new light on this matter.

B.—I believe that we could have explained the matter using expressions and comparisons very different from mine. But I hold that we will not be able to deny my account at bottom, if we meditate on it ever so little. It conforms with Saint Paul, Saint Augustine, and, in part, with the excellent work of Luther on servitude of the will,[159] which is extremely good, in my opinion, as long as one tones down some extravagant expressions, and which has seemed to me, from my childhood, to be the finest and most solid book he left to us.

A Specimen of Dynamics,

Toward Uncovering and Reducing to Their Causes Astonishing Laws of Nature Concerning the Forces of Bodies and Their Actions on One Another (1695)[160]

Leibniz had great trouble finishing his Dynamics. *But, as he explained in the opening sentence of the following essay, his friends were pressing him to publish. The result was the "*Specimen Dynamicum,*" "*A Specimen of Dynamics.*"*

---

158. Leibniz wrote, but then deleted, "nor known exactly by any finite mind."
159. Martin Luther, De servo arbitrio (1525), translated in J. Packer and O.R. Johnston, *Martin Luther on the Bondage of the Will.*
160. Dosch et al.; GM VI 234–54. Latin.

Part I was published in the Acta Eruditorum *in April 1695; however, part
II was not published in his lifetime. This is one of Leibniz's most important
publications; it is referred to often by Leibniz himself and by his contemporaries.*

Part I

EVER SINCE we made mention of establishing a *New Science of Dynamics*, many distinguished persons have requested a fuller explanation of this
doctrine in various places. Therefore, since we have not yet had the leisure to
put a book together, we shall here present some things that can shed light on
it, light that will perhaps even return to us with interest, if we elicit the views of
those who join power of thought with refinement of expression. We acknowledge that their judgments will be welcome to us, and hope that they help advance the work. Elsewhere we urged that in corporeal things there is something over and above extension, in fact, something prior to extension, namely,
that force of nature implanted everywhere by the Creator. This force does not
consist in a simple faculty, with which the schools seem to have been content,
but is further endowed with *conatus* or *nisus*,[161] attaining its full effect unless
it is impeded by a contrary *conatus*. This *nisus* frequently presents itself to
the senses and, in my judgment, is understood by reason to be everywhere in
matter, even where it is not obvious to sense. But if we should not attribute
this *nisus* to God, acting by miracle, then it is certainly necessary that he
produce that force in bodies themselves, indeed, that it constitute the innermost nature of bodies, since to act is the mark of substances, and extension means nothing but the continuity or diffusion of an already presup-
posed striving and reacting (that is, resisting) substance. So far is extension
from being able to constitute a substance itself! Nor does it matter that every
corporeal action derives from motion, and that motion itself comes only from
motion, either previously existing in the body or impressed from without.
For, strictly speaking, motion (and likewise time) never really exists, since the
whole never exists, inasmuch as it lacks coexistent parts. And furthermore,
there is nothing real in motion but a momentary something which must consist in a force striving [*nitente*][162] toward change. Whatever there is in corporeal
nature over and above the object of geometry or extension reduces to this.
And finally, this view takes both the truth and the doctrines of the ancients
into consideration. Just as our age has already saved from scorn Democritus'
corpuscles, Plato's ideas, and the Stoics' tranquility in light of the most perfect interconnection of things, so now we shall make intelligible the teachings
of the Peripatetics concerning forms or entelechies, notions which seemed
enigmatic for good reason, and were scarcely perceived by their own authors
in the proper way. Furthermore, we think that it is necessary not to destroy

---

161. 'Conatus' and 'nisus' are technical terms in this essay, to be defined later in the text. For the
most part we leave them untranslated. When Leibniz uses these terms in a nontechnical sense, they
are translated as 'effort' or 'striving', but in every such case the original Latin is given in brackets.
162. The verb Leibniz uses here is connected with the noun 'nisus.'

this philosophy accepted for so many centuries, but to explain it in such a way that it can be rendered self-consistent (where this is possible) and, further, to illuminate it, and augment it with new truths.

This plan of study seems to me to be the one best suited both for judiciousness in teaching and for the benefit of students. It prevents us from appearing more eager to destroy than to build, and it prevents the arrogance of bold minds from throwing us, daily, in our uncertainty, into perpetually changing our views; but rather, by restraining the whim of sects (which is encouraged by the empty glory of novelty) and by establishing doctrines with certainty, it enables the human race, at long last, to advance unhaltingly toward greater heights, no less in philosophy than in mathematics. For if you just omit the harsher things they say against others, there is usually much that is good and true in the writings of the distinguished ancients and moderns, much that deserves to be brought to light and deposited in the public treasury. And would that people chose to do this, rather than waste time with criticizing, which satisfies only their own vanity. Fortune has certainly favored me with certain novelties of my own, to such an extent that my friends constantly tell me to think about them alone. But nevertheless, many things others have done please me in a way, and I judge each in accordance with its worth, however it might vary. Perhaps this is because, by thinking about many things, I have learned not to despise anything. But we must now return to the proper path.

Active force (which might not inappropriately be called *power* [*virtus*], as some do) is twofold, that is, either *primitive*, which is inherent in every corporeal substance *per se* (since I believe that it is contrary to the nature of things that a body be altogether at rest), or *derivative*, which, resulting from a limitation of primitive force through the collision of bodies with one another, for example, is found in different degrees. Indeed, primitive force (which is nothing but the first entelechy) corresponds to the *soul or substantial form*. But, for that reason, it pertains only to general causes, which are insufficient to explain the phenomena. And so we agree with those who deny that we should appeal to forms when treating the individual and specific causes of sensible things. This is worth pointing out, so that when we restore forms, as if by birthright, in order to uncover the ultimate causes of things, at the same time, we don't seem to want to revive the verbal swordplay of the common schools. Nevertheless, a conception of forms is necessary for philosophizing properly, and no one can think that he sufficiently understands the nature of body unless he has turned his mind toward such things and understood that the crude notion of corporeal substance, which depends on the imagination alone and was carelessly introduced some years ago through an abuse of the corpuscular philosophy (by itself excellent and most true), is imperfect, not to say false. This can be established by the argument that since this notion of corporeal substance doesn't completely exclude inactivity or rest from matter, it cannot explain the laws of nature that regulate derivative force. Similarly, passive force is also twofold, either primitive or derivative. And indeed, the *primitive force of being acted upon* [*vis primitiva patiendi*] or of *resisting* constitutes that which is called *primary matter* in the schools, if correctly interpreted. This force is that by virtue of which it happens that a body cannot be penetrated by another body, but presents an obstacle to it, and at the same time is endowed with a certain laziness, so to speak, that is, an opposition to motion, nor, further, does it allow itself to be put into motion without somewhat diminishing the force of the body acting on it. As a result, the *derivative force of being acted upon* later shows itself to different degrees in *secondary matter*. But having distinguished and set out these general and basic considerations, considerations from which we learn that it is on account of form that every body always acts, and that it is on account of matter that every body is always acted upon and resists, we must now proceed deeper still and, in the doctrine of *derivative forces [virtus] and resistance*, deal with the extent to which bodies are empowered with different degrees of nisus, or the extent to which they offer resistance in various ways. For it is to these notions that the laws of action apply, laws which are understood not only through reason, but are also corroborated by sense itself through the phenomena.

Therefore, by derivative force, namely, that by which bodies actually act on one another or are acted upon by one another, I understand, in this context, only that which is connected to motion (local motion, of course), and which, in turn, tends further to produce local motion. For we acknowledge that all other material phenomena can be explained by local motion. Motion is the continual change of place, and so requires time. However, just as a mobile thing in motion has motion in time, so too at any given moment it has a *velocity*, which is greater to the extent that more space is traversed in less time. Velocity taken together with direction is called *conatus*. Furthermore, *impetus* is the product of the bulk *[moles]* of a body and its velocity, whose quantity is what the *Cartesians* usually call quantity of motion, that is, the momentary quantity of motion; although, more accurately speaking, the quantity of a motion, which exists in time, of course, arises from the sum over time of the impetuses (equal or unequal) existing in the mobile thing, multiplied by the corresponding times.[163] In arguing with the Cartesians, though, we have followed their terminology. But to speak in a way not inappropriate for scientific use, just as we can distinguish the progress we are now making from the progress we have made or will make, considering our present progress as an increment or element of progress, or just as we can distinguish the present descent from descent already made, descent which it augments, so too we can distinguish the present or instantaneous element of motion from that same motion extended through a period of time, and call the former *motio*. And so, what is commonly called quantity of motion would be called quantity of *motio*.[164] Although we can be casual in our use of words after having a proper

---

163. What the Cartesians call quantity of motion is size times speed; see Descartes's *Principles of Philosophy* II 36. The term '*moles*' that we translate as 'bulk' might also be translated as 'mass'. However, Leibniz appears to draw a distinction between '*moles*' and '*massa*' in some texts (e.g., in the Letter to Bernoulli, 20/30 September 1698, pp. 167–68 below); so we shall reserve 'mass' as a translation for '*massa*.'

164. The normal Latin word for motion is '*motus*'; in this passage Leibniz chooses a relatively rare synonym, '*motio*' to mark the distinction he is trying to make between instantaneous motion and motion extended over time.

understanding of them, beforehand, however, we must use them with care so as not to be deceived through ambiguity.

Furthermore, just as the numerical value of a motion [*motus*] extending through time derives from an infinite number of impetuses, so, in turn, impetus itself (even though it is something momentary) arises from an infinite number of increments successively impressed on a given mobile thing. And so impetus too has a certain element from whose infinite repetition it can only arise. Consider tube AC rotating around the immobile center C on the horizontal plane of this page with a certain uniform speed, and consider ball B in the interior of the tube, just freed from a rope or some other hindrance, and beginning to move by virtue of centrifugal force.[165] It is obvious that, in the beginning, the conatus for receding from the center, namely, that by virtue of which the ball B in the tube tends toward the end of the tube, A, is infinitely small in comparison with the impetus which it already has from rotation, that is, it is infinitely small in comparison with the impetus by virtue of which the ball B, together with the tube itself, tends to go from place D to (D), while maintaining the same distance from the center. But if the centrifugal impression deriving from the rotation were continued for some time, then by virtue of that very circumstance, a certain complete centrifugal impetus (D) (B), comparable to the rotational impetus D (D), must arise in the ball. From this it is obvious that the *nisus* is twofold, that is, elementary or infinitely

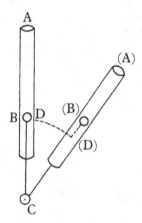

Figure 4

small, which I also call *solicitation*, and that which is formed from the continuation or repetition of elementary nisus, that is, *impetus* itself. Nevertheless, I wouldn't want to claim on these grounds that these mathematical entities are really found in nature, but I only wish to advance them for making careful calculations through mental abstraction.

From this it follows that *force* is also twofold. One force is elementary, which I also call *dead force*, since motion [*motus*] does not yet exist in it, but only a solicitation to motion [*motus*], as with the ball in the tube, or a stone in a sling while it is still being held in by a rope. The other force is ordinary force, joined with actual motion, which I call *living force*.[166] An example of dead force is centrifugal force itself, and also the force of heaviness [*vis gravitatis*] or centripetal force, and the force by which a stretched elastic body begins to restore itself. But when we are dealing with impact, which arises from a heavy body which has already been falling

---

165. Cf. Fig. 4.

166. An earlier version of this passage reads as follows:

Therefore, the force by which bodies actually act on one another is twofold, in my terminology, dead or inchoate, and living or formed. And indeed, dead force is to living force as a point is to a line, to the extent that living force arises from an infinity of impressions of dead force.

for some time, or from a bow that has already been restoring its shape for some time, or from a similar cause, the force in question is living force, which arises from an infinity of continual impressions of dead force. And this is what *Galileo* meant when he said, speaking enigmatically, that the force of impact is infinite in comparison with the simple nisus of heaviness.[167] But even though impetus is always joined to living force, we shall nevertheless show below that these two differ.

Living force in any aggregate of bodies must, again, be understood as twofold, namely *total force* or *partial force*, and *partial force*, again, is either relative or directive, that is, it either belongs to the parts or is common to the whole. *Relative* or *proper* force is that by which bodies contained in an aggregate can act on one another; *directive* or *common* force is that by which the aggregate itself can, in addition, act outside of itself. Moreover, I call it "directive" since the entire force embodied in the direction as a whole is conserved in this variety of partial force. If we imagine that the aggregate suddenly froze solid, having eliminated the motion of the parts with respect to one another, this force alone would remain. Whence the *total absolute force* consists of the relative and directive forces taken together. But these things will be better understood from the rules to be treated below.

So far as one can establish, the ancients had knowledge only of dead force, and this is what is commonly called mechanics, which deals with the lever, the pulley, the inclined plane (where accounts of the wedge and the screw belong), the equilibrium of bodies, and the like. There we treat only the first conatus of bodies acting on one another, before those bodies have received impetus through acting. And although one might, in a certain way, be able to transpose the laws of dead force over into living force, great caution is needed; those who confused force in general with the product of bulk [*moles*] and velocity because they discovered that dead force is proportional to that product were misled in just such a way. For, as we once warned, this fact[168] holds in this case for a special reason. For example, if different heavy bodies are falling, then at the very beginning of their motion, at least, the very descents or the very quantities of space traversed in descent, though, at that point, infinitely small or elementary, would be proportional to the speeds or to the conatus of descent. But once they have made some progress, and once living force has arisen, then the speeds acquired are no longer proportional to the spaces already traversed in descent (in terms of which force ought to be measured, as I once showed and will later show more fully), but are proportional only to the sum of their own elements. *Galileo* began to deal with *living force* (under a different name, granted, and, indeed, under a different conception) and was the first to explain how motion arises from the acceleration of heavy bodies in fall. *Descartes* correctly distinguished velocity

---

167. The relation between force of impact and the force of heaviness is discussed in the final day of Galileo's *Two New Sciences*, pp. 281f.

168. Their reference here is to the discussion of the special case of simple machines in the "Brief Demonstration," L 297–98.

from direction and also saw that what results in the collision of bodies is that which least changes the prior state. But he did not calculate the least change properly, first changing the direction alone, then the velocity alone, whereas the change must be determined by both at the same time. But how this could be escaped him; since he focused on modes, rather than things, things so heterogeneous seemed incapable of being compared or treated at the same time, not to speak of his other errors on this matter.[169]

Honoratus Fabri, Marcus Marci Joh. Alph. Borelli Ignatius Baptista Pardies, Claudius de Chales, and other very acute men have made contributions to the theory of motion that should not be despised, but they have not avoided these fatal mistakes. Huygens, who illuminated our age with his excellent discoveries, seems to be the first person I know of to have arrived at the pure and clear truth on this matter, and the first to have freed this subject from paralogisms through certain laws he once published. Wren, Wallis, and Mariotte, gentlemen excellent in these studies, though, granted, in different ways, all obtained virtually the same rules. But their views of the causes are not the same, and thus even these gentlemen, outstanding as they are in these studies, do not always draw the same conclusions. And, to that extent, the true sources of this science (which we have established)* have not yet been disclosed. Nor indeed, does everyone acknowledge what appears certain to me, that repercussion or reflexion arises from elastic force alone, that is, from resistance due to internal motion. Nor has anyone before us explained the notion of force. These matters have hitherto troubled the Cartesians and others who could not even grasp that the totality of motion or impetus (which they take to be quantity of force) might be different after a collision than it was before, because they believed that if that were to happen, the quantity of force would change as well.

In my youth, then believing (with *Democritus* and also with *Gassendi* and *Descartes*, who are among his followers on this question) that the nature of body consists in inert mass [*massa*] alone, I published a small book under the title *A Physical Hypothesis*,[170] in which I presented the theory of motion, both in abstraction from the organization of things in the world, and as it is connected with the organization of things in the world, a theory which, I see, pleased many distinguished people more than its insignificant worth deserved. There I established that if we assume such a notion of body, then every body entering into a collision gives its conatus to the body which receives it, that is, it gives its conatus to that which directly poses an obstacle as such. For,

---

169. The reference here is probably to Descartes's letter to Clerselier, 17 February 1645, AT IV, 183–88.

170. The book in question is the *Hypothesis Physica Nova*, published in 1671 and dedicated to the Royal Society of London (GM VI 17f; A VI, 2, 222f). Also relevant here is the closely connected *Theoria Motus Abstracti,* also from 1671 and dedicated to the French Academy of Sciences (GM VI 61f; A VI, 2, 261f; partly translated in L 139–42). In these works, Leibniz presents a series of geometrical laws of motion. Agreement with everyday observations is achieved through a hypothesis about the make-up of the physical world, which, together with the abstract laws of motion, is supposed to yield the world around us. The project failed and was abandoned by the late 1670s.

in the instant of collision, it tries[171] to proceed, and thus it tries to carry the receiving body along with it, and that conatus ought to have its full effect on the receiving body, unless hindered by a contrary conatus (for I then believed in the indifference of body to motion or rest), indeed, it ought to have its full effect even if hindered by a contrary conatus, since those different conatuses ought to be combined with one another. It was obvious that there is no reason why the body entering into the collision shouldn't attain the result toward which it strives, or why the receiving body shouldn't receive the entire conatus of the first. Therefore, it was obvious that the motion of the receiving body is the combination of its original motion with that it newly received, that is, the combination of its original motion with the conatus of the other body. From this, I further showed that if we understand there to be in body only mathematical notions, size, shape, place, and their change, or if we understand there to be strivings [conatus] for change in the body only at the very moment of collision, without their being any ground [ratio] for metaphysical notions, namely, no ground for active power [potentia actrix] in the form and laziness [ignavia] or resistance to motion in the matter, and thus, if it were necessary for the outcome of a collision to be determined by the geometrical composition of conatus alone, as we explained earlier, then I showed that it ought to follow that the conatus of a body entering into a collision, however small it might be, would be impressed on the whole receiving body, however large it might be, and thus, that the largest body at rest would be carried off by a colliding body however small it might be, without retarding it at all, since such a notion of matter contains not resistance to motion, but indifference. From this it follows that it would be no more difficult to put a large body into motion than a small one, and thus, that there would be action without reaction, and that there could be no measure of power [potentia], since anything could prevail over anything else. Since there were also many other things of this sort which are contrary to the order of things and which are opposed to the principles of the true metaphysics, I then thought (indeed, correctly) that, by way of the organization of things [structura systermatis], the Wisest Author of things had avoided the consequences that follow per se from the bare laws of motion derived from geometry.[172]

But after I examined all of this more deeply, I saw what a systematic explanation of things consists in, and noticed that my earlier hypothesis about the notion of body was imperfect. I also noticed, through other arguments as well as this one, that one can establish that something should be posited in body over and above size and impenetrability, something from which the consideration of forces arises, and that by adding the metaphysical laws of this something to the laws of extension, the laws of motion that I called systematic arise, namely, that all change comes about by stages, that all action has a reaction, that a new force is not produced unless an earlier one is diminished, and therefore that a body that carries another off with it is always

---

171. The verb Leibniz uses here is 'conor,' which is connected to the noun 'conatus.'
172. For a more careful development of this argument, see the fragment on the nature of bodies and the laws of motion, below, pp. 245–50.

slowed by the one it carries off, and that there is neither more nor less power [*potentia*] in an effect than there is in its cause. Since this law does not derive from the notion of bulk [*moles*], it is necessary that it follow from something else inherent in bodies, indeed from force itself, which always maintains its same quantity, even if it is realized in different bodies.[173] Therefore, I concluded from this that, because we cannot derive all truths concerning corporeal things from logical and geometrical axioms alone, that is, from large and small, whole and part, shape and position, and because we must appeal to other axioms pertaining to cause and effect, action and passion, in terms of which we can explain the order of things, we must admit something metaphysical, something perceptible by the mind alone over and above that which is purely mathematical and subject to the imagination, and we must add to material mass [*massa*] a certain superior and, so to speak, formal principle. Whether we call this principle form or entelechy or force does not matter, as long as we remember that it can only be explained through the notion of forces.

Today certain distinguished men, seeing this very fact, namely, that the common notion of matter is unsatisfactory, summon God *ex machina*, and withdraw all force for acting from things, like a certain Mosaic Philosophy (as Fludd once called it); but I cannot agree. I certainly grant their observation that there is no genuine influx of one created substance into another, if one considers the matter with metaphysical rigor, and I also admit freely that everything always proceeds from God through a continual creation. However, I believe that there is no natural truth in things whose explanation [*ratio*] ought to be sought directly from divine action or will, but that God has always endowed things themselves with something from which all of their predicates are to be explained. Certainly, it is agreed that God created not only bodies, but also souls, to which primitive entelechies correspond. But these things will be proven elsewhere, after their own grounds have been set out in greater depth.

However, even though I admit an active and, so to speak, vital principle superior to material notions everywhere in bodies, I do not agree with *Henry*

---

173. The following was in the original ms, and deleted before publication:

I also perceived the nature of motion. Furthermore, I also grasped that space is not something absolute or real, and that it neither undergoes change, nor can we conceive absolute motion, but that the entire nature of motion is relative, so that from the phenomena one cannot determine with mathematical rigor what is at rest, or the amount of motion with which some body is moved. This holds even for circular motion, though it appeared otherwise to Isaac Newton, that distinguished gentleman, who is, perhaps, the greatest jewel that learned England ever had. Although he said many superb things about motion, he thought that, with the help of circular motion, he could discern which subject contains motion from centrifugal force, something with which I could not agree. But even if there may be no mathematical way of determining the true hypothesis, nevertheless, we can, with good reason, attribute true motion to that subject, which would result in the simplest hypothesis most suitable for explaining the phenomena. For the rest, it is enough for practical purposes for us to investigate not the subject of motion as much as the relative changes of things with respect to one another, since there is no fixed point in the universe.

More and other gentlemen distinguished in piety and ability, who use an Archaeus (unintelligible to me) or hylarchic principle even for dealing with the phenomena, as if not everything in nature can be explained mechanically, and as if those who try to explain everything mechanically are thought to eliminate incorporeal things, not without the suspicion of impiety, or as if it were necessary, with Aristotle, to attach intelligences to the rotating spheres, or as if one ought to say that the elements rise or fall by virtue of form, a concise, but useless doctrine. With these views, I say, I do not agree, and such a philosophy pleases me no more than that theology of certain men, who believed that Jupiter thundered and caused the snow to such an extent that they even defamed those who investigated more particular causes with the charge of atheism. In my opinion, the middle way in which one satisfies both piety and knowledge is the best. That is, we acknowledge that all corporeal phenomena can be derived from efficient and mechanical causes, but we understand that these very mechanical laws as a whole are derived from higher reasons. And so we use this higher efficient cause only in establishing general and distant principles. But once these principles have been established, then afterwards, whenever we deal with the immediate and specific efficient causes of natural things, we should take no account of souls or entelechies, no more than we should drag in useless faculties or inexplicable sympathies. For that first and most general efficient cause should not enter into the treatment of particulars, except insofar as we contemplate the ends which divine wisdom had in thus ordering things, so that we might lose no opportunity for singing his praises and for singing most beautiful hymns.

Indeed, one can even bring final causes to bear from time to time with great profit in particular cases in physics (as I showed with the clearly remarkable example of an optical principle, which that most celebrated *Molyneux* greatly applauded in his Dioptrics),[174] not only the better to admire the most beautiful works of the Supreme Author, but also in order that we might sometimes discover things by that method [*via*] that are either less evident or follow only hypothetically on the method of efficient causes. Perhaps philosophers have not yet sufficiently seen just how useful this is. In general, we must hold that everything in the world can be explained in two ways: through the *kingdom of power*, that is, through *efficient causes,* and through the *kingdom of wisdom*, that is, through *final causes*, through God, governing bodies for his glory, like an architect, governing them as machines that follow the *laws of size* or *mathematics*, governing them, indeed, for the use of souls, and through God governing for his glory souls capable of wisdom, governing them as his fellow citizens, members with him of a certain society, governing them like a prince, indeed like a father, through *laws of goodness* or *moral laws*. These two kingdoms everywhere interpenetrate each other without confusing or disturb-

---

174. See William Molyneux, *Dioptrica nova* (London, 1692), pp. 192ff, where Molyneux discusses at length "Leibnutz's [*sic*] universal principle in opticks, &c," which Molyneux drew from Leibniz's "*Unicum Opticae, Catopticae, et Diopticae Principium . . .*" published in the *Acta Eruditorum* in June 1682.

ing their laws, so that the greatest obtains in the kingdom of power at the same time as the best in the kingdom of wisdom. But we had promised to establish here the general rules of effective forces, rules which we can then use in explaining particular efficient causes.

Next, I arrived at the true way of measuring forces, indeed, I arrived at the very same measure but in widely different ways, the one *a priori*, from a very simple consideration of space, time, and action (which I shall explain elsewhere), the other, *a posteriori*, namely, through measuring the force by the effect it produces in consuming itself.[175] By *effect* here I understand not any arbitrary effect, but one for which the force has to be expended, or one in which the force has to be consumed, an effect which one can therefore call *violent*. This kind of effect is unlike the effect a heavy body traversing a perfectly horizontal plane produces, since the same force always remains when such an effect is produced. Although we might have obtained this way of estimating forces of ours even from such an *effect*, properly called a *harmless effect*, so to speak, we shall set such effects aside for now. Moreover, I have chosen from among violent effects the one which is most conducive to homogeneous division, that is, the one most capable of being divided into similar and equal parts, as in the ascent of a body endowed with heaviness. For the elevation of a heavy body by two or three feet is precisely double or triple the elevation of the same body by one foot, and the elevation of a heavy body, double in size, by one foot is exactly double the elevation of a single heavy body to a height of one foot. As a result, the elevation of a heavy body, double in size, by three feet is precisely six times the elevation of a single body by one foot. This assumes, of course, that the heavy bodies are unchanged in weight when more or less distant from the horizon, an assumption we can make for the sake of exposition, at least, even if things are, perhaps, different in reality, though the error here is insensible. On the other hand, homogeneity is not as easily found in an elastic body. Then, when I wanted to compare different bodies, or bodies endowed with different speeds, I easily saw that if body A were single and body B double in size, and both had the same speed, then the one would have a single unit of force, and the other two units, since, in the other body, there is precisely twice of whatever there is in the one, for B is a body twice the size of A, moving with equal speed, and nothing more.[176] But if A and C are equal in size, and A has a single unit of speed, and C has two units, I saw that C does not have precisely twice of whatever there is in A, since it is speed and not the size of the body that is doubled, of course. And I saw that those who believed that force itself is doubled by the mere doubling of a modality made a mistake at this point.[177] In just this way I observed and warned long ago that the true art of measuring, hitherto untreated, despite the fact that numerous books on the Universal Elements of

---

175. See the "Preliminary Specimen to the Dynamics," pp. 105–11 above. The first three demonstrations there are *a posteriori*, the last is the *a priori* demonstration to which Leibniz is referring.

176. Cf. Fig. 5.

177. The reference here is to the Cartesians, for whom force is equated with quantity of motion, size times speed, so when speed, or modality, is doubled, so is force.

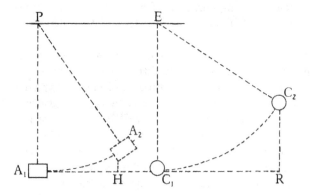

Figure 5

Mathematics have been written, consists in arriving, at last, at something homogeneous, that is, at an exact and complete repetition not only of modes, but also of realities. One can give no better illustration or example of this method than what this very argument shows.

Therefore, in order to obtain a measure of force, I considered whether those two bodies A and C, equal in size but different in speed, could produce any effects equal in power to their causes, and homogeneous with each other. For things which cannot easily be compared directly can at least be compared accurately through their effects. Moreover, I assumed that an effect ought to be equal to its cause, if that effect is produced by expending or consuming the entire power [*virtus*] of that cause; in this circumstance, it does not matter how much time it takes to produce the effect. Therefore, let us assume that bodies A and C are heavy, and that their force is converted into ascent, which would come about if, at the very moment when they had the speeds they were said to have, a single unit of speed in A, and double that in C, they were understood to be at the ends of the vertical pendula PA_1 and EC_1.[178] Now, it is well known from the demonstrations of Galileo and others that if body A, with a speed of one unit, ascends at its highest point above the horizon HR to a height A_2H of one foot, then body C, with a speed of two units, could ascend (at its highest) to a height C_2R of four feet. From this it already follows that a heavy body with two units of speed has four times as much power as a heavy body with one unit of speed, since by expending its entire power, it can bring about exactly four times the effect. For raising a pound (that is, raising the body itself) four feet raises one pound one foot precisely four times. In the same way one can conclude, in general, that the forces in equal bodies are proportional to the squares of their speeds, and thus that in general the forces in bodies are jointly proportional to the size of the bodies and the squares of the speeds.

---

178. Cf. Fig. 5.

I have confirmed this by reducing to absurdity (indeed, to perpetual motion) the contrary view commonly accepted, especially among the Cartesians, according to which forces are believed to be jointly proportional to the size of a body and its speed. I have also used this method repeatedly to define *a posteriori* two *states of unequal power* [*virtus*] and, at the same time, to find a sure mark for distinguishing greater power from less. For, when perpetual mechanical motion or an effect that is greater than its cause arises from substituting one thing for another, these states are hardly of equal power. Rather, that which was substituted for the other was more powerful since it caused something greater to appear. Moreover, I take it to be certain that nature never substitutes things unequal in their forces for one another, but that the entire effect is always equal to the full cause. And in turn, we can safely substitute things equal in force for one another in our calculations with complete freedom, just as if we had made that substitution in actuality, with no fear of perpetual mechanical motion arising as a consequence. Thus, if it were true, as people are commonly persuaded, that a heavy body A, two units in size (as we might now assume) and endowed with one unit of speed, and a heavy body C, one unit in size and endowed with two units of speed, are equal in power, then we should safely be able to substitute the one for the other. But this is not the case. For let us suppose that A, two units in size, has acquired its one unit of speed by descending along the path A_2A_1, from a height A_2H of one foot, and at the moment it was at A_1, that is, on the horizontal, let us substitute for it the weight C, one unit in size, two units in speed, equal in power, as they would have it, which ascends to C_2* or to a height of four feet. And so, merely through the fall of a two-pound weight A from a height A_2H of one foot, and by substituting for this something equal in power, we would have brought about the ascent of a one-pound body by four feet, which is double the power of the prior state. Thus we would have gained as much force as we started with, that is, we would have brought about perpetual mechanical motion, which is absurd. It does not matter whether we can actually bring this substitution about through the laws of motion, for we are safely able to substitute things equal in power for one another, even mentally. However, I have thought up various ways by which one can, as conveniently as you like, actually bring it about that the total force of a body A is transferred to body C, which was previously at rest but which now (having reduced A to rest) is alone in motion.[179] Hence, it could happen that a one-pound weight with two units of speed takes the place of a two-pound weight with one unit of speed, if they were equal in power; but from this we showed that an absurdity arises. These questions are not empty, nor is this a mere argument over words; on the contrary, these things are of the greatest utility for comparing machines and motions. For if anyone were to have, from water or animals or some other cause, force enough to keep a heavy body of one hundred pounds in constant motion, by which it could complete a horizon-

---

179. See the third demonstration in the "Preliminary Specimen to the Dynamics," pp. 109–10 above.

tal circle thirty feet in diameter in a quarter of a minute of time, and if another person, in its place, were to offer force enough to double the weight to complete only half the circle in the same time, with less expenditure of force, and reckoned this advantageous to you, he would have deceived you and shrewdly tricked you out of half of your force. But now, having eliminated the errors, let us set forth the true and, indeed, wonderful laws of nature a bit more distinctly in the second part of this sketch.

Part II

THE FACT that the nature of body, indeed of substance in general, is not known sufficiently well (as I have already touched upon) has brought it about that the distinguished philosophers of our times, locating the notion of body in extension alone, are thus forced to appeal to God for explaining the union between soul and body, and indeed for explaining the interaction of bodies with one another. For we must admit that it is impossible that bare extension, containing geometrical notions alone, is capable of action and passion. And so, this one position seemed to be the only one left for them, that when a person thinks and tries to move his arm, God moves the arm for him as if by primeval agreement, and, conversely, that when there is motion in the blood and [animal] spirits, God excites a perception in the soul. But these very consequences, so foreign to correct reasoning in philosophy, ought to have warned these writers that they were depending on a false principle, and that the notion of body from which such consequences were derived had been improperly explicated. Therefore, we have shown that there is a force of acting in every substance, and that there is also a force of being acted upon [*patiendi*] in every created substance, and that the notion of extension is incomplete in itself, but is relative to something which is extended, something whose diffusion or continuous repetition extension indicates; further, we have shown that the notion of extension presupposes the substance of body, which involves the power of acting and resisting, and exists everywhere as corporeal mass [*massa*], and that the diffusion of this substance is contained in extension. From this we shall, at some later time, shed new light on the explanation of the union of the soul and the body. But now we must show how, from this, follows wonderful and most useful practical theorems in dynamics, that is, the science which deals chiefly with the laws [*regulae*] governing corporeal forces.

We must realize, above all, that force is something absolutely real in substances, even in created substances, while space, time, and motion are, to a certain extent, beings of reason, and are true or real, not *per se*, but only to the extent that they involve either the divine attributes (immensity, eternity, the ability to carry out works), or the force in created substances. From this it immediately follows that there is no empty place and no empty moment in time. Moreover, it follows that motion taken apart from force, that is, motion insofar as it is taken to contain only geometrical notions (size, shape, and their change), is really nothing but the change of situation, and furthermore, that *as far as the phenomena are concerned, motion is a pure relation*, something

Descartes also recognized when he defined motion as the translation from the neighborhood of one body into the neighborhood of another. But in drawing consequences from this, he forgot his definition and set up the laws of motion as if motion were something real and absolute. Therefore, we must hold that however many bodies might be in motion, one cannot infer from the phenomena which of them really has absolute and determinate motion or rest. Rather, one can attribute rest to any one of them one may choose, and yet the same phenomena will result. From this follows something that Descartes did not notice, that *the equivalence of hypotheses is not changed even by the collision of bodies with one another*, and thus, that the laws of motion must be fixed in such a way that the relative nature of motion is preserved, so that one cannot tell, on the basis of the phenomena resulting from a collision, where there had been rest or determinate motion in an absolute sense before the collision. As a result, Descartes's law, the law in accordance with which he holds that a body at rest cannot in any way be moved from its place by another smaller body, is hardly adequate, nor are other things of this sort, which are as far from the truth as one can go.[180] It also follows from the relative nature of motion that *the mutual action or impact of bodies on one another is the same, provided that they approach one another with the same speed.* That is, if we keep the appearances in the given phenomena constant, then whatever the true hypothesis might finally be, to whichever body we might in the end truly ascribe motion or rest, the same outcome would be found in the phenomena in question, that is, the same outcome would be found in the resulting phenomena, even as regards the action of bodies on one another. And indeed, this is just what we experience, for we would feel the same pain whether we hit our hand against a stone at rest, suspended, if you like, from a string, or whether the stone hit our resting hand with the same speed. However, we speak as the situation requires, in accordance with the more appropriate and simpler explanation of the phenomena. It is in just this sense that we use the motion of the *primum mobile* in spherical astronomy, while in the theoretical study of the planets we ought to use the Copernican hypothesis. As an immediate consequence of this view, those disputes conducted with such enthusiasm, disputes in which even the theologians were involved, completely disappear.[181] For even though force is something real and absolute, motion belongs among phenomena and relations, and we must seek truth not so much in the phenomena as in their causes.

It also follows from our notions about bodies and forces that *what happens in a substance can be understood to happen of that substance's own accord, and in an orderly way.* Connected to this is *the fact that no change happens through a leap.* Assuming this, it also follows that

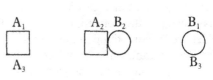

Figure 6

---

180. The reference is to Descartes's fourth rule of impact, *Principles of Philosophy* II 49.
181. See "On Copernicanism and the Relativity of Motion," pp. 90–94 above.

atoms cannot exist. In order to grasp the force of this consequence, let us assume that bodies A and B collide as in figure 6, so that A_1 arrives at A_2 and
likewise B_1 arrives at B_2, and so colliding at A_2B_2, they are reflected from A_2
to A_3 and from B_2 to B_3. However, if we were to imagine that there are atoms,
that is, bodies of maximal hardness and therefore inflexible, it would follow
that there would be a change through a leap, that is, an instantaneous change.
For at the very moment of collision the direction of the motion reverses itself,
unless we assume that the bodies come to rest immediately after the collision,
that is, lose their force; beyond the fact that it would be absurd in other ways,
this contains, again, a change through a leap, an instantaneous change from
motion to rest, without passing through the intermediate steps. And so, we
must acknowledge that if bodies A and B collide as in figure 7, and come from
A_1 and B_1 to the place A_2B_2, where they collide, they will, little by little,
be compressed there, just like two
inflated balls, and approach one
another more and more, continually increasing the internal pressure. By that very circumstance
the motion itself is weakened, the
force of the conatus having been
transformed into their elasticity,
until they are altogether at rest. Then, finally, restoring themselves through
their elasticity, they rebound from one another; having started a retrograde
motion from rest, a motion that continually increases, in the end they move
apart, having regained the same speed with which they originally approached
one another, but directed oppositely, and they return to A_3 and B_3, which
coincide with the places A_1 and B_1, if the bodies are assumed to be of the
same size and the same velocity. From this it is already obvious how no
change happens through a leap; rather, the forward motion diminishes little
by little, and after the body is finally reduced to rest, the backward motion at
last arises. In just the same way one shape does not arise from another (for
example, an oval from a circle), unless it passes through innumerable intermediate shapes, nor does anything pass from one place to another, or from
one time to another except by passing through all of the intermediate places
and times. And so, rest will not arise from motion, much less will motion in
an opposite direction arise, unless a body passes through all intermediate degrees of motion. Since this is of such importance in nature, I am amazed that
it has been so little noticed. From this follows something Descartes opposed in
his letters,[182] something many gentlemen of great reputation are even now
unwilling to admit, that *all rebound arises from elasticity*, which explains many
elegant experiments that show that *a body is deformed before it is impelled*, as
Mariotte nicely demonstrated. And finally, a most wonderful conclusion follows from this, that no body is so small that it is without elasticity, and

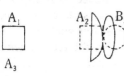

Figure 7

---

182. In the manuscript the letters against Hobbes are indicated. See AT III 289–90. Elasticity is
discussed in Mariotte's *Traité de la percussion ou choc des corps* (Paris, 1673).

furthermore, each body is permeated by a fluid even subtler than it is. And thus, *there are no elements of bodies*, nor is there maximally fluid matter, nor are there little solid globes (unintelligible to me) of the second element, both determinate in shape and hard. Rather, the analysis proceeds to infinity.

It is also in agreement with that *law of continuity*, or the law excluding a leap in changing, that the case of rest can be considered as a special case of motion, indeed, the case of vanishing or minimal motion, and that the case of equality can be considered as a case of vanishing inequality. From this it follows that the laws of motion ought to be formulated in such a way that there is no need for special laws for equal bodies and bodies at rest. Rather, these laws arise *per se* from the laws of [un]equal bodies and motions, or, if we want to formulate special laws for rest and equality, we must be careful not to formulate laws that are inconsistent with the hypothesis that takes rest as the limit of motion or equality as the least inequality, otherwise we will violate the harmony of things, and our laws will not be consistent with one another. I first published this new tool for examining our laws and those of others in the *Nouvelles de la république des lettres*[183] in July 1687, article 8, and called it a general principle of order that arises from the notions of infinity and continuity, something that suggests the axiom that, as the givens are ordered, so is that which is sought. I expressed the matter in a general way as follows: *if one case continually approaches another case among the givens, and finally vanishes into it, then it is necessary that the outcomes of the cases continually approach one another in that which is sought and finally merge with one another.* This is just as it is in geometry, where the case of the ellipse continually approaches that of the parabola; fixing one focus, if we assume the other to be moved farther and farther away, finally, in the case where the other focus is infinitely distant, the ellipse disappears into a parabola. From this it follows necessarily that all of the laws of the ellipse hold for the parabola, taken as an ellipse whose other focus is infinitely distant. And so, we can conceive of parallel rays intersecting a parabola as if they came from the other focus [at infinity] or proceed toward it. Therefore, the case in which body A collides with the moving body B can be continuously varied so that, holding the motion of A fixed, the motion of B is assumed to be smaller and smaller, until finally it is assumed to vanish into rest, and then increase once again in the opposite direction. I say that, in the same way, the outcome of the collision, or that which results either in A or in B, when both are in motion, continuously approaches the outcome of the collision that results when B is at rest, until finally the one case disappears into the other. Thus the case of rest, both in the givens and in the outcomes (that is, in that which is sought), is the limit of the cases of motion in a straight line, or, the common limit of continuous rectilinear motion, and thus, it is a special instance of it. When I examine the Cartesian laws of motion with respect to this touchstone, which I transposed from geometry into physics, it happens, much to my surprise, that a certain

---

183. The piece in question is "A Letter of Mr. Leibniz on a General Principle Useful in Explaining the Laws of Nature," G III 51–55, translated in L 351–53.

gap or leap, entirely abhorrent to the nature of things, displays itself. For, representing quantities by lines,[184] and taking the motion of B before the collision as the given case, represented in the abscissa, and its motion after the collision as the outcome sought, represented in the ordinate, and extending a line from one end of the ordinate to the other in accordance with Descartes's laws, this line was not a single continuous line, but was something wondrously gaping and leaping in an absurd and incomprehensible way. And since I noted on that occasion that even the laws proposed by the Rev. Father Malebranche do not entirely bear up under this examination, the distinguished gentleman, having considered the matter a second time, confessed in all candor that this is what gave him the occasion for altering the laws, which he presented to the public in a little book. However, one must admit that because he has not yet sufficiently attended to the use of this new tool, there remain things which even now do not sufficiently square up in every respect.[185]

Something else wonderfully follows from what I have said, *that every passion of a body is of its own accord, that is, arises from an internal force, even if it is on the occasion of something external.* I understand here the body's own passion, the passion that arises from collision, that is, the passion that remains the same, whichever hypothesis we finally adopt, that is, to whatever things we ascribe

---

184. The following is the sort of diagram Leibniz has in mind here:

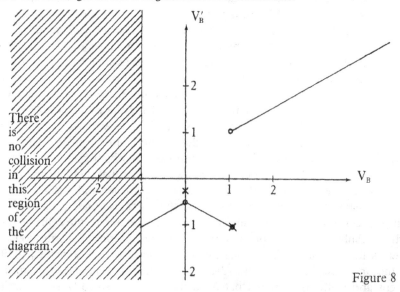

Figure 8

This diagram is made under the assumption that A and B are equal in size and that A is moving from right to left with one unit of speed; v_B is B's velocity before the collision and v_B' is B's velocity afterward, where a positive value represents motion from left to right. This diagram was constructed using Descartes's first, third, sixth, and seventh rules of impact; see Descartes, *Principles of Philosophy* II 46, 48, 51, 52.

185. For Malebranche's attempts to formulate laws of motions and Leibniz's critiques, see Paul Mouy, *Les lois du choc des corps d'apres Malebranche* (Paris, 1927).

absolute rest or motion in the end. For, since the impact is the same, wherever the true motion in the end belongs, it follows that the effect of the impact is equally distributed between the two, and thus that *in impact, both bodies are equally acted upon, and equally act,* and that half the effect arises from the action of the one, and half from the action of the other. And since half the effect or half of the passion is in one, and half in the other, it is also sufficient for us to derive the passion in the one from its own action, and we do not need any influx of the one into the other, even if the action of the one provides the occasion for the other to produce a change in itself. For example, in Figure 7, when A and B collide, the resistance of the bodies joined with their elasticity results in their being compressed on account of the impact, and there is equal compression in both and according to any hypothesis. Experience also shows this. If one imagines that two inflated balls collide, then whether both are in motion, or one of the two is at rest, or even if the body at rest is suspended from a string so that it can rebound as easily as possible, as long as the speed with which they approach one another, that is, the relative speed, is always the same, the compression or the intensity of the elasticity will also be the same and equal in both. Furthermore, when balls A and B restore themselves through the force of their considerable elasticity, that is, through the force of the compression they contain, they will repel one another and burst forth as if from a bow, and each will repel itself from the other through forces equal to one another; thus each body will rebound, not through the force of the other, but through its own. What we have said about inflated balls must also be understood to apply to every body insofar as it is acted upon in impact, namely, that the repercussion and bursting apart arises from the elasticity it contains, that is, from the motion of the fluid aetherial matter permeating it, and thus it arises from an internal force or a force existing within itself. I understand here the *proper motion* of bodies (as I have called it) as opposed to the *common motion* that can be ascribed to the center of gravity. As a result, we should conceive of their proper motion (conceive of it in a hypothetical way, I say) as if the bodies are being carried on a boat which has the motion of their common center of gravity, and on the boat, we should imagine, they move in such a way that from the composite motion of the boat, which they have in common (that is, the motion of the center of gravity), and from their own proper motion, the phenomena can be saved. From what we have said we can also understand that *the action of bodies is never without reaction, and both are equal to one another, and directed in opposite directions.*

Also, since only force and the nisus arising from it exist at any moment (for motion never really exists, as we discussed above), and since every nisus tends in a straight line, it follows that *all motion is either rectilinear or composed of rectilinear motions.* From this it not only follows that what moves in a curved path always tries [*conari*] to proceed in a straight line tangent to it, but also—something utterly unexpected—that the *true notion of solidity* derives from this. (Nothing is really solid or fluid, absolutely speaking, and everything has a certain degree of solidity or fluidity; which term we apply to a thing derives from the predominant appearance it presents to our senses.) For if we assume something we call solid is rotating around its center, its parts will try [*conabun-*

tur] to fly off on the tangent; indeed, they will actually begin to fly off. But since this mutual separation disturbs the motion of the surrounding bodies, they are repelled back, that is, thrust back together again, as if the center contained a magnetic force for attracting them, or as if the parts themselves contained a centripetal force. Thus, the rotation arises from the composition of the rectilinear nisus for receding on the tangent and the centripetal conatus among the parts. Thus, all curvilinear motion arises from rectilinear nisuses composed with one another, and at the same time, it is understood that all solidity is caused by surrounding bodies pushing a body together; if matters were otherwise, then it could not happen that all curvilinear motion is composed of pure rectilinear motions. From this we also get a new argument against atoms that is no less unexpected than the one before. Moreover, nothing can be imagined farther from things than the claim that solidity derives from rest, for *there is never any true rest in bodies,* nor can anything come from rest but rest.[186] Let us grant that A and B are at rest with respect to one another, if not truly at rest, then at least relatively (although this couldn't ever exactly happen, for *no body preserves exactly the same distance from another no matter how short the time elapsed*) and let us grant that whatever is at rest at one time will always be at rest, unless put into motion by a new cause. But it does not follow on that account that, since B resists being impelled, it also resists being separated from the other body, so that if one were to overcome the resistance of B, that is, if one were to put B into motion, A would immediately follow. But if there were *attraction,* something not found in nature, attraction explained either from primitive solidity, or through rest or something similar, then this would certainly have followed. And so, we should not explain solidity except through the surrounding bodies pushing a body together. For [mutual] pressure alone is insufficient to explain the matter, as if only A hindered the departure of B. But we must understand that the bodies do indeed separate from one another. However, one is driven back to the other by the surrounding bodies, and thus from the combination of these two motions the conjunction is preserved. And so, those who imagine certain planks or insensible plates in bodies (on the model of two polished marble plates which are carefully placed on one another),[187] planks or plates whose separation is made difficult because of the resistance of the surrounding bodies, and from this explain the solidity of hard, sensible bodies, even if they might often be right, these people don't give the ultimate explanation of solidity since they assume some solidity in the plates. From this we can also understand why, on this matter, I cannot agree with certain philosophical opinions of certain important mathematicians, who, beyond the fact that they admit empty space and don't seem to shrink from attraction, also take motion to be an absolute thing, and strive to prove this from rotation and the centrifugal force that arises from it.[188] But since rotation also arises only from a

---

186. It is Descartes's account of solidity that Leibniz has in mind here. See Descartes's *Principles of Philosophy* II 55.

187. Such an account is suggested by Galileo in his *Two New Sciences*, pp. 17ff.

188. In a deleted passage, Newton is identified as the sole target.

combination of rectilinear motions, it follows that if the equivalence of hypotheses is preserved in rectilinear motions, however they might be placed in things, then it will also be preserved in curvilinear motions.

From what was said one can also understand that *motion common to many bodies does not change their actions with respect to one another*, since the speed with which they approach one another, and therefore the force of impact by which they act on one another, is not altered. And from this follows those excellent experiments Gassendi related in his letters on motion impressed by a mover in motion in order to satisfy those who thought they could infer from the motion of projectiles that the earth is at rest.[189] However, it is certain that if some people were carried on a large boat (enclosed, if you please, or, at least, set up in such a way that things outside of the boat could not be seen by the passengers), then, however great the speed of the boat might be, as long as it moved peacefully and evenly, they would have no criterion for discerning (on the basis of that which happens on the boat, of course) whether the boat was at rest or in motion, even if they played vigorously with a ball or produce other motions. And this must be noted for the sake of those who, incorrectly understanding the opinion of the Copernicans, believe that according to them, things projected from the earth into the air are carried around by the air rotating with the earth, and because of that, follow the motion of the ground and fall back to earth as if they were at rest. This is correctly judged to be insufficient. However, the most learned gentlemen who use the Copernican hypothesis conceive that whatever is on the surface of the earth moves with the earth, and thus, when something is shot out of a bow or a catapult* it carries the impetus impressed by the rotation of the earth together with the impetus impressed by projecting it. As a result, since the motion of projectiles is twofold, one common with the earth, the other pertaining to the projection, it is not surprising that the common motion changes nothing. However, we must not hide the fact that if projectiles can be thrown far enough, or if we imagine a boat large enough, moving with sufficient speed, so that before the descent of the heavy body, the earth or the boat would describe an arc notably different from the rectilinear, then a criterion for discriminating motion and rest could be found, since then, indeed, the (circular) motion of the earth or ship would not remain in common with the (rectilinear) motion impressed on the missile by the rotation of the boat or the earth. And in addition, the nisus heavy bodies have toward the center [of the earth] adds an external action that can produce a distinction within the phenomena no less than if, enclosed in the ship, one had a compass that pointed to the pole, something that, at very least, would indicate when the boat turned. But, whenever we are dealing with the equivalence of hypotheses, we must take into account everything relevant to the phenomena. From these things we also understand that we can safely apply the composition of motions, or the resolution of one motion into two or however many more motions, even though a certain most ingenious

---

189. See P. Gassendi, "Three Letters Concerning the Motion Imparted by a Moving Body," translated in Bush, ed., *Selected Works of Gassendi*, pp. 119–50.

gentleman expressed doubts about this in the presence of Wallis, and not absurdly. For the matter warrants a proof, in any case, and it cannot be assumed as if it were self-evident, as many have done.

A New System of the Nature and Communication of Substances, and of the Union of the Soul and Body (1695)[190]

Leibniz published the "New System of Nature" anonymously in 1695, in the Journal des Savants. It was the first public statement of his philosophy, a particularly interesting statement because of the autobiographical or historical style adopted by Leibniz. The publication of the "New System of Nature" stimulated much discussion, with Foucher, de Beauval, Bayle, and others publishing criticisms of it, and Leibniz answering them; please refer to the "Note on Foucher's Objection" and the "Postscript of a Letter to Basnage de Beauval." Leibniz's manuscript copy contains some material thought to be later additions that does not appear in the published version. These are given in the double-bracketed passages, when possible, and otherwise in the notes.

A FEW YEARS have already passed since I conceived this system and communicated with some learned men about it, especially with one of the greatest theologians and philosophers of our time,[191] who had learned about some of my opinions through a person of the highest nobility, and had found them extremely paradoxical. But having received my explanations, he changed his attitude in the most generous and edifying way possible; and, having approved some of my propositions, he withdrew his censure regarding the others, with which he still disagreed. Since that time I have continued my meditations, as circumstances allow, so as to give the public only well-examined opinions; I have also tried to satisfy objections raised against my essays on dynamics, which are connected with this system.[192] Finally, since some important persons have desired to see my opinions further clarified, I have risked publishing these meditations, even though they are not at all popular, nor can they be appreciated by all sorts of minds. I have decided upon this mainly to profit from the judgments of persons enlightened in these matters, since it would be too troublesome to seek out and call individually upon all those who would be disposed to give me instruction—which I shall always be glad to receive, provided that it contains the love of truth, rather than a passion for preconceived opinions.

Although I am someone who has done much work on mathematics, I have continued to meditate on philosophy since my youth, for it always seemed to

---

190. G IV 477–87. French.

191. Leibniz indicates in his copy that he is referring to Arnauld. See the selections from the Letters to Arnauld, above.

192. See the "Preliminary Specimen to the *Dynamics*" and the "Specimen of Dynamics."

me that one can establish something solid there through clear demonstrations. I had penetrated far into the territory of the Scholastics, when mathematics and the modern authors made me withdraw from it, while I was still young. I was charmed by their beautiful ways of explaining nature mechanically, and I rightly despised the method of those who use only forms or faculties, from which one can learn nothing. But since then, having attempted to examine the very principles of mechanics in order to explain the laws of nature we learn from experience, I perceived that considering *extended mass* alone was not sufficient, and that it was necessary, in addition, to make use of the notion of *force*, which is very intelligible, despite the fact that it belongs in the domain of metaphysics. It also seemed to me that although the opinion of those who transform or degrade animals into pure machines may be possible, it is improbable, and even contrary to the order of things.

In the beginning, when I had freed myself from the yoke of Aristotle, I accepted the void and atoms, for they best satisfy the imagination. But on recovering from that, after much reflection, I perceived that it is impossible to find *the principles of a true unity* in matter alone, or in what is only passive, since everything in it is only a collection or aggregation of parts to infinity. Now, a multitude can derive its reality only from *true unities*, which have some other origin and are considerably different from [[mathematical]] points [[which are only the extremities and modifications of extension,]] which all agree cannot make up the *continuum*. Therefore, in order to find these *real entities* I was forced to have recourse to a formal atom, since a material thing cannot be both material and, at the same time, perfectly indivisible, that is, endowed with a true unity.[193] Hence, it was necessary to restore, and, as it were, to rehabilitate the *substantial forms* which are in such disrepute today, but in a way that would render them intelligible, and separate the use one should make of them from the abuse that has been made of them. I found then that their nature consists in force, and that from this there follows something analogous to sensation and appetite, so that we must conceive of them on the model of the notion we have of *souls*. But just as soul must not be used to explain the particular details of the economy of the animal's body, I judged that we must not use these forms to explain the particular problems of nature, even though they are necessary to establish the true general principles. Aristotle calls them *first entelechies*; I call them, perhaps more intelligibly, *primitive forces*, which contain not only act or the completion of possibility, but also an original activity.

I saw that these forms and souls must be indivisible, as our mind is; I remembered that this was Saint Thomas's view on the souls of animals.[194] But

---

193. A later version read as follows: "Therefore, in order to find these *real unities*, I was forced to have recourse to a *real and animated point*, so to speak, or to an atom of substance which must include something of form or activity to make a complete being."

194. Leibniz seems to have in mind the *Summa Theologiae* I, q. 76, art. 8, in which St. Thomas states that the souls of animals are "not able to be divided accidentally, that is, by a quantitative division." But it would not be accurate to attribute the immortality of animal souls to St. Thomas. See, e.g. *Summa Contra Gentiles* II, chap. 82: That the souls of brute animals are not immortal.

this truth revived the great difficulties about the origin and duration of souls and forms. For, since every [[*simple*]] *substance* which has a true unity can begin and end only by miracle, it follows that they can begin only by creation and end only by annihilation. Thus I was forced to recognize that, except for the souls that God wishes to create expressly, the forms constitutive of substances must have been created together with the world, and must always subsist. Moreover, certain Scholastics, like Albertus Magnus and John Bacon,[195] glimpsed a part of the truth about the origin of these forms. This should not appear extraordinary, since we ascribe to forms only duration, which the Gassendists grant their atoms.

I judged, however, that we must not indiscriminately confuse *minds* or rational souls [[with other forms or souls]], for they are of a higher order, and have incomparably greater perfection than the forms thrust into matter [[(which, in my view, are found everywhere)]], minds being like little gods in comparison with them, made in the image of God, and having in them some ray of the light of divinity. That is why God governs minds as a prince governs his subjects, and even as a father cares for his children, whereas he disposes of other substances as an engineer handles his machines. Thus minds have particular laws, which place them above the upheavals [*revolutions*] in matter, [[through the very order which God has put in them]]; and we can say that everything else is made only for them, and that these tumultuous motions themselves are adjusted for the happiness of the good and the punishment of the wicked.

However, returning to ordinary forms, or to material souls,[196] the duration that we must attribute to them, in place of the duration that had been attributed to atoms, might make us suspect that they pass from body to body—which would be *metempsychosis*—somewhat as some philosophers have believed in the transmission of motion and species. But this fancy is far removed from the nature of things. There is no such passage; this is where the *transformations* of Swammerdam, Malpighi, and Leeuwenhoek, the best observers of our time, have come to my aid, and have made it easier for me to admit that animals and all other organized substances have no beginning, although we think they do, and that their apparent generation is only a development, a kind of augmentation. I have also noticed that the author of the *Search after Truth*,[197] Régis, Hartsoeker and other able persons have held opinions not far removed from this.

But the greatest question still remained: what becomes of these souls or forms at the death of the animal or at the destruction of the individual organized substance? This question is most perplexing, since it hardly seems reasonable that souls should remain uselessly in a chaos of confused matter.

---

195. Albertus Magnus, Bishop of Ratisbon, and John Bacon of Baconthorpe were, respectively, thirteenth- and fourteenth-century Scholastics. Leibniz's statement is too vague to enable one to fix a reference to precise passages of which he might be thinking.

196. A later version reads: "brute souls."

197. Nicholas Malebranche. For Leibniz's criticisms of Malebranche, see the "Conversation of Philarète and Ariste," below.

This made me judge that there is only one reasonable view to take—namely, the conservation not only of the soul, but also of the animal itself and its organic machine, even though the destruction of its larger parts reduces it to a smallness which escapes our senses, just as it was before its birth. Moreover, no one can specify the true time of death, which for a long time may pass for a simple suspension of noticeable actions, and is basically never anything else in simple animals—witness the *resuscitations* of drowned flies buried under pulverized chalk, and several other similar examples which are sufficient to show that there would be many other resuscitations, and greater ones, if men were in a position to restore the machine. This may be similar to something the great Democritus discussed, complete atomist that he was, though Pliny made fun of him.[198] It is therefore natural that an animal, having always been alive and organized (as some persons of great insight are beginning to recognize), always remains so. And since there is no first birth or entirely new generation of an animal, it follows that there will not be any final extinction or complete death, in a strict metaphysical sense. Consequently, instead of the *transmigration* of souls, there is only a transformation of the same animal, according to whether its organs are differently enfolded and more or less developed.

However, rational souls follow much higher laws, and are exempt from anything that might make them lose the quality of being citizens of the society of minds; God has provided so well that no changes of matter can make them lose the moral qualities of their personhood. And we can say that everything tends not only toward the perfection of the universe in general, but also toward the perfection of these creatures in particular, creatures who are destined for such a degree of happiness that the universe finds itself benefited by virtue of the divine goodness that is communicated to each, to the extent that supreme wisdom can allow.

With respect to ordinary animal bodies and other corporeal substances, whose complete extinction has been accepted until now, and whose changes depend on mechanical rules rather than moral laws, I noted with pleasure that the ancient author of the book *De diaeta*, attributed to Hippocrates,[199] had glimpsed something of the truth when he stated explicitly that animals are not born and do not die, and that things we believe to begin and perish merely appear and disappear. This was also the opinion of Parmenides and Melissus, according to Aristotle.[200] For these ancients were much more solid than people believe.

I am the most readily disposed person to do justice to the moderns, yet I find that they have carried reform too far, among other things, by confusing

---

198. In book vii, chap. 55, of his *Natural History*, Pliny mocks Democritus' theory of resuscitation, referring to "the false opinion of resuscitation, promulgated by Democritus, who himself did not come back to life."

199. See *The Regimen*, 1.4: "So of all things nothing perishes and nothing comes into being that did not exist before. Things change merely by mingling and being separated."

200. . Parmenides of Elea and his follower, Melissus of Samos, were two Presocratic philosophers (ca. 450 B.C.) who denied the reality of all change.

natural things with artificial things, because they have lacked sufficiently grand ideas of the majesty of nature. They think that the difference between natural machines and ours is only the difference between great and small. Recently this led a very able man, the author of the *Conversations on the Plurality of Worlds*,[201] to assert that when we examine nature more closely we find it less admirable than previously thought and more like the workshop of a craftsman. I believe that this conception does not give us a sufficiently just or worthy idea of nature, and that my system alone allows us to understand the true and immense distance between the least productions and mechanisms of divine wisdom and the greatest masterpieces that derive from the craft of a limited mind; this difference is not simply a difference of degree, but a difference of kind. We must then know that the machines of nature have a truly infinite number of organs, and are so well supplied and so resistant to all accidents that it is not possible to destroy them. A natural machine still remains a machine in its least parts, and moreover, it always remains the same machine that it has been, being merely transformed through the different enfolding it undergoes, sometimes extended, sometimes compressed and concentrated, as it were, when it is thought to have perished.

In addition, by means of the soul or form there is a true unity corresponding to what is called the *self* [*moy*] in us. Such a unity could not occur in the machines made by a craftsman or in a simple mass of matter, however organized it may be; such a mass can only be considered as an army or a herd, or a pond full of fish, or like a watch composed of springs and wheels. Yet if there were no true *substantial unities*, there would be nothing substantial or real in the collection. That was what forced Cordemoy to abandon Descartes and to embrace the Democritean doctrine of atoms in order to find a true unity. But *atoms of matter* are contrary to reason. Furthermore, they are still composed of parts, since the invincible attachment of one part to another (if we can reasonably conceive or assume this) would not eliminate diversity of those parts. There are only *atoms of substance*, that is, real unities absolutely destitute of parts, which are the source of actions, the first absolute principles of the composition of things, and, as it were, the final elements in the analysis of substantial things. We could call them *metaphysical points*: they have *something vital*, a kind of *perception*, and *mathematical points* are the *points of view* from which they express the universe. But when corporeal substances are contracted, all their organs together constitute only a *physical point* relative to us. Thus physical points are indivisible only in appearance; mathematical points are exact, but they are merely modalities. Only metaphysical points or points of substance (constituted by forms or souls) are exact and real, and without them there would be nothing real, since without true unities there would be no multitude.

After I established these things, I thought I was entering port; but when I began to meditate about the union of soul and body, I felt as if I were thrown again into the open sea. For I could not find any way of explaining how the

---

201. Bernard de Fontenelle.

body makes anything happen in the soul, or *vice versa*, or how one substance can communicate with another created substance. Descartes had given up the game at this point, as far as we can determine from his writings. But his disciples, seeing that the common opinion is inconceivable, judged that we sense the qualities of bodies because God causes thoughts to arise in the soul on the occasion of motions of matter, and that when our soul, in turn, wishes to move the body, it is God who moves the body for it. And since the communication of motions also seemed inconceivable to them, they believed that God imparts motion to a body on the occasion of the motion of another body. That is what they call *the system of occasional causes*, which has been made very fashionable by the beautiful reflections of the author of the *Search after Truth*.

I must admit that they have penetrated the difficulty by articulating what could not possibly be the case, but their explanation of what actually happens does not appear to eliminate the difficulty. It is quite true that, speaking with metaphysical rigor, there is no real influence of one created substance on another, and that all things, with all their reality, are continually produced by the power [*vertu*] of God. But in solving problems it is not sufficient to make use of the general cause and to invoke what is called a *Deus ex machina*. For when one does that without giving any other explanation derived from the order of secondary causes, it is, properly speaking, having recourse to miracle. In philosophy we must try to give reasons by showing how things are brought about by divine wisdom, but in conformity with the notion of the subject in question.

Therefore, since I was forced to agree that it is not possible for the soul or any other true substance to receive something from without, except by divine omnipotence, I was led, little by little, to a view that surprised me, but which seems inevitable, and which, in fact, has very great advantages and rather considerable beauty. That is, we must say that God originally created the soul (and any other real unity) in such a way that everything must arise for it from its own depths [*fonds*], through a perfect *spontaneity* relative to itself, and yet with a perfect *conformity* relative to external things. And thus, since our internal sensations (meaning those in the soul itself, and not those in the brain or in other subtle parts of the body) are merely phenomena which follow upon external beings, or better, they are true appearances and like well-ordered dreams, these internal perceptions in the soul itself must arise because of its own original constitution, that is, they must arise through the representative nature (capable of expressing external things as they relate to its organs) given to the soul from its creation, which constitutes its individual character. This is what makes every substance represent the whole universe exactly and in its own way, from a certain point of view, and makes the perceptions or expressions of external things occur in the soul at a given time, in virtue of its own laws, as if in a world apart, and as if there existed only God and itself (to make use of the manner of speaking used by a certain person of great spiritual elevation whose piety is renowned).[202] There will be a perfect

---

202. Leibniz probably has St. Theresa in mind here. See the note to sec. 32 of the "Discourse on Metaphysics" above.

agreement among all these substances, producing the same effect that would be noticed if they communicated through the transmission of species or qualities, as the common philosophers imagine they do. In addition, the organized mass, in which the point of view of the soul lies, being expressed more closely by the soul, is in turn ready to act by itself, following the laws of the corporeal machine, at the moment when the soul wills it to act, without disturbing the laws of the other—the spirits and blood then having exactly the motions that they need to respond to the passions and perceptions of the soul. It is this mutual relation, regulated in advance in each substance of the universe, which produces what we call their *communication*, and which alone brings about *the union of soul and body*. We can thus understand how the soul has its seat in the body by an immediate presence which could not be greater, since the soul is in the body as unity is in the resultant of unities, which is a multitude.

This hypothesis is entirely possible. For why should God be unable to give substance, from the beginning, a nature or an internal force that can produce in it, in an orderly way (as would happen in a *spiritual* or *formal* automaton, but *free* in the case where it has a share of reason), everything that will happen to it, that is, all the appearances or expressions it will have, without the help of any created being? This is especially so since the nature of substance necessarily requires and essentially involves progress or change, without which it would not have the force to act. And since this nature that pertains to the soul is representative of the universe in a very exact manner (though more or less distinctly), the series of representations produced by the soul will correspond naturally to the series of changes in the universe itself, just as the body, in turn, has also been accommodated to the soul for the situations in which the soul is thought to act externally. This is all the more reasonable insofar as bodies are made only for minds capable of entering into community with God and celebrating his glory. Thus, once we see the possibility of this *hypothesis of agreements*, we also see that it is the most reasonable hypothesis, and that it gives us a marvelous idea of the harmony of the universe and the perfection of the works of God.

It also has this great advantage, that instead of saying that we are free only in appearance and in a way sufficient for practical purposes, as several intelligent persons have believed,[203] we should rather say that we are determined only in appearance, and that, in rigorously metaphysical language, we have a perfect independence relative to the influence of every other creature. This also throws a marvelous light on the immortality of our soul and the always uniform conservation of our individual being, which is perfectly well regulated by its own nature and protected from all external accidents, appearances to the contrary notwithstanding. Never has any system made our eminence more evident. Since every mind is like a world apart, self-sufficient, independent of any other creature, containing infinity, and expressing the universe, it is as durable, subsistent, and absolute as the universe of creatures

---

203. Leibniz probably has Spinoza in mind here. See the appendix to *Ethics* I (Geb II 78).

itself. Thus we should judge that it must always behave in the way most proper to contribute to the perfection of the society of all minds, which is their moral union in the City of God. There is also a new proof for the existence of God in our system, one which has extraordinary clarity. For the perfect agreement of so many substances which have no communication among them can only come from the common source.

Besides all the advantages that recommend this hypothesis, we can say that it is something more than a hypothesis, since it hardly seems possible to explain things in any other intelligible way, and since several serious difficulties which, until now, have troubled minds, seem to disappear by themselves when we properly understand the system. Ordinary ways of speaking are also preserved. For we can say that the substance, whose disposition accounts for change intelligibly, in the sense that we may judge that the other substances have been accommodated to this one in this regard from the beginning, according to the order of God's decree, is the substance we must consequently conceive as *acting* upon the others. Furthermore, the action of one substance on another is neither the emission nor the transplanting of an entity, as commonly conceived, and can reasonably be taken only in the manner just stated. It is true that we readily conceive emissions and receptions of parts in matter, by which we can reasonably explain all the phenomena of physics mechanically. But since material mass is not a substance, it is clear that action with respect to substance itself can only be as I have just described.

These considerations, however metaphysical they may seem, have yet another marvelous use in physics, in order to establish the laws of motion, as our *Dynamics* will be able to show. For we can say that in the impact of bodies, each body suffers only through its own elasticity, caused by the motion already in it. And as for absolute motion, nothing can fix it with mathematical rigor, since everything terminates in relations. This makes for the perfect equivalence of hypotheses, as in astronomy, so that no matter how many bodies we take, we may arbitrarily assign rest or a particular degree of speed to any body we choose, without being refuted by the phenomena of rectilinear, circular, or composite motion. However, it is reasonable to attribute some true motions to bodies, in accordance with the assumption that accounts for the phenomena in the most intelligible way, this denomination being in conformity with the notion of action we have just established.[204]

Note on Foucher's Objection (1695)[205]

In the September 1695 edition of the Journal des Savants, *Simon Foucher published a letter containing a number of objections to the "New System." Leibniz replied to Foucher's objections in the April 1696 edition of the same*

---

204. See "On Copernicanism and the Relativity of Motion," pp. 90–94 above.
205. The following is only part of Foucher's objection together with Leibniz's answer. G IV 491–92. French.

*journal. The following is only one of Foucher's objections together with
Leibniz's reply to it. We have emphasized the words to which Leibniz is
replying. Foucher's objection: "I agree with you, that we are right to require **the
unities that make up the composition and reality of extension**. For
without them, as you so correctly remark, an extension that is always divisible is
only a chimerical composite whose bases [principes] do not exist, since without
unities there can really be no multitude. However, I am surprised that anyone
would be so complacent with regard to this question; **for the essential bases
of extension cannot really exist**. In fact, there can be no points without
parts in the universe, and two points joined together cannot form any extension.
It is impossible for there to be any length without width nor any surface without
depth. And it serves no purpose to bring up physical points, since these points
are extended and contain all the difficulties one wishes to avoid."*

I T SEEMS THAT the author of the objection has not properly grasped
my opinion. Extension or space and the surfaces, lines, and points one can
conceive in it are only relations of order or orders of coexistence, both for
the actually existing thing and for the possible thing one can put in its place.
Thus they have no bases of composition, any more than does number. A number divided, $1/2$ for example, can be further divided into two fourths or four
eighths, etc. to infinity, without our being able to arrive at any smallest fractions or to conceive of the number as a whole that is formed by the coming
together of ultimate elements. It is the same for a line, which can be divided
just as this number can. Also, properly speaking, the number $1/2$ in the abstract
is an entirely simple ratio [*rapport*], in no way formed through the composition of other fractions, though in things numbered two fourths equal one half.
And one can say the same for the *abstract* line. Composition is only in *concretes*,
that is, in masses whose relations are marked by these abstract lines. And it
is in this way that mathematical points have their place; they are only modalities, that is, extremities. And since everything is indefinite in the abstract
line, we are dealing with everything that is possible, as in the fractions of a
number, without having to bother with divisions actually made, which fix
these points in a different way. But, in actual substantial things, the whole is
a result or coming together of simple substances, or rather of a multitude of
real unities. It is the confusion of the ideal with the actual which has muddled
everything and caused the labyrinth of *the composition of the continuum*. Those
who make up a line from points have looked for the first elements in ideal
things or relations, something completely contrary to what they should have
done; and those who found that relations like number or space (which contain
the order or relation of possible coexistent things) cannot be formed by the
coming together of points were wrong, for the most part, to deny that substantial realities have first elements, as if the substantial realities had no primitive
unities, or as if there were no simple substances. However, number and line
are not *chimerical* things, even though there is no such composition, for they

are relations that contain eternal truths, by which the phenomena of nature are ruled. In this way one can say that ½ and ¼ taken abstractly are independent of one another, or rather that the total ratio ½ is prior (in the sign of reason, as the Scholastics say) to the partial ratio ¼, since it is by the subdivision of the half that we come to the fourth, when considering the ideal order; and it is the same for the line, in which the whole is prior to the part because the part is only possible and ideal. But in realities in which only divisions actually made enter into consideration, the whole is only a result or coming together, like a flock of sheep. It is true that the number of simple substances which enter into a mass, however small, is infinite, since besides the soul, which brings about the real unity of the animal, the body of the sheep (for example) is actually subdivided—that is, it is, again, an assemblage of invisible animals or plants which are in the same way composites, outside of that which also brings about their real unity. Although this goes on to infinity, it is evident that, in the end, everything reduces [*revenir à*] to these unities, the rest or the results being nothing but well-founded phenomena.

Postscript of a Letter to Basnage de Beauval (1696)[206]

One of Foucher's comments on the "New System of Nature" was that "it can be granted that God, the great Maker of the universe, can so well adjust all the organic parts of a man's body that they may be capable of all the motions that the soul joined to that body would have produced in the course of its life, without the soul having had the power to change these motions or to modify them in any manner [... and similarly for the soul]—that is no more impossible than making two clocks agree so well and act so uniformly that at the moment clock A strikes twelve, clock B strikes twelve also, so that we imagine the two clocks being made to work by the same weight or the same spring" (G IV, 488–89). Leibniz turned to the image a year later, in a postscript to a letter to Basnage de Beauval. See also the "Response to Father Toumemine, on Harmony."

I SEE CLEARLY by your reflections that my thoughts inserted by a friend in the *Journal de Paris* require clarification.[207] You can say that you do not understand how I can prove what I have advanced about the communication or harmony of two substances as different as the soul and the body. It is true that I thought that I had given the way to do this. And here is how I hope to satisfy you.

Consider two clocks or watches in perfect agreement. Now this can happen in *three ways*: the *first* is that of a natural influence. This is what Huygens

206. G IV 498–500. French.
207. The reference is to the "New System of Nature."

experienced, to his great surprise.[208] He had suspended two pendula from the same piece of wood, and the constant swinging of the pendula transmitted similar vibrations to the particles of wood. But since these vibrations could not continue in an orderly way without interfering with each other, at least while the two pendula were not in accord with one another, it happened in a marvelous way that even when the swings of the pendula had been intentionally disturbed, they came to swing together again, almost as if they were two strings in unison. *The second way* to make two faulty clocks always agree would be to have them watched over by a competent workman, who would adjust them and get them to agree at every moment. *The third way* is to construct these two clocks[209] from the start with so much skill and accuracy that one can be certain of their subsequent agreement.

Let us now put the soul and the body in place of these two watches; their agreement or sympathy will also come about in one of these three ways. *The way of influence* is that of the common philosophy; but since we can conceive neither material particles nor immaterial qualities or species that can pass from one of these substances to the other, we must reject this opinion. *The way of assistance* is that of the system of occasional causes. But, I hold, that is to appeal to a *Deus ex machina* in a natural and ordinary matter, where, according to reason, God should intervene only in the sense that he concurs with all other natural things. Thus there remains only my hypothesis, that is, *the way of pre-established harmony*, through a prior divine artifice, which has formed each of these substances from the beginning in such a way that by following only its own laws, laws which it received with its being, it nevertheless agrees with the other, as if there were a mutual influence, or as if God always meddled with it, over and above his general concourse. Beyond this I do not think that I need to prove anything else, unless someone wishes me to prove that God is skillful enough to be able to make use of this prior artifice; we even see some examples of this among humans, in proportion to their ability. And assuming that God can do it, one sees clearly that it is the finest way, the way most worthy of him. You had some worry that my explanation would be in contradiction with the different ideas we have of the mind and of the body. But you now see clearly that nobody has better established their independence. For as long as their communication needed to be explained by way of miracle, it always gave some people the opportunity to fear that the distinction was not as great as it was thought to be, since we are forced to go to such lengths in order to maintain it. Now all these qualms will cease. My essays on dynamics are related to this.[210] There I had to fathom the notion of corporeal substance, which I placed in the force to act or resist, rather than in extension, which is merely the repetition or diffusion of something prior, that is, the repetition or diffusion of this force. And these thoughts, which

---

208. One of Huygens's major works was the *Horologium Oscillatorium, sive de motu pendulorum ad horologia adapto* (1673) about pendulum clocks.

209. The text reads '*pendules,*' which can mean clock, but Leibniz may have intended to write '*montre*' or '*horologe.*'

210. See, e.g., the "Specimen of Dynamics" above.

some people have found paradoxical, have led to an exchange of letters with several famous people; I could publish a collection of letters sometime later, in which my correspondence with Arnauld of which I have spoken in my previous letter, could appear. It would contain a curious mix of philosophical and mathematical thoughts which would perhaps have the charm of novelty. I let you judge whether these explanations I have just given would be suitable for sounding the opinions of enlightened persons through the medium of your Journal; however, I wish the work to remain anonymous, as was the item in the *Journal de Paris*.[211]

On the Ultimate Origination of Things
(23 November 1697)[212]

BEYOND THE WORLD, that is, beyond the collection of finite things, there is some One Being who rules, not only as the soul is the ruler in me, or, better, as the self is the ruler in my body, but also in a much higher sense. For the One Being who rules the universe not only rules the world, but also fashions or creates it; he is above the world, and, so to speak, extramundane, and therefore he is the ultimate reason for things. For we cannot find in any of the individual things, or even in the entire collection and series of things, a sufficient reason for why they exist. Let us suppose that a book on the elements of geometry has always existed, one copy always made from another. It is obvious that although we can explain a present copy of the book from the previous book from which it was copied, this will never lead us to a complete explanation, no matter how many books back we go, since we can always wonder why there have always been such books, why these books were written, and why they were written the way they were. What is true of these books is also true of the different states of the world, for the state which follows is, in a sense, copied from the preceding state, though in accordance with certain laws of change. And so, however far back we might go into previous states, we will never find in those states a complete explanation [*ratio*] for why, indeed, there is any world at all, and why it is the way it is.

I certainly grant that you can imagine that the world is eternal. However, since you assume only a succession of states, and since no reason for the world can be found in any one of them whatsoever (indeed, assuming as many of them as you like won't in any way help you to find a reason), it is obvious that the reason must be found elsewhere. For in eternal things, even if there is no cause, we must still understand there to be a reason. In things that persist, the reason is the nature or essence itself, and in a series of changeable things (if, *a priori*, we imagine it to be eternal), the reason would be the

---

211. The *Journal de Paris* is the *Journal des Savants*, in which the *New System* was first published. Basnage de Beauval was editor of the *Histoire des Ouvrages des Sçavans*, which was the title he gave the *Nouvelles de la République des Lettres*, when he took it over from Pierre Bayle in 1687.
212. G VII 302–8. Latin.

superior strength of certain inclinations, as we shall soon see, where the reasons don't necessitate (with absolute or metaphysical necessity, where the contrary implies a contradiction*) but incline. From this it follows that even if we assume the eternity of the world, we cannot escape the ultimate and extramundane reason for things, God.

Therefore, the reasons for the world lie hidden in something extramundane, different from the chain of states, or from the series of things, the collection of which constitutes the world. And so we must pass from physical or hypothetical necessity, which determines the later things in the world from the earlier, to something which is of absolute or metaphysical necessity, something for which a reason cannot be given. For the present world is physically or hypothetically necessary, but not absolutely or metaphysically necessary. That is, given that it was once such and such, it follows that such and such things will arise in the future. Therefore, since the ultimate ground must be in something which is of metaphysical necessity, and since the reason for an existing thing must come from something that actually exists, it follows that there must exist some one entity of metaphysical necessity, that is, there must be an entity whose essence is existence, and therefore something must exist which differs from the plurality of things, which differs from the world, which we have granted and shown is not of metaphysical necessity.

Furthermore, in order to explain a bit more distinctly how temporal, contingent, or physical truths arise from eternal, essential or metaphysical truths, we must first acknowledge that since something rather than nothing exists, there is a certain urge for existence or (so to speak) a straining toward existence in possible things or in possibility or essence itself; in a word, essence in and of itself strives for existence. Futhermore, it follows from this that all possibles, that is, everything that expresses essence or possible reality, strive with equal right for existence* in proportion to the amount of essence or reality or the degree of perfection they contain, for perfection is nothing but the amount of essence.

From this it is obvious that of the infinite combinations of possibilities and possible series, the one that exists is the one through which the most essence or possibility is brought into existence. In practical affairs one always follows the decision rule in accordance with which one ought to seek the maximum or the minimum: namely, one prefers the maximum effect at the minimum cost, so to speak. And in this context, time, place, or in a word, the receptivity or capacity of the world can be taken for the cost or the plot of ground on which the most pleasing building possible is to be built, and the variety of shapes [therein] [*formarum . . . varietates*] corresponds to the pleasingness of the building and the number and elegance of the rooms. And the situation is like that in certain games, in which all places on the board are supposed to be filled in accordance with certain rules, where at the end, blocked by certain spaces, you will be forced to leave more places empty than you could have or wanted to, unless you used some trick. There is, however, a certain procedure through which one can most easily fill the board. Thus, if, for example, we suppose that we are directed to construct a triangle, without being given any other directions, the result is that an equilateral triangle would be drawn; and if we suppose that we are to go from one point to another, without being directed to use a particular path, the path chosen will be the easiest or the shortest one. And so, assuming that at some time being is to prevail over nonbeing, or that there is a reason why something rather than nothing is to exist, or that something is to pass from possibility to actuality, although nothing beyond this is determined, it follows that there would be as much as there possibly can be, given the capacity of time and space (that is, the capacity of the order of possible existence); in a word, it is just like tiles laid down so as to contain as many as possible in a given area.

From this we can already understand in a wondrous way how a certain Divine Mathematics or Metaphysical Mechanism is used in the very origination of things, and how the determination of a maximum finds a place. The case is like that in geometry, where the straight angle is distinguished from all angles, or like the case of a liquid placed in another of a different kind, which forms itself into the most capacious shape, namely that of a sphere, or best of all, like the case in common mechanics where the struggling of many heavy bodies with one another finally gives rise to a motion through which there results the greatest descent, taken as a whole. For just as all possibles strive with equal right for existence in proportion to their reality, so too all heavy things strive with equal right to descend in proportion to their heaviness, and just as the one case results in the motion which contains as much descent of heavy things as is possible, the other case gives rise to a world in which the greatest number of possibles is produced.

And so, we now have physical necessity derived from metaphysics.[213] For even if the world is not metaphysically necessary, in the sense that its contrary implies a contradiction or a logical absurdity, it is, however, physically necessary or determined, in the sense that its contrary implies imperfection or moral absurdity. And just as possibility is the foundation [*principium*] of essence, so perfection or degree of essence (through which the greatest number of things are compossible) is the foundation of existence. From this it is at the same time obvious how the Author of the World can be free, even though everything happens determinately, since he acts from a principle of wisdom or perfection. Indeed, indifference arises from ignorance, and the wiser one is, the more one is determined to do that which is most perfect.

But, you say, this comparison between a certain determining metaphysical mechanism and the physical mechanism of heavy bodies, though it seems elegant, is faulty insofar as the heavy bodies striving really exist, while possibilities or essences before, or rather outside of existence, are imaginary or fictional, and therefore, one cannot seek a reason for existence in them. I respond that neither those essences nor the so-called eternal truths pertaining to them are fictitious. Rather, they exist in a certain realm of ideas, so to speak, namely, in God himself, the source of every essence and of the existence

---

213. Leibniz's Latin is ambiguous here; he can also be read as claiming that physical necessity is drawn from metaphysical necessity.

of the rest. The very existence of the actual series of things shows that we seem not to have spoken without grounds. For the reason for things must be sought in metaphysical necessities or in eternal truths, since (as I showed above) it cannot be found in the actual series of things. But existing things cannot derive from anything but existing things, as I already noted above. So it is necessary that eternal truths have their existence in a certain absolute or metaphysically necessary subject, that is, in God, through whom those things which would otherwise be imaginary are realized, to use a barbaric but graphic expression.[214]

And indeed, we observe that everything in the world takes place in accordance with laws that are eternally true, laws that are not merely geometrical, but also metaphysical, that is, not only in accordance with material necessities, but also in accordance with formal reasons. This is true not only in very general terms, in the explanation [ratio] we have just now given for why the world exists rather than not, and why it exists this way rather than some other way (which is certainly to be sought in the striving of possibles for existence), but in descending to particulars we also see the wonderful way in which metaphysical laws of cause, power and action, have their place in the whole of nature, and we see that these metaphysical laws prevail over the purely geometrical laws of matter. As I found to my great astonishment in explaining the laws of motion, this is true to such an extent that I was finally forced to abandon the law of the geometrical composition of conatus, which I once defended in my youth, when I was more materialistic, as I have explained at greater length elsewhere.[215]

And so, the ultimate reason for the reality of both essences and existences lies in one thing, which must of necessity be greater than the world, higher than the world, and must have existed before the world did, since through it not only existing things, which make up the world, but also possibles have their reality. Moreover, it can be sought in but one source, because of the interconnection among all of these things. Furthermore, it is obvious that, from this source, things are continually flowing forth, are being produced and were produced, since it is not clear why one state of the world any more than another, yesterday's any more than today's, should flow from it. It is also obvious how God acts not only physically, but freely, how in him there is not only the efficient cause of things, but the final cause, and how in him we have not only the reason for the greatness or power in the mechanism of the universe as now constituted, but also the reason for the goodness or wisdom in constituting it.

And lest anyone think that I am here confusing moral perfection or goodness with metaphysical perfection or greatness, and grant the latter while denying the former, one must realize that it follows from what I have said that not only is the world physically (or, if you prefer, metaphysically) most perfect, that is, that the series of things which has been brought forth is the one in which there is, in actuality, the greatest amount of reality, but it also follows

---

214. 'Realiso,' the verb Leibniz uses for 'realize' or 'make real,' is corrupt Latin.
215. See *A Specimen of Dynamics*, above, pp. 117–38.

that the world is morally most perfect, since moral perfection is in reality physical perfection with respect to minds. From this it follows that the world is not only the most admirable machine, but insofar as it is made up of minds, it is also the best republic, the republic through which minds derive the greatest possible happiness and joy, in which their physical perfection consists.

But, you ask, don't we experience quite the opposite in the world? For the worst often happens to the best, and not only innocent beasts but also humans are injured and killed, even tortured. In the end, the world appears to be a certain confused chaos rather than a thing ordered by some supreme wisdom, especially if one takes note of the conduct of the human race. I confess that it appears this way at first glance, but a deeper look at things forces us to quite the contrary view. From those very considerations which I brought forward it is obvious *a priori* that everything, even minds, is of the highest perfection there can be.

And indeed, it is unjust to make a judgment unless one has examined the entire law, as lawyers say. We know but a small part of the eternity which extends without measure, for how short is the memory of several thousand years which history gives us. But yet, from such meager experience we rashly make judgments about the immense and the eternal, like people born and raised in prison or, if you prefer, in the subterranean saltmines of the Sarmatians, people who think that there is no light in the world but the dim light of their torches, light scarcely sufficient to guide their steps. Look at a very beautiful picture, and cover it up except for some small part. What will it look like but some confused combination of colors, without delight, without art; indeed the more closely we examine it the more it will look that way. But as soon as the covering is removed, and you see the whole surface from an appropriate place, you will understand that what looked like accidental splotches on the canvas were made with consummate skill by the creator of the work. What the eyes discover in the painting, the ears discover in music. Indeed, the most distinguished masters of composition quite often mix dissonances with consonances in order to arouse the listener, and pierce him, as it were, so that, anxious about what is to happen, the listener might feel all the more pleasure when order is soon restored, just as we delight in small dangers or in the experience of misfortune for the very feeling or manifestation they provide of our power or happiness, or just as we delight in the spectacle of ropewalkers or sword dancing for their very ability to incite fear, or just as we ourselves laughingly half toss children, as if we are about to throw them off. (It was also for this reason that when Christian, King of Denmark, was still an infant, wrapped in swaddling clothes, an ape carried him to the edge of the roof, and then, while all were in distress, the ape, almost as if he were laughing, put him safely back into the cradle.) On that same principle it is insipid to always eat sweet things; sharp, acidic, and even bitter tastes should be mixed in to stimulate the palate. He who hasn't tasted bitter things hasn't earned sweet things, nor, indeed, will he appreciate them. Pleasure does not derive from uniformity, for uniformity brings forth disgust and makes us dull, not happy: this very principle is a law of delight.

But what we said about the part, which can be disordered without detract-ing from the harmony of the whole, should not be taken to mean that there is no reason for the parts, or that it would be (as it were) sufficient for the world as a whole to be perfect of its kind, even if the human race were miserable, and no attention paid to justice in the universe, or no provision made for us, as certain persons of poor judgment believe about the totality of things.[216] For one must realize that just as in the best constituted republic, care is taken that each individual gets what is good for him, as much as possible, similarly, the universe would be insufficiently perfect unless it took individuals into account as much as could be done consistently with preserving the harmony of the uni-verse. It is impossible in this matter to find a better standard than the very law of justice, which dictates that everyone should take part in the perfection of the universe and in his own happiness in proportion to his own virtue and to the extent that his will has thus contributed to the common good. This exon-erates what we call the charity and love of God, in which the entire force and power of the Christian religion alone consists, in the judgment of wise theolo-gians. Nor should the fact that minds get such deference in the universe ap-pear astonishing, since they are produced in the exact image of the Supreme Creator, and relate to him not only as machines to their builder (as other things do), but also as citizens to their prince. Likewise, they are to persist as long as the universe itself does, and they express the whole in a certain way and concentrate it in themselves, so that it might be said that they are parts that are wholes.

We must also hold that afflictions, especially those the good have, only lead to their greater good. This is true not only in theology, but in nature [*physice*] as well, since a seed flung to the ground must suffer before it bears fruit. And, all in all, one can say that afflictions that are bad in the short run are good in their effect, since they constitute a short path to greater perfection. It is just as in physics, where liquids that ferment slowly also improve more slowly, but those in which there is more violent disturbance improve more quickly because they eliminate [impure] parts with greater force. And this is what you might call stepping back in order to leap forward with greater force (one retreats the better to leap forward). These considerations must be held to be not only pleasing and consoling, but most true. I think that in the universe nothing is truer than happiness, nor is anything happier or sweeter than truth.

In addition to the beauties and perfections of the totality of the divine works, we must also recognize a certain constant and unbounded progress in the whole universe, so that it always proceeds to greater development [*cultus*], just as a large portion of our world is now cultivated [*cultura*] and will be-come more and more so. And while certain things regress to their original wild state and others are destroyed and buried, we must, however, understand this in the same way that we interpreted affliction a bit earlier. Indeed, this very destruction and burying leads us to the attainment of something better, so that we make a profit from the very loss, in a sense.

---

216. See, e.g., Spinoza, appendix to *Ethics* I.

And there is a ready answer to the objection that if this were so, then the world should have become Paradise long ago. Many substances have already attained great perfection. However, because of the infinite divisibility of the continuum, there are always parts asleep in the abyss of things, yet to be roused and yet to be advanced to greater and better things, advanced, in a word, to greater cultivation. Thus, progress never comes to an end.

On Nature Itself

Or, on the Inherent Force and Actions of Created Things, Toward Confirming and Illustrating Their Dynamics (1698)[217]

The publication of a pamphlet by Johann Christopher Sturm, a minor figure in the history of physics and a correspondent of Leibniz's, was the occasion for this piece, published in the September 1698 issue of the Acta Eruditorum. *It is one of Leibniz's most important writings, and it was often cited in his later works. It offers some of the clearest statements of Leibniz's arguments against Descartes, Spinoza, and the occasionalist tendencies of some of Descartes's followers; it nicely articulates the metaphysical view that underlies Leibniz's new science of dynamics, the view that force, activity, is in the body itself, and not merely in God. It is in this context that the term 'monad' makes its first appearance in Leibniz's published writings. When reading it in translation, it is important to remember that Latin, in which it is written, lacks a definite article. Leibniz is concerned here with both nature in the sense of the created world, and the natures that its individual constituents are usually taken to have.*

(1) RECENTLY I RECEIVED a defense of his dissertation, *De Idolo Naturae* (published in Altdorf), from Johann Christopher Sturm, that celebrated gentleman, distinguished in mathematics and physics; it had been challenged by that excellent and most accomplished physician of Kiel, Gunther Christopher Schelhammer in his book, *De Natura*.[218] Now, I too once pondered the same question, and there was something of a dispute in letters that passed between me and the distinguished author of the dissertation, a dispute which he recently mentioned in a respectful way, publishing several of the transactions that passed between us in his *Physica Electiva* (vol. I, bk. 1, chap. 3, epilogue, sec. 5, pp. 119, 120).[219] So, all the more willingly I applied my mind and attention to that question, important in and of itself, judging it necessary to present both my own view as well as the entire matter a bit more distinctly in terms of those principles which I have already made known on several

---

217. G IV 504–16. Latin.

218. What Leibniz refers to as Sturm's *De Idolo Naturae* is his *Idolum naturae . . . sive de naturae agentis ... conceptibus dissertatio* (1692); Schelhammer's *De Natura* is his *Natura sibi et medicis vindicata sive de natura liber bipartitus* (1697). The defense, later referred to as Sturm's apologetic dissertation, is his "De natura sibi incassum vindicata" (1698), which appeared in volume II of Sturm's *Physica eclectica* (1698).

219. Johann Christopher Sturm, *Physica electiva sive hypothetica*, tomus I (1697).

occasions. Sturm's apologetic dissertation seemed to provide an appropriate occasion for undertaking this project, since one might judge that the author has presented there, in a few words and in summary, what is most important to the matter. But I am not entering into other aspects of that controversy between these distinguished gentlemen.

(2) Above all, I think that we should investigate two questions: first, what constitutes the nature we customarily attribute to things, whose generally accepted properties the celebrated Sturm thinks reek of something pagan; and second, whether there is any *energeia* in created things, which he seems to deny. As to the first question, *on nature itself* (if we may reflect on what it is not, as well as what it is), I certainly agree that there is no such thing as the soul of the universe. I also agree that those wonders which present themselves daily, and about which we customarily say (quite rightly) that the work of nature is the work of intelligence, should not be ascribed to certain created intelligences endowed with wisdom and power [*virtus*] only in proportion to the task at hand, but rather that the whole of *nature* is, so to speak, the *workmanship of God*, indeed, so much so that any natural machine you may choose consists of a completely infinite number of organs (which is the true and insufficiently appreciated distinction between the natural and the artificial), and therefore requires the infinite wisdom and power of the author and ruler. And so, I think that the omniscient heat of Hippocrates, and Avicenna's Cholcodean giver of souls, the exceedingly wise plastic virtue of Scaliger and others, and the hylarchic principle of Henry More are in part impossible, and in part unnecessary. I hold that it is enough for the machine of things to have been constructed with such wisdom that, through its very development, those very wonders come to pass, chiefly (as I believe) by means of organisms unfolding themselves through some predetermined plan. And so I approve of the fact that the distinguished gentleman rejects the fiction of any sort of created, wise nature, fashioning and governing the mechanisms of bodies. But I do not think that it follows from this, nor do I think that it is in agreement with reason to deny all created, active force inherent in things.

(3) We have spoken of what isn't the case. Now let us examine a bit more directly* what that nature is, that nature which Aristotle not inappropriately called the *principle of motion and rest*; though, having taken the phrase rather broadly, that philosopher seems to me to understand not only local motion or rest in a place, but *change* in general and stasis or persistence. From this it also follows, as I might note in passing, that the definition of motion he gives, though more obscure than it ought to be, is not, however, as silly as it appears to those who understand it as if he wanted only to define local motion. But on to the matters at hand. Robert Boyle, a distinguished gentleman well versed in the careful observation of nature, wrote a little book called *On Nature Itself* whose main point was, if I remember rightly, that we ought to judge that nature is the very mechanism of bodies itself.[220] This can, indeed,

---

220. The work in question is Boyle's *A Free Inquiry into the Vulgularly Received Notion of Nature* (1682). Leibniz is citing it here in its Latin edition, *Tractatus de Ipsa Natura ...*, which appeared in 1688.

be approved of in a broad sense. But investigating the matter with greater care, we must distinguish the ultimate causes [*principia*] in this mechanism from that which is derived from them. So, for example, in explaining a clock, it is not sufficient to say that it is driven by a mechanical principle [*ratio*] unless you distinguish whether it is driven by a weight or by a spring. And I have already said a number of times that the source of the mechanism itself flows, not from material principles and mathematical reasons alone, but from some higher and, so to speak, metaphysical source, something that I think will be of use in preventing the mechanical explanation of natural things from being extended too far, to the detriment of piety, as if matter can stand by itself and as if mechanism required no intelligence or spiritual substance.

(4) *The foundation of the laws of nature*, among other things, provides a notable indication of this. That foundation should not be sought in the conservation of the same quantity of motion, as it has seemed to most, but rather in the fact that it is necessary that *the same quantity of active power be preserved*, indeed (something I discovered happens for a most beautiful reason) that the *same quantity of motive action* also be conserved, a quantity whose measure is far different from that which the Cartesians understand as quantity of motion. And when two mathematicians, who are clearly among the most talented, fought with me about this matter, in part through letters, in part in public, one came over entirely into my camp, and the other came to the point of abandoning all his objections after much careful airing and candidly confessed that he did not yet have a response to one of my arguments.[221] For that reason, I was very surprised that the distinguished gentleman [Sturm], explaining the laws of motion in the published part of his *Physica Electiva*, took the common view of them for granted, as if they were untouched by any objection (though he himself acknowledged that this view rests on no demonstration, but only on a certain probability [*verisimilitudo*], something he also repeats in his latest dissertation, chap. 3, sec. 2). Perhaps he wrote before my work came out, and then either did not have the leisure to review what he had written, or it did not cross his mind to review it, especially since he believed that the laws of motion are arbitrary, a view that seems to me not to be altogether coherent. For I believe that God came to decree those laws observed in nature through considerations of wisdom and reasons of order. And I think that it is apparent from this (something that I once noted, using an opportunity afforded by the laws of optics, something that was afterwards greatly applauded by the distinguished Molyneux in his *Dioptrics*) that final causes not only advance virtue and piety in ethics and natural theology, but also help us to find and lay bare hidden truths in physics itself. And so, when the most celebrated Sturm listed my view among the hypotheses during his treatment of the final cause in his *Physica Eclectica*, I wish that he had considered it sufficiently in his discussion, for it can scarcely be doubted that in such a discussion he would have taken the occasion to assert many things in favor of the excellence

---

221. The two "mathematicians" in question are probably Malebranche and Johann Bernoulli. See G III 56–57.

of the argument, things both remarkable for their fruitfulness and also beneficial for piety.

(5) But now we must consider what he himself says about the notion of a nature in his apologetic dissertation, and what seems yet to be lacking in what he says. He grants, in chapter 4, sec. 2, 3 and in other places throughout the work, that the motions now existing happen *by virtue of the eternal law* God once set up, a law he then calls a volition and *command*. He also grants that there is no need for a new divine command, a new volition, not to speak of a new effort [*conatus*], or for any other labors (sec. 3), and Sturm rejects the view that God moves a thing as a woodcutter moves an ax, or as a miller operates a mill, either by holding back the water or diverting it to the wheel, a view he rejects as having been wrongly imputed to him by his opponent. But yet, it certainly seems to me that this explanation is insufficient. For, I ask, has that volition or command, or, if you prefer, divine law that was once laid down, bestowed a mere *extrinsic denomination*, as it were, on things? Or, on the other hand, has it conferred some kind of enduring impression produced in the thing itself, that is, as that gentleman Schelhammer (as admirable in judgment as he is in experience) puts it, quite nicely, has it conferred an inherent law [*lex insita*] (even if it is not known to the creatures in which it exists), from which both actions and passions follow? The first seems to be the doctrine of the inventors of the system of occasional causes, principally that of that very acute Malebranche, while the latter is the received view, and, as I judge, the one that contains the most truth.

(6) For, since that past command does not now exist, it cannot now bring anything about unless it left behind some subsistent effect at the time, an effect which even now endures and is now at work. Whoever thinks otherwise, in my judgment, renounces all distinct explanation of things; anything could equally well be said to follow from anything else if something absent in place or time could be at work here and now, without an intermediary. And so, it is not sufficient to say that God, creating things in the beginning, willed that they follow a certain definite law in their change [*progressus*] if we imagine his will to have been so ineffective that things were not affected by it and no lasting effect was produced in them. And indeed, it contradicts the notion of that pure and absolute divine power and will to suppose that God wills and yet produces or changes nothing through willing, to suppose that he always acts but never accomplishes anything and leaves behind no work or accomplishment at all. Certainly, if nothing had been impressed on creatures by the divine words, "let the earth be fruitful and let the animals multiply," if things were disposed after that command just as if no command had intervened, then, since there must be some connection between cause and effect, either immediate or through some intermediary, it follows that either nothing now obeys that command or that the command held only at the time it was given and must always be renewed in the future, something the distinguished author correctly rejects. But if, indeed, the law God laid down left some trace of itself impressed on things, if by his command things were formed in such a way that they were rendered appropriate for fulfilling the will of the command

then already we must admit that a certain efficacy has been placed in things, a form or a force, something like what we usually call by the name 'nature,' something from which the series of phenomena follow in accordance with the prescript of the first command.

(7) Now, this inherent force can indeed be understood distinctly, but it cannot be explained through the imagination, nor, of course, should it be explained in that way, any more than the nature of the soul should be. For *force* is among those things which are reached, not by the imagination, but by the intellect. And so, when that distinguished gentleman (in chap. 4, sec. 6 of his apologetic dissertation) seeks an explanation in terms of the imagination for the way in which an inherent law works in bodies ignorant of that law, I interpret him to mean that he wants it to be explained through the intellect, for one certainly cannot believe that he requires us to picture sounds or hear colors. Furthermore, if difficulty in explaining things were a sufficient reason for rejecting them, then something he complains is wrongly imputed to him (chap. 1, sec. 2) would follow,* namely, that he would rather hold that everything is moved by divine power [*virtus*] alone, than admit anything called a nature, of whose nature he is ignorant. Indeed, even Hobbes and others who hold everything to be corporeal could depend on this principle with equal right since they persuade themselves that nothing can be explained distinctly and through the imagination, except body. But they are correctly refuted by the very fact that there is a force for acting in things, a force which is not derived from things that can be imagined. And simply to thrust this force back into a command of God's, given once in the past, affecting things in no way nor leaving an effect after itself, is so far from making the matter more easily explicable that it is, rather, to set aside the role of the philosopher altogether and cut the Gordian knot with a sword. But a more distinct and more correct explanation of active force than has yet been attained can be derived from our dynamics and from the account of the laws of nature and motion it contains, which is both true and in accordance with the facts.

(8) But if some defender of the new philosophy which introduces inertness [*inertia*] and inactivity [*torpor*] into things were to go so far as to deprive God's commands of all lasting effects and the ability to produce things in the future, and didn't even care that he required new labors of God all the time (which Sturm prudently professes to be foreign to his meaning), he himself may judge how worthy he thinks this is of God. But we cannot exempt him from criticism unless he can explain how it is that things themselves can endure through time, even while those attributes of things, which we call by the name 'nature' in them, cannot endure, since it is fitting that just as the words "let there be" [*fiat*] leave something behind, indeed, the very thing that persists, so should the no less *wonderful* word "*blessing*" have left something behind in things, a fecundity or a nisus for producing their actions and for being effectual, something from which a result follows if nothing prevents it. To this I can add something which I have already explained elsewhere, even if, perhaps, I have not yet made it sufficiently obvious to all, namely, that the very substance of things consists in a force for acting and being acted upon.

From this it follows that persisting things cannot be produced if no force lasting through time can be imprinted on them by the divine power. Were that so, it would follow that no created substance, no soul would remain numerically the same, and thus, nothing would be conserved by God, and consequently everything would merely be certain vanishing or unstable modifications and phantasms, so to speak, of one permanent divine substance. Or, what comes to the same thing, God would be the very nature or substance of all things, the sort of doctrine of ill repute which a recent writer, subtle indeed, though profane, either introduced to the world or revived.[222] Indeed, if corporeal things contained nothing but that which is material, they could quite rightly be said to be in constant change, but they would not have anything substantial, as the Platonists also once correctly recognized.

(9) The *other question* is whether creatures can properly and truly be said to act. Once we understand that the inherent nature is no different from the force of acting and being acted upon, this question reduces to the earlier one. For there can be no action [*actio*] without a force for acting, and, conversely, a power [*potentia*] which can never be exercised is empty. Since, nevertheless, action and power are different things, the former successive, the latter persisting, let us look then at action. Here, I confess, I find some difficulty in explaining the views of the celebrated Sturm. For he denies that created things, properly speaking, act in and of themselves, but then, however, he admits that they do act, insofar as he disavows, in a certain sense, the comparison between creatures and an ax moved by a woodcutter. From this I can't infer anything with certainty, nor do I see him explain with sufficient clarity just how far he departs from the received views, or what distinct notion of action he might have had in mind; as it is well known from the debates of the metaphysicians, this is no clear or easy matter. To the extent that I have made the notion of action clear to myself, I believe that the widely received doctrine of philosophy, that *actions pertain to supposita*, follows from that notion and is grounded in it. Furthermore, I believe that we must grasp the fact that this also holds reciprocally, so that not only is it the case that everything that acts is an individual substance [*substantia singularis*], but also that every individual substance acts without interruption, including even body itself, in which one never finds absolute rest.

(10) But now we must consider a bit more closely the view of those who deny true and proper action to created things, as Robert Fludd, author of the Mosaic Philosophy, did long ago, and as now do certain of the Cartesians, who think that things do not act, but that God acts directly on things [*in rerum praesentiam*] in accordance with what is appropriate for them, and who thus think that things are occasions, not causes, and that things receive but do not bring anything about or produce anything. Although Cordemoy, de la Forge, and other Cartesians had proposed this doctrine, Malebranche, above all, adorned it with a certain rhetorical luster, commensurate with his acumen. But no one, so far as I know, has brought forward any solid reasons. Indeed,

---

222. The reference here is to Spinoza and the doctrine developed in *Ethics* I.

if this view were extended so far as to eliminate even the *immanent actions* of substances (something which Sturm rightly rejects in his *Physica Electiva*, book I, chap. 4, epilogue, sec. 11, p. 176, and in this he shows his circumspection quite nicely), then it would be as distant as it could possibly be from reason. For who would call into doubt that the mind thinks and wills, that we elicit in ourselves many thoughts and volitions, and that there is a spontaneity that belongs to us? If this were called into doubt, then not only would human liberty be denied and the cause of evil things be thrust into God, but it would also fly in the face of the testimony of our innermost experience and consciousness, testimony by which we ourselves sense that the things my opponents have transferred to God, without even a pretense of reason, are ours. But if we were to attribute an inherent force to our mind, a force for producing immanent actions, or to put it another way, a force for acting immanently, then nothing forbids, in fact, it is reasonable to suppose that the same force would be found in other souls or forms, or, if you prefer, in the natures of substances—unless someone were to think that, in the natural world accessible to us, our minds alone are active, or that all power for acting immanently, and further, as I put it, all power for acting *vitally* is joined to an intellect, assertions that are neither confirmed by any rational arguments, nor can they be defended except by distorting the truth. In another place I shall give a better account of what can be said about the *transeunt actions of created things*. Indeed, elsewhere I have already explained a part of it, namely, that the *interaction* between *substances* or monads arises not from an influx, but through an agreement derived from divine preformation, accommodating each thing to things outside of itself while each follows the inherent force and laws of its own nature; in this also consists the *union of the soul and the body*.

(11) Moreover, it is indeed true that bodies are in and of themselves inert [*inertia*], if this is properly understood, namely, in the sense that what is assumed to be at rest at some time and in some respect cannot put itself into motion in that respect, nor will it allow itself to be put into motion by another thing without resistance—any more than it can spontaneously change either its degree of velocity or direction at any given time, or any more than it can allow itself to be changed by another thing easily and without resistance. And furthermore, we must admit that extension, or that which is geometrical in bodies, if taken by itself, has nothing in itself from which action and motion can arise. Indeed, we must admit, rather, that matter resists being moved through a certain *natural inertia* it has (as Kepler nicely named it), so that it is not indifferent to motion and rest, as is commonly believed, but requires more active force for motion in proportion to its size. Hence it is in this very passive force of resisting (which includes impenetrability and something more) that I locate the notion of primary matter or bulk [*moles*], which is everywhere the same in a body and proportional to its size, and I show that from this follow laws of motion far different than they would be if only impenetrability and extension were in bodies and their matter. And just as there is natural *inertia* opposed to *motion* in matter, so too in body itself, indeed in all substance, there is a natural *constancy* opposed to *change*. Indeed, this doctrine

does not support, but rather opposes those who deny activity [*actio*] to things. For, as certain as it is that matter cannot initiate motion through itself, it is just as certain that a body conceived in and of itself retains an impetus once it is imparted, and remains constant in its mobility [*levitas*], that is, it has the tendency to persevere in that series of its changes, which it has once entered upon, as admirable experiments on motion impressed by a mover in motion also show. And since these activities and entelechies certainly cannot be modifications of primary matter or bulk [*moles*], something essentially passive, as the most judicious Sturm has clearly acknowledged (how he did this we shall discuss in the following paragraph), we must judge even from this that a *first entelechy* must be found in corporeal substance, a first subject of activity, namely a primitive motive force which, added over and above extension (or that which is merely geometrical), and over and above bulk (or that which is merely material), always acts but yet is modified in various ways in the collision of bodies through conatus and impetus. And this substantial principle itself is what is called the soul in living things and *the substantial form* in other things; insofar as, together with matter, it constitutes a substance that is truly one, or something one *per se*, it makes up what I call a monad, since, if these true and real unities were eliminated, only entities through aggregation, indeed (it follows from this), no true entities at all would be left in bodies. For, although there are atoms of substance, namely monads, which lack parts, there are no atoms of bulk [*moles*], that is, atoms of the least possible extension, nor are there any ultimate elements, since a continuum cannot be composed out of points. In just the same way, there is nothing greatest in bulk nor infinite in extension, even if there is always something bigger than anything else, though there is a being greatest in the intensity [*intensio*] of its perfection, that is, a being infinite in power [*virtus*].

(12) However, I see that in this apologetic dissertation (chap. 4, sec. 7 and following) the celebrated Sturm has attempted to attack the motive force inherent in bodies through certain arguments. "From numerous considerations," he says, "I shall here show that corporeal substance is indeed incapable of any *actively* motive power" (though I don't understand what a power nonactively motive might be). He also says that he will use two similar arguments, one from the nature of matter and body, the other from the nature of motion. The former reduces to this: that matter is, in its nature, an essentially passive substance, and so it is no more possible for it to be given an active force than it would be for God to will a stone to be alive and rational, that is, to be a nonstone, while it remains a stone. Thus the things that are in body are only modifications of matter, and a modification of a thing that is essentially passive cannot render a thing active (this, I grant, is nicely put). But one can give an appropriate reply from the philosophy which is commonly received, no less than it is true. I understand matter as either secondary or primary. Secondary matter is, indeed, a complete substance, but it is not merely passive; primary matter is merely passive, but it is not a complete substance. And so, we must add a soul or a form analogous to a soul, or a first entelechy, that is, a certain urge [*nisus*] or primitive force of acting, which

itself is an inherent law, impressed by divine decree. I do not think that the celebrated and ingenious gentleman who recently defended the view that body is made up of matter and spirit shrinks from this view. But spirit is to be understood, not as an intelligent being (as he usually does elsewhere), but as a soul or as a form analogous to a soul, not as a simple modification, but as something constitutive, substantial, enduring, what I usually call a *monad*, in which there is something like perception and appetite. This received doctrine, which is also consistent with the doctrine of the schoolmen, properly interpreted, must first be refuted, in order for the argument of the distinguished gentleman to have force. And in the same way, it follows from this that one cannot concede his assumption that whatever is in corporeal substance is a modification of matter. For it has been noted that, according to the received philosophy, there are souls in the bodies of living things which are certainly not modifications of matter. For despite the fact that the outstanding gentleman has settled on the opposite view, and seems to deny all true sensation and all soul, properly speaking, to brute animals, one cannot assume this opinion as a basis for demonstration before it itself is demonstrated. On the contrary, I believe that it is consistent with neither order nor with the beauty or reasonableness of things for there to be something living, that is, acting from within itself, in only the smallest portion of matter, when it would contribute to greater perfection for such things to be everywhere. Nor is there any reason why souls or things analogous to souls should not be everywhere, even if dominant and consequently intelligent souls, like human souls, cannot be everywhere.

(13) It seems to me that the second argument, which the distinguished gentleman derives from motion, does not have any greater necessity in its conclusion. He says that *motion* is only the successive existence of the moving thing in different places. Let us grant this for the moment, even if it is not entirely satisfactory, and even if it expresses what results from motion better than it expresses its formal definition [*formalis ratio*], as it is called. But motive force is not excluded on these grounds. For in the present moment of its motion, not only is a body in a place commensurate to itself, but it also has a conatus or nisus for changing its place, so that the state following from the present one results *per se* from the force of its nature. If things were otherwise, then at the present moment (and furthermore, at any moment whatsoever) a body A in motion would differ not at all from a resting body B, and the view of that distinguished gentleman (if his view of the matter is different from mine) would entail that there is no clear criterion in bodies for distinguishing them, since in a plenum, there is no criterion for distinguishing between masses uniform in themselves unless one is provided by motion. From this view it would also follow, finally, that absolutely nothing would change in bodies, and that everything would always remain the same. For if no portion of matter whatsoever were to differ from equal and congruent portions of matter (something that the distinguished gentleman should admit, since he has eliminated active forces or impetus, and with them all other qualities and modifications except "existing in this place" and "successively coming to exist in some other place"),

and furthermore, if one momentary state were to differ from another in virtue of the transposition of equal and interchangeable portions of matter alone,
portions of matter that agree in every way, then, on account of this perpetual substitution of indistinguishables, it obviously follows that in the corporeal
world there can be no way of distinguishing different momentary states from
one another. For the *denomination* by which one part of matter would be distinguished from another would be only *extrinsic*, indeed, it would derive from
what will happen, namely from the fact that the part of matter in question
will later be some other place or another. But in the present there is no distinguishing criterion. Indeed, we cannot even get such a criterion, properly
grounded, from the future, since even later on one will never arrive at any true
criterion of distinction for the present. This is because, under the assumption of perfect uniformity in matter itself, one cannot in any way distinguish
one place from another, or one bit of matter from another bit of matter in the
same place. It is also useless to turn to *shape* over and above motion. For in
a mass that is perfectly homogeneous, undivided, and full, no shape, that is,
no boundary or distinction between its different parts arises, unless through
motion itself. But if motion contains no mark for distinguishing things from
one another, then it likewise bestows no mark with respect to shape. And
since everything substituted for something prior would be perfectly equivalent, no observer, not even an omniscient one, would detect even the slightest
indication of change. And thus, everything would be just as if there were no
change or discrimination in bodies, nor could we ever explain the different appearances we sense. Things would be just as they would were we to imagine
two perfect and concentric spheres, perfectly similar to one another both in
whole and in part, the one enclosed in the other in such a way that there is
not even the smallest gap. Let us then assume that the enclosed sphere either
revolves or is at rest, and, to say nothing more, not even an angel could find
any difference between its states at different times, nor have any evidence for
discerning whether the enclosed sphere is at rest or revolves, and what law of
motion it follows. Indeed, because we lack both a *gap* and a criterion of distinction, we cannot even define the boundaries of the spheres, in much the
same way as we cannot determine motion because we lack a *criterion of distinction* alone. Even if those who have not penetrated these matters deeply
enough may not have noticed this, it ought to be accepted as certain that such
consequences are alien to the nature and order of things, and that *nowhere are
there things perfectly similar* (which is among my new and more important axioms). Another consequence of this is that, in nature, there are neither corpuscles of maximal hardness, nor a fluid of maximal thinness, nor a subtle
matter universally diffused, nor ultimate elements which certain people call
by the names 'primary' and 'secondary'. Because, I think, Aristotle (more
profound in my view than many think) saw several of these principles, he
judged that, over and above change in place, one must have alteration, and
that matter is not everywhere similar to itself, or else it would remain unchangeable. However, dissimilarity or qualitative difference, and also *alloiosis*
or alteration, which Aristotle explained insufficiently, derive from different

degrees and directions of nisus, and thus derive from modifications of the monads existing in things. From this I think it can be understood that we must necessarily place something in bodies over and above uniform mass and its transposition, which, at any rate, would change nothing. Those who accept *atoms* and the *void* do diversify matter, to be sure, insofar as they make some of it divisible, some indivisible, one place full, another empty. But having overthrown the prejudices of youth, I have realized for a long time now that atoms should be rejected, along with the void. The celebrated gentleman adds that the existence of matter through different moments should be attributed to the will of God. Thus, he asks, why not attribute the fact that it exists here and now to that same cause? I respond: it can scarcely be doubted that this very thing is due to God, as is everything else that involves perfection. But just as that first and universal cause conserving everything does not destroy, but rather causes the natural subsistence of a thing beginning to exist, or its perseverance in existence, once existence is granted, so in the same way he will not destroy, but will rather support the natural efficacy of a thing incited to motion or its perseverance in acting, once it is impressed.

(14) There are also many other things in that apologetic dissertation that are problematic, such as what he says in chapter 4, sec. 11, namely, assuming that motion is transferred from one ball through several intermediaries into another ball, the last ball is moved *by the same force* as the first. However, it seems to me that it is moved with equivalent force, but not by the same force. This might seem astonishing, but this happens because each and every thing pushed by a neighboring body pressing on it is put into motion by *its very own force*, namely by elastic force (I am not now discussing the cause of this elasticity, and I do not deny that it ought to be explained mechanically through the motion of a fluid existing in bodies and flowing through them). Also, what he says in sec. 12 will seem truly astonishing, that something that cannot begin motion in itself cannot continue that motion of its own accord. For, quite the contrary, it is well known that, just as force is necessary for producing motion, so too, once an impetus is given, far from requiring a new force for continuing the motion, one needs a force to stop it. For conservation by a universal cause necessary to things is not at issue here—a conservation which, as we have already warned, if it removed the efficacy of things, would also remove their existence.

(15) From this it again follows that the doctrine of occasional causes defended by several persons can lead to dangerous consequences (unless it is explained in such a way that certain moderating changes are brought to bear, as the distinguished Sturm admitted in part, and in part seems to be on the verge of admitting), though these consequences are, doubtless, unintended by its most learned defenders. For this view is so far from increasing the glory of God by removing the idol of nature that, quite the contrary, it seems with Spinoza to make of God the very nature of things, while created things disappear into mere modifications of the one divine substance, since that which does not act, which lacks active force, which is robbed of discriminability, robbed finally of all reason and basis for existing, can in no way be a

substance. I am most firmly persuaded that the distinguished Sturm, a gentleman outstanding in both piety and his teachings, is very far from conveying such thoughts. And so, there is no doubt that he will either show clearly how some substance or even some change remains in things on his doctrine, or he will surrender to the truth.

(16) Certainly many things make me suspect* all the more that his views are not sufficiently clear to me, nor mine to him. Somewhere he confessed to me that a certain *small part of the divine power* (that is, I should think, an expression, likeness, proximate effect of the divine power, since the divine force certainly cannot be divided into parts) can, and in fact in a certain way even ought, to be understood as belonging to things and attributed to things. (The material sent to me which he repeated in his *Physica Electiva* can be seen in the passage I cited above near the beginning of this essay.) If, as would appear from his words, this is to be understood in the sense in which we speak of the soul as a small part of the divine breath, then the disagreement between us up to this point is already removed. But the fact that I see him relate such a view hardly anywhere else, and I do not see him set forth its consequences, makes me less willing to attribute it to him. On the other hand, I observe that what he writes in numerous places is hardly consistent with this view, and also that the apologetic dissertation leads to things altogether different. To be sure, when, in certain letters, he first objected to my views on the inherent force, as expressed in the *Acta Eruditorum* of Leipzig in March 1694 (further illustrated by a specimen of my dynamics in the same Journal, April 1695), but having received my response, he soon judged kindly that we differ only in the way we express ourselves.[223] But when, taking note of this, I cautioned him about a few other things, he immediately turned in the other direction and cited many differences between us, differences which I acknowledge. But, having only just discounted these differences, he quite recently returned to writing, again, that any differences between us are only verbal, something that would have been most gratifying to me. Therefore, on the occasion of this latest apologetic dissertation, I wanted to set the matter out so that we can finally get clear about our views and their truth with greater ease. For, in general, this distinguished gentleman has both skill in perceiving and perceptiveness in setting things out, and so I might expect that no small light could be brought to bear on such an important issue through his application to it. Furthermore, I might expect that my labors would not therefore be useless to the extent that or because they might perhaps give him an opportunity to weigh and illuminate with his usual industriousness and power of judgment, several things of some importance in the present matter missed up until now by many authors, things, if I am not mistaken, I have filled out with new, more profound, and more broadly grounded axioms. From this, it seems, there could arise a restored and corrected system of philosophy, a

---

223. The first is "On the Correction of Metaphysics and the Concept of Substance," GIV, 468–70, translated in L 432–33; the second is part I of *A Specimen of Dynamics*, translated above.

philosophy midway between the formal and the material, a system that correctly joins and preserves both.

From the Letters to Johann Bernoulli (1698–99)[224]

A. Leibniz to Johann Bernoulli, August–September 1698(?) [excerpts]

WITH REGARD to the nature of body, I have often said (something which you don't seem to disapprove of) that all phenomena in bodies, even the force of elasticity, can be explained mechanically. But the principles of mechanism or of the laws of motion cannot be derived from the consideration of extension and impenetrability alone; and so there must be something else in bodies from whose modification conatus and impetus arise, as shapes arise from the modification of extension. By monad I understand a substance truly one, namely, one which is not an aggregate of substances. Matter in itself, or bulk [*moles*], which you can call primary matter, is not a substance; indeed, it is not an aggregate of substances, but something incomplete. Secondary matter, or mass [*massa*], is not a substance, but [a collection of] substances; and so not the flock but the animal, not the fish pond but the fish is one substance. Moreover, even if the body of an animal, or my organic body is composed, in turn, of innumerable substances, they are not parts of the animal or of me. But if there were no souls or something analogous to them, then there would be no I [*Ego*], no monads, no real unities, and therefore there would be no substantial multitudes; indeed, there would be nothing in bodies but phantasms. From this, one can easily judge that there is no part of matter in which monads do not exist.

B. Leibniz to Johann Bernoulli, 20/30 September 1698 [excerpts]

YOU ASK, first, how I understand matter in itself, that is, primary matter, or bulk [*moles*], as separated from secondary matter. I respond: it is that which is merely passive, and separated from souls or forms.

You ask, second, what is 'incomplete' for me here? I respond: it is the passive without the active, and the active without the passive.

(3) You ask me to divide for you a portion of mass [*massa*] into the substances of which it is composed. I respond, there are as many individual substances in it as there are animals or living things or things analogous to them. And so, I divide it in the same way one divides a flock or fish pond, except that I think that the fluid [i.e., air or water] that lies between the animals of the flock, or between the fishes, and also the fluid (indeed, any remaining mass

---

224. GM III 536–37, 541–42, 551–53, 560–61, 565. Latin.

[*massa*]) contained in any fish or animal, ought to be divided again as if it were a new fish pond, and so on to infinity.

(4) What I call a complete monad or individual substance [*substantia singularis*] is not so much the soul, as it is the animal itself, or something analogous to it, endowed with a soul or form and an organic body.

(5) You ask how far one must proceed in order to have something that is a substance, and not [a collection of] substances. I respond that such things present themselves immediately and even without subdivision, and that every animal is such a thing. For none of us is composed of the parts of our bodies.

(6) You fear that matter is composed of that which is not quantitative. I respond, it is no more composed of souls than it is composed of points.

C. Leibniz of Johann Bernoulli,
18 November 1698 [excerpts]

ON 1. When I said that *primary matter* is that which is merely passive and separated from souls or forms, I said the same thing twice; that is, for me to have said that it is merely passive is just the same as if I had said that it is separated from all activity. For forms are for me nothing but activities or entelechies, and substantial forms are primitive entelechies.

On 2. I chose to say that what is incomplete is the active without the passive and the passive without the active, rather than matter without form or *vice versa*, so that I might use things that are already explained rather than ones that must be explained, and so that I might, in a sense, make use of your advice before you give it, since most moderns are offended less by the word 'activity' than by 'form.'

On 3. We shouldn't pause over the Cartesians, who deny that there is anything in bodies analogous to the soul, since they have no reason for denying it, nor does it follow that what we can't *imagine* doesn't exist.

On 4. It has long seemed ridiculous to me to suppose that the nature of things has been so poor and stingy that it provided souls only to such a trifling mass of bodies on our globe, like human bodies, when it could have given them to all, without interfering with its other ends.

On 5. I hardly know how far the flint should be divided so that organic bodies (and therefore monads) might occur; but I readily declare that our ignorance on the matter has no effect on nature.

On 6. I think that there is no smallest animal or living thing, that there is none without an organic body, none whose body is not, in turn, divided into many substances. Therefore, one will never arrive at living points, that is, points endowed with forms.[225]

If you have a clear idea of a soul, you will also have a clear idea of a form; for it is of the same genus, though a different species.

---

225. This is in response to Bernoulli's claim that on his view, Leibniz is committed to the position that "an individual substance is a point with a form, not a quantity with a form, otherwise it could be divided into many substances" (GM III 546–47).

You quite rightly judge that what we don't perceive clearly and distinctly should not be rejected on that account.

Those good Cartesians, whatever they may boast about their clear and distinct perception, don't seem to me to perceive extension in this way.

Futhermore, if we conceive of the soul or form as the primary activity, from whose modification secondary forces arise as shapes arise from the modification of extension, then, I think, we take sufficient account of the intellect.

Indeed there can be no active modifications of that which is merely passive in its essence, since modifications limit rather than increase or add. And so beyond extension, which is the seat or principle of shapes, we ought to posit a seat or first subject of actions, namely a soul, a form, a life, a first entelechy, as I would like to call it.

I completely approve of your advice, that among Cartesians and the like, we should abstain from mentioning primary matter and substantial form, and be satisfied with mentioning mass, that is, something *per se* passive, and entelechy, that is, a primitive activity, soul, life.

You also rightly believe that all bodies in the world arise from the mixture of inherent forces; I do not doubt that these forces are coeval with matter itself, since I think that matter *per se* cannot persist without forces. However, I think that primitive entelechies, that is, lives, are different from dead forces. Dead forces perhaps always arise from living forces, as it appears from the fact that the conatus for receding from a center, which ought to be counted among dead forces, arises from the living force of rotation. But life or the primary entelechy is something more than some simple dead conatus; for I think that it contains perception and appetite, as in an animal, both corresponding to the present state of the organs.

You discuss and confirm what I have said, that changes do not happen through a leap, something entirely to my liking. Furthermore, I am not joking, but clearly admit, that there are animals in the world as much larger than ours are, as ours are larger than those tiny animals of the microscopists, for nature knows no boundary. And, on the other hand, there could be, indeed, there have to be, worlds not inferior in beauty and variety to ours in the smallest motes of dust, indeed, in tiny atoms. And (what could be considered even more amazing) nothing prevents animals from being transported to such worlds by dying, for I think that death is nothing but the contraction of an animal, just as generation is nothing but its unfolding.

D. Leibniz to Johann Bernoulli,
17 December 1698 [excerpt]

I DON'T SAY that bodies like flint, which are commonly called inanimate, have perceptions and appetition; rather they have something of that sort in them, as worms are in cheese. . . .

You rightly judge that the passive is never actually separated from the active in creatures. What God could have done, I don't venture to say. The passive alone and the vacuum seem, at least, incompatible with his wisdom, even if they aren't incompatible with his power. Neither is it certain that there are intelligences completely separated from bodies except for God. Many Church Fathers have also inclined to the contrary, attributing bodies to angels.

It can scarcely be doubted that God is pure act [*purus actus*], since he is most perfect. But imperfect things are passive, and if you conceive of them otherwise, you consider them only incompletely.

Man is a substance; his body or matter is [a collection of] substances. I would say the same about the living things which lie hidden in flint.

Just as we somehow conceive other souls and intelligences on analogy with our own souls, I wanted whatever other primitive entelechies there may be remote from our senses to be conceived on analogy with souls. I confess that they are not conceived perfectly.

It is hardly necessary for all souls and entelechies to be rational; those Cartesians who draw this conclusion seem to me to be very much overhasty in judging the unknown from the known.

I also readily admit that there are animals, taken in the ordinary sense, that are incomparably larger than those we know of, and I have sometimes said in jest that there might be a system like ours which is the pocketwatch of some enormous giant.

I think that I have indicated, and even publicly admitted, that entelechies, that is, atoms of substance, so to speak, cannot arise or perish naturally, and that even the destruction of an organic body is nothing but the shrinking [*involutio*] of its organs. From my view it follows that it is possible for a thing to be transported into a tiny system, where everything could be equally as good, indeed, could be even better than in ours. But I do not proceed beyond possibility. I don't approve of metempsychosis [i.e., the transference of a soul] into a new animal, but rather metamorphosis, the increase or decrease of the same animal. Furthermore, when I spoke about the origin of the soul or the changes in an animal, I clearly declared that I said nothing definite about the origin and state of the rational soul, and that the Kingdom of Grace has special laws, laws besides those by which the Kingdom of Nature is governed.

E. From Leibniz to Johann Bernoulli, 13/23 January 1699 [excerpts]

I CONFESS that there are parts in cheese in which there appear to be no worms. But what prevents there from being other smaller worms or plants in those parts in turn, or other organic things that are *sui generis*, and so *ad infinitum*, so that there would be nothing in the cheese free from such things? One can also say the same thing about the flint.

I don't say that the vacuum, the atom, and other things of this sort are impossible, but only that they are not in agreement with divine wisdom. For even if God were to produce only that which is in accordance with the laws of wisdom, the objects of power and of wisdom are different, and should not be confused. From an infinity of possibles, God chose, in accordance with his wisdom, that which is most appropriate. However, it is obvious that the vacuum (and likewise atoms) leaves sterile and uncultivated places, places in which something additional could have been produced, while preserving everything else. For such places to remain contradicts wisdom. I think that there is nothing sterile and uncultivated in nature, even if many things seem that way to us.

It can scarcely be doubted that entelechies have an origin common with other things. Moreover, they cannot be naturally produced *de novo*.

I confess that certain organs of animals, namely the gross ones, are destroyed and broken up. But I believe that something else always survives, so that the animal (shrunken, I allow) remains still endowed with the prior entelechy; for entelechies don't migrate from matter to matter and are never found without organs. . . .

I have dared say nothing about the human soul, as far as its origin and its state after death, since rational souls, that is, intelligences like ours, created in a special sense in the image of God, are governed by laws far different from those by which those lacking intellect are governed. For God's relation to spirits is not only like that of a craftsman to his work, but also like that of a prince to his subjects. But as for entelechies subject only to natural laws, as I have said, I believe that they are never entirely separated from all matter, once joined to it.

From the Letters to de Volder (1699–1706)[226]

A. Leibniz to de Volder, 24 March/3 April 1699 [excerpts]

I DON'T THINK that substance consists of extension alone, since the concept of extension is incomplete. And I don't think that extension can be conceived through itself, but I think it is a notion that is resolvable and relative. For it is resolvable into plurality, continuity, and coexistence, that is, the existence of parts at one and the same time. Plurality is also found in number, and continuity is also found in time and motion, but coexistence is really present alone in an extended thing. But from this it appears that a something must always be assumed which is either continued or diffused, as whiteness is in milk, color, ductility and weight are in gold, and resistance is in matter.[227] For continuity taken by itself (for extension is nothing but simultaneous continuity) no more constitutes a complete substance than does multitude or number, where there must be something numbered, repeated, and continued. And so I believe that our thought is completed and terminated

---

226. G II 169–72, 248–53, 268–70, 275–78, 281–83. Latin.

227. Alternatively, Leibniz may be saying that there must be a *suppositum* (in the Scholastic sense) which is contained or diffused, etc. See the discussion to section 8 of the "Discourse on Metaphysics," note 73, p. 40.

more in the notion of the dynamic than in that of extension, and one should seek no notion of power or force but that of an attribute from which change follows, change whose subject is the substance itself. And I don't see what might be escaping the intellect here. The nature of the business doesn't allow anything more explicit, like a picture, for instance. I think that the unity of an extended thing lies only in its having been abstracted, namely, when we withdraw the mind from the internal motion of the parts, by virtue of which each and every part of matter is, in turn, actually subdivided into different parts, something that plenitude [i.e., the fact that all place is occupied] does not prevent. The parts of matter don't differ only modally if they are sprinkled with souls and entelechies, things which always exist.

I noticed that somewhere in his letters Descartes also recognized inertia in matter, on the example of Kepler.[228] You deduce inertia from the force any given thing has for remaining in its state, something that doesn't differ from its very nature. So you judge that the simple concept of extension suffices even for this phenomenon. But the very axiom concerning the preservation of a state must be modified, since, for example, what moves in a curved path doesn't preserve its curvedness, but only its direction. But even if there is a force in matter for preserving its state, that force certainly cannot in any way be derived from extension alone. I admit that each and every thing remains in its state until there is a reason for change; this is a principle of metaphysical necessity. But it is one thing to retain a state until something changes it, which even something intrinsically indifferent to both states does, and quite another thing, much more significant, for a thing not to be indifferent, but to have a force and, as it were, an inclination to retain its state, and so resist changing. And so once, when a youth, in a certain booklet I published, holding matter to be indifferent, in and of itself, to motion and rest, I inferred from this that the largest body at rest ought to be moved by a colliding body, however small, without weakening the colliding body, and from this I inferred rules of motion abstracted from the system of things.[229] Such a world, at any rate possible, in which matter at rest obeys that which puts it in motion without any resistance [renisus] can indeed be imagined, but such a world would be merely chaos. And so, two things on which I always rely here, success in experience and the principle [ratio] of order, brought it about that I later came to see that God created matter in such a way that it contains a certain repugnance to motion, and, in a word, a certain resistance, by which a body opposes motion per se. And so, a body at rest resists every motion, and motion, indeed, resists greater motion, even in the same direction, so that it

228. Kepler held that bodies in motion tend to come to rest, and the feature of bodies that causes this is what he called *inertia*. Descartes rejected this view; for him, bodies in motion tend to remain in motion, as he argued in *Principles* II 37–38. But he did grant that there is a sense in which bodies may be said to have inertia, insofar as in collision, a body at rest must slow the moving body that sets it into motion. See AT II 466–67, 543–44, 627.

229. See the discussion of this early view and its abandonment in the "Specimen of Dynamics" above, pp. 117–38, and in the fragment on the nature of body and the laws of motion below, pp. 245–50.

weakens the force of the thing that impels it. Therefore, since matter resists motion *per se* by means of a general passive force of resistance, but is put into motion through a special force of action, that is, through the special force of an entelechy, it follows that inertia also resists through the enduring motion of the entelechy, that is, through a perpetual motive force. From this I showed (in the preceding letter) that a unified force is stronger, that is, that the force is twice as great if two degrees of speed are united in a one-pound body as it would be if the two degrees of speed were divided between two one-pound bodies, and thus that the force of a one-pound body moving with two degrees of velocity is twice as great as the force of two one-pound bodies moving with a single degree of velocity, since, although there is the same amount of velocity in both cases, in the one-pound body inertia hinders it only half as much. The inequality of forces between bodies of one and two pounds having velocities inversely proportional to their masses [*moles*] has been demonstrated in another way from our way of calculating forces, but it can also be elegantly derived from the consideration of inertia, so completely does everything harmonize. And so the resistance of matter contains two things, impenetrability or antitypy and resistance or inertia, and since they are everywhere equal in body or proportional to its extension, it is in these things that I locate the nature of the passive principle or matter. In just the same way I recognize a primitive entelechy in the active force exercising itself in various ways through motion and, in a word, something analogous to the soul, whose nature consists in a certain eternal law of the same series of changes, a series which it traverses unhindered. We cannot do without this active principle or ground of activity, for accidental or mutable active forces and motions themselves are certain modifications of a substantial thing, but forces and actions cannot be modifications of a thing merely passive, such as matter is. Therefore, it follows that there is a first or substantial active thing modified by the added disposition [*dispositio*] of matter, or that which is passive. As a result, secondary or motive forces and motion itself should be attributed to secondary matter, that is, to the complete body that results from the active and the passive.

And so, I come to the interaction between the soul, or any entelechy of an organic body, and the machine of organs. I am gratified that my hypothesis concerning this matter does not altogether displease you, a person of understanding and judgment. And indeed, you illustrate the point quite nicely, attributing to the soul an adequate idea of the corporeal machine; it is this very thing that I intend when I say that the nature of the soul is to represent the body. As a result, it is necessary that the soul represent to itself, in order, whatever follows from the laws of the body, some distinctly, others confusedly (namely those which involve a multitude of bodies); the former is to understand, the latter to sense. However, I think that we are in agreement that the soul is one thing, the idea of the body another. For the soul remains the same, while the idea of the body is constantly changing in accordance with the changes in body itself, whose present modifications it always displays. Of course, the idea of the present state of the body is always in the soul, but it is not simple, nor is it to any extent purely passive, but it is joined to a tendency [*tendentia*] to give rise to a new idea from a prior one, so that the soul is the source and ground of the different ideas of the same body, ideas that arise through a prescribed law. However, if you take the name 'adequate idea' in such a way that it signifies not that thing which is changed, but the persisting law of change itself, I do not oppose you. In that sense, I will say that the idea of body is in the soul, together with the phenomena which result from it.

B. Leibniz to de Volder, 20 June 1703 [excerpts]

I TURN FIRST to your earliest letter, in which you desire a necessary connection between matter (that is, resistance) and active force, so that they will not be joined gratuitously. But the cause of the connection is the fact that every substance is active, and every finite substance is passive, and resistance is connected to passivity [*passio*]. The nature of things therefore requires such a connection; nature cannot be so impoverished that it lacks a principle of action, and it doesn't allow a vacuum in forms any more than it allows one in matter—not to mention (for now) the fact that action and unity have the same sources.

I don't entirely approve of the doctrine of attributes which they are formulating today, as if a single simple and absolute predicate (which they call an attribute) constitutes a substance, for I don't find among notions any predicates that are entirely absolute, predicates that don't involve a connection with others. Certainly none are less so than those attributes, thought and extension, which they commonly put forward as examples, as I have often shown. Nor is a predicate the same as the subject unless it is considered concretely; and so the mind coincides with that which is thinking (even if not by definition [*formaliter*]), but not with thought. For the subject must contain, beside present thoughts, future and past ones as well.

You believe that those who place the distinction among bodies principally in what they think of as the modes of extension (as almost everyone does today) by excluding the vacuum don't disavow the view that bodies differ only modally. But two individual substances [*substantiae singulares*] should be distinguished more than modally. Futhermore, as things are commonly conceived, bodies can't even be distinguished modally. For, if you take two bodies, A and B, equal and with the same shape and motion, it will follow from such a notion of body, namely one derived from the putative modes of extension alone, that they have nothing by which they can be distinguished intrinsically. Is it therefore the case that A and B are not different individuals? Or is it possible that there are different things that cannot, in any way, be distinguished intrinsically? This and innumerable other things of this sort indicate that the true notions of things are completely turned on their heads by that new philosophy which forms substances from what is only material and passive. Things that differ ought to differ in some way, that is, have an intrinsic difference that can be designated; it is amazing that people have not made use of this most obvious axiom, along with so many others. But content to satisfy the imagination, people don't usually attend to reasons, and from this, many monstrosities have been introduced, contrary to the true philosophy. Indeed, they have made use only of notions that are incomplete and abstract or mathematical, notions which thought supports but which nature doesn't know, taken by themselves. Take, for example, the notion of time, likewise space or purely mathematical extension, the notion of purely passive mass [*massa*], of motion considered mathematically, etc. In these cases people can imagine things that are different without diversity, for example, two equal parts of a straight line, since, of course, a straight line is something incomplete and abstract—which must be considered for the sake of teaching [*doctrina*]. But in nature, every straight line is distinguished from every other by what it contains. Hence, in nature, there cannot be two bodies at the same time perfectly similar and equal. Also, things that differ in place must express their place, that is, they must express the things surrounding, and thus they must be distinguished not only by place, that is, not by an extrinsic denomination alone, as is commonly thought. Hence bodies, like the atoms of the Democriteans or the perfect globes of the Cartesians, cannot, as commonly understood, be found in nature,[230] nor are they anything but the incomplete thoughts of philosophers who have not inquired sufficiently well into the natures of things. Futhermore, in my most recent response to the distinguished Sturm, I have demonstrated by an invincible argument that, assuming a plenum, it is impossible that matter as commonly conceived, matter as formed of modifications of extension or passive mass [*massa*] alone (if you prefer), suffices for filling the universe, but rather it is plainly necessary that we posit something else in matter, at any rate, something from which we can get a principle of variation and a principle for distinguishing phenomena.[231] And thus, beside augmentation, diminution, and motion, we must have alteration, and so matter must be heterogeneous. However, I will not admit the generation and corruption of substance.

Now I proceed to your other letter. Although I say that a substance, even though corporeal, contains an infinity of machines, at the same time, I think that we must add that a substance constitutes one machine composed of them, and furthermore, that it is activated by one entelechy, without which there would be no principle of true unity in it. Moreover, I think that it is obvious from what I have said that evident necessity forces us to admit entelechies. Also, I don't see how one can have real entities and substances without having true unities. Arbitrary unities, which the mathematicians use, are not relevant here; they are applicable even to apparent entities, such as all entities by aggregation are, for example, a flock or an army, whose unity derives from thought. The same holds for any aggregate, since you will find nothing that is truly one if you take away the entelechy.

Properly and rigorously speaking, perhaps one cannot say that the primitive

---

230. The reference here is to Descartes's second element. See his *Principles of Philosophy* III 52, 75.
231. See "On Nature Itself," sec. 13, above pp. 163–65.

entelechy impels the mass of its body. Rather, it is joined with a primitive passive power that it completes, that is, with which it constitutes a monad, but it cannot really flow into other entelechies and substances, even those existing in the same mass. However, in the phenomena, that is, in the resulting aggregate, everything is explained mechanically, and masses are understood to impel one another. We need consider nothing but derivative forces in these phenomena, once it is agreed where they come from, namely, the phenomena of aggregates come from the reality of monads.

In my judgment an organic machine new to nature never arises, since it always contains an infinity of organs so that it can express, in its own way, the whole universe; indeed, it always contains all past and present times, something in the very nature of all substance. And it is agreed that whatever is expressed in the soul is also expressed in the body. Hence both the soul and the machine it animates, as well as the animal itself, are as indestructible as the universe itself. Because of this, such a machine cannot be constructed by any mechanism any more than it can be destroyed. No primitive entelechy whatsoever can ever arise or be destroyed naturally, and no entelechy ever lacks an organic body. As far as my consideration of these matters goes, these things could not be otherwise; they are not derived from our ignorance of the formation of fetuses, but from higher principles.

What I take to be the indivisible or complete monad is the substance endowed with primitive* power, active and passive, like the 'I' or something similar,[232] and not those derivative forces which are continually found first in one way and then another. But if there is nothing *truly one*, then every *true* thing will be eliminated. The forces which arise from mass and velocity are derivative and belong to aggregates, that is, to phenomena. And when I speak of the primitive force that persists, I don't understand the conservation of total motive power about which we were once concerned, but the entelechy that always expresses that total force, as well as other things. And indeed, derivative forces are only the modifications and resultants of the primitive forces.

Hence you understand, esteemed Sir, that corporeal substances cannot be constructed from derivative forces alone, that is, from vanishing modifications joined with resistance. Every modification presupposes something that endures. Therefore, when you say, "let us suppose that nothing is found in bodies except derivative forces," I respond that the hypothesis is not possible, and futhermore, that from that hypothesis comes error, since we substitute incomplete notions for the full concepts of things.

Properly speaking, I don't admit the action of substances on one another, since there appears to be no way for one monad to flow into another. But who

---

232. In a letter written to de Volder in 1699, Leibniz wrote: ". . . You understand something when the Cartesians speak of the human soul, which does not differ in kind from other entelechies. And so, to your first question, what is the active principle, I answer in the same way as I would to the question as to what the soul is, though I can respond a bit more distinctly. However, I see that preconception and authority can bring it about that many deny that they can understand what they seem to understand in Descartes." (G II 194).

would deny impact and impulse in the appearances of aggregates, which are certainly only phenomena (though grounded and regulated)? However, I also find it to be true in phenomena and derivative forces that masses don't give other masses new force, so much as they direct the force already existing in them, so that a body repels itself from another by its own force, rather than being propelled by the other.

Entelechies must necessarily differ, that is, they must not be entirely similar to each other. Indeed, they must be sources [*principia*] of diversity, for different ones express the universe differently, each from its own way of viewing things; it is their duty to be so many living mirrors of things, that is, so many concentrated worlds. However, it is correct to say that the souls of animals with the same name (like humans) are of the same species, not in the mathematical, but in the physical sense, the sense in which father and son are held to be of the same species.

If you take mass [*massa*] to be an aggregate containing many substances, you can, however, conceive in it one substance that is preeminent, if that mass makes up an organic body, animated by its primary entelechy. Furthermore, along with the entelechy, I don't put anything into the monad or the complete simple substance, but the primitive passive force, a force corresponding to [*relatus ad*] the whole mass [*massa*] of the organic body. The remaining subordinate monads placed in the organs don't constitute a part of the substance, but yet they are immediately required for it, and they come together with the primary monad in a corporeal substance, that is, in an animal or plant. Therefore I distinguish: (1) the primitive entelechy or soul; (2) the matter, namely, the primary matter or primitive passive power; (3) the monad made up of these two things; (4) the mass [*massa*] or secondary matter, or the organic machine in which innumerable subordinate monads come together; and (5) the animal, that is, the corporeal substance, which the dominating monad in the machine makes one.

You doubt, esteemed Sir, whether a thing that is one and simple is liable to change. But since only simple things are true things, what remain are only entities by aggregation; to that extent they are phenomena, and, as Democritus put it, exist by convention and not by nature. So it is obvious that unless there were change in simple things, there would be no change in things at all. Indeed, not even change can come from without, since, on the contrary, an internal tendency to change is essential to finite substance, and change could not arise naturally in monads in any other way. But in phenomena or aggregates, all new change derives from the collision of bodies in accordance with laws prescribed, in part, by metaphysics and, in part, by geometry, for abstractions are needed to explain things scientifically. Hence, in mass, we regard the individual parts as incomplete things, each contributing its own certain something, while we regard the whole mass as made up of the coming together of them all. And therefore, any body whatsoever is understood, in and of itself, to tend in a straight, tangent line, even if curvilinear motion results through the continual impressions of other things. But the substance, which is complete in itself and envelops everything, contains and expresses the way that curved line is brought about, since everything that will happen is also predetermined in the present state of a substance. Indeed, there is as much difference between substance and mass as there is between complete things, things as they are in themselves, and incomplete things, things as we grasp them through abstraction. In the phenomena we can define through abstraction whatever we want to ascribe to each part of mass, and everything can be distinguished and explained rationally, something that necessarily requires abstractions.

You seem to have quite nicely grasped my view on how every body whatsoever expresses everything else, and how every soul or entelechy whatsoever expresses both its body and, through it, everything else. But as soon as you have pondered the force of my view, you will see that I have said nothing that does not derive from it.

I said that extension is the order of coexisting possibles, and that time is the order of inconsistent possibilities. If this is so, you say that it astonishes you how time is found in everything, both spiritual and corporeal, but extension is found only in bodies. I respond that the reason is the same in both cases and for both sorts of things, namely, for all changes, of both spiritual and material things, there is a place, so to speak, in the order of succession, that is, in time, and for all changes, of both spiritual and material things, there is a place in the order of coexistents, that is, in space. For even if they are not extended, monads have a certain kind of situation in extension, that is, they have a certain ordered relation of coexistence to other things, namely, through the machine in which they are present. I think that no finite substances exist separated from every body, and to that extent they do not lack situation or order with respect to other coexisting things in the universe. Extended things contain many things endowed with situation. But things that are simple ought to be situated in extension, even if they don't have extension, though it may be impossible to designate it exactly, as, for example, we can do in incomplete phenomena.

C. Leibniz to de Volder, 30 June 1704 [excerpts]

. . . FROM THE FACT that a mathematical body cannot be resolved into first constituents we can, at any rate, infer that it isn't real, but something mental, indicating only the possibility of parts, not anything actual. Indeed, a mathematical line is like the arithmetical unit [i.e., the number 1]: for both, the parts are only possible and completely indefinite. A line is no more an aggregate of the lines into which it can be divided than the number 1 is an aggregate of the fractions into which it can be broken up. And just as a number that enumerates things is not a substance taken apart from the things that are counted, so a mathematical body, that is, extension, is not a substance without active and passive things, that is, without motion. But in real things, namely, in bodies, the parts are not indefinite (as they are in space, a mental thing), but are actually assigned in a certain way, in accordance with how nature has actually instituted divisions and subdivisions as a result of various motions; and although these divisions might proceed to infinity, nonetheless, everything results from certain first constituents, that is, real unities, though infinite in number. However, properly speaking, matter isn't composed of constitutive unities, but results from them, since matter, that is, extended mass [*massa*] is only a phenomenon grounded in things, like a rainbow or a parhelion, and all reality belongs only to unities. Thus, phenomena can always be divided into lesser phenomena, phenomena that can be seen by other smaller animals, and we will never arrive at the least phenomena. Substantial unities aren't really parts, but the foundations of phenomena.

I come now to your objection, esteemed Sir. "I conceive innumerable properties of mathematical body that are very evident," you say. I grant it, indeed, for number or time, which are also only orders or relations pertaining to the possibility and the eternal truths of things, orders or relations that are then to be applied to actual things as circumstances arise. You add: "I conceive of the mathematical body as existing and inhering in nothing else." This I don't grant, except in the way we conceive of time as existing or inhering in nothing else. If by the mathematical body you mean *space*, it must be compared with *time*; if you mean *extension*, it must be compared with *duration*. Indeed, *space* is only the order of existing for possibles that exist simultaneously, just as *time* is the order of existing for possibles that exist successively. And the state or series of things relates to time just as the physical body relates to space. Body and the series of things add motion to space and to time, that is, they add action and passion and their source [*principium*]. Indeed, as I have often reminded you (although you seem not to have noticed), extension is an abstraction from the extended thing, and it is no more a substance than number or multitude can be considered to be a substance; it represents only a certain nonsuccessive ([unlike] duration) and simultaneous diffusion or repetition of a certain nature, or what comes to the same thing, it represents a multitude of things of the same nature, existing simultaneously, with a certain order among themselves. It is this nature, I say, that is said to be extended or diffused. And so the notion of extension is relative, that is, extension is the extension of something, just as we say that a multitude or duration is a multitude of something or the duration of something. Furthermore, the nature which is supposed to be diffused, repeated, continued, is that which constitutes the physical body; it cannot be found in anything but the principle of acting and being acted upon [*patiendi*], since the phenomena provide us with nothing else. But what sort of thing this action or passion is, I will say later. So you see, if we undertake an analysis of notions, in the end we always reach the view I am pressing on you. It is not surprising that the Cartesians did not understand the nature of corporeal substance and did not penetrate to true principles as long as they accepted extension as something absolute, ineffable, unresolvable, and primitive. Indeed, considering only the imagination, and perhaps also eager for people's approbation, they wished to remain silent whenever the imagination stopped, even though they boasted otherwise that they had correctly distinguished that which is imaginable from that which is intelligible.

"By forces, I have always understood something not substantial, but which inheres in substance," you say. You are right, at any rate, when you understand changeable forces. But when force is taken for the principle of action and passion, and is therefore something modified through derivative forces, that is, something modified through that which is momentary in action, you can understand well enough from what has been said that this principle is bound up with the very notion of extension, a notion in and of itself relative, and that, as a consequence, in the end you must arrive at this same conclusion on your own analysis of corporeal substance. The same conclusion is even more apparent (as I showed above) through a consideration of the analysis of multitude and phenomena into unities and reality.

You add: "regarded without a foundation from which they flow, I have always considered forces as being like an external denomination." I prefer to consider derivative forces with respect to their foundation, as shape is considered with respect to extension, that is, as a modification. And you know from my method of calculation, the one with which I demonstrated *a priori* the true way of measuring (derivative) forces, that the force (as I claimed), multiplied by the time in which it is exerted, makes up action, and that, therefore, force is what is momentary in action, though it bears a relation to the succeeding state.[233] I have often said, and I do not remember having deviated from the view, that unless there is some active principle in us, there cannot be derivative forces and actions in us, since everything accidental or changeable ought to be a modification of something essential or perpetual, nor can it contain anything more positive than that which it modifies, since every modification is only a limitation, shape a limitation of that which is varied, and derivative force a limitation of that which brings about the variation.

You continue: "The very foundation which is to be in a thing is perhaps the same as that which you call the primitive forces, from which the derivative forces flow." I believe this is absolutely true. So it appears we agree here on this matter.

You suggest: "But how weak are powers of understanding, for of primitive forces I perceive nothing but the fact that you assert that all remaining mutations flow from them." But you are being overly modest, since you grasp the matter as well as its nature allows. For do you wish to imagine things that can only be understood, to see sounds and hear colors? And indeed, I believe that you don't deny what I asserted (that from it mutations flow); do you think that knowing this is knowing nothing?

Moreover, it is worthwhile to consider that this principle of action is most intelligible, since in it there is something analogous to what there is in us, namely perception and appetite. This is because the nature of things is uni-

---

233. See the fourth demonstration in the "Preliminary Specimen to the *Dynamics*" above, pp. 110–11.

form, and our substance cannot differ altogether from the other simple substances of which the whole universe consists. Indeed, considering the matter carefully, we must say that there is nothing in things but simple substances, and in them, perception and appetite. Moreover, matter and motion are not substances or things as much as they are the phenomena of perceivers, the reality of which is situated in the harmony of the perceivers with themselves (at different times) and with other perceivers.

D. Leibniz to de Volder,
1704 or 1705[234]

Y OUR LETTERS could not be more welcome to me, for they always either teach me something, or at least give me an opportunity to consider or set things out. You say that you noticed many surprising things in my most recent letters. But you will perhaps observe that the same views had already been suggested in previous letters, and only prejudice has prevented you from coming to this point some time ago and at long last stopping your search for substance and for the source of forces where it isn't to be found. And so, I was forced to impress certain of my views on you more explicitly, and to respond, if not to what you asked, at least to what you should have been asking. You say, "I had asked where the forces in corporeal substances flow from, but indeed you seem to eliminate bodies completely and place them in appearances [*visus*], and to substitute for things only forces, not even corporeal forces, but perception and appetite." I don't really eliminate body, but reduce [*revoco*] it to what it is. For I show that corporeal mass [*massa*], which is thought to have something over and above simple substances, is not a substance, but a phenomenon resulting from simple substances, which alone have unity and absolute reality. I relegate derivative forces to the phenomena, but I think that it is obvious that primitive forces can be nothing but the internal strivings [*tendentia*] of simple substances, strivings by means of which they pass from perception to perception in accordance with a certain law of their nature, and at the same time harmonize with one another, representing the same phenomena of the universe in different ways, something that must necessarily arise from a common cause. It is necessary that these simple substances exist everywhere and that they be self-sufficient (with respect to one another), since an influx of one into another is unintelligible, beyond the fact that such an influx is something placed in things for no purpose, and established by no argument. For, since everything ought to be deduced from the phenomena, by what evidence, I ask, might you prove that there is something real in things beyond these things, something substantial beside these substances, by which appearances that conform to the eternal laws of metaphysics and mathematics arise in things from themselves? Whoever adds anything to these brings nothing about, works vainly at explaining things, and will be faced by inextricable difficulties. And so the Academics have

---

234. The double brackets '[[...]]' contain material in Leibniz's copy not actually sent to de Volder.

argued, not altogether improperly, against what we imagine to be outside of us, that is, outside of souls or simple substances, even if they were improperly understood or used good arguments badly.[235] Indeed, everywhere and throughout everything, I place nothing but what we all acknowledge in our souls on many occasions, namely, internal and spontaneous changes. And so, with one stroke of mind, I draw out the entirety of things. Moreover, I also put corporeal forces where I put bodies, namely, among the phenomena, if they are understood as adding something over and above simple substances or their modifications. In just the same way a rainbow is not improperly said to be a thing, even though it is not a substance, that is, it is said to be a phenomenon, [[a real or well-founded phenomenon that doesn't disappoint our expectations based on what precedes]]. And indeed, not only sight but also touch has its phenomena. [[And corporeal masses [*massa*] are like entities of aggregation, things whose unity derives from perceiving.]]

In the *mass* [*massa*] *of extension*, or rather, of extended things, or, as I prefer, in the multitude of things, I say that there is *no unity*, but rather innumerable unities.

I did not say that "the corporeal universe is composed of one substance affected with an infinity of different modes," although it can be said that matter regarded in itself (that is, insofar as it is passive) is everywhere similar to itself. [[For it can be said that matter is real to the extent that, in simple substances, there is a reason for the passivity observed in phenomena.]] The true substance is not in the whole aggregate but in individual unities, just as in the ocean there is not one substance or one thing, but every drop contains other things, although every drop is assumed to be made of similar mass. However, even before it is formed into drops, the water is actually divided, as is the mass of ivory you proposed even before it is formed into statues; it is the same way in every mass. However, in mathematical extension, through which possibles are understood, there is no actual division nor any parts except those we make through thought, nor are there any first elements, any more than there is a smallest fraction, the element, as it were, for the rest. [[Hence number, hour, line, motion or degree of velocity, and other ideal quantities or mathematical entities of this sort are not really aggregated from parts, since there are no limitations at all on how anyone might wish to assign parts in them. Indeed, these notions must necessarily be understood in this way since they signify nothing but the mere possibility of assigning parts any way one likes.]]

If there were no divisions of matter in nature, there would be no things that are different; indeed there would be nothing but the mere possibility of things. It is the actual division into masses that really produces things that appear distinct, and this presupposes simple substances. Some believe (I think many commonly do) that, at some time, there was or could have been a certain matter or mass everywhere uniform and at rest, and that things arose from its division and, restored to rest, these things could return to it; but whoever

---

235. The reference here is to the Academic school of skeptics.

believes this greatly errs. Those who have minds possessed by such a crude picture give insufficient consideration not only to other matters, but especially to the fact that no basis for distinction in corporeal things would arise were that the case (something I once demonstrated to Sturm),[236] since if anyone were to imagine such a mass as being in motion, equivalents would always be substituted for one another. How remarkable it is that an opinion which overturns all of the phenomena could have gathered such support! How much less likely, however, that from such a mass, souls or perceiving things will arise, which are not only in us, but everywhere in things, as nature's uniformity in diversity will easily convince the wise. Those who imagine matter such as I have spoken of, who imagine such an origin of things from matter, grasp at shadows instead of things, and take extension, a thing in itself ideal, consisting in relation like number and time, for a substance, and fashion things from ideas, as from Pythagorean numbers. And even if we grant that impenetrability is added to extension, nothing complete is brought about on that account, nothing from which a reason for *motion*, and especially for the laws of motion, can be given, indeed, not even a reason for the apparent *difference* among things.

The *diffusion* that I conceive of in extension and that seems to have put into you the suspicion of some hidden paradox, I know not what, is, I claim, nothing but the continuity [*continuatio*] in which a part is similar to the whole, as, for example, we conceive of whiteness as diffused in milk, the same direction as diffused everywhere in a straight line, and equal curvedness as diffused in the circumference of a circle. But my unities, that is, my simple substances, are not diffused (as we commonly conceive of the flowing of a point), nor do they constitute a homogeneous whole, for the homogeneity of matter is brought about only through an abstraction of the mind, when it is considered as being only passive and therefore incomplete.

I thought that I had brought forward "the reason why derivative forces and actions presuppose something active" some time ago; certainly I brought it forward publicly in the response to Sturm.[237] I am glad that you now approve of it.

Individuals [*singularia*] involve infinity; in forming *universals* the soul only abstracts certain circumstances by concealing innumerable others. And so it is only in an individual that there is a notion so complete that it also includes all of its changes. A *spherical body* complete in all respects is nowhere in nature; the soul forms such a notion by concealing aberrations. And it is the same for any other shape that a finite mind can grasp, namely, such a shape can never exist exactly. The *essential ordering of individuals*, that is, their relation to *time and place*, must be understood from the relation they bear to those things contained in time and place, both nearby and far, a relation which must necessarily be expressed by every individual, so that a reader can read the universe in it, if he were infinitely sharp-sighted.

---

236. The reference here is to the argument in section 13 of "On Nature Itself" above, pp. 163–65.
237. The reference here is again to "On Nature Itself."

And finally you ask, "why are these appearances produced in me or in other true substances?" I say: those that follow are produced from the preceding appearances in accordance with metaphysical and mathematical laws of eternal truth. But the reason why there are any such appearances at all is the same as the reason why the universe exists. For you can easily see that the simple substances can be nothing but the sources and principles [[and, at the same time, the subjects]] of as many series of perception unraveling themselves in order, expressing the same universe of phenomena with the greatest order and variety. In this way the Supreme Substance has spread his perfection as widely as possible into the many substances that depend upon him, substances which must be conceived of as individual concentrations of the universe and (some more than others) as likenesses of divinity. I think that no other reasons for things can be understood nor, briefly, can they be hoped for; things ought to have existed either in this way or in no way at all.

E. Leibniz to de Volder, 19 January 1706

Y OU RIGHTLY despair of obtaining from me something, the hope for which I am not responsible for raising, something I neither hope for nor even desire. In the schools they commonly look for things which are not so much ultramundane as utopian. Recently the clever French Jesuit Tournemine supplied me with an elegant example of this. When he praised my preestablished harmony somewhat, which seemed to explain the agreement that we perceive between the soul and the body, he said that there is one thing he still desires, namely, the reason for the *union*, something that certainly differs from the agreement.[238] I answered that that metaphysical union, I know not what, that the schools add, over and above agreement, is not phenomenon, and we do not have any notion of it or acquaintance with it. And so I could not have intended to explain it.[239]

---

238. See the "Remark of the Author of the System of Pre-established Harmony" below, pp. 196–97.
239. In the first draft, the first paragraph of this letter continues as follows:

The situation is the same in those matters we are concerned with. I believe that that primitive or derivative force [*virtus*] which is conceived in extension or mass as outside of perceivers is not a thing but a phenomenon, as is extension itself, as well as mass and motion, which are things no more than an image in a mirror or a rainbow in a cloud are. But to seek something here beyond the phenomena, it seems to me, is just as if someone were to deny that he was satisfied with an explanation of the phenomena of an image, as if there were some unknown essence of the image that remained to be explained.

Arguments, in my judgment, can prove the existence of nothing but perceivers and perceptions (if you put aside their common cause), as well as the existence of those things which must be admitted in them, namely, in the perceiver, the passage from perception to perception while the same subject remains, and, in the perceptions, the harmony of the perceivers. We impose other things on nature and we then struggle with the chimeras of our mind, as with ghosts. In every perceiver there is active and passive force: active force in the passage to what is more perfect, passive force in its opposite. Moreover, perceivers are infinite in number, indeed, there are as many as there are simple substances or monads. Their order with respect to one another, clearly exhibited by our phenomena, gives rise to

I am afraid that that force, which is conceived in extension or mass [*moles*] as outside of perceivers or their phenomena, is of just this sort. For there can be nothing real in nature but simple substances and the aggregates that result from them. Moreover, we have acknowledged nothing but perceptions or their grounds [*rationes*] in these simple substances. Anyone who postulates more things must have marks by which they can be proved and revealed. As I have written several times (though I granted that everything is not yet organized in such a way that I easily place the demonstration before the eyes of others), I take it to have been demonstrated that it is essential to substance that its present state contain its future states and vice versa; we can derive neither force nor the reason for the passing to new perceptions from anywhere else.

It is also obvious from what I have said that, in actual things, there is only discrete quantity, namely a multitude of monads or simple substances, indeed, a multitude greater than any number you choose in every sensible aggregate, that is, in every aggregate corresponding to phenomena. But continuous quantity is something ideal, something that pertains to possibles and to actual things considered as possible. The continuum, of course, contains indeterminate parts. But in actual things nothing is indefinite, indeed, every division that can be made has been made in them. Actual things are composed as a number is composed of unities, but ideal things are composed of fractions: there are actually parts in a real whole, but not in an ideal whole. As long as we seek actual parts in the order of possibles and indeterminate parts in aggregates of actual things, we confuse ideal things with real substances and entangle ourselves in the labyrinth of the continuum and inexplicable contradictions. However, the science of continua, that is, the science of

---

the notions of time and space. That which results from the perceivers and limits the very phenomena produces, in general, the appearance [*idolum*] of mass [*moles*], *that is, the appearance of the passive force of bodies.*

Futhermore, although these things can be demonstrated once a subject whose perceptions change has been admitted, it is sufficient for me to assume what is usually conceded, that a perceiver has a certain ability [*vis*] to form new perceptions for himself from prior ones, which is to say that from some prior perception a new one sometimes follows. This, commonly acknowledged in some circumstances by philosophers both ancient and modern, namely, in the voluntary operations of the soul, this, I think, is found always and everywhere, and I think that it is sufficient to explain all the phenomena with great uniformity and simplicity among things.

Furthermore, you can easily understand from this that material substances are not eliminated, but conserved. However, we should look for them in that which is dynamic, something that reveals itself through the phenomena, that is, we should look for them in the active and passive force of perceivers, and not outside. However, extension, like time, mass [*moles*] and that which is made up of their variations, as well as motion, vanish into the phenomena, no less than real qualities do, and exist by convention [*nomos*] more than in reality [*physis*], as Democritus put it. The transitory and relative nature of motion also provides an adequate proof of this in another way, as does the notorious labyrinth of the continuum, in which we ourselves were entangled because of a false conception of time, space, and mass.

In real things there is only discrete quantity, that is, a multitude resulting from true unities. A continuous quantity, which is not merely apparent but exact, pertains to ideal things and possibilities since it involves something indefinite or indeterminate, which is not allowed by the actual nature of things.

possible things, contains eternal truths, truths which are never violated by actual phenomena, since the difference [between real and ideal] is always less than any given amount that can be specified. And we don't have, nor should we hope for, any mark of reality in phenomena, but the fact that they agree with one another and with eternal truths.

Letter to Queen Sophie Charlotte of Prussia, On What Is Independent of Sense and Matter (1702)[240]

John Toland (1670–1722), author of Christianity Not Mysterious *(1696), visited the courts of Hanover and Berlin around 1702, and took the opportunity to expound upon his empiricist and hermeticist views. Leibniz's pupil and friend, Queen Sophie Charlotte of Prussia (1668–1705), submitted one of Toland's letters to Leibniz for criticism. This started a brief three-cornered correspondence among Leibniz, Toland, and Queen Sophie Charlotte. In all probability, Leibniz's criticism of Toland was meant to apply to John Locke as well. See also the "Letter to Samuel Masson."*

I FOUND TRULY INGENIOUS and beautiful the letter that was sent some time ago from Paris to Osnabruck, which I recently read, at your command, in Hanover. And since it treats of two important questions, *whether there is something in our thoughts that does not arise from the senses*, and *whether there is something in nature that is not material*, questions about which, I admit, I do not entirely share the opinion of the author of the letter, I should like to be able to explain myself with the gracefulness equal to his, in order to obey your commands and to satisfy the curiosity of your majesty.

We use the external senses as a blind man uses his stick, following the comparison used by an ancient writer,[241] and they allow us to know their particular objects, which are colors, sounds, odors, flavors, and the tactile qualities. But they do not allow us to know what these sensible qualities are, nor what they consist in, for example, whether red is the rotation of certain small globes which, it is claimed, make up light, whether heat is a vortex of very fine dust, whether sound is produced in air as circles are in water when a stone is tossed in, as some philosophers claim. We do not see these things, and we cannot even understand why this rotation, these vortices, and these circles, if they are real, should bring about exactly the perceptions we have of red, heat, and noise. Thus it can be said that *sensible qualities* are in fact *occult qualities*, and there must be others *more manifest* that can render them more understandable. Far from understanding only sensible things, it is

---

240. G VI, 499–508. French.
241. The reference is to a view that seems to have been held by certain Stoics. See, e.g., the accounts in Diogenes Laertius, *Lives of the Eminent Philosophers* VII 157 (Loeb ed., Vol. II, p. 261), and Galen, *De Placitis*, 7.7.

precisely these we understand the least. And although they are familiar to us, we do not understand them any better for it, just as a pilot does not understand the nature of the magnetic needle that turns toward the north any better than anyone else does, though it is always before his eyes in the compass, and as a result, it hardly astonishes him.

I do not deny that many discoveries have been made about the nature of these occult qualities; for example, we know what kind of refraction produces blue and yellow, and that the mixing of these two colors produces green. But for all this we do not yet understand how the perception we have of these three colors results from these causes. Also, we do not even have nominal definitions of such qualities, definitions by which to explain the terms. The purpose of nominal definitions is to give marks sufficient for recognizing things. For example, assayers have marks by which they distinguish gold from any other metal, and even if a person had never seen gold, he can be taught these infallible marks for recognizing it, should he encounter it one day. But it is not the same with these sensible qualities. For example, one cannot give marks for recognizing blue, if one has not seen it. Hence, blue is its own mark, and in order for someone to know what blue is, we must necessarily show it to him.

It is for this reason that it is usually said that the *notions* of these qualities are *clear*, for they help us to recognize the qualities, but that these same notions are not *distinct*, because we can neither distinguish nor unfold what they contain. What we perceive is a *something I know not what*, but a something for which we cannot give an account. On the other hand, we can make another person understand what the thing is when we have a description or nominal definition, even though we do not have the thing at hand to show him. Yet we must do justice to the senses by acknowledging that, besides these occult qualities, they allow us to recognize other, more manifest, qualities which furnish us with more distinct notions. These are the notions we attribute to the *common sense* because there is no external sense to which they are particularly attached and belong. It is here that definitions of the terms or words we use can be given. Such is the idea of *number*, which is found equally in sounds, colors, and tactile qualities. It is in this way that we also perceive *shapes* which are common to colors and tactile qualities, but which we do not observe in sounds. However, it is true that in order to conceive numbers, and even shapes, distinctly, and to build sciences from them, we must have recourse to something which the senses cannot provide and which the understanding adds to the senses.

Therefore, since our soul compares the numbers and shapes that are in color, for example, with the numbers and shapes that are in tactile qualities, there must be an *internal sense* in which the perceptions of these different external senses are found united. This is called *imagination*, which contains both the *notions of the particular senses*, which are *clear but confused*, and the *notions of the common sense*, which are *clear and distinct*. And these clear and distinct ideas, subject to imagination, are the objects of the *mathematical sciences*, namely arithmetic and geometry, which are *pure* mathematical sciences, and the objects of these sciences as they are applied to nature, which make up applied [*mixtes*] mathematics. We also see that particular sensible qualities are capable of being explained and reasoned about only insofar as they contain what is common to the objects of several external senses, and belong to the internal sense. For those who attempt to explain sensible qualities distinctly always have recourse to the ideas of mathematics, and these ideas always contain *magnitude*, or multitude of parts. It is true that the mathematical sciences would not be demonstrative and would consist only in simple induction or observation (which would never assure us the perfect generality of the truths found there) if something higher, something that intelligence alone can provide, did not come to the aid of *imagination* and *senses*.

Therefore, there are objects of still another nature which are not in any way included in what we notice among the objects of either the particular senses or common sense, and which, consequently, are not objects of the imagination, either. Thus, besides the *sensible* and the *imaginable*, there is that which is only *intelligible*, the *object of the understanding alone*; and such is the object of my thought when I think of myself.

The thought of *myself*, who perceives sensible objects, and the thought of the action of mine that results from it, adds something to the objects of the senses. To think of some color and to consider that one thinks of it are two very different thoughts, just as much as color itself differs from the "I" who thinks of it. And since I conceive that other beings can also have the right to say "I", or that it can be said for them, it is through this that I conceive what is called *substance* in general. It is also the consideration of myself that provides me with other notions of *metaphysics*, such as cause, effect, action, similarity, etc., and even those of *logic* and *ethics*. Thus it can be said that there is nothing in the understanding that did not come from the senses, except the understanding itself, or that which understands.

Therefore, there are three levels of notions: *those that are only sensible*, which are the objects attributed to each sense in particular; *those that are both sensible and intelligible*, which belong to the common sense, and *those that are only intelligible*, which belong to the understanding. Those in the first and second level are both imaginable, but those in the third are above the imagination. Those in the second and third are intelligible and distinct; but those in the first are confused, although they are clear or recognizable.

Being itself and *truth* are not known wholly through the senses. For it would not be impossible for a creature to have long and orderly dreams resembling our *life*, such that everything it believed it perceived by the senses was nothing but mere *appearances*. There must therefore be something beyond the senses which distinguishes the true from the apparent. But the truth of the demonstrative sciences is exempt* from these doubts, and must even serve to judge the truth of sensible things. For, as able ancient and modern philosophers have already remarked, even if everything I believed I saw were only a dream, it would always still be true that I (who in dreaming thinks) would be something, and would, in fact, think in many ways, for which there must always be some reason.

Thus, what the ancient Platonists have remarked is very true, and very worthy of consideration, that the existence of intelligible things, and particularly of this I who thinks and is called mind or soul, is incomparably more certain than the existence of sensible things, and thus, that it would not be impossible, speaking with metaphysical rigor, that, at bottom, there should only be these intelligible substances, and that sensible things should only be appearances. However, our lack of attention lets us take sensible things for the only true things. It is also worth observing that, if in dreaming I should discover some demonstrative truth, mathematical or otherwise (as, in fact, can be done), it would be as certain as if I had been awake. This allows us to see the extent to which intelligible truth is independent of the truth or the existence of sensible and material things outside of us.

This conception of *being* and *truth* is, therefore, found in this I and in the understanding, rather than in the external senses and in the perception of external objects.

We also discover there what it is to affirm, deny, doubt, will, and act. But above all, we find there the *force of the conclusions* of reasoning, which are part of what is called the *natural light*. For example, from the premise *no wise man is vicious*, one can, by converting the terms, derive the conclusion that *no vicious man is wise*. Whereas from the premise *every wise man is praiseworthy*, it cannot be concluded, by conversion, that *every praiseworthy man is wise*, but only that *some praiseworthy man is wise*. Even though particular affirmative propositions can always be converted—for example, if some wise man is rich, it must be the case that some rich man is wise—this cannot be done with particular negative propositions. For example, we may say that there are charitable men who are not just, which happens when the charity is somewhat irregular, but we cannot infer from this that there are just men who are not charitable; for charity and the rule of reason are included at the same time in justice.

It is also by this *natural light* that the *axioms* of mathematics are recognized, for example, that if we take away the same quantity from two equal things, the things remaining are equal; similarly, that if everything is equal on both sides of a balance, neither side will incline—a thing we can easily predict without ever having experienced it. And it is on such foundations that we establish arithmetic, geometry, mechanics, and other demonstrative sciences, where the senses are indeed necessary for having certain ideas of sensible things, and experience is necessary for establishing certain facts, and even useful for verifying our reasonings as by a kind of proof. But the force of the demonstrations depends upon intelligible notions and truths, which alone are capable of allowing us to judge what is necessary. In the conjectural sciences they are even capable of demonstratively determining the degree of probability, given certain assumptions, so that we may reasonably choose, among opposing appearances, the one which is most probable. But this part of the art of reasoning has not yet been developed as much as it should be.

But, to return to *necessary truths*, it is generally true that we know them only by this natural light, and not at all by the experiences of the senses. For the senses can, in some way, make known what there is, but they cannot make known what must be or what cannot be otherwise.

For example, although we have experienced countless times that heavy bodies fall toward the center of the earth, and are not sustained in the air, we are not certain that this is necessary as long as we do not understand the reason for it. Thus we cannot be certain that the same thing would happen in the air at a higher altitude, at a hundred or more leagues above us. There are philosophers who imagine that the earth is a magnet, and since an ordinary magnet does not attract a needle when it is a little removed from it, they think that the attractive force of the earth does not go much farther, either. I do not say that they are right, but only that one cannot proceed with much certainty beyond one's experiences when not aided by reason.

That is why geometers have always held that what is proved by *induction* or by example in geometry or in arithmetic is never perfectly proved. For example, experience teaches us that the odd numbers continually added together in order produce in order the perfect squares, that is, the numbers that come from multiplying a number by itself. Thus 1 and 3 make 4, that is, 2 times 2; and 1 and 3 and 5 make 9, that is, 3 times 3; and 1 and 3 and 5 and 7 make 16, that is, 4 times 4; and 1 and 3 and 5 and 7 and 9 make 25, that is, 5 times 5; and so forth.

However, if one tried a hundred thousand times, extending the calculation very far, one might well reasonably judge that this will always turn out. But one can never be absolutely certain of this unless one learned the demonstrative reason for it, something mathematicians discovered long ago. And on the grounds of the uncertainty of induction, but carried a little too far, an Englishman has lately attempted to maintain that we can avoid death. For, he said, from the fact that my father, grandfather, and great-grandfather have died, and so have all the others who have lived before us, it cannot be inferred that we too will die.[242] For their death has no influence on us. The problem with this reasoning is that we resemble them a little too much, insofar as the causes of their death also exist in us. So, similarity is insufficient for drawing consequences with certainty, without the consideration of the same reasons.

In fact, there are *experiments* that succeed countless times, and ordinarily succeed, yet in some extraordinary cases we find that there are *instances* where the experiment does not succeed. For example, even after having experienced a hundred thousand times that iron placed on the surface of water sinks to the bottom, we are not assured that this must always happen. And without having recourse to the miracle of the prophet Elisha, who made iron float, we know that one can make an iron pot so hollow that it floats, and can even carry a considerable weight, as do boats of copper and tin. Even abstract sciences like geometry provide cases in which what happens ordinarily no

---

242. David Norton has suggested that the writer in question is John Asgill (1659–1738), who in 1700 published a pamphlet entitled *An argument proving that according to the covenant of eternal life revealed in the scriptures, man may be translated from hence, into that eternal life, without passing through death.*

longer happens. For example, one finds ordinarily that two lines that continually approach finally intersect, and many people would be ready to swear that this could not be otherwise. However, geometry provides extraordinary lines, called *asymptotes* for this reason, that when extended to infinity approach continually and yet never intersect.

This consideration also shows that there is *an inborn light within us*. For since the senses and induction can never teach us truths that are fully universal, nor what is absolutely necessary, but only what is, and what is found in particular examples, and since, nonetheless, we know some universal and necessary truths in the sciences, a privilege we have over the beasts, it follows that we have derived these truths, in part, from what is within us. Thus one can lead a child to them in the way Socrates did, by simple questions, without telling him anything, and without having him experiment at all about the truth of that which is asked of him. And this can very easily be carried out with numbers and other similar matters.

Yet I agree that, in the present state, the external senses are necessary for our thinking, and that if we did not have any, we would not think. But that which is necessary for something does not, for all that, constitute its essence. Air is necessary for our life, but our life is something other than air. The senses provide us material for reasoning, and we never have thoughts so abstract that something from the senses is not intermixed with them; but reasoning requires something else besides that which is sensible.

As for the *second question*, whether there are *immaterial substances*, to answer it one must first explain what one means. Up until now matter has been understood to include only purely passive and indifferent notions, namely, extension and impenetrability, which need to be given some determinate form or activity [*action*] by something else. Thus when one says that there are immaterial substances, one means that there are substances which include other notions, namely, perception and the principle of action or of change, notions that cannot be explained either by extension or by impenetrability. When these beings have sensation they are called *souls*, and when they are capable of reason they are called *minds*. Thus, if someone says that force and perception are essential to matter, he is taking matter as the complete corporeal substance, which includes form and matter, or soul together with organs. It is as if he said that there are souls everywhere. This could be true and would not be contrary to the doctrine of immaterial substances. For this doctrine does not require that these souls be outside matter, but only that they be something more than matter and not produced or destroyed by the changes which matter undergoes, or be subject to dissolution, since they are not composed of parts.

Yet it must also be admitted that there is some *substance separate from matter*. For this we need only consider that there is an infinity of possible modes [*façons*] that all matter could have received, instead of the sequence of variations which it actually received. It is clear, for example, that stars could have moved otherwise, since space and matter are indifferent to every kind of motion and shape.

Therefore, the reason or universal determining cause that makes things be, and makes them be this way and not otherwise, must be outside matter. And even the existence of matter depends on it, since in its notion we do not find that it carries with it a reason for its own existence.

Now, this ultimate reason for things, common to all and universal because of the connection between all parts of nature, is what we call *God*, who must necessarily be an infinite and absolutely perfect substance. I am inclined to think that all finite immaterial substances (even the genii or angels according to the opinion of the old Church Fathers) are joined to organs and accompany matter; I am even inclined to think that souls or active forms are found everywhere. And in constituting a complete substance, matter cannot do without them, since force and action are found everywhere, and since the laws of force depend upon some marvelous principles of metaphysics or upon intelligible notions, and cannot be explained by material notions or the notions of mathematics alone or by those falling under the jurisdiction of imagination.

Perception cannot be explained by a mechanism either, whatever it may be. One can therefore conclude that there is also something immaterial everywhere in created things, and particularly in us, where force is accompanied by a perception that is sufficiently distinct, and also by that light which I spoke of above. This makes us resemble God in a small way, as much through our knowledge of order as through the order we ourselves can give to things within our grasp, in imitation of the order God gives the universe. It is also in this that our *virtue* and perfection consists, just as our *felicity* consists in the pleasure we take in it.

And since every time we penetrate to the bottom of things we find there the most beautiful order that can be desired, surpassing even what we expected, as all those who have worked in the sciences know, we can conclude that it is the same for everything else, and that not only do immaterial substances always exist, but also that their lives, progress, and changes are directed toward a definite end, or rather, directed so as to approach an end more and more, as asymptotes do. And although we sometimes slip back, as do lines that turn away, the advance must finally prevail and win.

The natural light of reason is insufficient to let us know the details of this, and our experiences are too limited to let us glimpse the laws of this order. However, the revealed light guides us through faith. But there is room to believe that in the future we will know more by experience itself, and that there are minds that already know more of this than we do.

However, philosophers and poets, lacking this knowledge, have thrown themselves into the fictions of metempsychosis or the Elysian Fields to provide some ideas which might make an impression on the common folk. But the consideration of the perfection of things, or, what is the same, of the supreme power, wisdom, and goodness of God, who does everything for the best, that is, with the greatest order, is sufficient to make all reasonable people content, and to convince them that contentment should be greater to the extent that we are disposed to follow order or reason.

Letter to Coste, on Human Freedom
(19 December 1707)[243]

Late in his life, Leibniz tried to establish his ideas in England through a correspondence with such figures as Lady Masham, Thomas Burnett, and Pierre Coste (see the section on Locke, especially the Preface to the New Essays*). Coste was very useful for that purpose, since, as the translator of various English authors (Locke, Shaftesbury, and others), he maintained good communications across the Channel.*

I THANK YOU very much for forwarding Mr. Locke's latest additions and corrections, and I am also very pleased to learn about his last dispute with Mr. Limborch. The freedom of indifference on which this dispute turned, and about which you asked my opinion, contains a certain subtlety that few take care to understand, although many people reason about it. It reduces to the consideration of necessity and contingency.

A truth is *necessary* when its opposite implies a contradiction; and when it is not necessary, it is called *contingent.* That God exists, that all right angles are equal to one another, etc., are necessary truths, but that I exist and that there are bodies in nature that actually appear to have right angles are contingent truths. For the whole universe could have been made otherwise, since time, space, and matter are absolutely indifferent to motions and to shapes, and God has chosen from an infinity of possibles that which he judged most suitable.

But once he has chosen, we must confess that everything is included in his choice and that nothing can be changed, since he has foreseen and regulated everything once and for all, for he would not regulate things by bits and pieces. Consequently, sins and evils, which he has judged permissible in order to allow greater goods, are included in some way in his choice. It is this necessity that we can now attribute to things to come, a necessity which we call *hypothetical* or *consequential,* that is, necessity based on a consequence of the hypothesis of the choice made. This necessity does not destroy the contingency of things and does not produce the absolute necessity that contingency cannot allow. And almost all theologians and philosophers (that is, except the Socinians) acknowledge the hypothetical necessity I have just explained and acknowledge that we cannot oppose it without upsetting God's attributes and the very nature of things.

However, although all facts of the universe are now certain with respect to God, or (what comes to the same thing) determined in themselves and even linked among themselves, it does not follow that their interconnection is always truly necessary, that is, that the truth which asserts that one fact

---

243. Editors' title. G III 400–4. French.

follows from another is necessary. And it is this fact we must especially apply to the case of voluntary actions.

When we present a choice to ourselves, for example, whether to leave or not to leave, given all the internal or external circumstances, motives, perceptions, dispositions, impressions, passions, inclinations taken together, there is a question as to whether I am still in a state of contingency, or whether I make the choice to leave, for example, by necessity—that is, whether in fact this true and determined proposition, that *in all these circumstances taken together, I will choose to leave*, is contingent or necessary. I reply that it is contingent, because neither I nor any other more enlightened mind could demonstrate that the opposite of this truth implies a contradiction. And assuming that by *freedom of indifference* we understand a freedom opposed to necessity (as I have just explained), I agree about this freedom. For, I am actually of the opinion that our freedom, as well as that of God and the blessed spirits, is not only exempt from coercion, but also from absolute necessity, even though it cannot be exempt from determination and certainty.

But I find that we need to be very cautious here so that we do not fall into a chimera which shocks the principles of good sense, namely, what I call an *absolute indifference* or *indifference of equilibrium*, an indifference that some people imagine freedom to involve, and that I believe to be chimerical. We must therefore consider that this interconnection about which I have just spoken is not necessary, absolutely speaking, but that it is certainly true, nevertheless, and that, in general, every time that the circumstances, taken together, tip the balance of deliberation more on one side than on the other, it is certain and infallible that the former side will be chosen. God or a perfectly wise person will always choose the best that they know of, and if one side were not better than the other, they would choose neither the one nor the other. The passions often take the place of reason in other intelligent substances, and we can always assert, with respect to the will in general, that *choice follows the greatest inclination* (by which I understand both passions and reasons, true or apparent).

However, I see that there are people who imagine that sometimes we set ourselves for the lesser option, that God sometimes chooses the lesser good, everything considered, and that a person sometimes chooses without grounds [*sujet*] and against all his reasons, dispositions, and passions, and finally, that we sometimes choose without any reason determining the choice. But I hold that to be false and absurd, because one of the greatest principles of good sense is that nothing ever happens without a cause or determining reason. Thus when God chooses, it is by reason of the best, and when a person chooses, it is the option that struck him the most. If he chooses what he sees as less useful and pleasant in some respects, perhaps it becomes more agreeable to him through a whim, or contrariness, or for similar reasons which belong to a depraved taste; these are determining reasons, even though they are not conclusive reasons. And we will never be able to find a contrary example.

Thus, although we have a freedom of indifference which saves us from necessity, we never have an indifference of equilibrium which exempts us from determining reasons. There is always something which inclines us and makes us choose, but without being able to necessitate us. And just as God is always infallibly led to the best, even though he is not led to it necessarily (other than by a moral necessity), we are always infallibly, but not necessarily, led to what strikes us the most; since the contrary does not imply any contradiction, it was neither necessary nor essential that God created, nor that he created this world in particular, even though his wisdom and goodness led him to it.

That is what Mr. Bayle, subtle as he was, did not consider well enough when he held that a case similar to Buridan's ass was possible, and that a man placed in circumstances of perfect equilibrium could nevertheless choose. For we must say that the case of a perfect equilibrium is chimerical, and never happens, since the universe is incapable of being divided or split into two equal and similar parts. The universe is not like an ellipse or other such oval, where a straight line drawn through its center can cut it into two congruent parts. The universe has no center, and its parts are infinitely varied; thus the case never arises in which everything is perfectly equal and strikes equally on all sides. And although we are not always capable of perceiving all the small impressions that contribute to determining us, there is always something that determines us [to choose] between two contradictories, without the case ever being perfectly equal on all sides.

However, although our choice *ex datis*, with respect to all internal and external circumstances taken together, is always determined, and although, for the present, we cannot alter our will, it is true, nevertheless, that we have great power with respect to our future volitions, by choosing to be attentive to certain objects and by accustoming ourselves to certain ways of thinking. In this way we can accustom ourselves to resist impressions better and have our reason behave better, so that we can contribute to making ourselves will what we should. Moreover, I have also shown that when we take things in a certain metaphysical sense, we are always in a state of perfect spontaneity, and that what we attribute to the impressions of external things arises only from confused perceptions in us corresponding to them, perceptions that cannot fail to be given to us from the first in virtue of pre-established harmony, which relates each substance to all the others.

If it were true, sir, that your Cevennois were prophets, this circumstance would not be contrary to my hypothesis of pre-established harmony, indeed, it would strongly agree with it.[244] I have always said that the present is pregnant with the future, and that there is a perfect interconnection between things, no matter how distant they are from one another, so that someone who is sufficiently acute could read the one from the other. I would not even oppose someone who maintains that there are spheres in the universe in which prophecies are more common than in ours, just as there might be a world in which dogs have noses sufficiently acute to smell their game at 1,000 leagues;

---

244. Cf. G III 393, where Coste refers to Cevennois rebels against Louis XIV who prophesized and spoke in tongues.

perhaps there may also be spheres in which genii have greater leave than they have here below to interfere with the actions of rational animals. But when it is a question of reasoning about what actually happens here, our presumptive judgment must be based on what is usual in our sphere, where these kinds of prophetic views are extremely rare. We cannot swear that there are no such prophets, but, it seems to me, it is a good bet that those in question aren't. One of the reasons that could best lead me to judge favorably with respect to them would be Mr. Fatio's judgment, but we would need to know what he judges, without getting it from a newspaper. If you yourself have observed, with all due attention, a gentleman with a yearly income of two thousand pounds sterling who prophesies well in Greek, Latin, and French, although he only knows English well, there would be nothing to criticize. Thus I beg you to send me some more information about this very curious and important matter; I zealously await your response, etc.

Remark of the Author of the System of Pre-established Harmony on a Passage from the Mémoires de Trévoux of March 1704 (1708)[245]

This piece is in response to a criticism found in René-Joseph de Tournemine, "Conjectures sur l'Union de l'Ame et du Corps," published in Mémoires pour l'Histoire des Sciences et des Beaux Arts *(commonly known as the* Mémoires de Trévoux*), May 1703, pp. 864–75. Tournemine had objected to pre-established harmony as an account of mind-body unity. Referring to the two-clock example Leibniz often used to illustrate pre-established harmony, Tournemine noted: "Thus correspondence, harmony, does not bring about either union or essential connection. Whatever resemblance one might suppose between two clocks, however justly their relations might be considered perfect, one can never say that the clocks are united just because the movements correspond with perfect symmetry "(pp. 869–70). For the two-clock example, see also the "Postscript to a Letter to Basnage de Beauval." The date in Leibniz's title probably refers to the date on which the issue actually appeared.*

FATHER TOURNEMINE has spoken of me so obligingly in one of his *Conjectures* presented in the *Mémoires de Trévoux* (conjectures which are, in general, ingenious) that it would be wrong of me to complain that he attributes to me an objection against the Cartesians which I do not remember having made, an objection which can clearly be turned against me. However, I declare that if I did ever make it, I renounce it from now on, and would have made the following assertion instead, if I had not been so tardy in noticing the passage from the *Mémoires*.

---

245. G VI 595–96. French.

I must admit that it would have been very wrong of me to object to the Cartesians that the agreement God immediately maintains, between soul and body, according to them, does not bring about a true union, since, to be sure, my pre-established harmony would do no better than it does.

My intent was to explain naturally what they explain by perpetual miracles, and I tried to account only for the phenomena, that is, for the relation that is perceived between soul and body.

But since the metaphysical union one adds is not a phenomenon, and since no one has ever given an intelligible notion of it, I did not take it upon myself to seek a reason for it.

However, I do not deny that there is something having this nature. Its nature would be something almost like that of *presence*, whose notion has also not yet been explained when applied to incorporeal things, and which is distinguished from the *relations of harmony* that accompany it, which are also *phenomena* capable of marking the *location* of incorporeal things.

After having conceived of a union and a presence in material things, we judge that *there is something I know not what analogous* in immaterial things. But to the extent that we cannot conceive those notions further than this, we have only obscure notions of them.

This is as it is with respect to the *Mysteries*. There we also attempt to *elevate* what we conceive in the ordinary course of creatures to something more sublime, something that can correspond to those mysteries with regard both to nature and to divine power, without being able to conceive anything in them distinct enough and sufficiently characteristic of them to form an intelligible definition of the whole.

This is also why we cannot perfectly account for the Mysteries, nor completely understand them here below. There is something more to them than simple words; however, we do not have anything by which we can arrive at an exact explanation of the terms.[246]

From the Letters to Des Bosses (1712–16)[247]

Leibniz first met the Jesuit theologian and mathematician Bartholomaeus Des Bosses in January 1706. They soon were to start an important correspondence that was to last to the end of Leibniz's life. Although they discussed numerous subjects, the correspondence is most important for the lengthy and detailed discussions of the metaphysical status of body that begins in the letters of 1712. Indeed, these letters contain, by far, the most detailed account of corporeal substance in Leibniz's later writings. In these letters, and apparently only in these letters, Leibniz introduces the notion of a substantial chain to explain how

---

246. A brief paragraph on another issue that appeared in the *Mémoires* concerning the history of the invention of the calculus has been omitted from the translation.
247. G II, 435–36, 438–39, 444, 515–21. Latin.

simple substances can come together and compose a genuine composite
substance.

I READ your discussion of corporeal substance with great pleasure. If a corporeal substance is something real, over and above monads, just as a line is held to be something over and above points, then we will have to say that corporeal substance consists in a certain union, or better, in a real unifying thing that God superadds to the monads. Primary matter, namely, that which is required for extension and antitypy, that is, for diffusion and resistance, arises from the union of the passive power of the monads, and from the union of the monadic entelechies arises substantial form. But what can arise in this way can also be destroyed, and it will be destroyed when that union ceases to exist, unless it is miraculously preserved by God. Furthermore, such a form will not be a soul, which is a simple and indivisible substance. This form (and thus this matter as well) is in perpetual flux, since one can't really designate any point in matter that stays in the same place for more than a moment and that doesn't recede from neighboring things as much as you like. But a soul stays the same in its changes by remaining the same subject. However, the situation is quite different in a corporeal substance. And so one must say one of the following two things: either bodies are mere phenomena, and so extension will also be only a phenomenon and the monads alone will be real, the union will be provided by the operation of the perceiving mind on the phenomena, or, if faith compels us to accept corporeal substances, we must say that the substance consists in that unifying [*unionalis*] reality that adds *something complete* [*absolutus*] (and therefore substantial), though in flux, to those things that are to be united. Your transubstantiation must be located in its change, for monads aren't really ingredients of this thing which is added, but requisites for it, although they are required not by absolute and metaphysical necessity, but things merely needed for it. And so the monads can remain, as well as the sensible phenomena grounded on them, even if the substance of the body is changed. An accident that is not a mode seems difficult to explain, and I do not hold extension to be one. Even though monads aren't accidents, one can say that it happens that the unifying substance has them (with physical necessity), just as it can happen that a body is touched by another body, even though a body is not an accident. The extension of body seems to be nothing but the continuity or diffusion of matter through parts beyond parts. However, were the "beyond parts" supernaturally to cease, the extension which belongs to this body will also cease. What will remain is only a phenomenal extension, grounded in the monads, along with the other things that result from them; they alone exist if there is no unifying substance. If that substantial chain [*vinculum substantiale*][248] for monads did not exist, all

---

248. This appears to be the first public use of the term "substantial chain" in Leibniz's writings, although it should be noted that it also appears in the notes for this letter which follow.

bodies, together with all of their qualities, would be nothing but well-founded phenomena, like a rainbow or an image in a mirror, in a word, continual dreams perfectly in agreement with one another, and in this alone would consist the reality of those phenomena. For one should no more say that monads are parts of bodies, that they touch one another, that they compose bodies, than that points and souls do the same. And a monad, like a soul, is, as it were, a certain world of its own, having no connections of dependency except with God. Therefore, if a body is a substance, it is a making real of the phenomena over and above their agreement.

Notes for Leibniz to Des Bosses, 5 February 1712

IF BODIES are phenomena and judged in accordance with how they appear to us, they will not be real since they will appear differently to different people. And so the reality of bodies, of space, of motion, and of time seem to consist in the fact that they are phenomena of God, that is, the object of his knowledge by intuition [*scientia visionis*]. And the distinction between the appearance bodies have with respect to us and with respect to God is, in a certain way, like that between a drawing in perspective and a ground plan. For there are different drawings in perspective, depending upon the position of the viewer, while a ground plan or geometrical representation is unique. Indeed, God sees things exactly as they are in accordance with geometrical truth, although he also knows how everything appears to everything else, and so he eminently contains in himself all other appearances.

Furthermore, God not only sees individual monads and the modifications of every monad whatsoever, but he also sees their relations, and in this consists the reality of relations and of truth. Of these, one of the most important relations is duration, or the order of successive things, and position, or the order of coexisting things, and interaction, or mutual action for as long as we conceive the ideal mutual dependence of monads on one another to last; moreover, position without a thing mediating is presence. Beyond presence and interaction comes connection, when things move one another. Through these relations things seem to us to make one thing, and truths can really be asserted of a whole, truths which hold even for God. But over and above these real relations one more perfect relation can be conceived, a relation through which one new substance arises from many substances. And this will not be a simple resultant, that is, it will not be built up from true or real relations alone, but will add, besides, a certain new substantiality, that is, a substantial chain, and will be an effect, not only of the divine intellect, but also of the divine will. This addition to the monads does not arise in just any way, otherwise any scattered monads at all might be united into a new substance, and nothing definite might arise in contiguous bodies. But it is sufficient that this thing unite monads that are under the domination of one monad, those which make up one organic body, that is, one machine of nature. And in this consists the metaphysical chain between the soul and the body, which constitute one subject [*suppositum*], to which the union of natures in Christ is analogous. And these are what constitute a *per se* unity, that is, one subject.

Things are either concrete or abstract. Concrete things are either substances or *substantiata*.[249] Every substance is alive. Substances are either simple or composite. Simple substances or monads are either intelligent or without reason. Intelligent monads are called spirits and are either uncreated or created. A created intelligent monad is either angelic or human and is also called a soul. Again, monads can be understood either as separated, such as God and, in the opinion of certain people, an angel, or they can be understood as connected to a body, that is, they can be understood as souls; we know of souls both with reason and without. Monads without reason are either sentient or only vegetative. Composite substances are those which constitute a *per se* unity, composed of a soul and an organic body, which is a machine of nature resulting from monads. *Substantiata* are aggregates that are either natural or artificial, connected or unconnected. Many substances can make up a single subject [*suppositum*], as indeed can many *substantiata*, or substances together with *substantiata*, for example, souls together with the organs of a body. Abstract things are either absolute or relative, and the absolute ones are either essential or added on. Essential things are either primitive, like active and passive force, or derivative, that is, affections, which add only relations to the prior things. Those added on are either *per se*, that is, natural (which a thing requires and has unless it is prevented), or those which are attributed *per accidens*. Such things are modifications, that is, qualities and actions. Relative things are relations. There are certain entities built up from the preceding abstract things, built up, as it were, from the essentials, from the naturals, from the modifications, and from relations; and so, they will be aggregate accidents.

Terms extend further than things, since many terms are attributed to the same thing, for example, a man is learned, prudent, laughing.

Why is 'man' more a substance than 'learned' is? Why is 'animal' more a substance than 'rational' is? Namely, because it involves a thing, as if I were to say "animal, that is, rational thing." But 'substance' isn't usually* attributed to everything, and we do not make substantive words from everything, even though from 'white' we could make 'the white,' that is, the white thing. But is 'the white' in the category of substance? I think not, since not everything that can be attributed to the white subject [*subjectum*] is a modification of whiteness, while what can be attributed to a man are modifications of humanity.

Leibniz to Des Bosses, 26 May 1712 [excerpts]

IF YOU DENY that what is added to monads to produce a union is substantial, it immediately follows that one cannot call body a substance, for

---

249. In an undated essay, Leibniz wrote: "An aggregate of substances is what I call a *substantiatum*, like an army of men or a flock of birds, and such are all bodies" (C 13). The term is left in Latin for lack of an appropriate translation.

then it will be an aggregate of monads, and I am afraid that you will fall back into the mere phenomena of bodies. For monads, in and of themselves, have no position with respect to one another, that is, no real position which extends beyond the order of the phenomena. Each is, as it were, a certain separate world, and they agree among themselves through their phenomena, having no other intercourse or connection *per se*.

If you call an accident whatever presupposes a complete substance, in such a way that it cannot naturally be without it, you do not explain what is essential to an accident, and how it ought to be distinguished in its supernatural state from a substance. The Peripatetics certainly recognize something substantial besides monads, otherwise there would be no substances besides monads for them. And monads do not constitute a complete composite substance, since they make up, not something one *per se*, but only a mere aggregate, unless some substantial chain is added.

One cannot prove from harmony that there is anything in bodies but phenomena. For from other considerations it is clear that the harmony of phenomena in souls does not arise from the influx of bodies, but is pre-established. And this would be enough if there were only souls or monads, in which case all real extension (not to mention motion) would vanish, and its reality would be reduced to mere mutations of phenomena.

Leibniz to Des Bosses, 29 May 1716 [excerpts]

JUST AS it sometimes happens in geometry that, from the very fact that we assume that something is different, it follows that it is not different (Cardano, Clavius and others have disputed this kind of reasoning, sometimes found in Euclid), so, if anyone were to imagine the world to have been created sooner, he would find that it had not been made any sooner, since there is no absolute time, and time is nothing but the order of successive things. In the same way, if anyone were to imagine the whole universe to be moved from its place* without changing the mutual distances of things with respect to one another, nothing will have happened, since absolute space is something imaginary, and there is nothing real in it but the distances of bodies. In a word, they are orders, not things. Such assumptions arise from false ideas. And so, as long as the world isn't eternal, it doesn't matter when the world is said to have started: and unless we agree to this, we shall fall into absurdity, and we will not be able to answer those who argue for the eternity of the world. For it would then follow that God did something contrary to reason, since it is impossible to give a reason for this rather than that initial time, because one cannot point to any distinction here. But, from the fact that one cannot point to any distinction, I also judge that there is no difference. Therefore, if the world could have arisen sooner, then we must conclude that it is eternal.

For matter naturally to require extension is for its parts naturally to require an order of coexistence among themselves. Will you deny this?

When points are situated in such a way that there are no two points between which there is no midpoint, then, by that very fact, we have a continuous extension.

In your judgment the chain that makes a composite real is called a substantial mode. But then you make use of 'mode' in a sense different from the customary one. For such a mode will really be the foundation for a composite substance. But this mode is an enduring thing, not a modification which arises and passes away. However, it isn't a mode of the monads, since nothing is changed in the monads whether you place it there or take it away.

I do not say that there is a chain midway between matter and form, but that the substantial form and primary matter of the composite, in the Scholastic sense, that is, the primitive power, active and passive, are in the chain, just as they are in the essence of the composite. However, this substantial chain is naturally, not essentially, a chain. For it requires monads, but it does not involve them essentially, since it can exist without monads, and monads without it.

If making phenomena real didn't presuppose anything besides monads, then the composite would already have been made real, contrary to the hypothesis. Whatever exists besides monads and the modifications of monads is a consequence of making phenomena real.

Also, true composite substances don't come into being except with respect to sense. For, as I have often said, not only the soul but also the animal survives. Only modifications and (from *substantiata*) aggregates, that is, accidents or accidental things, arise or perish.

But we judge that we are not alone from a reason derived from things, even without regard to divine wisdom, since there appears to be no reason to favor just one thing. Nor is there any other way you could use reason to change the mind of someone who contended that he alone exists and that others are only dreamed by him. But there is reason why existing things are favored over nonexisting things, that is, there is reason why not every possible thing exists. Furthermore, even if no creatures were to exist except a perceiving creature, the perceived order would show divine wisdom. And so, even though we can also grasp the wisdom of God *a priori*, and not from the order of the phenomena alone, there is no circle here. For, from the fact that there are contingent things, there is a necessary thing—an intelligent thing, as I showed in the *Theodicy*.[250] If bodies were mere phenomena, the senses would not deceive us on that account, for the senses put nothing forward concerning metaphysical matters. The veracity of the senses consists in the fact that phenomena agree with one another, and that we are not deceived by events if we properly follow the regularities [*rationes*] built up from experience.

Substance acts insofar as it can, unless it is impeded; moreover, even a simple substance is impeded, but it is not impeded naturally except from within itself. And when a monad is said to be impeded by another, this must be understood as concerning the representation of the other in the one. The author of things has accommodated them to one another, and the one is said

---

250. See *Theodicy*, part I, sec. 7.

to be acted upon in the case when its consideration gives way before the consideration of the other.

An aggregate, but not a composite substance, is resolved into parts. A composite substance only needs the coming together of parts, but is not essentially constituted of them, otherwise it would be an aggregate. It acts mechanically, since it contains primitive or essential forces and derivative or accidental forces.

It is the echo of monads, which, from its nature [*ex sua constitutione*], once posited, requires monads, but does not depend on them. The soul is also the echo of external things, but yet it is independent of external things.

Since neither monads nor partial, composite substances taken apart from the whole composite substance are the active essence [of a composite substance], the composite substance can be eliminated, leaving behind the monads or other ingredients, and *vice versa.*

If bodies were mere phenomena, they would nevertheless exist as phenomena, like the rainbow.

You say that bodies can be something other than phenomena, even if they aren't substances. I believe that unless there are corporeal substances, bodies are transformed into phenomena. And aggregates themselves are nothing but phenomena, since things other than the monads making them up are added by perception alone, by virtue of the very fact that they are perceived at the same time. Furthermore, if only monads were substances, then it would be necessary either that bodies are mere phenomena, or that a continuum arise from points, which, it is agreed, is absurd. Real continuity can arise only from a substantial chain. If nothing substantial existed beside monads, that is, if composites were mere phenomena, then extension itself would be nothing but a phenomenon resulting from simultaneous and mutually ordered appearances, and by virtue of that very fact, all of the controversies concerning the composition of the continuum would cease. What is to be added to monads in order to make the phenomena real is not a modification of the monads, since it changes nothing in their perceptions. For orders, or relations which join two monads, are not in one monad or the other, but equally well in both at the same time, that is, really in neither, but in the mind alone. You will not understand this relation unless you add a real chain, that is, something substantial which is the subject of their common predicates and modifications, that is, the subject of the predicates and modifications joining them together. For I don't believe that you have established the existence of an accident that can, at the same time, be in two subjects and has one foot in one, so to speak, and one foot in the other.

Continuous quantity does not add impenetrability (for continuous quantity is also attributed to place), but matter does. And you yourselves have established that matter only requires impenetrability, though impenetrability is not part of its essence.

Composite substance does not formally consist in monads and their subordination, for then it would be a mere aggregate or a being *per accidens.* Rather, it consists in primitive active and passive force, from which arise the qualities and the actions and passions of the composite which are discovered by the senses, if they are assumed to be more than phenomena.

You say that to be *substantially modified* is for the monads to have a mode which makes them a natural principle of their operations. But what, I ask, is this mode? Is it a quality? Is it an action? Does it change the perceptions of the monads? One should say no such thing. It is really a substance, and not a mode of the monads, even if the monads naturally correspond to it. For monads aren't a principle of operation for things outside of themselves. I don't know what could force you to make the substantiality of the composite a mode of the monads, that is, really an accident. It is not necessary for us to hold that substances arise and pass away; indeed if we were to hold that, then we would demolish the nature of substance, and fall back into aggregates or things *per accidens*. What are commonly called substances are really only *substantiata*. Peripatetic philosophers, as long as they believed in the true generation and corruption of substances, fell into inexplicable difficulties surrounding the origin of forms and other matters, all of which difficulties cease on my way of explaining things.

And so it is, as you say, whenever the complete [*absoluta*] substance that makes phenomena real is posited, one immediately has a composite substance.* But that substance is not posited by God, acting in a regular way, unless the ingredients are present, namely the monads or other composite and partial substances. However, these ingredients are not formally in the substance; they are needed, but they are not required by necessity. And so, through a miracle they can be lacking, which is to say that these ingredients are not formally constitutive [of the composite substance]; they are constitutive in aggregates but not in true substances. You say that when the composite substance is present* while the monads or ingredients are not present, then no one would say that the composite is present. I answer, no one would say that unless he had been informed that it is a miracle. Thus no one would say that the body of Christ is present in the Eucharist unless he had been informed that this happens miraculously.

Forgive the fact that I write in fits and starts, and for that reason do not, perhaps, always satisfy, for I cannot go back to what I wrote earlier. Because of that, perhaps certain sorts of contradiction will arise from time to time. But once the matter is examined, the contradiction will be more in the way I express myself than in the account. I don't know whether, when, or in what way I might have said that a modification of a nonextended thing produces an extended thing.

In my judgment, every perfection pertains to the path of wisdom. Furthermore, the path of wisdom leads toward the introduction of the greatest perfection a thing can have. And so, if some perfections are compatible with the others, they will not be omitted. Such is the perfection of pre-established harmony, which also rests on certain higher considerations. But this very relation between each and every monad brings it about that monads don't act on one another, since each is sufficient for everything that happens in itself; whatever you add in them is unnecessary.

You ask, finally, how my composite substance differs from an entelechy. I say that it differs from it only as a whole does from its part, that is, the first entelechy of a composite is a constitutive part of the composite substance, namely its primitive active force. But it differs from a monad, since it makes phenomena real. Monads can, indeed, exist, even if bodies are only phenomena. However, the entelechy of a composite substance always naturally accompanies its dominant monad. And so, if a monad is taken with an entelechy, it will contain the substantial form of an animal.

Nothing prevents an echo from being able to be the foundation of other things, especially if it is an originary [*originaria*] echo.

If monads, strictly speaking, are accidental to composite substances, even if they are only naturally connected to them, then to want them to be eliminated is to revive the overnicety of certain Greeks who hold that even the accidents of the bread and the wine are eliminated. In short, miracles should not be increased beyond necessity. Monads really pertain to quantity, something that the Scholastics themselves hold to be left behind [in the Eucharist]; and it is no slight matter that everything in the one substance which makes phenomena real is present, while everything in the other substance which makes phenomena real is absent. Briefly: my entire view here is derived from these two positions, that there is composite substance, endowing the phenomena with reality, and that substance cannot naturally arise or perish, though it is true that the Peripatetic philosophy as corrected now* seems really to be demonstrable from the first position alone, that is, from the postulate that the phenomena have reality outside of a perceiver. Indeed, the fact that substance does not arise or perish can also be derived from the fact that otherwise we will fall into perplexities. Furthermore, the formal distinction between composite substance and the monad and, on the other hand, the distinction between the composite substance and the aggregate, derives from these considerations, and also the independence of the composite substance from the ingredients, by virtue of which it is called composite, even though it is not aggregated from them. And it is also on this basis that the substance and the composite itself (for example, that of a man or of an animal) are said to remain numerically the same, not only in appearance, but also in reality, even though the ingredients are always changing and in continual flux. And thus, since we posit that the ingredients are separated from the substance, through nature, little by little and piecemeal, why don't you admit, through miracle, a separation, so to speak, all at once, all at the same time, taking the entire composite substance away (that is, everything that makes the phenomena real) that's in the terrestrial thing [i.e., the bread], and substituting the thing that makes the phenomena real in the celestial thing [i.e., the body of Christ]? And so, I don't think that I depart from the doctrine of the schools on corporeal substance except in this one thing, that I eliminate the generation and corruption of a true substance, whether it is simple or composite, since I find that such a view is neither necessary nor explicable, and so I free that philosophy from innumerable difficulties. But I thus restrict corporeal or composite substance to living things alone, that is, to organic machines of nature alone. Other things are, for me, mere aggregates of substances, which I call *substantiata*; aggregates really constitute something one only *per accidens*.

To what you have said about Zeno's points, I add that they are only boundaries, and so they can make up nothing. But monads alone do not make up a continuum, since, in and of themselves, they lack all connection, and each monad is, as it were, a world apart. But primary matter (for secondary matter is an aggregate), that is, that which is passive in the composite substance, contains the foundation of continuity, whence true continuity arises from composite substances placed next to one another, unless God supernaturally removes the extension by removing the order among those coexistents which are thought to penetrate each other. And it was in this sense, perhaps, that I said that extension is a modification of primary matter, that is, a modification of that which is formally nonextended. But this kind of modality is intermediate between an essential attribute and an accident, for it consists in an attribute that is perpetually natural, an attribute that cannot be changed except supernaturally.[. . .]

I have considered from time to time what one would say to one of your Order [i.e., the Jesuits] who wanted to eliminate every composite substance, that is, everything that makes phenomena real, as superfluous. Assuming that, the substance of body itself would consist in the phenomena that constitute it, as accidents might consist in the phenomena that result. In just the same way, the nature of a white thing might consist in balls having some texture like foam or something similar, the perception of which is insensible in us. But the accident might, in a different way, consist in the observed perception through which we recognize a white thing. And so, if God wanted to substitute a black thing for a white thing, preserving the accidents of the white thing, he would bring it about that all perceivers (for in the mutual agreement of perceivers consists the truth of the phenomena) retain the observed perception of the white thing and its effect, that is, the perception of what results from that which constitutes the white thing. But they wouldn't have the unobserved perception of the foam or the little mountains (that is, the textures producing a white thing); rather, they would have the unobserved perception of valleys, that is, the unobserved perception of textures producing a black thing. And so, all observable perceptions of the bread would remain, but substituted for the phenomena constituting the bread (which are also perceived by us, though insensibly) would be the general perception of the phenomena that constitute the flesh, that is, the general perception of the insensible phenomena of the flesh.

Principles of Nature and Grace, Based on Reason (1714)[251]

The "Principles of Nature and Grace" and the "Monadology" were written at Vienna in 1714. They were both part of Leibniz's attempts, toward the end of his life, to seek a wider audience for his views than that of his scholarly

---

251. . RPM; G VI 598–606. French.

correspondents. He seems to have looked to Prince Eugene of Savoy, in Vienna, and to Nicolas Remond, the chief counselor of the Duke of Orleans, in Paris, for the propagation of his ideas in the circles of powerful and influential persons. Toward that end, he appears to have acquiesced to a request from Prince Eugene to write a condensation of his philosophy. The result was probably the "Principles of Nature and Grace," which he also sent to Remond.

1. *A SUBSTANCE* is a being capable of action. It is simple or composite. *A simple substance* is that which has no parts. *A composite substance* is a collection of simple substances, or *monads. Monas* is a Greek word signifying unity, or what is one. Composites or bodies are multitudes; and simple substances—lives, souls, and minds—are unities. There must be simple substances everywhere, because, without simples, there would be no composites. As a result, all of nature is full of life.

2. Since the monads have no parts, they can neither be formed nor destroyed. They can neither begin nor end naturally, and consequently they last as long as the universe, which will be changed but not destroyed. They cannot have shapes, otherwise they would have parts. As a result, a monad, in itself and at a moment, can be distinguished from another only by its internal qualities and actions, which can be nothing but its *perceptions* (that is, the representation of the composite, or what is external, in the simple) and its *appetitions* (that is, its tendencies to go from one perception to another) which are the principles of change. For the simplicity of substance does not prevent a multiplicity of modifications, which must be found together in this same simple substance, and which must consist in the variety of its relations to external things. Similarly, in a *center* or point, though entirely simple, we find an infinity of angles formed by the lines that meet there.

3. Everything is full in nature. There are simple substances everywhere, actually separated from one another by their own actions, which continually change their relations; and each distinct simple substance or monad, which makes up the center of a composite substance (an animal, for example) and is the principle of its unity, is surrounded by a mass composed of an infinity of other monads, which constitute the *body belonging* to this central monad, through whose properties [*affections*] the monad represents the things outside it, similarly to the way a center does. And this body is organic when it forms a kind of automaton or natural machine, which is not only a machine as a whole, but also in its smallest distinguishable parts. And since everything is connected because of the plenitude of the world, and since each body acts on every other body, more or less, in proportion to its distance, and is itself affected by the other through reaction, it follows that each monad is a living mirror or a mirror endowed with internal action, which represents the universe from its own point of view and is as ordered as the universe itself. And the perceptions in the monad arise from one another by the laws of appetites, or by the laws of the *final causes of good and evil*, which consist in notable perceptions, ordered or disordered. Similarly, changes in bodies and external

phenomena arise from one another by the laws of *efficient causes*, that is, the laws governing motions. Thus there is perfect *harmony* between the perceptions of the monad and the motions of bodies, pre-established from the first between the system of efficient causes and that of final causes. And in this consists the agreement and the physical union of soul and body, without the one being able to change the laws of the other.

4. Each monad, together with a particular body, makes up a living substance. Thus, there is not only life everywhere, joined to limbs or organs, but there are also infinite degrees of life in the monads, some dominating more or less over others. But when a monad has organs that are adjusted in such a way that, through them, there is contrast and distinction among the impressions they receive, and consequently contrast and distinction in the perceptions that represent them [in the monad] (as, for example, when the rays of light are concentrated and act with greater force because of the shape of the eye's humors), then this may amount to *sensation*, that is, to a perception accompanied by *memory*—a perception of which there remains an echo long enough to make itself heard on occasion. Such a living thing is called an *animal*, as its monad is called a *soul*. And when this soul is raised to the level of *reason*, it is something more sublime, and it is counted among the minds, as I will soon explain.

It is true that animals are sometimes in the condition of simple living things, and their souls in the condition of simple monads, namely when their perceptions are not sufficiently distinct to be remembered, as happens in a deep, dreamless sleep or in a fainting spell. But perceptions which have become entirely confused must be unravelled again in animals, for reasons I shall give shortly (cf. section 12). Thus it is good to distinguish between *perception*, which is the internal state of the monad representing external things, and *apperception*, which is *consciousness*, or the reflective knowledge of this internal state, something not given to all souls, nor at all times to a given soul. Moreover, it is because they lack this distinction that the Cartesians have failed, disregarding the perceptions that we do not apperceive, in the same way that people disregard imperceptible bodies. This is also what leads the same Cartesians to believe that only minds are monads, that there are no souls in beasts, still less other *principles of life*. And after having shocked common opinion too much by refusing sensation to beasts, they have, in the opposite direction, accommodated themselves too much to the prejudice of the masses by confusing a *long stupor*, which arises from a great confusion of perceptions, with *death strictly speaking*, in which all perception ceases. This has confirmed the ill-founded belief in the destruction of some souls, and the evil opinion of some so-called freethinkers who have denied the immortality of our soul.

5. There is interconnection among the perceptions of animals which bears some resemblance to reason, but this interconnection is only founded in the memory of *facts* or effects, and not at all in the knowledge of *causes*. That is why a dog runs away from the stick with which he was beaten, because his memory represents to him the pain which the stick caused him. And men, to the extent that they are empirical, that is, in three fourths of their actions,

act only like beasts. For example, we expect the day to dawn tomorrow because we have always experienced it thus; only an astronomer foresees it by reason, and even this prediction will finally fail, when the cause of day dawning, which is not eternal, shall cease.

But *true reasoning* depends on necessary or eternal truths, such as those of logic, numbers, and geometry, which bring about an indubitable connection of ideas and infallible consequences. Animals in which these consequences are not noticed are called *beasts*; but those who know these necessary truths are those that are properly called *rational animals*, and their souls are called *minds*. These souls are capable of performing reflective acts, and capable of considering what is called "I", substance, soul, mind—in brief, immaterial things and immaterial truths. And that is what makes us capable of the sciences or of demonstrative knowledge.

6. Modern investigations have taught us, and reason confirms it, that living things whose organs are known to us, that is, plants and animals, do not come from putrefaction or chaos, as the ancients believed, but from *preformed* seeds, and consequently, from the transformation of preexistent living beings.

There are small animals in the seeds of large ones, which, through conception, assume new vestments that they appropriate for themselves, which give them the means to nourish themselves and grow in order to pass to a larger stage [*théatre*] and to bring about the propagation of the large animal. It is true that the souls of the human spermatic animals are not rational and do not become rational until conception settles that these animals will have a human nature. And since animals generally are not fully born in conception or *generation*, they do not fully perish in what we call *death*, for it is reasonable that what does not begin naturally does not end in the order of nature. Thus, abandoning their mask or their tattered dress, they merely return to a smaller stage, where they can, nevertheless, be just as sensitive and as well-ordered as in the larger. Moreover, what we have just said about the large animals is also true of the generation and death of spermatic animals themselves. That is, they grow from other, smaller, spermatic animals, in proportion to which they may be considered large; for everything goes to infinity in nature.

Thus, not only souls, but also animals cannot be generated and cannot perish. They are only unfolded, enfolded, reclothed, unclothed, and transformed; souls never entirely leave their body, and do not pass from one body into another that is entirely new to them. There is therefore no *metempsychosis*, but there is *metamorphosis*. Animals change, but they acquire and leave behind only parts. In nutrition this happens a little at a time and by small insensible particles, though continually, but it happens suddenly, visibly, but rarely, in conception or in death, which causes animals to acquire or lose a great deal all at once.

7.[252] So far we have just spoken as simple *physicists*; now we must rise to *metaphysics*, by making use of the *great principle*, little used, commonly, that

---

252. Originally, the "Principles of Nature and Grace" was divided into two chapters. Leibniz began chapter 2 here.

nothing takes place without sufficient reason, that is, that nothing happens without it being possible for someone who knows enough things to give a reason sufficient to determine why it is so and not otherwise. Assuming this principle, the first question we have the right to ask will be, *why is there something rather than nothing?* For nothing is simpler and easier than something. Furthermore, assuming that things must exist, we must be able to give a reason for *why they must exist in this way,* and not otherwise.

8. This sufficient reason for the existence of the universe cannot be found in the series of contingent things, that is, in the series of bodies and their representations in souls; for, since matter is in itself indifferent to motion and rest, and to one motion rather than another, we cannot find in matter the reason for motion, still less the reason for a particular motion. And although the present motion found in matter comes from the preceding motion, and it, in turn, comes from a preceding motion, we will not make any progress in this way, however far back we go, for the same question always remains. Thus *the sufficient reason,* which needs no other reason, must be outside this series of contingent things, and must be found in a substance which is its cause, and which is a necessary being, carrying the reason of its existence with itself. Otherwise, we would not yet have a sufficient reason where one could end the series. And this ultimate reason for things is called *God.*

9. This simple primitive substance must eminently include the perfections contained in the derivative substances which are its effects. Thus it will have perfect power, knowledge, and will, that is, it will have omnipotence, omniscience, and supreme goodness. And since *justice,* taken very generally, is nothing other than goodness in conformity with wisdom, there must also be supreme justice in God. The reason that made things exist through him, makes them still depend on him while they exist and bring about their effects; and they continually receive from him that which causes them to have any perfection at all. But the imperfection that remains in them comes from the essential and original limitation of created things.

10. It follows from the supreme perfection of God that he chose the best possible plan in producing the universe, a plan in which there is the greatest variety together with the greatest order.[253] The most carefully used plot of ground, place, and time; the greatest effect produced by the simplest means; the most power, knowledge, happiness, and goodness in created things that the universe could allow. For, since all the possibles have a claim to existence in God's understanding in proportion to their perfections, the result of all these claims must be the most perfect actual world possible. And without this, it would not be possible to give a reason for why things have turned out in this way rather than otherwise.

11. God's supreme wisdom has led him, above all, to choose *laws of motion* that are best adjusted and most suitable with respect to abstract or metaphysical reasons. The same quantity of total and absolute force, or of action, is

---

253. Leibniz originally wrote: "in the greatest possible variety together with the greatest possible order."

preserved, the same quantity of respective force, or of reaction; and finally, the same quantity of directive force.[254] Furthermore, action is always equal to reaction, and the whole effect is always equivalent to its full cause. And it is surprising that, by a consideration of *efficient causes* alone, or by a consideration of matter, we cannot give the reason for the laws of motion discovered in our time, some of which I myself have discovered. For I have found that we must have recourse to *final causes* for this, and that these laws do not depend upon the *principle of necessity*, as do logical, arithmetical, and geometrical truths, but upon the *principle of fitness*, that is, upon the choice of wisdom. And this is one of the most effective and most evident proofs of the existence of God for those who can delve deeply into these matters.

12. It also follows from the perfection of the supreme author that not only is the order of the whole universe as perfect as possible, but also that each living mirror that represents the universe according to its own point of view, that is, each *monad*, each substantial center, must have its perceptions and its appetites as well ordered as is compatible with all the rest. From this it also follows that *souls*, that is, the most dominant monads, or rather animals themselves, cannot fail to awaken from the state of stupor, into which death or some other accident may put them.

13. For everything is ordered in things once and for all, with as much order and agreement as possible, since supreme wisdom and goodness can only act with perfect harmony: the present is pregnant with the future; the future can be read in the past; the distant is expressed in the proximate. One could know the beauty of the universe in each soul, if one could unfold all its folds, which only open perceptibly with time. But since each distinct perception of the soul includes an infinity of confused perceptions which embrace the whole universe, the soul itself knows the things it perceives only so far as it has distinct and heightened [*revelées*] perceptions; and it has perfection to the extent that it has distinct perceptions. Each soul knows the infinite—knows all—but confusedly. It is like walking on the seashore and hearing the great noise of the sea: I hear the particular noises of each wave, of which the whole noise is composed, but without distinguishing them.

But confused perceptions are the result of impressions that the whole universe makes upon us; it is the same for each monad. God alone has distinct knowledge of the whole, for he is its source. It has been said quite nicely that he is like a center that is everywhere, but that his circumference is nowhere, since all is present to him immediately, without any distance from this center.

14. As for the rational soul, or *mind*, there is something more in it than in monads, or even in the simple souls. It is not only a mirror of the universe of created things, but also an image of the divinity. The mind not only has a perception of God's works, but it is even capable of producing something that resembles them, although on a small scale. For to say nothing of the wonders of dreams, in which we effortlessly (but also involuntarily) invent things which we would have to ponder long to come upon when awake, our soul is

---

254. See above, "A Specimen of Dynamics," part I.

also like an architect in its voluntary actions; and in discovering the sciences according to which God has regulated things (*by weight, measure, number,* etc.), it imitates in its realm and in the small world in which it is allowed to work, what God does in the large world.

15. That is why all minds, whether of men or genies, entering into a kind of society with God by virtue of reason and eternal truths, are members of the City of God, that is, members of the perfect state, formed and governed by the greatest and best of monarchs. Here there is no crime without punishment, no good action without proportionate reward, and finally, as much virtue and happiness as is possible. And this is accomplished without disordering nature (as if what God prepared for souls disturbed the laws of bodies), but through the very order of natural things, in virtue of the harmony pre-established from all time between the kingdoms of nature and grace, between God as architect and God as monarch. Consequently, nature itself leads to grace, and grace perfects nature by making use of it.

16. Thus although reason cannot teach us the details of the great future, which are reserved for revelation, reason itself assures us that things are made in a way that surpasses our wishes. Since God is the most perfect and happiest, and consequently, the substance most worthy of love, and since *genuinely pure love* consists in the state that allows one to take pleasure in the perfections and felicity of the beloved, this love must give us the greatest pleasure of which we are capable whenever God is its object.

17. And it is easy to love him as we ought to, if we know him as I have just spoken of him. For although God cannot be sensed by our external senses, he does not cease to be extremely worthy of love and to give great pleasure. We see the extent to which honors are pleasurable to men, although they do not at all consist in qualities derived from the external senses.

Martyrs and fanatics (although the affection of the latter is ill-regulated) show what power the pleasure of the mind has. And further, even the pleasures of the senses reduce to intellectual pleasures known confusedly.

Music charms us, even though its beauty consists only in the harmonies of numbers and in a calculation that we are not aware of, but which the soul nevertheless carries out, a calculation concerning the beats or vibrations of sounding bodies, which are encountered at certain intervals. The pleasures that sight finds in proportions are of the same nature, and those caused by the other senses amount to something similar, even though we might not be able to explain it so distinctly.

18. One can even say that the love of God gives us, in the present, a foretaste of future felicity. And although it is disinterested, it constitutes, by itself, our greatest good and our greatest interest, even when we are not seeking these things in it, and when we consider only the pleasure it gives, without regard to the utility it produces. For it gives us perfect confidence in the goodness of our author and master, which produces real tranquility of mind, unlike the Stoics, who are forced to be patient, but one that is produced by present contentment, which also assures us future happiness. And beside the present pleasure, nothing can be more useful for the future.

For the love of God also fulfills our hopes, and leads us down the road of supreme happiness, because by virtue of the perfect order established in the universe, everything is done in the best possible way, both for the general good and for the greatest individual good of those who are convinced of this, and who are content with divine government, which cannot fail to be found in those who know how to love the source of all good. It is true that supreme felicity (with whatever *beatific vision* or knowledge of God it may be accompanied) can never be complete, because, since God is infinite, he can never be entirely known.

Thus our happiness will never consist, and must never consist, in complete joy, in which nothing is left to desire, and which would dull our mind, but must consist in a perpetual progress to new pleasures and new perfections.

The Principles of Philosophy, or, the Monadology (1714)[255]

The "Monadology" was probably meant as an elaboration of the "Principles of Nature and Grace"; Leibniz might have started the "Monadology" before the "Principles of Nature and Grace," but he certainly finished writing it after. It should be stressed that the "Monadology" was not intended as an introduction to Leibniz's philosophy, but rather as a condensed statement of the main principles of his philosophy and an elucidation of some of the passages of his Theodicy.

1. THE *MONAD*, which we shall discuss here, is nothing but a simple substance that enters into composites—simple, that is, without parts (*Theodicy,* sec. 10).

2. And there must be simple substances, since there are composites; for the composite is nothing more than a collection, or *aggregate,* of simples.

3. But where there are no parts, neither extension, nor shape, nor divisibility is possible. These monads are the true atoms of nature and, in brief, the elements of things.

4. There is also no dissolution to fear, and there is no conceivable way in which a simple substance can perish naturally.

5. For the same reason, there is no conceivable way a simple substance can begin naturally, since it cannot be formed by composition.

6. Thus, one can say that monads can only begin or end all at once, that is, they can only begin by creation and end by annihilation, whereas composites begin or end through their parts.

7. There is also no way of explaining how a monad can be altered or changed internally by some other creature, since one cannot transpose anything in it, nor can one conceive of any internal motion that can be excited, directed,

255. "Principles . . ." was probably Leibniz's title. RPM and G VI 607–23. French. References to the *Theodicy* are not found in the final copy, but are taken from an earlier draft.

augmented, or diminished within it, as can be done in composites, where there can be change among the parts. The monads have no windows through which something can enter or leave. Accidents cannot be detached, nor can they go about outside of substances, as the sensible species of the Scholastics once did. Thus, neither substance nor accident can enter a monad from without.[256]

8. However, monads must have some qualities, otherwise they would not even be beings.[257] And if simple substances did not differ at all in their qualities, there would be no way of perceiving any change in things, since what there is in a composite can only come from its simple ingredients; and if the monads had no qualities, they would be indiscernible from one another, since they also do not differ in quantity. As a result, assuming a plenum, in motion, each place would always receive only the equivalent of what it already had, and one state of things would be indistinguishable from another[258] (Pref.***.2.b).

9. It is also necessary that each monad be different from each other. For there are never two beings in nature that are perfectly alike, two beings in which it is not possible to discover an internal difference, that is, one founded on an intrinsic denomination.

10. I also take for granted that every created being, and consequently the created monad as well, is subject to change, and even that this change is continual in each thing.

11. It follows from what we have just said that the monad's natural changes come from an *internal principle*, since no external cause can influence it internally (sec. 396, 400).

12. But, besides the principle of change, there must be *diversity* [*un détail*] *in that which changes*, which produces, so to speak, the specification and variety of simple substances.

13. This diversity must involve a multitude in the unity or in the simple. For, since all natural change is produced by degrees, something changes and something remains. As a result, there must be a plurality of properties [*affections*] and relations in the simple substance, although it has no parts.

14. The passing state which involves and represents a multitude in the unity or in the simple substance is nothing other than what one calls *perception*, which should be distinguished from apperception, or consciousness, as will be evident in what follows. This is where the Cartesians have failed badly, since they took no account of the perceptions that we do not apperceive. This is also what made them believe that minds alone are monads and that there are no animal souls or other entelechies. With the common people, they have confused a long stupor with death, properly speaking, which made them fall again into the Scholastic prejudice of completely separated

---

256. Deleted from the first draft: "Monads are not mathematical points. For these points are only extremities, and the line cannot be composed of points."

257. Deleted from earlier drafts: "and if simple substances were nothings, the composites would reduce to nothing."

258. Cf. "On Nature Itself," sec. 13, above pp. 163–65.

souls, and they have even confirmed unsound minds in the belief in the mortality of souls.[259]

15. The action of the internal principle which brings about the change or passage from one perception to another can be called *appetition*; it is true that the appetite cannot always completely reach the whole perception toward which it tends, but it always obtains something of it, and reaches new perceptions.

16. We ourselves experience a multitude in a simple substance when we find that the least thought we ourselves apperceive involves variety in its object. Thus, all those who recognize that the soul is a simple substance should recognize this multitude in the monad; and Mr. Bayle should not find any difficulty in this as he has done in his *Dictionary* article, "Rorarius."[260]

17. Moreover, we must confess that the *perception*, and what depends on it, is *inexplicable in terms of mechanical reasons*, that is, through shapes and motions. If we imagine that there is a machine whose structure makes it think, sense, and have perceptions, we could conceive it enlarged, keeping the same proportions, so that we could enter into it, as one enters into a mill. Assuming that, when inspecting its interior, we will only find parts that push one another, and we will never find anything to explain a perception. And so, we should seek perception in the simple substance and not in the composite or in the machine. Furthermore, this is all one can find in the simple substance— that is, perceptions and their changes. It is also in this alone that all the *internal actions* of simple substances can consist.

18. One can call all simple substances or created monads entelechies, for they have in themselves a certain perfection (*echousi to enteles*); they have a sufficiency (*autarkeia*) that makes them the sources of their internal actions, and, so to speak, incorporeal automata (sec. 87).

19. If we wish to call *soul* everything that has *perceptions* and *appetites* in the general sense I have just explained, then all simple substances or created monads can be called souls. But, since sensation is something more than a simple perception, I think that the general name of monad and entelechy is sufficient for simple substances which only have perceptions, and that we should only call those substances *souls* where perception is more distinct and accompanied by memory.

20. For we experience within ourselves a state in which we remember nothing and have no distinct perception; this is similar to when we faint or when we are overwhelmed by a deep, dreamless sleep. In this state the soul does not differ sensibly from a simple monad; but since this state does not last, and since the soul emerges from it, our soul is something more (sec. 64).

---

259. For Leibniz's critique of Descartes on the immortality of the soul, see the "Letter to Molanus," below, pp. 240–45.

260. Leibniz's *Theodicy* was, to a large extent, an attempt to answer the skeptical arguments, from Bayle's *Historical and Critical Dictionary*, regarding the impossibility of reconciling faith with reason. "Rorarius," an article of the *Dictionary*, was Bayle's occasion for a discussion of the problem of the souls of animals: Jerome Rorarius (1485–1566) wrote a treatise maintaining that

21. And it does not at all follow that in such a state the simple substance is without any perception. This is not possible for the previous reasons; for it cannot perish, and it also cannot subsist without some property [*affection*], which is nothing other than its perception. But when there is a great multitude of small perceptions in which nothing is distinct, we are stupefied. This is similar to when we continually spin in the same direction several times in succession, from which arises a dizziness that can make us faint and does not allow us to distinguish anything. Death can impart this state to animals for a time.

22. And since every present state of a simple substance is a natural consequence of its preceding state, the present is pregnant with the future (sec. 360).

23. Therefore, since on being awakened from a stupor, we apperceive our perceptions, it must be the case that we had some perceptions immediately before, even though we did not apperceive them; for a perception can only come naturally from another perception, as a motion can only come naturally from a motion (secs. 401–403).

24. From this we see that if, in our perceptions, we had nothing distinct or, so to speak, in relief and stronger in flavor, we would always be in a stupor. And this is the state of bare monads.

25. We also see that nature has given heightened perceptions to animals, from the care she has taken to furnish them organs that collect several rays of light or several waves of air, in order to make them more effectual by bringing them together. There is something similar to this in odor, taste, and touch, and perhaps in many other senses which are unknown to us. I will soon explain how what occurs in the soul represents what occurs in the organs.

26. Memory provides a kind of sequence in souls, which imitates reason, but which must be distinguished from it. We observe that when animals have the perception of something which strikes them, and when they previously had a similar perception of that thing, then, through a representation in their memory, they expect that which was attached to the thing in the preceding perception, and are led to have sensations similar to those they had before. For example, if we show dogs a stick, they remember the pain that it caused them and they flee (Prelim., sec. 65).

27. And the strong imagination that strikes and moves them comes from the magnitude or the multitude of the preceding perceptions. For often a strong impression produces, all at once, the effect produced by a long *habit* or by many lesser, reiterated perceptions.

28. Men act like beasts insofar as the sequence of their perceptions results from the principle of memory alone; they resemble the empirical physicians who practice without theory. We are all mere Empirics in three fourths of our actions. For example, when we expect that the day will dawn tomorrow,

---

men are less rational than the lower animals. In "Rorarius" Bayle criticizes Leibniz's views; see Bayle, "Rorarius," notes H and L.

we act like an Empiric,[261] because until now it has always been thus. Only the astronomer judges this by reason (Prelim., sec. 65).

29. But the knowledge of eternal and necessary truths is what distinguishes us from simple animals and furnishes us with *reason* and the sciences, by raising us to a knowledge of ourselves and of God. And that is what we call the rational soul, or *mind*, in ourselves.

30. It is also through the knowledge of necessary truths and through their abstractions that we rise to *reflective acts*, which enable us to think of that which is called "I" and enable us to consider that this or that is in us. And thus, in thinking of ourselves, we think of being, of substance, of the simple and of the composite, of the immaterial and of God himself, by conceiving that that which is limited in us is limitless in him. And these reflective acts furnish the principal objects of our reasonings (*Theod.* Preface *.4.a).

31. Our reasonings are based on *two great principles, that of contradiction*, in virtue of which we judge that which involves a contradiction to be false, and that which is opposed or contradictory to the false to be true (sec. 44, 169).

32. And that of sufficient reason, by virtue of which we consider that we can find no true or existent fact, no true assertion, without there being a sufficient reason why it is thus and not otherwise, although most of the time these reasons cannot be known to us (sec. 44, 196).

33. There are also two kinds of *truths*, those of *reasoning* and those of *fact*. The truths of reasoning are necessary and their opposite is impossible; the truths of fact are contingent, and their opposite is possible. When a truth is necessary, its reason can be found by analysis, resolving it into simpler ideas and simpler truths until we reach the primitives (sec. sec. 170, 174, 189, 280–282, 367, Abridgment, objection 3).

34. This is how the speculative *theorems* and practical *canons* of mathematicians are reduced by analysis to *definitions, axioms* and *postulates*.

35. And there are, finally, *simple ideas*, whose definition cannot be given. There are also axioms and postulates, in brief, *primitive principles*, which cannot be proved and which need no proof. And these are *identical propositions*, whose opposite contains an explicit contradiction.

36. But there must also be a *sufficient reason* in *contingent truths*, or *truths of fact*, that is, in the series of things distributed throughout the universe of creatures, where the resolution into particular reasons could proceed into unlimited detail because of the immense variety of things in nature and because of the division of bodies to infinity. There is an infinity of past and present shapes and motions that enter into the efficient cause of my present writing, and there is an infinity of small inclinations and dispositions of my soul, present and past, that enter into its final cause (sec. 36, 37, 44, 45, 49, 52, 121, 122, 337, 340, 344).

37. And since all this *detail* involves nothing but other prior or more detailed

---

261. The Empirics were a sect of physicians before Galen (ca. A.D. 150). In later times, the epithet "Empiric" was given to physicians who despised theoretical study and trusted tradition and their own experience.

contingents, each of which needs a similar analysis in order to give its reason, we do not make progress in this way. It must be the case that the sufficient or ultimate reason is outside the sequence or *series* of this multiplicity of contingencies, however infinite it may be.

38. And that is why the ultimate reason of things must be in a necessary substance in which the diversity of changes is only eminent, as in its source. This is what we call God (*Theod.* sec. 7).

39. Since this substance is a sufficient reason for all this diversity, which is utterly interconnected, *there is only one God, and this God is sufficient.*

40. We can also judge that this supreme substance which is unique, universal, and necessary must be incapable of limits and must contain as much reality as is possible, insofar as there is nothing outside it which is independent of it, and insofar as it is a simple consequence of its possible existence.

41. From this it follows that God is absolutely perfect—*perfection* being nothing but the magnitude of positive reality considered as such, setting aside the limits or bounds in the things which have it. And here, where there are no limits, that is, in God, perfection is absolutely infinite (*Theod.* sec. 22; *Theod.* Preface, sec. 4.a).

42. It also follows that creatures derive their perfections from God's influence, but that they derive their imperfections from their own nature, which is incapable of being without limits. For it is in this that they are distinguished from God (*Theod.* sec. 20,27–31, 153, 167, 377 et seq.; sec. 30, 380, Abridgment, objection 5).[262]

43. It is also true that God is not only the source of existences, but also that of essences insofar as they are real, that is, or the source of that which is real in possibility. This is because God's understanding is the realm of eternal truths or that of the ideas on which they depend; without him there would be nothing real in possibles, and not only would nothing exist, but also nothing would be possible (*Theod.* sec. 20).

44. For if there is reality in essences or possibles, or indeed, in eternal truths, this reality must be grounded in something existent and actual, and consequently, it must be grounded in the existence of the necessary being, in whom essence involves existence, that is, in whom possible being is sufficient for actual being (sec. 184, 189, 335).

45. Thus God alone (or the necessary being) has this privilege, that he must exist if he is possible. And since nothing can prevent the possibility of what is without limits, without negation, and consequently without contradiction, this by itself is sufficient for us to know the existence of God *a priori.* We have also proved this by the reality of the eternal truths. But we have also just proved it *a posteriori* since there are contingent beings, which can only have their final or sufficient reason in the necessary being, a being that has the reason of its existence in itself.

46. However, we should not imagine, as some do, that since the eternal truths

---

262. The following appears in the second draft, but is missing in the final copy: "This *orginal imperfection* of creatures is noticeable in the *natural inertia* of bodies."

depend on God, they are arbitrary and depend on his will, as Descartes appears to have held, and after him Mr. Poiret.[263] This is true only of contingent truths, whose principle is *fitness* [*convenance*] or the choice of the *best*. But necessary truths depend solely on his understanding, and are its internal object (sec. 180, 184, 185, 335, 351, 380).

47. Thus God alone is the primitive unity or the first [*originaire*] simple substance; all created or derivative monads are products, and are generated, so to speak, by continual fulgurations of the divinity from moment to moment, limited by the receptivity of the creature, to which it is essential to be limited (sec. 382-391, 398, 395).

48. God has *power*, which is the source of everything, *knowledge*, which contains the diversity of ideas, and finally *will*, which brings about changes or products in accordance with the principle of the best (sec. 7, 149, 150). And these correspond to what, in created monads, is the subject or the basis, the perceptive faculty and the appetitive faculty. But in God these attributes are absolutely infinite or perfect, while in the created monads or in entelechies (or *perfectihabies*, as Hermolaus Barbarus translated that word)[264] they are only imitations of it, in proportion to the perfection that they have (sec. 87).

49. The creature is said to *act* externally insofar as it is perfect, and to *be acted upon* [*patir*] by another, insofar as it is imperfect. Thus we attribute *action* to a monad insofar as it has distinct perceptions, and *passion*, insofar as it has confused perceptions (*Theod.* sec. 32, 66, 386).

50. And one creature is more perfect than another insofar as one finds in it that which provides an *a priori* reason for what happens in the other; and this is why we say that it acts on the other.

51. But in simple substances the influence of one monad over another can only be ideal, and can only produce its effect through God's intervention, when in the ideas of God a monad reasonably asks that God take it into account in regulating the others from the beginning of things. For, since a created monad cannot have an internal physical influence upon another, this is the only way in which one can depend on another (*Theod.* sec. 9, 54, 65, 66, 201, Abridgment, objection 3).

52. It is in this way that actions and passions among creatures are mutual. For God, comparing two simple substances, finds in each reasons that require him to adjust the other to it; and consequently, what is active in some respects is passive from another point of view: *active* insofar as what is known distinctly in one serves to explain what happens in another; and *passive* insofar as the

---

263. For Leibniz's critique of Descartes's concept of God, see the "Letter to Molanus," below, pp. 240–45. Pierre Poiret (1646–1719) was initially one of Descartes's followers; he published a book of reflections on God, soul and evil, *Cogitationum rationalium de Deo, anima, et malo libri quattuor* (1677), which was attacked by Bayle.

264. Hermolaus Barbarus (1454–93) was an Italian scholar who attempted, through retranslations of Aristotle, to recover Aristotle's original doctrine from under the layers of Scholastic interpretations. His works include popular compendia of ethics and natural philosophy, drawn from the writings of Aristotle.

reason for what happens in one is found in what is known distinctly in another (sec. 66).

53. Now, since there is an infinity of possible universes in God's ideas, and since only one of them can exist, there must be a sufficient reason for God's choice, a reason which determines him towards one thing rather than another (*Theod.* sec. 8, 10, 44, 173, 196 & seq., 225, 414–16).

54. And this reason can only be found in fitness, or in the degree of perfection that these worlds contain, each possible world having the right to claim existence in proportion to the perfection it contains (sec. 74, 167, 350, 201, 130, 352, 345 & seq., 354).[265]

55. And this is the cause of the existence of the best, which wisdom makes known to God, which his goodness makes him choose, and which his power makes him produce (*Theod.* sec. 8,78,80,84 119,204,206,208; Abridgment, objection 1, objection 8).

56. This interconnection or accommodation of all created things to each other, and each to all the others, brings it about that each simple substance has relations that express all the others, and consequently, that each simple substance is a perpetual, living mirror of the universe (sec. 130, 360).

57. Just as the same city viewed from different directions appears entirely different and, as it were, multiplied perspectively, in just the same way it happens that, because of the infinite multitude of simple substances, there are, as it were, just as many different universes, which are, nevertheless, only perspectives on a single one, corresponding to the different points of view of each monad (sec. 147).

58. And this is the way of obtaining as much variety as possible, but with the greatest order possible, that is, it is the way of obtaining as much perfection as possible (sec. 120, 124, 241 & seq., 214, 243, 275).

59. Moreover, this is the only hypothesis (which I dare say is demonstrated) that properly enhances God's greatness. Mr. Bayle recognized this when, in his *Dictionary* (article "Rorarius"), he set out objections to it; indeed, he was tempted to believe that I ascribed too much to God, more than is possible. But he was unable to present any reason why this universal harmony, which results in every substance expressing exactly all the others through the relations it has to them, is impossible.[266]

60. Furthermore, in what I have just discussed, we can see the *a priori* reasons why things could not be otherwise. Because God, in regulating the whole, had regard for each part, and particularly for each monad, and since the nature of the monad is representative, nothing can limit it to represent only a part of things. However, it is true that this representation is only confused as to the detail of the whole universe, and can only be distinct for a small portion of things, that is, either for those that are closest, or for those that are greatest with respect to each monad, otherwise each monad would be a divinity. Monads are limited, not as to their objects, but with respect to the

---

265. The following appears in the second draft: "Thus there is nothing that is completely arbitrary."
266. . See note to sec. 16, above.

modifications of their knowledge of them. Monads all go confusedly to infinity, to the whole; but they are limited and differentiated by the degrees of their distinct perceptions.

61. In this respect, composites are analogous to simples. For everything is a plenum, which makes all matter interconnected. In a plenum, every motion has some effect on distant bodies, in proportion to their distance. For each body is affected, not only by those in contact with it, and in some way feels the effects of everything that happens to them, but also, through them, it feels the effects of those in contact with the bodies with which it is itself immediately in contact. From this it follows that this communication extends to any distance whatsoever. As a result, every body is affected by everything that happens in the universe, to such an extent that he who sees all can read in each thing what happens everywhere, and even what has happened or what will happen, by observing in the present what is remote in time as well as in space. "All things conspire [*sympnoia panta*]," said Hippocrates. But a soul can read in itself only what is distinctly represented there; it cannot unfold all its folds at once, because they go to infinity.

62. Thus, although each created monad represents the whole universe, it more distinctly represents the body which is particularly affected by it, and whose entelechy it constitutes. And just as this body expresses the whole universe through the interconnection of all matter in the plenum, the soul also represents the whole universe by representing this body, which belongs to it in a particular way (sec. 400).

63. The body belonging to a monad (which is the entelechy or soul of that body) together with an entelechy constitutes what may be called a *living being*, and together with a soul constitutes what is called an *animal*. Now, the body of a living being or an animal is always organized; for, since every monad is a mirror of the universe in its way, and since the universe is regulated in a perfect order, there must also be an order in the representing being, that is, in the perceptions of the soul, and consequently, in the body in accordance with which the universe is represented therein (sec. 403).

64. Thus each organized body of a living being is a kind of divine machine or natural automaton, which infinitely surpasses all artificial automata. For a machine constructed by man's art is not a machine in each of its parts. For example, the tooth of a brass wheel has parts or fragments which, for us, are no longer artificial things, and no longer have any marks to indicate the machine for whose use the wheel was intended. But natural machines, that is, living bodies, are still machines in their least parts, to infinity. That is the difference between nature and art, that is, between divine art and our art (sec. 134, 146, 194, 483).

65. And the author of nature has been able to practice this divine and infinitely marvelous art, because each portion of matter is not only divisible to infinity, as the ancients have recognized, but is also actually subdivided without end, each part divided into parts having some motion of their own; otherwise, it would be impossible for each portion of matter to express the whole universe (Prelim., sec. 70, *Theodicy*, sec. 195).

66. From this we see that there is a world of creatures, of living beings, of animals, of entelechies, of souls in the least part of matter.

67. Each portion of matter can be conceived as a garden full of plants, and as a pond full of fish. But each branch of a plant, each limb of an animal, each drop of its humors, is still another such garden or pond.

68. And although the earth and air lying between the garden plants, or the water lying between the fish of the pond, are neither plant nor fish, they contain yet more of them, though of a subtleness imperceptible to us, most often.

69. Thus there is nothing fallow, sterile, or dead in the universe, no chaos and no confusion except in appearance, almost as it looks in a pond at a distance, where we might see the confused and, so to speak, teeming motion of the fish in the pond, without discerning the fish themselves (Preface *** 5.b* *** b).

70. Thus we see that each living body has a dominant entelechy, which in the animal is the soul; but the limbs of this living body are full of other living beings, plants, animals, each of which also has its entelechy, or its dominant soul.

71. But we must not imagine, as some who have misunderstood my thought do, that each soul has a mass or portion of matter of its own, always proper to or allotted by it, and that it consequently possesses other lower living beings, forever destined to serve it. For all bodies are in a perpetual flux, like rivers, and parts enter into them and depart from them continually.

72. Thus the soul changes body only little by little and by degrees, so that it is never stripped at once of all its organs. There is often metamorphosis in animals, but there is never metempsychosis nor transmigration of souls; there are also no completely *separated souls*, nor spirits [*Génies*] without bodies. God alone is completely detached from bodies (sec. 90, 124).

73. That is why there is never total generation nor, strictly speaking, perfect death, death consisting in the separation of the soul. And what we call *generations* are developments and growths, as what we call deaths are enfoldings and diminutions.

74. Philosophers have been greatly perplexed about the origin of forms, entelechies, or souls. But today, when exact inquiries on plants, insects, and animals have shown us that organic bodies in nature are never produced from chaos or putrefaction, but always through seeds in which there is, no doubt, some *preformation*, it has been judged that, not only the organic body was already there before conception, but there was also a soul in this body; in brief, the animal itself was there, and through conception this animal was merely prepared for a great transformation, in order to become an animal of another kind. Something similar is seen outside generation, as when worms become flies, and caterpillars become butterflies (sec. 86, 89; Preface ***5.b. ff; sec. 90, 187, 188, 403, 86, 397).

75. Those *animals*, some of which are raised by conception to the level of the larger animals, can be called *spermatic*. But those of them that remain among those of their kind, that is, the majority, are born, multiply, and are destroyed,

just like the larger animals. There are but a small number of Elect that pass onto a larger stage [*théatre.*]

76. But this was only half the truth. I have, therefore, held that if the animal never begins naturally, it does not end naturally, either; and not only will there be no generation, but also no complete destruction, nor any death, strictly speaking. These *a posteriori* reasonings, derived from experience, agree perfectly with my principles deduced *a priori*, as above (sec. 90).

77. Thus one can state that not only is the soul (mirror of an indestructible universe) indestructible, but so is the animal itself, even though its mechanism often perishes in part, and casts off or puts on its organic coverings.

78. These principles have given me a way of naturally explaining the union, or rather the conformity of the soul and the organic body. The soul follows its own laws and the body also follows its own; and they agree in virtue of the harmony pre-established between all substances, since they are all representations of a single universe (Preface ***6; sec. 340, 352, 353, 358).

79. Souls act according to the laws of final causes, through appetitions, ends, and means. Bodies act according to the laws of efficient causes or of motions. And these two kingdoms, that of efficient causes and that of final causes, are in harmony with each other.

80. Descartes recognized that souls cannot impart a force to bodies because there is always the same quantity of force in matter. However, he thought that the soul could change the direction of bodies. But that is because the law of nature, which also affirms the conservation of the same total direction in matter, was not known at that time. If he had known it, he would have hit upon my system of pre-established harmony (Preface ****; *Theod.* sec. 22, 59, 60, 61, 63, 66, 345, 346 & seq., 354, 355).

81. According to this system, bodies act as if there were no souls (though this is impossible); and souls act as if there were no bodies; and both act as if each influenced the other.

82. As for *minds* or rational souls, I find that, at bottom, what we just said holds for all living beings and animals, namely that animals and souls begin only with the world and do not end any more than the world does. However, rational animals have this peculiarity, that their little spermatic animals, as long as they only remain in this state, have only ordinary or sensitive souls. But that as soon as the Elect among them, so to speak, attain human nature by actual conception, their sensitive souls are elevated to the rank of reason and to the prerogative of minds (sec. 91, 397).

83. Among other differences which exist between ordinary souls and minds, some of which I have already noted, there are also the following: that souls, in general, are living mirrors or images of the universe of creatures, but that minds are also images of the divinity itself, or of the author of nature, capable of knowing the system of the universe, and imitating something of it through their schematic representations [*échantillons architectoniques*] of it, each mind being like a little divinity in its own realm (sec. 147).

84. That is what makes minds capable of entering into a kind of society with God, and allows him to be, in relation to them, not only what an inventor is

to his machine (as God is in relation to the other creatures) but also what a prince is to his subjects, and even what a father is to his children.

85. From this it is easy to conclude that the collection of all minds must make up the city of God, that is, the most perfect possible state under the most perfect of monarchs (see 146, Abridgment, Objection 2).

86. This city of God, this truly universal monarchy, is a moral world within the natural world, and the highest and most divine of God's works. The glory of God truly consists in this city, for he would have none if his greatness and goodness were not known and admired by minds. It is also in relation to this divine city that God has goodness, properly speaking, whereas his wisdom and power are evident everywhere.

87. Since earlier we established a perfect harmony between two natural kingdoms, the one of efficient causes, the other of final causes, we ought to note here yet another harmony between the physical kingdom of nature and the moral kingdom of grace, that is, between God considered as the architect of the mechanism of the universe, and God considered as the monarch of the divine city of minds (sec. 62, 74, 118, 248, 112, 130, 247).

88. This harmony leads things to grace through the very paths of nature. For example, this globe must be destroyed and restored by natural means at such times as the governing of minds requires it, for the punishment of some and the reward of others (sec. 18 & seq., 110, 244, 245, 340).

89. It can also be said that God the architect pleases in every respect God the legislator, and, as a result, sins must carry their penalty with them by the order of nature, and even in virtue of the mechanical structure of things. Similarly, noble actions will receive their rewards through mechanical means with regard to bodies, even though this cannot, and must not, always happen immediately.

90. Finally, under this perfect government, there will be no good action that is unrewarded, no bad action that goes unpunished, and everything must result in the well-being of the good, that is, of those who are not dissatisfied in this great state, those who trust in providence, after having done their duty, and who love and imitate the author of all good, as they should, finding pleasure in the consideration of his perfections according to the nature of genuinely *pure love*, which takes pleasure in the happiness of the beloved. This is what causes wise and virtuous persons to work for all that appears to be in conformity with the presumptive or antecedent divine will, and nevertheless, to content themselves with what God brings about by his secret, consequent, or decisive will, since they recognize that if we could understand the order of the universe well enough, we would find that it surpasses all the wishes of the wisest, and that it is impossible to make it better than it is.[267] This is true not only for the whole in general, but also for ourselves in particular, if we are attached, as we should be, to the author of the whole, not only as the architect and efficient cause of our being, but also as to our

---

267. The distinction between God's antecedent and consequent will can be found in Thomas Aquinas, *Summa Theologiae* I, q. 19, art. 6, ad 1.

master and final cause; he ought to be the whole aim of our will, and he alone can make us happy (sec. 134 end, Preface *4.a.b.; *Theodicy*, sec. 278, Preface *.4.b).

Letter to Samuel Masson, on Body (1716)[268]

This is one of the last philosophical pieces composed by Leibniz. He is writing to Samuel Masson, the editor of the Histoire Critique de la République des Lettres, *thanking him for having just published some of his essays, and responding to an anonymous critic, whose essay was also published in the same issue.*

I AM INDEBTED to you, as well as to Mr. Des Maizeaux, for the publication of some pieces concerning my system in vol. XI of your journal.[269] His learned reflections on the passage from the author of the *De diaeta, attributed to Hippocrates*, deserve to be preserved.[270] Perhaps that ancient author, in denying true generation and true destruction, had in mind the atoms of Democritus, which are supposed to persist forever. But perhaps these words: *a living being cannot die unless the whole universe dies* (or perishes) *as well*,[271] also say something more. For taking them literally, I cannot find better words to express my own opinion. I do not know whether it is likely that by the word *zoon, living being*, the author meant us to understand all reality, as, for example, atoms, on the view of those who admit them. It is true that on my view, everything that one can truly call a *substance* is a living being; thus the

---

268. G VI 624-29. French.
269. Leibniz had written to Abbot Antonio Conti, forwarding some essays, comments, and explanations about the "system of pre-established harmony." Conti transmitted them to Des Maizeaux, a future editor of Leibniz's works (*Recueil de diverses Pièces sur la Philosophie, la Religion naturelle, l'Histoire, les mathematiques, etc., par Mrs Leibniz, Clarke, Newton, et autres auteurs célèbres*—1720). Des Maizeaux had shown some interest in Leibnizian philosophy, having written a critique of Leibniz's "New System of Nature" and having corresponded with Leibniz, asking for copies of Bayle's critique of Leibnizian philosophy. Conti's letter was the occasion for the renewal of the correspondence between Des Maizeaux and Leibniz. Des Maizeaux then forwarded the essays, together with a fragment of his critique of Leibniz and a letter from Leibniz, to Jean Masson. The latter gave them to his brother, Samuel Masson, editor of the *Histoire Critique de la République des Lettres*, to have them published. Volume XI (1716) of the *Histoire Critique* contained article 3: "Lettre de Mr. Leibniz à Mr. Des Maizeaux, contenant quelques Eclaircissements sur l'Explication précédente et sur d'autres endroits du Systéme de l'Harmonie préétablie. Hanovre, ce Juillet 1711."
270. Volume XI, article 2: "Explication d'un passage d'Hippocrate, dans le livre de la Diète, et du sentiment de Melisse et Parménide sur la durée des Substances, etc.: pour servir de Réponse à un endroit du nouveau Système de Mr. le Baron Leibnitz, de la Nature de la Communication des Substances ou de l'Harmonie préétablie. Par M. Des Maizeaux, à Mr. Jean Masson, Ministre de l'Eglise Anglicane, etc." Des Maizeaux's article is a scholarly analysis of ancient opinions; he makes a reasonable case for the proposition that no ancient, including the author of *The Regimen*, ever held the thesis of the indestructibility of animals.
271. *The Regimen* I.4.

author, it seems, would agree with me in this, if by *zoon* he understood every true substance. But I don't wish to argue this point with Mr. Des Maizeaux, and it appears difficult to completely decipher the opinions of the ancients, when they give little detail. However, it is good to notice and mark the traces of the truth from the time it begins to show itself to men.

I am also indebted to you, and to him, for having preserved my *Reply to Bayle's Second Objections*.[272] If this excellent man had replied to it, he would no doubt have given me some opportunities to say something better than what I can say about the *Critical Remarks* given to this *Reply*, which follow it in your journal.[273] The author of these *Remarks* appears to be a man of wit and learning, but he does not show here the exactitude and depth of thought that one recognizes in the writings of Bayle, and it seems that he wanted to turn the matter into a pleasantry. He may have spoken to the late Queen of Prussia[274] against my system, and Her Majesty may have told him to put his objections in writing. But I can truly say that I have never had knowledge of it; and it seems that this great princess, who had much good will toward me and who was capable of great depth of understanding, did not judge it appropriate to show it to me, either because she judged the writing too superficial, or because she found that it did not please her well enough.

The author begins by saying that he did not understand my writing. But Foucher, Father Lami, the Benedictine, Bayle, and even Arnauld, who have addressed objections to me, did not accuse me of obscurity. And Father Malebranche, whose doctrine may be well known to the learned author of the *Remarks*, having read my writings, found them sufficiently clear, even though we are not completely of the same opinion. I believe that this author did not want to take the trouble to read what I published previously about this matter. He compares my opinion with the *Cabbala* as interpreted by the Rabbis, which an able man published at Sulzbach.[275] The latter called himself Mr. Knorr of Rosenroth, Director of the Prince's Chancellery; he had wide-ranging erudition, and was a good friend of Francis Mercurius van Helmont, falling in a little with the opinion of this singular man.[276] I do not have the

---

272. The "Réponse de Mr. Leibnitz aux Réflexions contenues dans la second Edition du Dictionnaire Critique de Mr. Bayle, article Rorarius, sur le Système de l'Harmonie préétablie," was published in a subsequent volume of the journal (and, as Des Maizeaux tells us, unfortunately after Leibniz's death).

273. Article 4 was an anonymous essay, said to have been written on January 14, 1703, in Berlin: "Remarques Critiques sur le Système de Monsr. Leibnitz de l'Harmonie préétablie, où l'on recherche en passant pourquoi les Systèmes Métaphysiques des Mathématiciens ont moins de clarté, que ceux des autres: écrites par ordre de sa Majesté la feue Reine de Prusse."

274. "The late Queen of Prussia" is a reference to Queen Sophie Charlotte. This remark, along with the alleged date and place of composition and the contents of the anonymous critique, allow us to speculate that the anonymous author was John Toland (or, at least, that Leibniz thought so). See also above, the "Letter to Sophie Charlotte, On What Is Independent of Sense and Matter."

275. Knorr von Rosenroth (d. 1689) was the Latin translator of the *Kabbala denudata* (1677–84).

276. Francis van Helmont (1614–98) was an alchemist who believed in the transmigration of souls. Leibniz had met and corresponded with him. Despite the distance Leibniz wishes to place

time to consult this latter work and compare its opinions with mine. But perhaps by examining it, we would find in it as much or more difference than Des Maizeaux found between the work of the Greek author of the *De diaeta* and mine. But even when our views agreed, there wouldn't be any problem at all. However, I would not say, as has been imputed to me, *that there is a single substance for all things,* and that this substance is mind. For there are as many completely distinct substances as there are monads, and not all the monads are minds, and these monads do not make up a whole that is truly one, and the whole, were they to make one up, would not be a mind. I am also far from saying that matter is a *shadow* and even a *nothing.* These expressions go too far. Matter is an aggregate, *not a substance but a substantiatum*[277] as would be an army or a flock; and, insofar as it is considered as making up *one* thing, it is a phenomenon, very real, in fact, but a thing whose *unity* is constructed by our conception.

The term *pre-established harmony* has seemed sufficiently intelligible to people without my having to explain what Aristoxenes meant to say when he called the soul a harmony to make them understand it; for that notion one can have a glance at Plato's *Phaedo.* The author, who did not wish to meditate sufficiently to understand what has seemed extremely clear to others, did not go so far as to understand what *entelechies* and *living mirrors* meant. It was, no doubt, all gibberish [*Hiroquois*] to him. The mirror gives us a figurative expression, one suitable enough and already used by philosophers and theologians when they speak of an infinitely more perfect mirror, that is, of *the mirror of divinity,* which they made the object of the beatific vision. I do not say, as is imputed to me, that matter is a *mode,* still less that it is a mode of mind. An interpreter who explains the opinions of others in this way is extremely apt to warp their thoughts. It is true that what allows one to conceive the unity of a piece of matter is, no doubt, only a modification, in particular motion and shape, which make up its entire essence when entelechies are set aside. Likewise, this piece is only a fleeting thing and never remains the same more than a moment, always losing and acquiring parts. That is why the Platonists said of material things that they are always becoming, and never are, nor do they exist at any time. The author of the *Remarks* said that *my hypothesis upsets the common notions, because it establishes that there is an infinity of minds that have no more thought or perception than the particles of matter have.* He is right to say that he does not understand *my hypothesis, for he represents it very badly.* According to me, all minds have thought and all monads, or simple substances that are truly one, have perception. If the author had

---

between himself, on the one hand, and Francis van Helmont and Knorr von Rosenroth, on the other, Leibniz was considerably influenced by them, and especially by van Helmont. In 1697, with Leibniz's help, van Helmont published two volumes, including an older German translation of Boethius's *Consolation of Philosophy* that he had done some years before with Knorr von Rosenroth, and some commentaries on Genesis to which Leibniz himself may have contributed.

277. A *substantiatum* is an aggregate of substances that is not itself a substance. See the note to p. 200 above.

given some attention to my discourses, he would have seen how each simple substance acts without constraint, since it is entirely the principle of its actions; he would have also seen how there are always characters in the imagination that correspond to the most abstract thoughts—witness arithmetic and algebra; and he would have seen how these mirrors he calls magic for a pleasantry, how these monads represent the universe. Only God has the penetration to see everything in them. But that does not prevent everything from being represented there, and one must know that even in the least portion of matter, he who knows all reads the whole universe in virtue of the harmony of things. It is true that this could not be if matter were not actually subdivided to infinity. But it is impossible that things are not this way. One finds that everything conspires in the universe, as Hippocrates says of the human body. I have denied that beasts are capable of reflection; the author states that they demonstrate by their actions that they are. He should have brought forth some proofs of this. Up until now people have distinguished between the perceptions we grant them and the reflective acts we do not.

I confess that my opinion, according to which matter cannot pass for a real substance, will surprise some minds who think superficially, having been led to believe that *matter is the only substance in the universe*; but my hypothesis is no less true for this. To say that souls are *intelligent points* is to use an expression that is insufficiently exact. When I call them centers or concentrations of external things, I am speaking analogically. Points, strictly speaking, are extremities of extension, and not, in any way, the constitutive parts of things; geometry shows this sufficiently.

When the author of the objection says that *particular bodies have no reality,* for a different reason than mine, he goes further than I do in opposition to the reality of bodies. But continuity,* which always places something between any two things, does not prevent distinctness. When there is a flock of sheep, one sheep is distinct from another, and there is something other than sheep between two of them. He says that he does not understand *how an indivisible point can have a composite tendency*. But that can always be found in mechanics; since bodies often have composite tendencies, their points or extremities, which go as the bodies go, also have composite tendencies. But the tendency of which I speak is of another nature; it is internal to the soul, which is not a point. It is the progress of one thought to another, and since thoughts (though in a soul not composed of parts) represent things composed of parts, it is only in this sense that these perceptions are called composite, as are their tendencies or appetites—that is, they contain a multitude of modifications and relations all at once. It seems that the author of the objection denies the immateriality of the soul when he states: *according to me thought is accomplished by a composite being*. I would have to go on too long to refute this; thus I content myself for the time being in having on my side all those who believe the soul immaterial and indivisible: the Aristotelians (at least the Thomists) and the Cartesians agree on this. It is true that, on my view, the soul is always accompanied by a composite being, or organs. However, the simplicity of a substance does not prevent several modes from being in it all at once. There are successive perceptions, but there are also simultaneous ones, for, when there is a perception of the whole, at the same time there are perceptions of its actual parts, and it is even the case that each part has more than one modification. There is a perception all at once, not only of each modification, but also of each part. These perceptions, however much they are multiplied, are different from one another, even though our attention cannot always distinguish them, and that is what makes confused perceptions, of which each distinct one contains an infinity because of its relation to everything external. Finally, that which is composition of parts outside is represented only by the* composition of modifications in the monad; without this, simple beings could not be distinguished internally from one another, and they would have no relation to external things. And finally, since everywhere there are only simple substances whose composites are only aggregates, there would be no variation or differentiation among things if simple substances did not have any internal variation. What follows in the *Remarks* contains no other objections, only exaggerations of the supposed obscurity, together with some clever and ingenious pleasantry.

Finally, the author of the *Critical Remarks*, a man of wit no doubt, but one whose wit is content with a superficial examination of things, even though he is capable of going deeper, ends with a reflection on a fact that appears doubtful, and even false, to many people. He claims that mathematicians who dabble in philosophy scarcely ever succeed; on the contrary, it seems that they should succeed best, since they are accustomed to thinking with exactitude. In our time, Gassendi and Descartes have been excellent mathematicians and also excellent philosophers, to the extent that they have become heads of sects. The ancients considered mathematics as the passage from physics to metaphysics or to natural theology, and they were right. The author does not present any example of his claim, and he seeks to explain an imaginary fact. Minds like his despise what requires deep meditation, which is necessary in mathematics. And here is the reason why he imagines that mathematicians do not succeed in philosophy. The Queen thought otherwise; she, as well as her mother, the elector, often regretted not having been initiated in mathematics. I do not agree at all with the reasons that the author of the *Remarks* puts forth to prove his opinion. He claims that mathematicians take abstract beings for real beings, or relative beings for absolute beings. *I* do not do this, at least, for I take the beings of pure mathematics, like space, and what depends upon them, to be relative beings, and not at all absolute, and I do not agree with those who make of space an absolute reality, as the supporters of the vacuum usually do. I am also far from *making extension up of mathematical points.* That is not a view commonly held by mathematicians, and the author is wrong to impute it to them; even though his slightly cavalier reason against this view does not prove anything, still, there are more solid reasons for it. And, notwithstanding my *infinitesimal calculus,* I do not admit any real infinite number, even though I confess that the multitude of things surpasses any finite number, or rather any number. The author is right to criticize the ideas of points composing [extension] and of an infinite number. But he no doubt believed that I held these, and these prejudices against me could have contributed to his wanting to refute me. But perhaps he will see that he went too fast. I would prefer to give this reason [for his zeal against me], rather than that he is biased toward the Epicurean System on the issue of souls, which seems to show through, and which would cause harm, if it were true. The infinitesimal calculus is useful with respect to the application of mathematics to physics; however, that is not how I claim to account for the nature of things. For I consider infinitesimal quantities to be useful fictions. I also approve of what is said here against those who claim that weight is essential to matter. If the author had wanted to speak to me about these matters before rejecting me (for it seems that we were within range), he would perhaps have saved me the bother of responding to him here, though it has not been a very great bother. I want people to give me objections that require me to go beyond what I have said already. These kinds of objections are instructive, and I take pleasure in them so that I might profit from them, and so that others can profit also; but they are not so easy to make.

From the Letters to Wolff (1714–15)[278]

Christian Wolff (1679–1754) was one of the dominant figures of German intellectual life in the eighteenth century, the author of a seemingly endless series of philosophical texts in German and Latin. In his youth, from 1704 until Leibniz's death in 1716, Wolff carried on an active correspondence with Leibniz. Leibniz was Wolff's sponsor at the Berlin Academy in 1711; Wolff, in turn, popularized many of Leibniz's ideas after the death of his elder sponsor.

A. From Wolff to Leibniz, 3 October 1714

FURTHERMORE I would be pleased to know how Your Excellency usually defines perfection. Indeed, various definitions come to my mind, but either the notions of use or end enter into them, or they are insufficient for some other reason.

B. From Leibniz to Wolff, Winter 1714–15

THE PERFECTION about which you ask is the degree of positive reality, or what comes to the same thing, the degree of affirmative intelligibility, so that something more perfect is something in which more things worthy of observation [*notatu digna*] are found.

C. From Wolff to Leibniz, February 1715

I HAVE already found that your definition of perfection answers my needs in many ways. Moreover, although I am confused over several things (for

---

278. GLW 160, 161, 163, 166–67, 170–72. Latin.

example, whether more things worthy of observation [*observabilia*] occur in a healthy body than in a sick body, since a healthy body is judged more perfect than a sick one), I shall easily satisfy myself as soon as I meditate on it more carefully. For I foresee that among the things worthy of observation one must include the things that follow in any way from the assumed state of the thing.

D. From Leibniz to Wolff, 2 April 1715

I AM GRATIFIED to know that you are not displeased with my very general definition of perfection. I have noticed from the *Acts* that, having accepted certain things from me, especially things concerning the definitions of similitude and of use, and things concerning the analysis of axioms into identical propositions and definitions, you have used them in your own distinguished work, which pleases me so much that I offer you my thanks on that account.[279]

One shouldn't doubt that there are more things worthy of observation [*observabilia*] in a healthy body than in a sick one. If everyone were sick, many remarkable observations would cease, namely, those constituting the ordinary course of nature, which is disturbed in disease; the more order there is, the more things worthy of observation there are. Imperfections are exceptions which disturb general rules, that is, *general observations.* If there were many exceptions to a rule, there would be nothing worthy of observation [*observatione dignum*], but only chaos. In my *Theodicy* I noted that wisdom always acts through principles, that is, through rules, and never through exceptions, except when rules interfere with one another, and one rule limits another.[280] And so one can also say that which is *more perfect* is that which is more regular, that is, that which admits of more observations, namely, more general observations. And so, my view is expressed more distinctly in this way, for the term 'observation' is commonly used even for exceptions. However, a multitude of regularities brings forth variety. So uniformity, that is, generality, and variety are reconciled.

E. From Wolff to Leibniz, 4 May 1715

I NEED the notion of perfection for dealing with morals. For, when I see that some actions tend toward our perfection and that of others, while others tend toward our imperfection and that of others, the sensation of perfection excites a certain pleasure [*voluptas*] and the sensation of imperfection a certain

---

279. Leibniz may be referring here to Wolff's "Meditatio de similitudine figurarum . . ." which was to appear in the *Acta Eruditorum* in the May 1715 issue (pp. 213–18). There (p. 214), Wolff makes prominent mention of a definition of 'similar' Leibniz communicated to him "about four years ago." Leibniz and his "On Nature Itself" also have a prominent part in a discussion of the question of occasionalism and activity in bodies Wolff published a few years earlier, "Defensio virium in corporibus existentiam contra nuperas objectiones," *Acta Eruditorwn*, Sept. 1711, pp. 400–05.
280. *Theodicy*, part II, sec. 208.

displeasure [*nausea.*] And the emotions [*affectus*], by virtue of which the mind
is, in the end, inclined or disinclined, are modifications of this pleasure and
displeasure; I explain the origin of natural obligation in this way. As soon
as the perfection toward which the action tends, and which it indicates, is
represented in the intellect, pleasure arises, which causes us to cling more
closely to the action that we should contemplate. And so, once circumstances
overflowing with good for us or for others have been noticed, the pleasure is
modified and is transformed into an emotion by virtue of which the mind is,
at last, inclined toward appetition. And from this inborn disposition toward
obligation, I deduce all practical morals, properly enough. From this also
comes the general rule or law of nature that our actions ought to be directed
toward the highest perfection of ourselves and others. Human nature forces
us to proceed in this direction and no other. Therefore, I need a notion of
perfection so that these principles can be illuminated. When I taught morality
in the Winter, many things that seem quite uncommon presented themselves
to me; but I don't think that it is necessary to tell you of them here. However,
most importantly, I then taught the foundation of civil obligation and its
distinction from natural obligation in a clearer way, and established more
certain limits on the love of others, so that in a particular case, one could
demonstrate what other person we should prefer when not everyone can
be satisfied at once. But when I transferred Your Excellency's notion of
perfection to this case, it seemed to me that the plurality of things worthy of
observation [*observabilia*] wasn't sufficient; I judged that we still need some
further delimitation, and I am perplexed about how it should be formulated.
For example, I must be shown that the divine intellect is supremely perfect.
I already assume that the divine intellect is the simultaneous and adequate
representation of all possible things, and I see that altogether more things
can be observed in it than in another intellect limited either on account of its
object or on account of its mode or form. However, it seems to me that I must
prove that in the divine intellect, everything which can be conceived in an
unlimited intellect is observed, and that the unlimited is more perfect than
the limited. Indeed, Your Excellency now adds another condition, namely
that things worthy of observation are to be calculated from regularity; but it
isn't known how regularity is to be calculated. For example, from what is the
regularity of the intellect to be calculated? It seemed to me that perfection
consists in the plurality of things worthy of observation in the essence. Of
course I take 'essence' to be a synonym of 'possibility', and thus I don't
distinguish the idea of an essence from the idea of a distinct possibility. But
yet the condition which* I should have derived from this didn't display itself
distinctly to me in every case.

F. From Leibniz to Wolff,
18 May 1715

F INALLY, I have not, as you think, given up my prior view in defining
perfection. What I wrote most recently is only an explanation and illustration of the prior view. When I say that something in which more is worthy of

observation is more perfect, I understand general observations or rules, not exceptions, which constitute imperfections. The more there is worthy of observation in a thing, the more general properties, the more harmony it contains; therefore, it is the same to look for perfection in an essence and in the properties that flow from the essence. I am astonished that you ask what it is to be more regular, since I have already shown that it is that which provides more general rules or general observations. Nothing is more regular than the divine intellect, which is the source of all rules, and produces the most regular, that is, the most perfect system of the world, the system that is as harmonious as possible and thus contains the greatest number of general observations.

You also see from this how the sense of harmony, that is, the observation of agreements [*consensus*] might bring forth pleasure, since it delights perception, makes it easier, and extricates it from confusion. Hence, you know that consonances please, since agreement is easily observable in them. Therefore, it seems to me that everything harmonizes quite beautifully in theory and in practice, and there is not the least bit of difficulty. Agreement is sought in variety, and the more easily it is observed there, the more it pleases; and in this consists the sense of perfection. Moreover, the perfection a thing has is greater, to the extent that there is more agreement in greater variety, whether we observe it or not. Therefore, this is what order and regularity come to. Spinoza didn't understand these things when he eliminated perfection from things as a chimera of our mind;[281] but it belongs to the divine mind not less but more [than it belongs in ours]. There are also animals capable of a certain sort of pleasure, as it were, since they observe agreement, though they do this empirically, not *a priori*, as we do, so that they cannot give reasons. I don't know whether it can be said more absolutely that the unlimited is more perfect than the limited. The unlimited is a certain sort of chaos, but its observation brings on discomfort [*molestia*], not pleasure. If the divine intellect were to produce good things and bad in equal measure, it would remain unlimited, but it would not remain perfect. It is more perfect for the better things among the possibles alone to exist than for good and bad things to exist equally and indiscriminately. But [God's] intellect is also unlimited in its kind with respect to the best, since it produces infinite harmonies.

In morals I set up our *happiness* [*felicitas*] as an end; this I define as a state of enduring joy [*laetitia*]. Joy I define as an extraordinary predominance of pleasure [*voluptas*], for in the midst of joy we can sense certain sorrows, but sorrows which are hardly to be considered in comparison with the pleasures, as, for example, if somewhere a kingdom were granted to an ambitious person suffering hopelessly from the gout.[282] Moreover, it is necessary that the joy be enduring, so that it not be withdrawn by a subsequent greater sadness [*tristitia*] by chance. Furthermore, *pleasure* is the sensation of perfection. *Perfection* is the harmony of things, or the state where everything is worthy

---

281. See the preface to part IV of Spinoza's *Ethics*, Geb. II 207–08.
282. It is interesting to note that Leibniz suffered from gout in his last years.

of being observed, that is, the state of agreement [*consensus*] or identity[283] in variety; you can even say that it is the degree of contemplatibility [*consider-abilitas*]. Indeed, order, regularity, and harmony come to the same thing. You can even say that it is the degree of essence, if essence is calculated from harmonizing properties, which give essence weight and momentum, so to speak. Hence, it also follows quite nicely that God, that is, the supreme mind, is endowed with perception, indeed to the greatest degree; otherwise he would not care about the harmonies.

---

283. This might be a slip of the pen for 'regularity.'

PART II

Leibniz on His Contemporaries

Descartes and Malebranche

Letter to Countess Elizabeth(?),
On God and Formal Logic (1678?)[284]

IF YOUR HIGHNESS had not ordered me to explain more distinctly what I said in passing about Descartes and his proof for the existence of God, it would have been presumptuous of me to try. For Your Highness's extraordinary intelligence (which I recognized far better when I had the honor of hearing you speak for a moment, than by reading what so many great men had published about you) anticipates everything one can tell you with respect to a subject which, no doubt, has long been the object of your most profound thoughts. Therefore, I undertake this discourse, not because I intend to propose something new to you, but in order to learn your judgment, which I do not aspire to solicit.[285]

Your Highness knows that there is nothing more trite today than demonstrations of God's existence; I observe that it is almost like proofs for squaring the circle and perpetual motion. The greenest student of mathematics and of mechanics lays claim to these sublime problems, and there is not a distiller, even the most ignorant, who does not promise himself the philosopher's stone. Similarly, all those who have learned a little metaphysics begin first with the demonstration of God's existence and the immortality of our souls, which, in my opinion, are the fruits of all our studies, since they constitute the foundation of our greatest hopes. I admit that Your Highness would have no reason to have a better opinion of me unless I told her that I came to these matters after having prepared my mind by extremely precise investigations in the rigorous sciences, which are the touchstone of our thoughts. Everywhere else people flatter themselves and find flatterers, but there are very few

---

284. A II, I, 433–38; G IV 290–96. French.
285. Leibniz addresses the noble recipient in the third person. We have changed this to second person.

mathematicians who have spread errors, and there are none who could get others to approve their mistakes. In my early years I was well enough versed in the subtleties of the Thomists and Scotists, and when I left school, I threw myself into the arms of jurisprudence, which required history as well. But my travels allowed me to know some great persons who gave me a taste for mathematics. I applied myself to it with an almost disproportionate passion during the four years I resided in Paris, which resulted in greater success and public praise than a novice and stranger could have expected. With respect to analysis, I am not so bold as to say how the men greatest in these matters today have judged my work, but with respect to mechanics, the arithmetical machine, whose model I showed to the two Royal Societies of France and England, appeared to be something completely extraordinary. It is not the Rabdology of Napier[286] (the Scottish Baron) transformed into a machine, as are some others that have been made public since. The two Academies saw an infinite difference between my machine and the others, which are, in fact, mere games and have only a name in common with mine, something people will recognize when it is perfected, as I am expecting it will be.

As for myself, I cherished mathematics only because I found in it the traces of the art of *invention in general*; and it seems to me that I discovered, in the end, that Descartes himself had not yet penetrated the mystery of this great science. I recall that he said somewhere that the excellence of his method, which only appears probable from his physics, is demonstrated by his geometry. But I must admit that I mainly recognized the imperfection of his method in his geometry itself. For, we should not be surprised if there is much to criticize in his physics, since Descartes did not have enough experiments at his disposal. But geometry depends only on ourselves; it does not need external help. I claim then that there is yet another analysis in geometry which is completely different from the analysis of Viète and of Descartes, who did not advance sufficiently in this, since its most important problems do not depend on the equations to which all of Descartes's geometry reduces. Despite what he had advanced too boldly in his geometry (namely, that all problems reduce to his equations and his curved lines), he himself was forced to recognize this defect in one of his letters; for de Beaune had proposed to him one of these strange but important problems of the inverse method of tangents, and he admitted that he did not yet see it clearly enough.[287] I fortunately discovered that this very problem can be resolved in three lines by the new analysis which

---

286. Leibniz is referring to John Napier (1560–1617), the inventor of logarithms, who published a book called *Rabdologiae, seu numerationis per virgulas, libri duo* in 1617. The book describes a mechanical aid to multiplication by "Napier's Bones," or numbering rods; Napier's Bones were modified in various ways during the seventeenth century so that they could be manipulated rapidly, in the fashion of an adding machine.

287. In an article in the *Acta Eruditorum* (1684), "Nova methodus pro maximis et minimis, itemque tangentibus, quae nec fractas, nec irrationales quantitates moratur, et singulare pro illis calculi genus" (GM V, 220–26), Leibniz specifies that the inverse tangent problem he can solve by means of his methods was one proposed by Florimond De Beaune (1601–52) to Descartes. Leibniz also observes that Descartes tried to solve it in his letter to De Beaune, 20 February 1639, AT II, 510–19.

I am using. But it would be premature of me to go into the details; it suffices to say that geometry, enriched by these new means, can surpass the geometry of Viète and Descartes as much and incomparably more than theirs surpassed the geometry of the ancients. And this is not only in curiosities, but in the solution of the most important problems for mechanics.

I do not wish to discuss physics here, even though I have demonstrated rules of motion that are quite different from those of Descartes. I come, then, to metaphysics, and I can state that it is for the love of metaphysics that I have passed through all these stages. For I have recognized that metaphysics is scarcely different from the true logic, that is, from the art of invention in general; for, in fact, metaphysics is natural theology, and the same God who is the source of all goods is also the principle of all knowledge. This is because the idea of God contains within it absolute being, that is, what is simple in our thoughts, from which everything that we think draws its origin. Descartes did not go about it in this way. He gave two ways of proving the existence of God. The *first* is that there is an idea of God in us since, no doubt, we think about God, and we cannot think of something without having its idea.[288] Now, if we have an idea of God, and if it is true [*véritable*], that is, if it is the idea of an infinite being, and if it represents it faithfully, it could not be caused by something lesser, and consequently, God himself must be its cause. Therefore, he must exist. The *other* reasoning is even shorter. It is that God is a being who possesses all perfections, and consequently, he possesses existence, which is to be counted as one of the perfections.[289] Therefore, he exists. It must be said that these reasonings are somewhat suspect, because they go too fast, and because they force themselves upon us without enlightening us. Real demonstrations, on the other hand, generally fill the mind with some solid nourishment. However, the crux of the matter is difficult to find, and I see that many able people who have formulated objections to Descartes were led astray.

Some have believed that there is no idea of God because he is not subject to imagination, assuming that idea and image are the same thing. I am not of their opinion, and I know perfectly well that there are ideas of thought, existence, and similar things, of which there are no images. For we think of something and when we notice in there what it is that allows us to recognize it, this is what constitutes the idea of the thing, insofar as it is in our soul. This is why there is also an idea of what is not material or imaginable.

Others agree that there is an idea of God, and that this idea contains all perfections, but they cannot understand how existence follows from it, either because they do not agree that existence is to be counted among the perfections, or because they do not see how a simple idea or thought can imply an existence outside us. As for me, I genuinely believe that anyone who has recognized this idea of God, and who sees that existence is a perfection, must admit that existence belongs to God. In fact, I do not question the idea of

---

288. Cf. Descartes, Meditation III.
289. Cf. Descartes, Meditation V.

God any more than I do his existence; on the contrary, I claim to have a demonstration of it. But I do not want us to flatter ourselves and persuade ourselves that we can arrive at such a great thing with such little cost. Paralogisms are dangerous in this matter; when they occur, they reflect on us, and they strengthen the opposite side. I therefore say that we must prove with the greatest imaginable exactness that there is an idea of a completely perfect being, that is, an idea of God. It is true that the objections of those who believed that they could prove the contrary because there is no image of God are worthless, as I have just shown. But we also have to admit that the proof Descartes gives to establish the idea of God is imperfect. How, he would say, can one speak of God without thinking of him, and how can one think of him without having an idea of him? Yes, no doubt we sometimes think about impossible things and we even construct demonstrations from them. For example, Descartes holds that squaring the circle is impossible, and yet we still think about it and draw consequences about what would happen if it were given. The motion having the greatest speed is impossible in any body whatsoever, because, for example, if we assumed it in a circle, then another circle concentric to the former circle, surrounding it and firmly attached to it, would move with a speed still greater than the former, which, consequently, would not be of the greatest degree, in contradiction to what we had assumed. In spite of all that, we think about this greatest speed, something that has no idea since it is impossible. Similarly, the greatest circle of all is an impossible thing, and the number of all possible units is no less so; we have a demonstration of this. And nevertheless, we think about all this. That is why there are surely grounds for wondering whether we should be careful about the idea of the greatest of all beings, and whether it might not contain a contradiction. For I fully understand, for example, the nature of motion and speed and what it is to be greatest, but, for all that, I do not understand whether all those notions are compatible, and whether there is a way of joining them and making them into an idea of the greatest speed of which motion is capable. Similarly, although I know what being is, and what it is to be the greatest and most perfect, nevertheless I do not yet know, for all that, whether there isn't a hidden contradiction in joining all that together, as there is, in fact, in the previously stated examples. In brief, I do not yet know, for all that, whether such a being is possible, for if it were not possible, there would be no idea of it. However, I must admit that God has a great advantage, in this respect, over all other things. For to prove that he exists, it would be sufficient to prove that he is possible, something we find nowhere else, as far as I know. Moreover, I infer from that that there is a presumption that God exists. For there is always a presumption on the side of possibility, that is, everything is held to be possible unless it is proven to be impossible. There is, therefore, a presumption that God is possible, that is, that he exists, since in him existence follows from possibility. This is sufficient for practical matters in life, but it is not sufficient for a demonstration. I have strongly disputed this matter with several Cartesians, but I finally succeeded in this with some of the most able of them who have frankly admitted, after having understood the force of my reasons, that this possibility is still to be demonstrated. There are even some who, challenged by me to do so, have undertaken this demonstration, but they have not yet succeeded.

Since Your Highness is intelligent, you see what the state of things is and you see we can do nothing unless we prove this possibility. When I consider all this, I take pity on man's weakness, and I take care not to exclude myself from it. Descartes, who was no doubt one of the greatest men of this century, erred in so visible a manner, and many illustrious people erred with him. Nevertheless, we do not question their intelligence or their care. All of this could give some people a bad opinion of the certainty of our knowledge in general. For, one can say, with so many able men unable to avoid a trap, what can I hope for, I, who am nothing compared to them? Nevertheless, we must not lose our courage. There is a way of avoiding error, which these able men have not condescended to use; it would have been contrary to the greatness of their minds, at least in appearance, and with respect to the common people. All those who wish to appear to be great figures and who set themselves up as leaders of sects have a bit of the acrobat in them. A tightrope walker does not allow himself to be braced in order to avoid falling; if he did so, he would be sure of his act, but he would no longer appear a skillful man. I will be asked, what then is this wonderful way that can prevent us from falling? I am almost afraid to say it—it appears to be too lowly. But I am speaking to Your Highness who does not judge things by their appearance. In brief, it is to construct arguments only in proper form [*in forma*], I seem to see only people who cry out against me and who send me back to school. But I beg them to be a little patient, for perhaps they do not understand me; arguments in proper form do not always bear the stamp of *Barbara Celarent*.[290] Any rigorous demonstration that does not omit anything necessary for the force of reasoning is of this kind, and I dare say that the account of an accountant and a calculation of analysis are arguments in proper form, since there is nothing missing in them and since the form or arrangement of the whole reasoning is the cause of their being evident. It is only the form that distinguishes an account book made according to the practice we commonly call Italian (of which Stevin has written a whole treatise) from the confused journal of someone ignorant of business. That is why I maintain that, in order to reason with evidence in all subjects, we must hold some consistent formalism [*formalité constante.*] There would be less eloquence, but more certainty. But in order to determine the formalism that would do no less in metaphysics, physics, and morals, than calculation does in mathematics, that would even give us degrees of probability when we can only reason probabilistically, I would have to relate here the thoughts I have on a new characteristic [*characteristique*], something that would take too long. Nevertheless, I will

---

290. *Barbara Celarent* is a reference to the first line of some thirteenth-century mnemonic nonsense verses enabling students to remember the rules governing the validity of syllogisms; the full line would be "Barbara, Celarent, Darii, Ferioque prioris." Leibniz's statement, "arguments in proper form do not always bear the stamp of *Barbara Celarent*," indicates that there are valid arguments whose validity cannot be established by syllogistic means.

say, in brief, that this characteristic would represent our thoughts truly and distinctly, and that when a thought is composed of other simpler ones, its character would also be similarly composed. I dare not say what would follow from this for the perfection of the sciences—it would appear incredible. And yet, there is a demonstration of this. The only thing I will say here is that since that which we know is from reasoning or experience, it is certain that henceforth all reasoning in demonstrative or probable matters will demand no more skill than a calculation in algebra does; that is, one would derive from given experiments everything that can be derived, just as in algebra. But for now it is sufficient for me to note that the foundation of my characteristic is also the foundation of the demonstration of God's existence. For simple thoughts are the elements of the characteristic and simple forms are the source of things. I maintain that all simple forms are compatible among themselves. That is a proposition whose demonstration I cannot give without having to explain the fundamentals of the characteristic at length. But if that is granted, it follows that God's nature, which contains all simple forms taken absolutely, is possible. Now, we have proven above that God exists, as long as he is possible. Therefore, he exists. And that is what needed to be demonstrated.

Letter to Molanus(?) On God and the Soul (ca. 1679)[291]

SINCE YOU WANT me to frankly tell you my thoughts on Cartesianism, I will hide nothing from you that I think, at least nothing that can be stated briefly; and I will make no claims without giving or being able to give a reason for them.

First, all those who completely surrender themselves to the opinions of any author become enslaved and raise suspicions of error on themselves; for to assert that Descartes is the only author who is exempt from significant error is to assert something that might be true, but is not likely. In fact, this kind of attachment belongs only to those who themselves do not have the strength or the leisure to meditate, or who do not wish to take the trouble to do so. That is why the three noted Academies of our time, England's Royal Society, which was established first, and then the *Académie Royale des Sciences* at Paris and the *Accademia del Cimento* at Florence, have openly asserted that they did not want to be Aristotelians, or Cartesians, or Epicureans, or followers of any author whatever.

Moreover, I have recognized from experience that those who are completely Cartesian are not capable of discovery; they merely undertake the job of interpreting or commenting upon their master, as the Scholastics did with Aristotle. There have been many beautiful discoveries since Descartes, but, as far as I know, not one of them has come from a true Cartesian. I know these people a little, and I defy them to name one such discovery from their

---

291. A II, 1, 499–504; G IV 297–303. French.

ranks. This is evidence that either Descartes did not know the true method, or else that he did not leave it to them.

Descartes himself had a rather limited mind. He excelled all people in speculation, but he discovered nothing useful for the portion of life which falls under the senses, and nothing useful in the practice of the arts. His meditations were either too abstract, as in his metaphysics and his geometry, or too much subject to the imagination, as in his principles of natural philosophy. The only useful things he thought he had produced were telescopic lenses, constructed according to hyperbolic curves, with which he promised to show us animals, or things as small as animals, on the moon. Unfortunately, he was never able to find workmen capable of executing his designs, and in any case, it has since been shown that the advantage of hyperbolic curves is not as great as he had thought.[292]

It is true that Descartes was a great genius and that the sciences owe him great debts, but not in the way the Cartesians believe. Therefore, I must go into some specifics and give examples of what he borrowed from others, what he himself accomplished, and what he left us to accomplish. We shall see in this way whether I speak without knowing what I am talking about. First, his morality is a composite of the opinions of the Stoics and Epicureans—something not very difficult to do, for Seneca had already reconciled them quite well.[293] Descartes wants us to follow reason, or else to follow the nature of things, as the Stoics said, something with which everybody will agree. He adds that we should not trouble ourselves with things that are not in our power. That is precisely the Stoic doctrine; it places the greatness and freedom of their much-praised wise man in his strength of mind to do without things that do not depend upon us, and endure things when they come in spite of ourselves. That is why I am accustomed to calling this morality the art of patience. The supreme good, according to the Stoics, and even according to Aristotle, is to act in accordance with virtue or prudence, and the pleasure resulting from this resolution is properly the tranquility of soul or indifference [indoleance] that both the Stoics and Epicureans sought for and recommended, under different names. We need only inspect the incomparable manual of Epictetus and the Epicurean of Laercia to admit that Descartes has not much advanced the practice of morality. But it seems to me that this art of patience, which for him constitutes the art of living, is not yet everything. Patience without hope cannot last and scarcely consoles; it is in this that Plato, in my opinion, surpasses all others, for he brings us to hope for a better life with good reason, and he is closest to Christianity. For one to have a high opinion of him, it is sufficient to read his excellent dialogue on the immortality of the soul (or on the death of Socrates), which Theophile has translated into French.[294] I think that Pythagoras did the same thing and that his metempsy-

---

292. See the 7th to 10th discourses of Descartes's *Optics*, in Ols.

293. Descartes's moral theory is presented in a series of letters to the Princess Elizabeth written in the 1640s. The relevant letters are collected and translated in Descartes (ed. and trans. John J. Bloom), *His Moral Philosophy and Psychology* (New York: New York University Press, 1978).

294. The reference here is to Plato's *Phaedo*.

chosis was only a device to accommodate the common people; among his disciples, I think, he reasoned differently. Thus, Ocellus Lucanus, who was one of his disciples, and from whom we have a small but excellent fragment of his *Universe*, does not say a word about metempsychosis. Someone might tell me that Descartes established the existence of God and the immortality of soul extremely well. But I fear that we are deceived by fine words, since Descartes's God, or perfect being, is not a God like the one we imagine or hope for, that is, a God just and wise, doing everything possible for the good of creatures. Rather, Descartes's God is something approaching the God of Spinoza, namely, the principle of things and a certain supreme power or primitive nature that puts everything into motion [*action*] and does everything that can be done. Descartes's God has neither *will* nor *understanding*, since according to Descartes he does not have the *good* as object of the will, nor the true as object of the understanding. Also, he does not want his God to act in accordance with some end; this is why he eliminates the search for final causes from philosophy, under the clever pretext that we are not capable of knowing God's ends.[295] On the other hand, Plato has nicely shown that if God acts in accordance with wisdom, since God is the author of things, then the true physics consists in knowing the ends and uses of things.[296] For science consists in knowing reasons, and the reasons for what was created by an understanding are the final causes or plans of the understanding that made them. These are apparent in their use and function, which is why considering the use parts have is so helpful in anatomy. That is why a God like Descartes's allows us no consolation other than that of patience through strength. Descartes tells us in some places that matter passes successively through all possible forms,[297] that is, that his God created everything that can be made, and passes successively through all possible combinations, following a necessary and fated order. But for this doctrine, the necessity of matter alone would be sufficient, or rather, his God is merely this necessity or this principle of necessity acting as it can in matter. Therefore, it is impossible to believe that this God cares for intelligent creatures any more than he does for the others; each creature will be happy or unhappy depending upon how it finds itself engulfed in these great currents or vortices. Descartes has good reason to recommend, instead of felicity, patience without hope.

But one of those good people among the Cartesians, deceived by the beautiful words of his master, will tell me that Descartes has, however, quite nicely established the immortality of the soul, and consequently, a better life. When I hear such things, I am surprised by the ease with which one can deceive people merely by playing around with pleasing words, though corrupting

---

295. On the claim that the world is good because God created it, and not *vice versa*, see Descartes's *Replies to Objections VI* (AT VII 432). On the denial of final causes, see *Principles of Philosophy* I 28; Meditation IV (AT VII 55) and the *Replies to Objections V* (AT VII 375).

296. See Plato, *Phaedo*, 97–98.

297. See Descartes, *Principles of Philosophy* III, 47; and Descartes to Mersenne, 9 January 1639 (AT II 485). These seem to be the only passages in which Descartes makes this claim. (The letter was published in Leibniz's lifetime and could well have been known to him.)

their meaning. For as hypocrites misuse piety, heretics the Scriptures, and seditious people the word 'freedom,' so Descartes has misused the important words, 'existence of God,' and 'immortality of the soul.' We must therefore elucidate this mystery and show them that Descartes's immortality of soul is worth no more than his God. I believe that I will not bring pleasure to some, for people are normally unhappy to be awakened from a pleasant dream. But what should I do? Descartes wishes us to uproot false thoughts before introducing true ones.[298] We must follow his example; and I believe I would be doing the public a service if I could disabuse people of such dangerous doctrines.

I therefore assert that the immortality of soul, as established by Descartes, is useless and could not console us in any way. For let us suppose that soul is a substance and that no substance perishes; given that, the soul would not perish and, in fact, nothing would perish in nature. But just as matter, the soul will change in its way, and just as the matter that composes a man has at other times composed other plants and animals, similarly, this soul might be immortal in fact, but it might pass through a thousand changes without remembering what it once was.[299] But this immortality without memory is completely useless to morality, for it upsets all reward and punishment. What good would it do you to become the King of China under the condition that you forget what you once were? Would that not be the same as if God created a King of China at the same time as he destroyed you? That is why, in order to satisfy the hopes of humankind, we must prove that the God who governs all is wise and just, and that he will allow nothing to be without reward and without punishment; these are the great foundations of morality. But the doctrine of a God who does not act for the good, and of a soul which is immortal without any memory, serves only to deceive simple people and to undo spiritual people.

I could even show some defects in Descartes's supposed demonstration, for there is still much to be proven in order to complete it. But I believe that it would be useless to bother with this now, since these demonstrations would not be of much use for anything even if they were good demonstrations, as I have just proven.

It remains for me to touch upon the other sciences that Descartes has treated, in order to show examples of what he has accomplished and what he has not. I begin with geometry, since it is believed to be Descartes's strength. We must do him justice; he was a capable geometer, but not so capable as to eclipse the others. He pretends not to have read Viète; however, Viète has

---

298. See Descartes, Meditation I.
299. Leibniz seems to have in mind the account of memory that Descartes gives in his *Treatise of Man*; see Descartes (trans. Hall), *Treatise of Man*, pp. 87ff. There Descartes conceives of memory as brain traces which cause the soul, a mental substance distinct from the brain, to perceive representations of past events. So, when a person dies and the immortal soul separates from the mortal body, it would seem that all memory would be lost. However, it should be noted that Descartes also recognizes a kind of memory that pertains to the soul alone, a kind of memory that is not lost in death. See, for example, K 73–74, 76, 134, 148–49. Leibniz does not seem to take this view into account.

said much, and what Descartes has added to this is, first, a more distinct inquiry into solid curved lines or curved lines that intersect solids, by means of equations referring to coordinates, and second, the method of tangents by two equal roots. However, he speaks in geometry with an unfounded lofti-ness. He boldly asserts that all problems can be resolved by his method. But he was obliged to admit in some exchanges, first, that the arithmetical problems of Diophantus were not in his power to solve, and second, that the inverse of tangents also surpassed it. Yet these inverses of tangents are the most sub-lime and useful part of geometry. I believe that few Cartesians will understand what I wish to say, for there are very few excellent geometers among them; they are satisfied with resolving some small problems using their master's methods of calculation, and the two or three great geometers of our time who are commonly counted among the Cartesians recognize only too well the things I have just said for them to be judged Cartesians.

Descartes's astronomy is, at its root, only the astronomy of Copernicus and Kepler, to which Descartes has added an improvement, explaining more distinctly the connection among planetary bodies by means of the fluid mat-ter that is pushed by their motion, in contrast with Kepler, who, having kept some residual Scholastic notions, still employed imaginary virtues. But Kepler had prepared this matter so well that the synthesis Descartes fashioned be-tween the corpuscular philosophy and Copernicus's astronomy was not very difficult. I say the same for the magnetic philosophy of Gilbert. And yet I rec-ognize that what Descartes says about the magnet, about the ebb and flow of the sea, and about meteors, is quite ingenious and surpasses everything that the Ancients said about them.[300] However, I still do not venture to say if he got matters exactly right. His *Optics* has some admirable passages, but it also has some indefensible passages. For example, he correctly established the proportion between sines [in refraction], but in a clumsy way, for the reasons he brought to bear in order to prove the laws of refraction are worthless. I believe that capable geometers are still in agreement about this.[301]

As for anatomy and the knowledge of man, Descartes is indebted to Harvey who discovered the circulation of the blood. But I do not find anything he discovered that is useful and demonstratively certain. He is too taken with reasoning about the invisible parts of our body, before having explored the parts that are visible. Steno has made it clear that Descartes was completely mistaken in his opinion about the movement of the heart and muscles.[302] Most unfortunately for physics and medicine, Descartes lost his life by believing himself extremely capable in medicine, putting aside the advice of others, and

---

300. Descartes's cosmology can be found in his treatise *The World* and in part III of the *Principles of Philosophy*. In his view, the planets are kept in their orbits and moved around the sun by virtue of a swirling mass of fluid matter. Descartes's theory of magnetism and other earthly phenomena is found in *The World*, in Part IV of the *Principles of Philosophy*, and in the *Meteorology* (trans. in Ols.).
301. See the Second Discourse of Descartes's *Optics*. The law in question is what has come to be called Snell's law of refraction.
302. Descartes gives an account of his theory of the heart and his relations to Harvey in Part V of the *Discourse on Method*.

at first refusing to allow himself to be cared for when he became ill in Sweden. We must admit that he was a great man, and that if he had lived, perhaps he would have corrected some of his errors (if his arrogance would have allowed it). Still, he would certainly have made some important discoveries. But it is just as certain that he would not have had the reputation he had in his time, when there were few able people capable of measuring up to him, or rather, when they were young people barely beginning. But since then we have discovered things in geometry that Descartes believed impossible, and in physics we are making discoveries that surpass in usefulness all his pretty fictions concerning imaginary vortices. In addition, Descartes was ignorant of chemistry, without which it is impossible to advance in applied physics. What he said about salts would deserve the pity of those who are knowledgeable on this, and one can clearly see that he did not understand their differences. If he had had less ambition to make a sect for himself, more patience in reasoning about sensible things, and less inclination to give himself over to the invisible, he would perhaps have put forth the foundations of the true physics, for he had the considerable talent necessary to succeed in this. But since he strayed from the true path, he harmed his reputation, which will not be as solid as that of Archimedes. We will soon forget the beautiful novel of physics which he has given us.[303] It is, therefore, left to posterity to start building on better foundations, incapable of being shaken, foundations that the illustrious Academies are busily putting forth. Let us therefore follow their example, and let us contribute to these beautiful plans, or else, if we are not capable of discovery, let us at least keep the freedom of mind that is so necessary for being rational.

On the Nature of Body and the Laws of Motion (ca. 1678–82)[304]

THERE WAS A TIME when I believed that all the phenomena of motion could be explained on purely geometrical principles, assuming no metaphysical propositions, and that the laws of impact depend only on the composition of motions. But, through more profound meditation, I discovered that this is impossible, and I learned a truth higher than all mechanics, namely, that everything in nature can indeed be explained mechanically, but that the principles of mechanics themselves depend on metaphysical and, in a sense, moral principles, that is, on the contemplation of the most perfectly effectual [*operans*], efficient and final cause, namely, *God*, and cannot in any way be deduced from the blind composition of motions. And thus, I learned that it is impossible for there to be nothing in the world except matter and its

---

303. The reference here is to the preface to the French edition of the *Principles of Philosophy* in which Descartes tells the reader that he would like the *Principles* "first to be read in its entirety, like a novel, without the reader forcing his attention too much or stopping at the difficulties which he may encounter in it...." (AT IX-2, 11–12).
304. Editors' title. G VII 280–83. Latin.

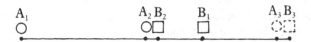

Figure 9

variations, as the Epicureans held. To make this clearer, I shall first briefly recall what I once believed could be established, and then I shall say what led me away from that view.

Let us suppose in Figure 9 that the two bodies A and B (which I consider no different from points for this purpose) directly collide with one another on the straight line AB; suppose that, having left places A_1 and B_1 at the same time and proceeding with uniform motion, they collide at places A_2 and B_2, so that their speeds are represented by the straight lines A_1A_2 and B_1B_2, which they complete in the same time. I said that the slower body B is carried off by the faster body A, and that they travel together from the place of impact A_2B_2 to A_3B_3 with speed A_2A_3 (or B_2B_3), which is the difference between the prior speeds A_1A_2 and B_1B_2. That is, after the collision, A would go from A_2 to A_3 and B would simultaneously go from B_2 to B_3 in as much time as it took, before the collision, for A to go from A_1 to A_2 and B from B_1 to B_2, and A_2A_3 (or B_2B_3) would each equal A_1A_2 minus B_1B_2. I sought a demonstration for this from my assumption that, in body, nothing can be considered except bulk [*moles*], that is, extension and impenetrability, or what comes to the same thing, the filling of space or place. Moreover, I assumed that nothing could be considered in motion except the change of those things we have mentioned, that is, the change of place. But if we want to assert only what follows from these notions, we will say that the reason [*causa*] why a body impels another must be sought in the nature of impenetrability, for while body A presses against body B and cannot penetrate it, it cannot continue its own motion unless it takes B with it. And since, at the very moment of impact, it tries [*conor*] to continue its motion, it will try to carry the other body with it, that is, it will begin to carry it off, that is, it will also impress upon the other the conatus of something moving with the same speed and direction.[305] For every conatus is the beginning of an action, and therefore contains the beginning of an effect or a passion in that toward which it is directed. And if only there is nothing to prevent it, that conatus will succeed fully, and A will, indeed, continue with the same speed and, moreover, after the collision, B will be moved with the same speed and direction with which A had moved. Nothing prevents this from happening if body B is assumed to be at rest before the collision, as in Figure 10 (where points B_1 and B_2 coincide), that

---

305. See "A Specimen of Dynamics" above for a discussion of the technical term '*conatus*' and the related Latin verb '*conor*.'

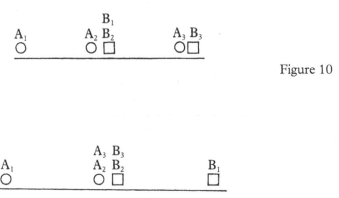

Figure 10

Figure 11

is, if B is assumed to be indifferent to receiving motion of any sort. And so, in the case of Figure 10, A_1A_2 will be equal to the straight lines A_2A_3 and B_2B_3. For to say that matter resists motion, and that the whole composed of A and B together now moves more slowly than A did before, is to claim that there is something that cannot be derived from the simple nature of body and motion of the sort we assumed above, if in that nature we understand nothing but the filling and change of space. If indeed, in Figure 11, we suppose that two bodies collide with equal speed, then both will be at rest after the collision, for at the moment of collision, body A will have two conatus, one conatus for continuing with the same speed with which it approached, that is, with speed A_1A_2, the other conatus for retreating with the same speed as the other body B approached A, that is, with B_1B_2, which is equal to the speed A_1A_2. And so, in order that each conatus might be understood to have an effect, we must understand A to be moved with two opposite and equal motions; that is, it will be at rest. For, if on the boat LM in Figure 12, ball C rolls from the prow toward the stern with speed C_1C_2, and meanwhile the boat advances with speed M_1M_2, which is equal to C_1C_2, then despite all of its conatus, the ball will not change its place, but will correspond to the same point N on the immobile bank. And what we said about A in Figure 11 must also be said about the other one, B. Indeed, if, as in Figure 9, one of the two bodies moves more quickly, it will prevail, and both will certainly continue in the direction of the faster body with the difference between their [original] speeds. For, at the moment of impact, body A will have two conatus, one a conatus for continuing with the greater speed A_1A_2, the other for retreating with the lesser speed B_1B_2; similarly, body B will have two conatus as well, but just the opposite, one for continuing with the lesser speed B_1B_2, the other for retreating with the greater speed A_1A_2. In order that all of those conatus attain their

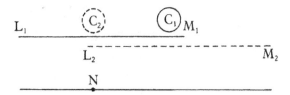

Figure 12

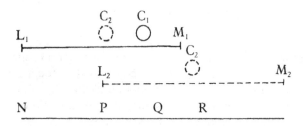

Figure 13

effect, we must again combine with one another the motions which the conatus demand. Moreover, it is always the case that if a body is moved with two opposite motions at the same time, it will, in the end, be moved in the direction of the greater motion, but with the difference between the speeds. That is, in Figure 9, it will move from A_2B_2 to A_3B_3 with speed A_2A_3 or B_2B_3 which is equal to A_1A_2* minus B_1B_2. Again, we can understand this by means of the example of the boat in Figure 13. For if NPQR is the bank, while boat LM on the river travels from L_1M_1 to L_2M_2 with speed NP, and carries with it body C, which is meanwhile traveling on the boat from the prow toward the stern with speed C_1C_2, it is obvious that the body is being moved with two opposite speeds, the greater one PR (equal to NP), the speed of the boat, and the lesser opposite speed QR (equal to C_1C_2), its own speed. Therefore, with respect to the bank, the body will in fact be moved from place Q to place R, in the same direction in which the boat is tending, that is, in the direction of the greater speed, and it will move with speed QR, which is the difference between the speeds PR and QP. One further case remains. If, in Figure 14, bodies A and B tend in the same direction on the same line, but the faster A catches up with the slower B, and thus collides with it, then both will travel together with the greater speed, that is, with speed A_2A_3 or B_2B_3, which is equal to speed A_1A_2. That is, as in the preceding cases where the difference

Figure 14

between the speeds must be subtracted from the greater speed when they collide head on with one another, so now the same quantity must be added to the lesser speed when the faster body runs into the slower. For the one drives against the other by virtue of its greater speed alone, for were they to have* the same speed, one does not act on the other. It is just as if they were being carried on the same boat with its common motion, and we assumed that on that boat the slower body was at rest and the larger body collided with it with a speed equal to the difference between the [original two] speeds. If we had simply assumed that the faster body impressed its entire speed on the slower body moving before it, then they would not travel together (which, however, always happens otherwise here), but the faster one would retain its velocity, and the slower one would move with the sum of the velocities and so would become the faster.

What we concluded in this way about the collision of bodies differs from experience, especially insofar as in Figure 10, for example, when the magnitude of the body to be moved is increased, it is not thereby determined that the speed is decreased. For in other respects, almost the same results occur if two soft bodies lacking elasticity (by virtue of which they would be forced to fly apart after a collision) are allowed to collide, as for example, two balls of clay wrapped in paper and suspended from strings—except that one must divide by the sum of the [bodies], that is, the speed must be halved when the bodies are equal. And furthermore, even if what I concluded were to hold with respect to the condition of bodies placed outside of an organized system, bodies in their untamed condition, so to speak, so that the greatest body at rest would be carried off by the smallest colliding body, with the same speed it has, however little that might be, I believed that in an organized system, that is, with respect to the bodies around us, such a thing would be utterly absurd, for in this way the slightest bit of work would produce maximal disorder. And thus, I believed, this result is blocked by various devices. For, I believed, bodies are endowed with elasticity and are flexible, and often a part is impelled without the whole being impelled. But when I considered how, in general, we could explain what we experience everywhere, that speed is diminished through an increase in bulk [*moles*] as, for example, when the same boat carried downstream goes more slowly the more it is loaded down, I stopped, and all my attempts having been in vain, I discovered that this, so to speak, inertia of bodies cannot be deduced from the initially assumed notion of matter and motion, where matter is understood as that which is extended or fills space, and motion is understood as change of space or place. But rather, over and above that which is deduced from extension and its variation or modification alone, we must add and recognize in bodies certain notions or forms that are immaterial, so to speak, or independent of extension, which you can call powers [*potentia*], by means of which speed is adjusted to magnitude. These powers consist not in motion, indeed, not in conatus or the beginning of motion, but in the cause or in that intrinsic reason for motion, which is the law required for continuing. And investigators have erred insofar as they considered motion, but not motive power or the reason for motion, which even if derived from God, author and governor of things, must not be understood as being in God himself, but must be understood as having been produced and conserved by him in things. From this we shall also show that it is not the same quantity of motion (which misleads many), but the same powers that are conserved in the world.

On Body and Force, Against the Cartesians (May 1702)[306]

I HAVE NOT YET published any book against Cartesian philosophy, though here and there in the *Acta Eruditorum* of Leipzig and in French and Dutch journals are found sketches I placed, by which I have made known my disagreement with it. But, not to mention other things for now, it was especially concerning the nature of body and the nature of the motive forces [*vis motricis*] in body, that I had to disagree. Cartesians, of course, place the essence of body in extension alone. But even though, with Aristotle and Descartes, and against Democritus and Gassendi, I admit no vacuum, and even though, against Aristotle, and with Democritus and Descartes, I consider all rarefaction or condensation to be only apparent, nevertheless, with Democritus and Aristotle, and against Descartes, I think that there is something passive in body over and above extension, namely, that by which body resists penetration. Furthermore, with Plato and Aristotle, and against Democritus and Descartes, I acknowledge a certain active force or entelechy in body. Consequently, it seems to me that Aristotle correctly defined nature as the principle of motion and rest, not because I think that any body can move itself or be put into motion by any quality such as heaviness, unless it is already in motion, but because I believe that every body always has motive force, indeed, actual intrinsic motion, innate from the very beginning of things. However, I agree with Democritus and Descartes, against the multitude of Scholastics, that the exercise of motive power [*potentia motricis*] and the phenomena of bodies can always be explained mechanically, except for the very causes of the laws of motion, which derive from a higher principle, namely, from entelechy, and cannot be derived from passive mass [*massa*] and its modifications alone.

---

306. Editors' title. G IV 393-400; GM VI 98-106. Latin.

But so that my view might better be understood and my several reasons for it made apparent, let me first say that I believe that the nature of body does not consist in extension alone; in unraveling the notion of extension, I noticed that it is relative to something which must be spread out [*extendi*], and that it signifies a diffusion or repetition of a certain nature. For every repetition (or collection of things of the same kind) is either discrete, as, for example, in things that are counted, where the parts of the aggregate are distinguished, or continuous, where the parts are indeterminate [*indeterminata*] and one can obtain parts in an infinite number of ways. Moreover, there are two kinds of continua, the one successive, like time and motion, and the other simultaneous, that is, made up of coexisting parts, like space and body. And indeed, just as in time we conceive nothing but the very order [*dispositio*] or series of changes that can take place in time, so too, we understand nothing in space but the possible order of bodies. And so, when space is said to be extended, we understand this in the same way as when time is said to endure or number is said to be counted. Indeed, time adds nothing to duration, nor does space add anything to extension, but just as successive changes are in time, there are different things [*varia*] in body which can be spread out [*diffundi*] at the same time. For, since extension is a continuous and simultaneous repetition (just as duration is a successive repetition), it follows that whenever the same nature is diffused through many things at the same time, as, for example, malleability or specific gravity or yellowness is in gold, whiteness is in milk, and resistance or impenetrability is generally in body, extension is said to have place. However, it must be confessed that the continuous diffusion of color, weight, malleability, and similar things that are homogeneous only in appearance is merely apparent [diffusion], and cannot be found in the smallest parts [of bodies]. Consequently, it is only the extension of resistance, diffused through body, that retains this designation on a strict examination. From this, it is obvious that extension is not an absolute predicate, but is relative to that which is extended or diffused, and therefore it cannot be separated from the nature of that which is diffused any more than a number can be separated from that which is counted. And thus, those who have taken extension to be some absolute and primitive attribute in body, indefinable and ineffable, have erred through a defect in analysis, and indeed have taken refuge in occult qualities (which they otherwise so condemn), as if extension were something that cannot be explained.

You ask, now, what is that nature whose diffusion constitutes body? We have already said, of course, that matter consists in the diffusion of resistance. But since on our view there is something besides matter in body, one might ask what its nature is. Therefore, we say that it can consist in nothing but the dynamicon, or the innate principle of change and persistence. From this it also follows that physics makes use of principles from two mathematical sciences to which it is subordinated, geometry and dynamics. (I have promised the elements of this latter science, which to this day have not been treated in a satisfactory way anywhere.) Moreover, geometry itself, or the science of extension, is, in turn, subordinated to arithmetic, since, as I said above, there is repetition or multitude in extension; and dymamics is subordinated to metaphysics, which treats cause and effect.

Furthermore, the *dynamicon* or power [*potentia*] in bodies is twofold, passive and active. Properly speaking, passive force [*vis*] constitutes matter or mass [*massa*], and active force constitutes entelechy or form. Passive force is resistance itself, by means of which a body resists not only penetration, but also motion, and through which it happens that another body cannot advance into its place unless the body withdraws from it, which it will not do without somewhat slowing the motion of the impelling body. And so, a body tries to persist in its prior state, not only in the sense that it will not leave that state of its own accord, but also in the sense that it resists [*repugno*] that which changes it. And so, there are two resistances or masses in body, first, *antitypia*, as it is called, or impenetrability, and second, resistance, or what Kepler calls the natural inertia of bodies, something Descartes somewhere in his letters also recognizes from the fact that it is only through force that bodies receive new motion, and further, that bodies resist that which presses upon them and weakens their force.[307] This would not happen if there were not in body, beyond extension, the *dynamicon* or the principle of the laws of motion, which brings it about that the quantity of forces cannot increase, and further, that a body cannot be impelled by another unless it opposes its force. Moreover, this passive force in body is everywhere the same and is proportional to its size. For, even if some bodies appear denser than others, this is only because the pores of the former are filled to a greater extent with matter that belongs to the body, while, on the other hand, the other rarer bodies have the makeup [*natura*] of a sponge, so that other, subtler matter, which is not considered part of the body, and neither follows nor awaits its motion, glides through their pores.

Active force, which one usually calls force in the absolute sense, should not be thought of as the simple and common potential [*potentia*] or receptivity to action [*actio*] of the schools. Rather, active force involves an effort [*conatus*] or striving [*tendentia*] toward action [*actio*], so that, unless something else impedes it, action results. And properly speaking, entelechy, which is insufficiently understood by the schools, consists in this. For such a potency involves act [*actus*] and does not persist in a mere faculty, even if it does not always fully attain the action [*actio*] toward which it strives, as of course happens whenever a hindrance is imposed. Furthermore, active force is twofold, primitive and derivative, that is, either substantial or accidental. Primitive active force, which Aristotle calls first entelechy and one commonly calls the form of a substance, is another natural principle which, together with matter or passive force, completes a corporeal substance. This substance, of course, is one *per se*, and not a mere aggregate of many substances, for there is a great difference between an animal, for example, and a flock. And further, this entelechy is either a soul or something analogous to a soul, and always naturally activates [*actuo*] some organic body, which, taken separately, indeed, set apart

---

307. See the discussion of this in the de Volder correspondence and its notes, above pp. 172–73.

or removed from soul, is not one substance but an aggregate of many, in a word, a machine of nature.

Moreover, a natural machine has the great advantage over an artificial machine, that, displaying the mark of an infinite creator, it is made up of an infinity of entangled organs. And thus, a natural machine can never be absolutely destroyed just as it can never absolutely begin, but it only decreases or increases, enfolds or unfolds, always preserving, to a certain extent, the very substance itself and, however transformed, preserving in itself some degree of life [*vitalitas*] or, if you prefer, some degree of primitive activity [*actuositas*]. For whatever one says about living things must also be said, analogously, about things which are not animals, properly speaking. However, we must grant that intelligences or higher souls, which are also called spirits, are ruled by God, not only as machines, but also as subjects, and that intelligences are not subject to those radical changes to which other living things are subject.*

Derivative force is what certain people call impetus, conatus, or a striving [*tendentia*], so to speak, toward some determinate motion, and therefore, it is that by which a primitive force or principle of action is modified. I have shown that derivative force is not conserved in the same quantity in a given body, but that it nonetheless remains the same in its totality, however it might be distributed among many things, and that derivative force differs from motion itself, whose quantity is not conserved. And this very derivative force is the impression a body receives in impact, that by virtue of which projectiles persist in their motion without needing a new impulse, as Gassendi also showed by way of elegant experiments performed on a boat.[308] And so, certain people who think that projectiles persist in their motion because of the air are wrong.[309] Furthermore, derivative force differs from action [*actio*] only as the instantaneous differs from the successive. For there is already force in the first instant, while action requires the passage of time, so that action is the product of force and time, considered in every part of a body. And so, action is jointly proportional to [the size of] a body, to time, and to force or power [*virtus*], even though the quantity of motion of the Cartesians is measured by the product of the speed and [size of] a body alone; forces are very different from speeds, as I shall soon discuss.

Moreover, many things force us to place active force in bodies, especially experience itself which shows that motions are in matter. Though in origin they ought to be attributed to God, the general cause of things, however, directly and in particular cases, they ought to be attributed to the force God placed in things. For to say that, in creation, God gave bodies a law for acting means nothing, unless, at the same time, he gave them something by means

---

308. See Gassendi's "Three Letters Concerning the Motion Imparted by a Moving Body," translated in Brush.

309. On the Aristotelian view, violent motion requires the continued presence of a mover, making it difficult to see how an arrow could continue to move after it leaves the bow. Aristotle (and some of his followers) suggested that currents set up by the moving body in the medium can be used to explain the continuation of projectile motion. See *Physics* VIII. 10, 266b.27–267a.20.

of which it could happen that the law is followed; otherwise, he himself would always have to look after carrying out the law in an extraordinary way. But indeed, his law is efficacious, and he did render bodies efficacious, that is, he gave them an inherent force. Furthermore, we must consider derivative force (and action) as something modal, since it admits of change. But every mode consists of a certain modification of something that persists, that is, of something more absolute. And just as shape is a certain limitation or modification of passive force or extended mass, so derivative force (and motive action) [actio motrix] is a modification, not of something merely passive (otherwise the modification or limit would involve more reality than that which is limited), but of something active, that is, of a primitive entelechy. Therefore, derivative and accidental or changeable force will be a certain modification of the primitive power [virtus] that is essential and that endures in each and every corporeal substance. Hence, since the Cartesians recognized no active, substantial, and modifiable principle in body, they were forced to remove all activity [actio] from it and transfer it to God alone, summoned ex machina, which is hardly good philosophy.

Moreover, through derivative force, primitive force is altered [variatur] in the collisions of bodies, namely, in accordance with whether the exercise of primitive force is turned inward or outward. For every body, in fact, has internal motion and can never be brought to rest. This internal force turns itself outward when it performs the function of elastic force, namely, when the internal motion is hindered in its usual course. From this it follows that every body is essentially elastic, even water, which rebounds with great violence, as even cannon balls show. And unless every body were elastic, the true and proper [debitus] laws of motion could not obtain. However, that force does not always make itself visible in the sensible parts of bodies, namely, when they are insufficiently solid. But the harder a body is, the more elastic it is and the more forcefully it rebounds. Indeed, when bodies mutually rebound in collision, this is brought about through elastic force. From this it follows that bodies, in fact, always gain their motion in collision from their very own force, to which the impulse of another body provides only the occasion for acting and a limitation [determinatio], so to speak.

From this we also understand that even if we admit this primitive force or form of substance (which, indeed, fixes shapes in matter at the same time as it produces motion), we must, nonetheless, proceed mechanically in explaining elastic force and other phenomena. That is, we must explain them through shapes, which are modifications of matter, and through impetus, which is a modification of form. And it is empty to fly immediately, and in all cases, to the form or the primitive force in a thing when distinct and specific reasons should be given, just as it is empty to resort to the first substance, or God, in explaining the phenomena of his creatures, unless his means or ends are, at the same time, explained in detail, and the proximate efficient or even the pertinent final causes are correctly assigned, so that he shows himself through his power and wisdom. For, all in all, whatever Descartes may have said, not only efficient causes, but also final causes, are to be treated in physics, just as a house would be badly explained if we were to describe only the arrangement of its parts, but not its use. I already warned earlier that, although we say that everything in nature is to be explained mechanically, we must exempt the explanation of the laws of motion themselves, or the principles of mechanism, which should not be derived from things merely mathematical and subject to the imagination, but from a metaphysical source, namely, from the equality of cause and effect and from other laws of this kind, which are essential to entelechies. Indeed, as I have already said, physics is subordinated to arithmetic through geometry, and to metaphysics through dynamics.

The Cartesians, confusing motive force with motion because they insufficiently understood the nature of forces, have greatly erred in establishing their laws of motion. For although Descartes understood that the same force should be conserved in nature, and understood that when a body gives part of its force (derivative force, of course) to another, it retains a part so that the total force remains the same, nevertheless, deceived by the example of equilibrium, or, as I call it, dead force (which doesn't enter into the reckoning here, and is only an infinitesimal part of living force, that which is at issue here), he believed that force is jointly proportional to mass and speed, that is, that force is the same as what he calls quantity of motion, by which name he understands the product of mass and speed, although I have elsewhere demonstrated *a priori* that forces are jointly proportional to the masses and the squares of the speeds. I know that recently, certain learned men, since they were finally forced to acknowledge, against the Cartesians, that quantity of motion is not conserved in nature,[310] since they considered quantity of motion alone to be absolute force, they also concluded that absolute force does not persist, and took refuge in the conservation of relative force [*vis respectiva*] alone. But we have grasped that nature has not forgotten its constancy and perfection in conserving absolute force. And although the Cartesian opinion that the quantity of motion is conserved conflicts with all the phenomena, ours is wonderfully confirmed by experiments.

Since the Cartesians don't understand the use of elastic force in the collision of bodies, they also err in thinking that changes happen through leaps, as if, for example, a body at rest could, in a moment, pass into a state of determinate motion, or as if a body placed in motion could suddenly be reduced to rest, without passing through intermediate degrees of velocity. If elastic force were lacking, then, I confess, what I call the law of continuity, through which leaps are avoided, would not be observed in things, nor would the law of equivalences by which absolute forces are conserved, nor would there be place for other excellent contrivances of the Architect of Nature, contrivances by which the necessity of matter and the beauty of form are united. Moreover, this very elastic force, inherent in every body, shows that there is internal motion in every body as well as a primitive and (so to speak) infinite force, although in collision itself it is limited [*determinetur*] by derivative force as circumstances demand. For, just as in an arch, each part sustains the full

---

310. Leibniz may have Malebranche in mind here. See RLM 333, 334–35, 337–38.

force of that which puts weight on it, and just as, in a taut string, each part sustains the full force of that which tightens it, and just as each portion of compressed air has as much force as the weight of the air pressing down, so too each and every corpuscle is aroused into action by the combined force of the entire surrounding mass, and awaits only an occasion for exercising its power, as the example of gunpowder shows.

There are many other matters in which I have had to distance myself from Descartes. But what I have now brought forward deals mainly with the very principles of corporeal substances, and is capable of vindicating the old philosophy of a sounder school, if interpreted properly, which, I see, has been abandoned, where it was not necessary to do so, by many of the most learned moderns, even those inclined toward it. The philosophy of the Reverend Father Ptolemaeus, a man well versed in the opinions of both the ancients and the moderns, whose distinguished doctrine I myself examined in Rome, a philosophy which I find most promising, has not yet reached us.

Furthermore,[311] in conclusion, I am pleased to add that even if many Cartesians rashly reject forms and forces in bodies, Descartes, however, spoke with greater moderation, and only claimed that he found no reason for using them.[312] For my part, I confess that if they were useless, they would be rejected with good reason; but I have shown that Descartes erred on this very point. For not only are the principles of mechanism, that by which everything in bodies is regulated, situated in entelechies or in the *dynamicon*, but I also showed with an irrefutable demonstration in the *Acta Eruditorum* (when I answered that most celebrated gentleman Johann Christopher Sturm, who, in his *Physica Eclectica*, attacked my view, which he did not sufficiently understand) that, assuming a plenum, if there were nothing in matter but mass itself and the change in position of its parts, then it would be impossible for there to be any perceptible change in anything, since things equivalent in boundary* would always be substituted for one another, and setting aside conatus or force striving for the future (that is, eliminating entelechies), a present state of things in one moment could not be distinguished from another.[313] I believe that Aristotle saw this when he saw that there has to be alteration, over and above local motion, in order to account for the phenomena. Moreover, alteration, though, like qualities, appears to be of many sorts, in the final analysis, reduces to the variation of forces alone. For all qualities of bodies, that is, except for shapes, all of their real and stable accidents (that is, those which do not exist merely in a transitory way, like motion, but which are understood to exist in the present, even if they make reference to the future) are in the end reduced [*revoco*] to forces, when analysis is undertaken. Furthermore, if we set forces aside, then nothing real remains in motion itself, since from change of place alone one cannot determine where the true motion or the cause of the change really is.

---

311. This paragraph was a later addition and is given in the manuscript as a note.
312. See the end of the First Discourse of the *Meteorology*, Ols. 268. See also AT III 491–92, K 126–27, where Descartes recommends a similar strategy to his then disciple, Henricus Regius.
313. See sec. 13 of "On Nature Itself" above.

Conversation of Philarète and Ariste,

Following the Conversation of Ariste and Théodore (1712 revised 1715)[314]

Ever since they first met in Paris, probably in 1675, when they were both quite young, Leibniz had been interested in the thought of Nicholas Malebranche, the oratorian, metaphysician, theologian, and, to a large extent, follower of Descartes. The following dialogue is one of Leibniz's most direct examinations of the metaphysical system Malebranche developed during his long career. It presents itself as a continuation of Malebranche's own Dialogues on Metaphysics, *first published in 1688, but, as with all of Malebranche's works, elaborated in later editions. Malebranche's conversation occurs between Théodore, who represents Malebranche himself, and Ariste, an impressionable friend. Leibniz's conversation begins after Théodore has left and Ariste is visited by Philarète, Leibniz's stand-in, who takes issue with some of the views Théodore (Malebranche) has presented. The text survives in two different drafts, which are quite distinct in places. The translation follows the later draft. The variants given in notes are passages from the earlier draft that were eliminated and replaced by the passages given in the body of the text.*

AFTER THÉODORE had left, Ariste received a visit from Philarète, an old friend and highly esteemed Doctor of the Sorbonne, who had once taught philosophy and theology in the Scholastic manner, yet who did not disdain the discoveries of the moderns, but approached them with much caution and precision. He had gone into a kind of retreat in order to better give himself to the exercises of piety, and, at the same time, he worked to illuminate the truths of religion, attempting to rectify and to perfect their proofs. This led him to rigorously examine the proofs produced in order to determine how they needed to be strengthened.

ARISTE, seeing him, exclaimed: What an appropriate time for you to come, my dear Philarète, after such a long interruption in our acquaintance! I have just finished a charming conversation, and I wish you had been there! Théodore, that profound philosopher, that excellent theologian, completely swept me away; he took me from this corporeal and corruptible world into an intelligible and eternal world. Yet, when I think about it without him, I easily fall back into my old prejudices, and sometimes I do not know where I stand. No one is more capable than you of settling me down and making my judgments sure and calm. For I admit that Théodore's great and fine expressions touch me and uplift me. But, after he leaves me, I no longer know how I had been lifted so high, and I sense a kind of dizziness that troubles me.

PHILARETE. Théodore's worthiness is known to me through his works, which

314. RML 434–61; G VI 579–94. French.

contain many great and fine thoughts. Many of these have been well confirmed, but there are also some, and these are among the most fundamental, that still need to be clarified further. I do not doubt that he said thousands of things appropriate for helping you in the fine resolution you have made, I gather, to leave the vanities of the world, the deafening noise of people and the vain and often pernicious conversations of the worldly, and to give yourself over to the solid meditations that bind us to virtue and lead us to felicity. What I heard said of your happy change has led me to pay you this visit to renew our old ties; and you couldn't have given me a better opportunity to begin and show you my zeal than by first speaking to me about what has long been the object of my meditations, and must be one of the most interesting objects of yours. If you can remember the substance of Théodore's discourse, perhaps I could help you in unfolding a few of the notions he has given you, notions he himself will later perfect by clarifying and settling what still appears obscure or doubtful to us.

A.   I am delighted for your help, and I will attempt to summarize the substance of what Théodore said to me; but do not expect from me the charm that came with everything he said. He first undertook to show me that the I who thinks is not a body, because thoughts are not ways of being that pertain to extension, in which the essence of body consists. I asked him to prove to me that my body is nothing but extension; it seemed to me that he did prove it, when I was listening to him, but I don't know how this proof escaped me. Yet, it does return to me bit by bit. Extension is sufficient to form body, he said to me. He also added that if God were to destroy extension, body would be destroyed.

P.   Philosophers who are not Cartesians do not agree that extension is sufficient to form body; they also require something else that the ancients call antitypy, that is, that which renders a body impenetrable to another. According to them, bare extension only makes up the place or space in which bodies are located. And, in fact, it seems to me that, when Descartes and his followers undertake to refute this opinion, they merely make assumptions, and—to call the thing by its proper name—they commit a *petitio principii*.

A.   But don't you find that the assumption that the destruction of extension entails the destruction of body proves that body consists only of extension?

P.   This proves only that extension enters into the essence or nature of body, but not that it constitutes its entire essence, a bit like the case of magnitude, which enters into the essence of extension, without being sufficient to constitute that essence, for number, time and motion also have magnitude, though they differ from extension. If God were to destroy all actual magnitude, he would destroy extension, but in producing magnitude, he might produce only time, perhaps, without producing extension. It is the same with extension and body. If God were to destroy extension, he would destroy body, but in producing only extension, he might produce only space without body, perhaps, at least according to the people that the Cartesians still have not properly refuted.

A.   I am sorry not to have noticed this difficulty before, but I will note it down to suggest it to Théodore. However, if I remember correctly, he put forward another argument for the same conclusion, but this one seemed very subtle to me, for it was taken from the nature of substance. Théodore proved to me that extension is a substance, and I believe that he wanted to infer from this that body could only be extension, otherwise, it would be composed of more than one substance. But I don't guarantee that this argument was Théodore's. I could be mistaken by putting his words together in a way different from what he had in mind; I shall find out about this.

P.   Once more I find difficulty in this conclusion you attributed, with some misgivings, to Théodore. For you know that, for the Peripatetics, body is composed of two substantial principles, matter and form. One must, then, prove that it is not possible for body to be composed of two substances at the same time, that is, of extension (if we grant that extension is a substance) and of some other substance as well. But let us see how Théodore proved that extension is a substance, for this point is important enough.

A.   I am trying to remember. Whatever can be conceived alone and without thinking of anything else, that is, without the idea we have of it representing anything else, or else, whatever we can conceive alone as existing independently of anything else, is a substance; and whatever we cannot conceive alone, that is, without thinking of something else, is a way of being or a *modification of substance.*

That is what we mean when we say that a substance is a being that subsists in itself; and we have no other way of distinguishing substances from modifications. Now, Théodore showed me that I could think of extension without thinking of anything else.

P.   This definition of substance is not free from difficulty. At bottom, only God can be conceived as independent of everything else. Should we say, then, as a well-known innovator does, that God is the only substance and that created things are only its modifications?

But[315] if you restrict your definition by adding that substance is that which can be conceived independently of any other created thing, we might find things that have as much independence as extension, without being substances. For example, active force, life, and antitypy are things essential

---

315. In an earlier version, this paragraph read as follows: "But if you restrict your definition by adding that substance is that which can be conceived independently of any other created thing, we might find things that have as much independence as substances themselves do, for we must take into consideration the fact that there is something beside substance and modification. We can distinguish realities into subjects and real or adjunct predicates, or rather, into concrete realities and abstract realities, the one essential to their subject, and the other accidental. Abstract accidental realities are modifications, as, for example, the motion of a body. But the adjunct or real predicates are primitive or derivative. Primitive predicates (that is, those taken in and of themselves) are ordinarily called attributes. Derivative predicates are called affections. But one will find that affections only add relations to the reality of the attributes, and that they are formalities [*formalités*] rather than forms. Attributes are sometimes constitutive principles of substances; for example, active force is an essential primitive predicate, or rather an attribute of substance, antitypy is an attribute of body, life is an attribute of the soul. Now if these attributes could be conceived as dependent on something else outside of substance, then so could substances, since substances are conceived by means of such attributes."

and at the same time primitive, and they can be conceived independently of other notions, and even of their subjects, through abstraction. Indeed, on the contrary, it is the subjects that are conceived by means of such attributes.

However, these attributes are different from the substances of which they are attributes. Therefore, there is something which is not a substance, yet which cannot be conceived of as being dependent, any more than substance itself. Therefore, the independence of a notion is not the criterion [*caractère*] of a substance, since the criterion should, furthermore, correspond to what is essential to substance.

A.   [316]I believe that abstracts cannot be conceived independently of something; they must, at least, be conceived in the concrete subject, which, joined to the sufficient essential primitive attribute, makes up the complete subject. But, to extricate ourselves from these thorns, let us say that the definition is understood only for concrete things. Thus, a substance will be a concrete thing which is independent of any other created concrete thing.

P.   That is a new restriction on your definition; but many difficulties still remain. For (1) perhaps the explanation of what it is to be concrete will presuppose substance, and thus, the definition will be circular. (2) I deny that extension is a concrete, for it is abstracted from the extended. (3) It follows that the exact and incomplete subject, or the simple and primitive concrete which, joined to the essential attribute, makes up the complete substance, alone deserves the name of substance, since the abstracts as well as the complete concrete things can neither be conceived nor exist without it. I will not insist, for now, (4) on the doctrine of the theologians who maintain that accidents can exist without their subject in the sacrament of the eucharist; these accidents are essentially independent of their subject, and consequently, your definition holds for them.

A.   We are delving into many subtleties, so it is a good thing that I was once in the College and have retained some of the Scholastic terms. I admit, however, that these subtleties are unavoidable here, and that you set them out quite intelligibly, which puts me in a position to reply to you. I therefore reply to the *first* point, that the definition of a concrete does not require that of substance, for accidents can also be concretes. For example, heat can be great or have magnitude; but, 'great' is a concrete. A number can be called great, proportional, commensurable, etc. As for the *second* point, I would say that, since extension, space, and body are one and the same thing according to Théodore, he would say that extension is a concrete. I reply to the *third* point that extension or body is properly this primary subject conceived as matter, given form by shapes and motions so as to make up a complete subject. Finally, I say to the *fourth* point that Théodore might not grant the possibil-

---

316. In an earlier version, this passage read as follows: "On this argument, no created substance could be conceived independently of some other created thing, since it could not be conceived independently of the realities that constitute it and which are its primitive attributes. But isn't it enough to say that a substance should be conceived independently of some other created substance?"

ity of the existence of accidents without a subject. Others who may wish to maintain the definition would say that *substance* is a concrete that is *naturally* independent of any other created concrete.

P. Your reply to the *first* point seems good to me. Yet the notions of concrete and abstract must be explained more distinctly. But one cannot grant, with respect to the *second* point, that the extended and extension are the same thing: among created things there is no example of the identity of the abstract and the concrete. The reply to the *third* can pass, and so can the one you gave to the *fourth* objection, with respect to those who deny that accidents subsist outside the subject. But those who wish to correct the definition by limiting it to what occurs naturally, make it resemble the definition of man attributed to Plato. It is said that he defined man as a featherless, two-legged animal, whereupon Diogenes plucked a cock and threw it into Plato's auditorium, saying, here is a Platonic man. A follower of Plato could similarly add that we were speaking of an animal such as it occurs naturally. But what is required are definitions taken from the essence of things. It is true that definitions taken from what happens naturally (*per se*) can be useful, and that three degrees of predicates can be distinguished, *the essential, the natural, and what is simply accidental*. But, in metaphysics, what is needed are essential attributes, or those taken from what is called a formal reason.

A. From what I can see, the only question left between us is whether extension is abstract or concrete.

P. Against your definition, I could also object that bodies are not at all independent of one another, and that they need, for example, to be compressed or to be put into motion by ambient bodies. But you could respond with my own reply, that that which is essential is sufficient, since God can make them independent of the ambient bodies and conserve them in their state, when all other bodies have been annihilated. Therefore, I insist on what I have just said, that extension is only an abstract thing, and that it requires something extended. It needs a subject; it is something relative to that subject, like duration. It even presupposes something prior to it in this subject, some quality, some attribute, some nature in this subject, which is extended, is expanded with the subject, and is continued. Extension is the diffusion of this quality or nature. For example, in milk there is an extension or diffusion of whiteness, in a diamond, an extension or diffusion of hardness, and in body in general, an extension or diffusion of antitypy or materiality. In this way you see at once that there is something prior to extension in bodies. And one can say that, in some sense, extension is to space as duration is to time. Duration and extension are attributes of things, but time and space are taken to be outside of things and serve to measure them.

A. Those who admit a space distinct from body conceive of it as a substance that makes up place. But the Cartesians and Théodore conceive of matter itself as you conceive of space, except that they give it mobility along with extension.

P. They therefore tacitly acknowledge that extension is not sufficient to constitute matter or body, since they must add to it mobility, which is a consequence of antitypy or resistance; otherwise, a body could not be pushed or moved by another body.

A. They would say that mobility is a consequence of extension, since all extension is divisible, so that its parts are separable from one another.

P. Those who claim that there is a void, or at least real space distinct from the matter that fills it, will not grant you this consequence. They will say that different parts in space can be indicated, but cannot be separated. As for me, even though I distinguish the notion of extension from that of body, I believe that there is no void, and also that there is no substance that can be called space. I would always distinguish between *extension* and the attribute to which extension or diffusion (a relative notion) relates, which would be situation or locality. Thus, the diffusion of place would form space, which would be like the *proton dektikon*, or the primary subject of extension, that through which it would also apply to other things in space. Thus, extension, when it is the attribute of space, is the diffusion or continuation of situation or locality, just as the extension of body is the diffusion of antitypy or materiality. For place is in points as well as in space, and consequently, there can be place without extension or diffusion. But diffusion simply in length makes up a local line endowed with extension. It is the same for matter; it is in points as well as in body, and its diffusion simply in length constitutes a material line. The other continuations or diffusions in width and in depth constitute the surface and the solid of geometry—in a word, space with respect to place, and body with respect to matter.

A. These comparisons between place and matter, and space and body, please me and help one speak properly. It is good to distinguish these things, just as it is good to distinguish duration from time, and extension from space. I must consult Théodore about this question.

P. Finally, to go further, I agree with the opinion that not only extension, but also body itself cannot be conceived independently of other things. Thus we must say that either bodies are not substances, or else that being conceived independently does not apply to all substances, even though it may be applicable only to substances. For, given that a body is a whole, it depends upon other bodies of which it is composed and which make up its parts. Only *monads*, that is, simple or indivisible substances, are truly independent of any other concrete created thing.

A. I would therefore say that *substance* is a concrete, which is independent of any concrete created outside of it. Thus the dependence of substance upon its attributes and its parts will not block our reasonings.

P. This is the third restriction on your definition. You are allowed to do it, but to tell the truth, some things that are allowable are not appropriate—not everything permitted is expedient. What does it matter whether the worm gnawing at me is within me or outside of me? Am I any less dependent on it? Only incorporeal substances are independent of all other created substances. Thus it seems that, in philosophical rigor, bodies do not deserve the name substances; this seems to have been Plato's view when he remarked that they are transitory beings that never subsist longer than a moment. But this is a point that requires more ample discussion, and I have still other important reasons for refusing bodies the title and name of substances, in metaphysical language. For, in a word, body does not have true unity; it is only an *aggregate*, what the schools call *one per accidens,* an assemblage like a flock; its unity arises from our perception. It is a *being of reason,* or, rather, of *imagination, a phenomenon.*

A.   I hope that Théodore will properly satisfy you on all these difficulties. However, let us assume that body and extension do not differ much, given that you do not admit the void; or at least, let us set the point aside for more ample discussion, and let us pass to the rest of Théodore's demonstration. It comes to this. *Everything that has modifications, which we are unable to explain by extension, is distinct from body,* assuming that bodies and extension are the same thing, or at least that they differ only as space does from that which is needed simply to fill it—that which, besides extension, also has some resistance and mobility, as you seem to grant. *Now the soul has modifications which are not modifications of extension,* nor, if you wish, of antitypy or of the simple filling of space. Théodore even proves this; for my pleasure, my desire, and all my thoughts are not relations of distance and cannot be measured by feet or inches, like space or that which fills it.

P.   I share Théodore's view when he maintains that the modifications of the soul are not modifications of matter, and consequently, that the soul is immortal. But his proof suffers from a certain difficulty, though. He holds that thoughts are not relations of distance because we cannot measure thoughts. But a follower of Epicurus would say that this is due to our lack of knowledge of them, and that if we knew the corpuscles that form thought and the motions necessary for this, we would see that thoughts are measurable and are the workings of some very subtle machines—just as the nature of color does not seem to consist internally of something measurable. And yet, if it is true that the reason for these qualities of objects comes from certain configurations and certain motions, as, for example, the whiteness of foam comes from little hollow bubbles that are polished like so many small mirrors, then these qualities would, in the end, reduce to something measurable, material, and mechanical.

A.   In this way you surrender to your opponents all the proofs that can be given for the distinction between soul and body?

P.   Not at all; my intention is merely to perfect them. To give you a small sample of this here, I consider that matter includes only what is passive. It seems to me that the Democriteans as well as other philosophers who think mechanistically must agree with this. For, not only extension, but also the antitypy attributed to bodies are purely passive things, and consequently, action cannot originate from a modification of matter. Therefore, both motion and thought must come from something else.

A.   I hope you can stand, in turn, my pointing out what seems defective to me in your argument, for you teach me to be exact to the point of rigor. I would say then that your argument is of no value except as an *ad hominem,* that is, against those who philosophize as Democritus and Descartes do. But followers of Plato and Aristotle, and some recent proponents of an arche-us, as well as the latest sympathists who maintain the attraction of bodies at a distance, place qualities in bodies that cannot be explained mechanically; consequently, they will not agree that bodies are purely passive. I also recall that a certain author, one of your friends, though he favors only the mechanical explanations of the phenomena of bodies, has undertaken to show, in some essays published in the *Acta Eruditorum* of Leipzig,[317] that bodies are endowed with some active force, and thus that bodies are composed of two natures, namely, primitive active force (called *first entelechy* by Aristotle) and matter, or primitive passive force, which seems to be antitypy. He holds, for this reason, that everything in material things can be explained mechanically, except the principles of mechanism, which cannot be derived solely from considerations of matter.

P. I am corresponding with this author and am fairly familiar with his opinions. This primitive active force, which one can call *life*, is, according to him, exactly what is contained in what we call a soul, or in simple substance. It is an immaterial, indivisible, and indestructible reality; he locates it everywhere in bodies, believing that there is no part of mass in which there is no organized body, endowed with some perception or with a kind of soul. Thus, this reasoning leads us directly to the distinction between soul and matter. And though some would call body what I prefer to call, with him, *corporeal substance*, composed of soul and mass, it is only a difference of terminology. Now, this active force is exactly what best shows the distinction between the soul and mass, and in a way that can easily be sensed, for the principles of mechanism, from which the laws of motion derive, cannot be derived from something purely passive, geometrical, or material, nor proven by the axioms of mathematics alone. For in more than one article in the *Journal des Savants* of Paris, the *Acts* of Leipzig, and elsewhere, when speaking of his *Dynamics*, and even more recently in his *Theodicy*, this author noted that, to justify the laws of dynamics, we must have recourse to the real metaphysics and to the principles of fitness which affect souls, and which are no less exact than those of geometry.

In the letters he exchanged with Hartsoeker, inserted in the *Mémoires de Trévoux*, you can also find how he destroyed the void and atoms through higher considerations, even making use of part of his *Dynamics* for this; others who occupy themselves instead with matter alone cannot settle the question. That is why the new philosophers, who are ordinarily too materialistic and not trained to combine metaphysics with mathematics, have not been in a position to decide whether or not there are atoms and void; and several have even been led to believe in them, that is, to believe that there is either a void with atoms, or at least, that there are atoms swimming in a fluid that excludes the void. But he shows that void, atoms, that is, perfect hardness, and finally, perfect fluidity, are equally opposed to fitness and order.

A. There is something to what you say, and with your assistance, I wish to

---

317. The reference is to part I of "A Specimen of Dynamics" above, pp. 117–38.

meditate further about these things, especially about dynamics, since it is so important for knowing both immaterial substances and the unseemliness of the void and atoms. But I still have something to object to you, namely, that God could do by himself, and immediately, everything you attribute to souls. Thus the modifications and operations that go beyond matter would not lead us to souls distinct from matter, since they would be the operations of God. It is true that this objection is also valid against Théodore himself, and perhaps more so than against others; for you know that he considers secondary causes to be occasional causes.

P.   Even if the operations in question were operations of God, the modifications we attribute to souls, and which we sense in our own soul, cannot be modifications of God. And, as for the operations, again, we cannot deny our internal actions to ourselves. They would be sufficient for us here, since matter is incapable of internal actions insofar as it is only passive. But this assumption, which gives all external actions to God alone, has recourse to miracles, and even to miracles that are unreasonable, hardly worthy of divine wisdom. We have as much right to construct such fictions, which only God's miraculous omnipotence could render possible, as we would to maintain that I am alone in the world and that God produces all the phenomena in my soul, just as if there were other things outside of me, without there being any such things. However, even if the present reasoning, which proves the distinction between soul and body based on external operations or on dynamics, were valid only under the assumption that things take place in the ordinary course of nature by natural forces, without God entering in except to conserve them, that would be a great achievement, for it would prove either the distinction between soul and body or the existence of divinity. We can go farther and show more distinctly how dynamics confirms both of these two great doctrines; but that would be a more extended discussion, which we do not need to enter into at the present.

A.   We must talk of this further some other time at your convenience; however, I find that it is already considerable that impious people would not be able to resist what you have just said about the immortality of souls, without having recourse to God, that is to say, to what they most shun. And once convinced of God's existence, that is, of the existence of an infinitely powerful and wise mind, it would not be difficult to infer from this that he also made finite minds that are immaterial like him, and further, that God would not be just if our souls perished with their bodies.

P.   There are even good grounds for doubting whether God made anything other than monads or substances without extension, and whether bodies are anything other than the phenomena resulting from these substances. My friend, whose opinion I have just related, gives enough evidence that he leans in this direction, since he reduces everything to monads, or to simple substances and their modifications, along with the phenomena that result from them, phenomena whose reality is indicated by their interconnections, something that distinguishes them from dreams. I have already touched a bit on this. But now it is time for me to listen to the rest of the reasonings of the worthy Théodore.

A.   After having established the distinction between the soul and the body as the foundation for the principal tenets of philosophy, and also the foundation for immortality of the soul, he drew my attention to the ideas perceived by the soul, and he maintained that these ideas are realities. He even went further and held that these ideas have an eternal and necessary existence, and that they are the archetype of the visible world, whereas the things we believe we see outside of us are often imaginary and always fleeting. He even advanced the following argument: assuming that God annihilates all the beings he has created, except you and me, and assuming further that God presents to our minds the same ideas presented to our minds in the presence of objects, we would see the same beautiful things as we see at present. Therefore, the beautiful things we see are not material, but intelligible beautiful things.

P.   I rather agree that these material things are not the immediate objects of our perceptions; but I find some difficulty in the proof and in the way the matter is explained, and I wish that it were developed a bit better. Does this hypothetical proposition, the major premise of the argument, contain a genuinely certain inference?—*If, in the case where external things are annihilated, we would see everything in an intelligible world, then we must also see everything at present in an intelligible world*—I repeat, is this inference genuinely trustworthy? Couldn't it be that our present and ordinary perception is of a different nature than this extraordinary perception? The minor premise is: *In the case of this annihilation, we would see everything in an intelligible world.* But this minor premise would also seem doubtful to many people. Wouldn't the opponent who believes that bodies have an influence on souls say that, in the case where bodies are annihilated, God would supply their lack and would produce in our souls the qualities that bodies produce there, without needing eternal ideas and an intelligible world? And even if everything happened in us in the ordinary case as it does in the case where everything is annihilated, that is to say, if it were granted that we ourselves produce in us (as I believe) or that God (as Théodore believes) produces there our internal phenomena, without the body having any influence on us, must this necessarily involve external ideas?[318] Isn't it sufficient for these phenomena simply to be new, fleeting modifications of our souls?

A.   I do not recall that Théodore proved to me in general terms that the ideas we see are eternal realities; he only undertook to do this for the idea of space, using a reasoning particular [to that case]. But this always establishes a presumption for the ideas of other things, where space is most often contained. He also replied very well to the arguments I gave against him. I objected to him that *the earth offers resistance to me, and that this is something solid.* He replied that this resistance could be imaginary, as in a vivid dream, whereas ideas do not deceive. He also enabled me to understand, very aptly, that if resistance is a mark of reality, there is also resistance in ideas, when we want to attribute to them what they cannot allow. But as I have already said, he

---

318. The first draft gives "eternal" ideas here. "External" may be a copyist's mistake.

proved to me that the idea of space is necessary, eternal, immutable, and the same in all minds.

P. It can be agreed that there are eternal truths; but not everyone will agree that eternal realities are present to our soul when it considers such truths. It will be said that it is enough for our thoughts to be related in this to those of God; in him alone are these eternal truths actualized.

A. Yet this is the argument that Théodore brought forth to prove his thesis. When we have the idea of space, we have the idea of the infinite, but the idea of the infinite is infinite, and an infinite thing cannot be a modification of our soul, which is finite;[319] therefore, some ideas we see are not modifications of our souls.

P. This argument seems important and deserves to be developed further. I agree that we have the idea of an infinite in perfection, since, for that, we only need to conceive the absolute, setting aside all limitations. And we have a perception of this absolute because we participate in it, insofar as we have some perfection. However, we can correctly doubt whether we have the idea of an infinite whole or of an infinite composed of parts; for a composite cannot be an absolute.

It may be said that we can conceive, for example, that every straight line can be lengthened, or that there is always a straight line greater than any given one; but however, we do not have any idea of an infinite straight line, or of one greater than all other lines that can be given.

A. Théodore's opinion is that the idea we have of extension is infinite, but that the thought we have of it, which is a modification of our soul, is not.

P. But how can we prove that we need something more than our thoughts and their objects in us, and that we need an infinite idea existing in God as our object, in order to have only a finite thought? If we must have ideas distinct from thoughts, isn't it enough that these ideas be proportionate to the thoughts? It should be said, thus, that there is no way of perceiving [s'appercevoir de] such ideas.

A. Here is the way Théodore provided. The mind does not see the infinite in the sense that it measures the infinite by its thought. However, it is not enough that the end not be in sight, for the mind could hope to find this end; but the mind understands that there is no such end. This is how geometers see that, although subdivision can be continued as far as one pleases, there will never be an aliquot part of the side of a square, no matter how small, that can also be aliquot to the diagonal, or can measure it exactly.[320] This is also how these geometers see the asymptotic lines of the hyperbola, which they know can never intersect it, though they approach it without end.

P. This way of knowing the infinite is certain and incontestable; it also proves that objects have no limits. But though we can conclude from it that there is no ultimate finite whole, it still does not follow that we see a complete infinite thing. There is no infinite straight line, but any line can always be lengthened

---

319. The text gives 'infinie.'
320. An aliquot part is one contained by an exact integral number of times in a magnitude.

or surpassed by a greater line. Thus the example of space does not prove, in particular, that we need the presence of certain subsisting ideas that differ from the fleeting modes of our thought. *Prima facie*, it seems that our thoughts are sufficient for this.

A. It is not myself that I see when I see space and shapes; therefore, I see something outside of me.

P. Why should I not see these things in me? It is true that I see their possibility even when I do not perceive their existence, and that even when we do not see them, these possibilities always subsist as eternal truths concerning possibles whose whole reality is based in something actual, that is, in God. But the question is whether we have grounds for saying that we see them in God. However, since I am sufficiently appreciative of Théodore's fine thoughts, here is how I believe one can justify his opinion on the matter, though it seems highly paradoxical to those who have not raised their minds beyond the senses. I am convinced that God is the only immediate external object of souls, since he alone acts immediately on the soul. And our thoughts, with all that is in us insofar as it includes some perfection, are produced without any interruption by his continued operation. Thus, insofar as we receive our finite perfections from his infinite perfections, we are immediately affected by them; and that is how our mind is immediately affected by the eternal ideas in God, when our mind has thoughts that relate to them and participate in them. It is in this sense that we can say that our mind sees all things in God.

A. I hope that your objections and elucidations will please Théodore, instead of displeasing him. He likes to communicate with others, and the account I will bring him will give him an opportunity to share more and more of his insights with us. I even flatter myself that I was able to gratify both of you by getting you to know one another; and I will be the one to profit the most from this.

Hobbes and Spinoza

Dialogue (August 1677)[321]

Leibniz was interested in the works of Thomas Hobbes from his youth on; indeed, one of the earliest letters we have is dated 1670, from the 24-year-old Leibniz to the aged Hobbes [G VII, 572–574; L 105–107]. While Hobbes is not explicitly named in this early dialogue, it is clearly Hobbes Leibniz is

---

321. VE I 60–64; G VII 190–93. Latin.

addressing here. Hobbes's name was associated with the doctrine that, insofar as all truth depends on definitions, and definitions are arbitrary, so is truth: True and false belong to speech, and not to things. . . . The first truths are arbitrarily made by those that first of all imposed names upon things. . . .
[Body, Man, and Citizen, *pp. 48–49*].

A. IF YOU WERE GIVEN a string and required to shape it in such a way that it turned back on itself and enclosed as much space as possible, how would you shape it?

B.   Into a circle. For the geometers show that the circle is the shape that has the greatest capacity for a given circumference. And if there were two islands that could be circumnavigated in equal times, one circular, the other square, the circular island would contain more territory.

A.   Do you think that this is true, even if you are not thinking about it?

B.   Of course. It was true even before geometers had demonstrated it or before people had observed it.

A.   So you think that truth and falsity are in things, and not in thoughts?

B.   Yes, indeed.

A.   Then a thing is false?

B.   Not a thing, I think, but a thought or proposition about a thing.

A.   And so falsity pertains to thoughts, not to things.

B.   I am forced to admit it.

A.   Therefore truth as well?

B.   So it seems. But I hesitate over whether this consequence holds.

A.   Now, when a question has been posed, and before you are certain of your opinion, aren't you in doubt about whether something is true or false?

B.   Certainly.

A.   Therefore, you know that the same subject is capable both of truth and falsity, until one of the two is determined by the particular nature of the question.

B.   I know and I admit that if falsity pertains to thoughts, then truth pertains to thoughts, and not to things.

A.   But this contradicts what you said earlier, that even something no one might be thinking of can be true.

B.   You have confused me.

A.   But we should try for a reconciliation. Do you think that all of the thoughts there can be are actually formed? Or, to speak more clearly, do you think that all propositions are being thought?

B.   I don't think so.

A.   Therefore, you see that truth pertains to propositions or to thoughts, but to propositions or thoughts that are possible, so that, at very least, we can be certain that if anyone were to think in this way or in its opposite, his thought would be true or false.

B.   You seem nicely to have rescued us from that slippery place.

A.   But since there must be reason [*causa*] why a given thought is going to be true or false, where, I ask, shall we look for it?

B.   In the nature of things, I think.

A.   What if it arises from your own nature?

B.   Certainly not from there alone. For it is necessary that my nature and the nature of the things I'm thinking about are such that, when I proceed using a legitimate method, I infer a proposition of the sort that is at issue, that is, I find a true proposition.

A.   You respond nicely. But there are difficulties.

B.   What are they, I beg of you?

A.   Certain learned men think that truth arises from decisions people make, and from names or characters.[322]

B.   This view is quite paradoxical.

A.   But they prove it in this way: Isn't a definition the starting place [*principium*] for a demonstration?

B.   I admit that it is, for some propositions can be demonstrated only from definitions joined to one another.

A.   Therefore, the truth of such propositions depends on definitions.

B.   I concede that.

A.   But definitions depend upon our decision.

B.   How so?

A.   Don't you see that it is a matter of decision among mathematicians to use the word 'ellipse' in such a way that it signifies a particular figure? Or that it was a matter of decision among the Latins to impose on the word '*circulus*' the meaning that the definition expresses?

B.   But what follows? There can be thoughts without words.

A.   But not without some other signs. See whether you can do any arithmetic calculation without numerical signs, I ask.[323]

B.   I am very disturbed, for I didn't think that characters or signs were so necessary for reasoning.

A.   Therefore, the truths of arithmetic presuppose certain signs or characters?

B.   That must be admitted.

A.   Therefore, they depend upon human decision.

B.   You seem to have trapped me through trickery, as it were.

A.   These views are not mine, but belong to quite an ingenious writer.[324]

B.   Can anyone depart so far from good sense [*bona mens*] as to convince himself that truth is arbitrary and depends on names, when it is agreed that the Greeks, the Latins, and the Germans all have the same geometry?

A.   What you say is right. Nevertheless, there is a difficulty that must be resolved.

B.   One thing troubles me, the fact that I notice that I never know, discover, or prove any truth without using words or other signs in my mind.

322. Hobbes.
323. In the margin Leibniz wrote: "When God calculates and exercises his thought, the world is made."
324. The reference, again, is to Hobbes.

A.   Indeed, if characters were lacking, we would never distinctly know or reason about anything.

B.   But when we examine figures in geometry, we often bring truths to light through a careful contemplation of them.

A.   Indeed so. But we must also realize that these figures must be regarded as characters, for a circle drawn on paper is not a true circle, nor is it necessary that it be, but it is sufficient that it be taken by us for a circle.

B.   But it does have a certain similarity with a circle, and that certainly isn't arbitrary.

A.   I admit that, and as a consequence, figures are the most useful of characters. But what similarity do you think there is between ten and the character '10'?

B.   There is some relation or order among the characters which is also found among things, especially if the characters are well designed.

A.   Indeed, but what similarity do the primary elements themselves have with things, for example, '0' with nothing, or 'a' with a line? You are forced to admit, at very least, that no similarity is necessary in these elements. This, for example, is the case with respect to the words 'light' and 'bearing' even though the composite word 'lightbearer' is related to the words 'light' and 'bearing', in a way that corresponds to the relation between the thing signified by 'lightbearer' and the things signified by 'light' and 'bearing'.

B.   But the Greek word *phosphoros* has the same relation to *phos* and *phero*.

A.   The Greeks could have used another word instead.

B.   True. But yet I notice that if characters can be applied to reasoning, there must be some complex arrangement, some order which agrees with things, an order, if not in individual words (though that would be better), then at least in their conjunction and inflection. And a corresponding variegated order is found in all languages in one way or another. This gives me hope that we can avoid the difficulty. For though the characters are arbitrary, their use and connection have something that is not arbitrary, namely, a certain correspondence [*proportio*] between characters and things, and certain relations among different characters expressing the same things. And this correspondence or this relation is the ground of truth. For it brings it about that whether we use these characters or others, the same thing always results, or at least something equivalent, that is, something corresponding in proportion always results. This is true even if, as it happens, it is always necessary to use some characters for thinking.

A.   Well done! You have completely untangled yourself in an excellent way. And the analytic or arithmetic calculus confirms this. For, with numbers, things will always come out the same way, whether one uses the decimal system or, as some have done, the duodecimal system. And if, after that, you use seeds or other countable things to show what you explained in a different way using the calculi, it will always come out the same. This is also true in analysis, even though using different characters, different properties of things may appear more easily. But the basis of truth is always in the very connection and arrangement of characters. For example, if you call 'a^2' the square of 'a',

then, by taking '$b + c$' for 'a', you will have as the square '$+ b^2 + c^2 + 2bc$.'
Or, by taking '$d - e$' for 'a', you will have as the square '$+ d^2 + e^2 - 2de$.'
In the prior case we express the relation of the whole a to its parts b and c,
and in the latter case we express the relation of the part a to the whole d and
to e, that which is in d over and above a. However, by substituting, it is obvious that it always comes to the same thing. For if in the formula $d^2 + e^2$
$- 2de$ (which is equivalent to a^2) we substitute for d its value, $a + e$, then for
d^2 we will have $a^2 + e^2 + 2ae$, and for $- 2de$ we will have $- 2ae - 2e^2$.
Therefore, by adding them together:

$$+ d^2 = a^2 + e^2 + 2ae$$
$$+ e^2 = e^2$$
$$- 2de = - 2e^2 - 2ae$$

we will get the sum $\ldots = a^2$

You see that, by whatever decision the characters are chosen, as long as a
certain order and measure is observed in their use, everything will always
agree. Therefore, although truths necessarily presuppose some characters,
indeed, sometimes they deal with the characters themselves (as with the
theorems about casting off nines), truths don't consist in what is arbitrary
in the characters, but in what is invariant [*perpetuus*] in them, namely, in the
relation they have to things. And it is always true, independent of any decision
of ours, that if, given such and such characters, such and such a reasoning
will succeed, then it will likewise succeed given others whose relation to
the former ones is known; however, the reasoning preserves a relation to
the former ones that results from the relation among the characters. This is
something obvious from substituting and comparing.

The End

Comments on Spinoza's Philosophy (1707?)[325]

*Leibniz corresponded with Spinoza from October 1671, and met him in
November 1676. Leibniz carefully studied Spinoza's* Ethics *(and other
writings) when Spinoza's* Opera Posthuma *appeared in 1677. He left many
notes and comments that date from this early confrontation with Spinoza's
thought. [See G I 113–152 and the translations in L 167–169, 196–205 for
some of the most important of these.] The following piece was written much
later, and dates from a period when Leibniz's thought was well developed. The
following translation is a long excerpt from a larger manuscript in which
Leibniz discusses Johann Georg Wachter's* Elucidarius cabalisticus, sive
Reconditae Hebraeorum philosophiae brevis & succincta recensio *(Rome,
1706). Leibniz's text appears to be his reading notes on Wachter; the passage
translated corresponds to a chapter in Wachter entitled "On the agreement*

---

325. Editors' title. FB, 22–70. Latin.

between the Cabala and Spinoza," in which Wachter attempts to relate
Spinoza's thought to that of the Cabala. Leibniz takes this opportunity to reflect
on Spinoza himself. In virtually every case, the choice of text and its
arrangement simply follows Wachter. References to Spinoza in parentheses
in the text are Leibniz's; the page and letter numbers are keyed to Spinoza's
Opera Posthuma (1677). We have added references to Gebhardt's standard
modern edition in the notes. When a passage given in Leibniz's text is an exact
quotation (or close to one), it is given in quotation marks; paraphrases are so
indicated. Significant departures from Spinoza's text are indicated in the notes.
In virtually every case, the quotations and references are borrowed, mistakes
and all, from Wachter's text, suggesting that Leibniz did not bother to turn to
his own copy of Spinoza.

THE AUTHOR [Wachter], then, in Chapter 4, compares Spinoza with the Cabbala. In *Ethics*, part 2, scholium to proposition 10, Spinoza says: "Everyone ought to concede that nothing is nor can be conceived without God. For all generally acknowledge that God is the only cause of both the essence and the existence of all things. That is, God is not only the cause of things coming to be [*secundum fieri*], but also of their being."[326] This is Spinoza's view, which the author seems to applaud. It is true that one shouldn't say anything about created things except that they are permitted by God's nature. But I don't think Spinoza fully understood this, in my view. Essences can, in some sense, be conceived without God, but existences involve God. The very reality of the essences, indeed, that by which they flow into existence, is from God. The essences of things are coeternal with God, and the very essence of God comprehends all other essences, to the extent that God cannot perfectly be conceived without them. But existence is inconceivable without God, who is the ultimate reason for things.

The axiom, "that without which a thing can neither be nor be conceived belongs to the essence of a thing,"[327] is to be used with regard to necessary things or species, but not with regard to individuals or contingent things, for individuals cannot distinctly be conceived. Thus, they have no necessary connection with God, but were produced freely. God was inclined toward them for a definite reason, but he was not necessitated.

Spinoza dismisses as false [*fictio*] the claim that something comes from nothing (*On the Improvement of the Intellect*, p. 374).[328] But modes which arise really come from nothing. Since there is no matter of modes, neither a mode nor part of a mode preexists, to be sure, but rather the mode that vanished, and which this one succeeds, is a different mode.

---

326. Geb II 93 ll.21–25. Spinoza's text is slightly altered, following Wachter.
327. This is a paraphrase of E 2 D 2, Geb II 84. In the notes, references to the *Ethics* are given in standard form, 'E' followed by the part of the *Ethics*, then the particular subdivision, 'P' for proposition, 'S' for scholium, 'D' for definition, 'A' for axiom, 'App' for appendix, and 'C' for corollary.
328. Geb II 22, 1. 24.

Cabalists seem to say that on account of the baseness of its essence, matter can neither be created nor can it exist, and thus that either there is no matter in the universe, or spirit and matter are one and the same, as Henry More held in his Cabalistic Theses.[329] Spinoza also denies that God could have created any corporeal and material mass to serve as the underpinnings [*subjectum*] of this world, since, he says, those who disagree "don't know from what divine power it could have been created."[330] There is something true in this, but, I think, it is something not sufficiently understood. Matter really exists, but it is not a substance, since it is an aggregate or the resultant of substances. I speak of matter insofar as it is secondary matter or extended mass, something that is hardly a homogeneous body. But that which we conceive of as homogeneous and call primary matter is something incomplete, since it exists merely in potency. On the other hand, a substance is a something complete and active.

Spinoza thought that matter, as commonly understood, does not exist. Thus he often warns that "Descartes badly defined matter through extension"[331] (letter 73),[332] and that extension is badly explained by a thing so base, a thing that must be in a place, that must be divisible (*On the Improvement of the Intellect*, p. 385),[333] since "matter ought to be explained through an attribute that expresses eternal and infinite essence."[334] I reply that extension, or, if you prefer, primary matter, is nothing but a certain indefinite repetition of things, insofar as they are similar or indiscernible with respect to one another. But just as number presupposes things numbered, extension presupposes things which are repeated and which contain properties, over and above those they have in common. These proper accidents produce actual limits in size and shape that, beforehand, are only possible limits. Matter that is merely passive is something very base; indeed, it lacks all power [*virtus*], and as such, it consists in something only incomplete or abstract.

Spinoza (*Ethics* part 1, corollary to prop. 13, and scholium to prop. 15) says that no substance, not even corporeal substance, is divisible.[335] This is not a remarkable thing for him to say, since for him there is only one substance. But it is true for me as well, even though I admit an infinity of substances, since all of them are indivisible, or what I call *monads*.

He also says (*Ethics* part 3, scholium to prop. 2) that mind and body are the same thing, only expressed in two ways, and (*Ethics* part 2, scholium to

---

329. Leibniz is probably referring here to an obscure passage in More's exposition of the "Philosophick Cabbala," found on p. 17 of his *Conjectura Cabbalistica*, bound in More's *A Collection of Several Philosophical Writings* (1662). There More writes: "The *Active* and *Passive* principles here are not two distinct *Substances*, the one *Material*, the other *Spiritual* . . . This *Passive* and *Active* principle are the *First* day's work: A *Monad* or a *Unite* being so fit a symbole of the *Immaterial* nature."

330. E I P 15S, Geb II 57 ll. 15–16.

331. Geb IV 334 ll. 24–25.

332. Wachter was misled by a typographical error in Spinoza's *Opera Posthuma*; the correct reference is letter 72, now letter 83 in Geb. Leibniz follows Wachter's mistake.

333. Geb II 33.

334. Geb IV 334 ll. 25–26.

335. This is a paraphrase of Wachter's quotation from Spinoza.

prop. 7) that "thinking substance and extended substance are one and the same substance, which is now conceived under the attribute of thought, and now conceived under the attribute of extension."[336] And in the same place he says: "certain of the Hebrews seem to have seen this as through a cloud, namely, those who thought that God, God's intellect, and the things understood by him are one and the same."[337] This is not right, in my view. Mind and body are no more the same thing than are the principle of action and the principle of passion. A corporeal substance has a soul and an organic body, that is, a mass composed of other substances. It is true that the same substance thinks and has extended mass joined to it; but it hardly consists of extended mass since any of those things could be taken away, leaving the substance intact. Furthermore, all substance perceives, but not all substance thinks. Thought really belongs to monads; indeed, all perception does, but extension belongs to composites. That God and the things understood by God are one and the same thing cannot be said any more than that the mind and the things perceived by the mind are the same. The author thinks that Spinoza assumed a common nature, in which there are the attributes, thought and extension, and that this common nature is *spirit* [*spiritus*]. But there is no extension in spirits unless you take the notion more broadly to include certain tiny animals, as the ancients took angels to be. The author adds that the modes of these attributes are mind and body. But how, I ask, can mind be a mode of thought when it is the principle of thought? And so, rather, mind is the attribute, and thought the modification of that attribute. It is also remarkable that Spinoza, as above (*On the Improvement of the Intellect*, p. 385)[338] seems to have denied that extension is divisible into parts and is composed of parts, which is without meaning except, perhaps, in the sense that space is not a divisible thing. But space and time are orders of things, not things.

The author rightly says that God discovered the beginnings of all things in himself, just as I once remember Julius Scaliger to have said that things don't derive from the passive power of matter, but from the active power of God. And I affirm this of forms, that is, active forms or entelechies.

I do not admit what Spinoza says (*Ethics* part 1 [proof of] prop. 34) that God, by the same necessity, "is his own cause and the cause of all things"[339] and (in the *Political Tract*, p. 270, chap. 2, no. 2)[340], that the power of things is the power of God. God necessarily exists, but he produces things freely. And while the power of things is produced by God, it is distinct from divine power, and things themselves operate, even if they may have received their forces for acting [from elsewhere].

Spinoza says in letter 21.[341] "I affirm with Paul, and perhaps also with all

---

336. This is a slight variant of Geb II 90 ll. 6–8; cf. Geb II 141 ll. 24–26.

337. E 2 P 7S, Geb II 90 ll. 9–12, slightly altered by Leibniz from Wachter's text.

338. Geb II 33.

339. Geb II 77 ll. 2–4.

340. Geb III 276.

341. Now letter 73, Geb IV 307 ll. 6–11 and 24–28. The variants between Spinoza's text and this one are not due to Wachter, but to Leibniz.

the remaining[342] philosophers, that everything is in God and moves in God, though in a different way [than they think]. And I have even ventured to speak, together with all of the ancient Hebrews, insofar as one can conceive[343] their view from certain traditions, though corrupted in every way." I should think that everything is in God not as a part is in a whole, nor as an accident is in a subject, but as a place is in that which contains it, a spiritual or a sustaining place, though, not a commensurate or shared place, but in such a way that God is immense or everywhere, and the world is present to him. And so, everything is in him, for he is where things are and where they aren't, and he remains when they depart, and is already there when they arrive.

The author says that the Cabalists agree in the view that God produced some things mediately, and others immediately. Hence, he next speaks of a certain first principle [*principiatum*] that God made flow immediately from himself, by whose mediation the rest of things were produced in succession and in order. This they usually call by various names, for example, Adam, Cadmon, Messiah, Christ, *logos*, word, firstborn, first man, heavenly man, leader, shepherd, mediator, etc. I shall give the reason for this assertion elsewhere. Spinoza knew that very doctrine, in such a way that nothing is lacking but the name. He says (*Ethics*, part 1, scholium to prop. 28): "It follows, secondly, that God cannot properly be called the remote cause of individual things, except perhaps, in order to distinguish them from those which he immediately produced, or better, from those that follow from his absolute nature."[344] Moreover, he thus explicates the sorts of things that are said to follow from the absolute nature of God ([*Ethics* part 1] prop. 21): "All that follows from the absolute nature of any attribute of God ought always to have existed and be infinite, that is, they are eternal and infinite through the same attribute."[345] The author cites these things, which lack all foundation, from Spinoza. God produces no infinite creature, nor can it be shown by any argument, nor can we specify how such an infinite creature would differ from God himself.

For what Spinoza imagines to himself, that from any attribute whatsoever comes an infinite thing, from extension a certain thing infinite in extension, from thought a certain infinite intellect, arises from the unsteady imagination of certain heterogeneous divine attributes, like thought and extension, and innumerable others, perhaps. For, since it is only a repetition of perceivings, extension is not, in and of itself, really an attribute.

An infinite extended thing is only imaginary. An infinite thinking thing is God himself. Things that are necessary, and that follow from the infinite nature of God, are eternal truths. A particular creature is produced by another, and this, again, by another. Thus, one will not arrive at God by reasoning in this way, even if the regress were imagined to go to infinity. But yet, the last one, no less than the other prior creatures, depends on God.

---

342. Spinoza wrote: "ancient."
343. Spinoza wrote: "conjecture."
344. Geb II 70 ll. 9-12.
345. Geb II 65 ll. 12-14.

Tatian says in his *Oration to the Greeks* that there are spirits in the stars, in angels, in plants, in waters, in men, and though it is one and the same spirit, there are distinctions within it.[346] But I don't approve of this doctrine at all. It is the error of the world soul, diffused through the world, which, like the air in pneumatic pipe organs, produces different sounds in different pipes. So, when the pipe is broken, that soul will be idle and return to the world soul. But it should be known that there are as many incorporeal substances, or if you prefer, souls, as there are natural organic machines. But, what Spinoza says in *Ethics* part 2, scholium to prop. 13, that everything is animated with as many different degrees of animation as you like, rests on a different and remarkable view, for he says, "there is necessarily in God an idea of each thing, of which God is the cause in the same way as he is the cause of the idea of the human body."[347] But it is completely alien to every sort of reason that a soul should be an idea. Ideas are purely abstract things, like numbers and shapes, and cannot act. Ideas are abstract and universal: the idea of any animal is a possibility, and it is a mockery to call souls immortal because ideas are eternal, as if the soul of a globe is to be called eternal because the idea of a spherical body is eternal. The soul is not an idea, but the source of innumerable ideas. For, over and above a present idea, the soul has something active, that is, the production of new ideas. But, according to Spinoza, at any given moment, a soul will be different, since, when the body changes, the idea of the body is different. Hence, we shouldn't be surprised if he takes creatures for vanishing modifications. Therefore, the soul is something vital, that is, something that contains active force.

Spinoza says, in *Ethics* part 1 prop. 16: "From the necessity of the divine nature there must follow infinitely many things in infinitely many ways (that is, everything which can fall under infinite intellect)."[348] This view is quite false, and makes the same mistake that Descartes insinuated, that matter successively accepts all shapes.[349] Spinoza begins where Descartes leaves off: *in naturalism*. Also, he wrongly holds that the world is an effect of the divine nature (Letter 58),[350] even though he almost adds that it was not made by chance. There is a midpoint between what is necessary and what is by chance, namely, that which is free. The world is a voluntary effect of God, but a voluntary effect due to inclining or prevailing reasons. And even if we imagine the world to be perpetual, it would still not be necessary. For God could either have not created or created the world otherwise; but this was something he did not do. He thinks (letter 49) that God produces the world with that necessity by which he knows himself.[351] However, we must respond that things are possible in many ways, but it was impossible that God not know

---

346. This is a quotation from Wachter, p. 50.
347. Geb II 96 ll. 28–30.
348. Geb II 60 ll. 17–19.
349. See Descartes, *Principles of Philosophy* III 47.
350. Now letter 54; cf. Geb IV 251 l. 29; Leibniz leaves out "*necessarium.*" which modifies "effect," departing from both Wächter and Spinoza.
351. Now letter 43; this is a paraphrase of Geb IV 221, ll. 16–18.

himself. Spinoza says, further (*Ethics* part 1 scholium to prop. 17): "I know
that there are many who think that they can demonstrate that a supreme intellect and a free will belong to God's nature. For they say that they know
nothing that can be attributed to God more perfect than that which is the
highest perfection in us. . . . Therefore, they preferred to hold God to be
indifferent to everything, creating nothing but what he decreed to create by
a certain absolute will. But I think that I have shown clearly enough that everything follows from God's supreme power with the same necessity, in the
same way that it follows from the nature of the triangle that its three angles
are equal to two right angles."[352] From the opening of this passage it is obvious
that Spinoza does not attribute intellect and will to God. He correctly denies
that God is indifferent and that he decides anything by an absolute [exer-
cise of the] will; he decides through will based on reasons. One cannot prove
by any argument that things follow from God as properties follow from the
triangle, nor is there an analogy between essences and existing things.

The same scholium to [*Ethics*, part 1] prop. 17 holds that the intellect and
will of God agree with ours in name alone, for ours are posterior to things,
while God's are prior. But from this it does not follow that they agree in name
alone. Nevertheless, he says elsewhere that thought is an attribute of God,
and that particular modes of thinking must be referred back to it (*Ethics* part
2, prop. 1). But then the author thinks that he is speaking of the external[353]
word of God because he says (*Ethics* part 5)[354] that our mind is a part of the
infinite intellect.

Spinoza says (*Ethics* part 5, proof of prop. 23):[355] "the human mind cannot
completely be destroyed with the body, but something of it, which is eternal,
remains"; moreover, this something has no relation to time, and so, he says,
"we do not attribute duration to mind except while the body endures." And
in the following scholium he says: "this idea, which expresses the essence of
body from the eternal point of view [*sub specie aeternitatis*], is a certain mode
of thinking which pertains to the essence of mind and which is necessarily
eternal."[356] This must be meant as a mockery. This idea is like the shape of a
sphere, whose eternity does not at all decide its existence one way or another, since it is the ideal possibility of a sphere. And so, it means nothing to say
that "our mind is eternal insofar as it involves the body from the eternal point
of view,"[357] and it would be equally eternal by virtue of understanding eternal
truths concerning the triangle. Our mind does not endure nor is it related to
time beyond the actual existence of the body.[358] So says Spinoza in the place

---

352. Geb II 62 ll. 3–7, 12–19 with some omissions and changes.
353. Wachter does refer to the '*lógo externo*' here (p. 54); it might it be a typographical error for '
lógo aeterno'.
354. Perhaps the reference is to the scholium to proposition 40 of *Ethics* part 5.
355. Actually, the quote is from the statement of the proposition. The mistake is Wachter's, which
Leibniz repeats.
356. Geb II 295, ll. 29–31.
357. E 5 P 23S, Geb II 296, ll. 8–9.
358. This is a paraphrase of Geb II 296, ll. 11–13.

cited*; he thinks that the mind perishes with the body, since he judged that the body itself always remains a single thing, even if it is transformed.

The author adds: I never read Spinoza to have clearly set forth the view that minds move from one body to another, and into various houses and dwelling places of eternity.[359] But, he says, this can be inferred from his view. Our author is in error. Just as the shape of a sphere is not the shape of a cylinder, the same soul, for Spinoza, cannot be the idea of another body. Therefore, Spinoza's soul is so transitory that it does not exist even for a moment, since the body also does not remain the same.* Spinoza (*Ethics* part 5 prop. 21 [proof]) says that memory and imagination vanish with the body. But I think that some imagination and memory always remain, and that there would be no soul without them. Nor should we think that a mind exists without sense or without a soul. Reason without imagination and memory is a consequence without its premises. Aristotle also thought that *nous*, mind, or active intellect endures, but not the soul. But it is also the soul that acts, and the mind that is acted upon.

Spinoza says (*On the Improvement of the Intellect*, p. 384) that the ancients "never, so far as I know, conceived of the soul (as we do here) as acting in accordance with certain laws, like some spiritual automa (he meant to say automaton)."[360] The author interprets this as having to do with the soul alone, and not the mind, and holds that the soul acts in accordance with the laws of motion and external causes. Both are wrong, for I say that the soul acts spontaneously and yet as a spiritual automaton, and that this is also true of the mind. The soul is no less exempt from the impulses of external things than is the mind, and it is not the case that the soul acts more determinately [*determinate*] than does the mind. Just as in bodies everything happens through motions in accordance with the laws of power, so too, in the soul everything happens through effort [*conatus*], that is, through desires in accordance with the laws of the good. The two kingdoms are in agreement. However, it is true that there are certain things in the soul that can only be explained in an adequate way through external things, and to that extent the soul depends upon external things; this happens not through a physical influx, but, so to speak, through a moral influx, insofar as, in creating the mind, God took things other than the mind itself into consideration to a greater extent. For, in creating and conserving each and every thing, God takes all other things into consideration.

The author improperly calls will the striving [*conatus*] each thing makes to persist in its being.[361] For the will tends toward something more particular, and toward a more perfect way of existing. He improperly says that the striving is the essence itself, although the essence is always the same and the striving varies.[362] I do not admit that affirmation is the mind's effort to preserve

---

359. '*Domus aetemitatis*' means the everlasting dwelling place, i.e., death. Wachter might be talking about the transmigration of souls after death.
360. Geb II 32 ll. 24–26. The parenthetical remark is Leibniz's.
361. E3P9S.
362. Cf. E 3 P 7.

itself in its being, that is, the mind's effort to conserve its ideas.[363] We also have this striving when we affirm nothing. Moreover, according to Spinoza, the mind is an idea and does not have ideas. He also improperly thinks that affirmation and negation are volition, although volition involves, in addition, the principle [*ratio*] of the good.[364]

Spinoza says (letter 2, to Oldenberg)[365] that "the will differs from this or that volition as whiteness differs from this or that white thing," and so the will is not the cause of a volition, just as humanity is not the cause of Peter and Paul. Therefore, particular volitions need another cause. The will is only a being of reason [*ens rationis*].[366] Spinoza said these things. But we take the will to be the power of willing, whose exercise is a volition. Therefore, it is, at any rate, through the will that we will, though, it is true, other particular causes are necessary for determining the will, that is, for it to produce a certain volition. It must be modified in a certain way. Therefore, the will is not related to volitions as a species or as something abstracted from a species is related to individuals. Errors are not free, nor are they acts of the will, even though we often contribute to our errors through free actions.

Then Spinoza says (*Political Treatise*, chapter 2, no. 6):[367] "Men conceive of themselves as being in nature like a kingdom within a kingdom (a *malcuth* within a *malcuth*, the author adds).[368] For they hold that the human mind cannot be produced by any natural causes, but is created immediately by God, and is, therefore, independent of everything else to such an extent that it has the absolute power of determining itself and using reason properly. But experience overwhelmingly shows[369] that having a sound mind is no more in our power than having a sound body."[370] This is what he says. My view is that every substance whatsoever is a kingdom within a kingdom, but one in precise harmony [*conspirans*] with everything else. No substance receives an influx from anything else whatsoever, except from God, but yet it depends upon everything else through God, its author; it proceeds immediately from God, and yet is produced agreeing with everything else. Still, not everything is equally in our power, for we are inclined more in one way than in another. The malcuth or kingdom of God eliminates neither divine nor human freedom, but only the indifference of equilibrium posited by those who think that the reasons for their actions, which they do not understand, are nonexistent.

Spinoza thinks that the mind can greatly be strengthened if it understands that what happens, happens necessarily.[371] But the mind [*animus*] of the

---

363. The reference might be to E 3 P 10D.
364. Cf. E 2 P 49.
365. Same number in Geb IV.
366. This is a quotation from Geb IV 9 ll. 12–13, followed by a paraphrase of ll. 14–17.
367. Cf. the preface to E 3, Geb II 137 ll. 10–11.
368. Leibniz adds this parenthetical remark to Wachter's quotation. "Malcuth" is a transliteration of Biblical Hebrew for kingdom. This word is used as an example in Spinoza's Hebrew grammar, Geb I 308 l 26.
369. Spinoza wrote: "teaches"; Wachter follows Spinoza.
370. Geb III 277 l. 32–278 l. 3.
371. See E 2 P 49S (Geb II 136); E 4 P 73S (Geb II 265); E 4 App (Geb II 276).

sufferer is not rendered content through this compulsion, nor does it feel its evils any the less on that account. The soul is happy if it understands that good follows from evil, and that what happens is the best for us, if we have wisdom.

From these things we can also understand that what Spinoza says about the intellectual love of God (*Ethics* part 4, prop. 28)[372] is only a sop to the masses, since there is nothing capable of being loved in a God who necessarily produces all good and bad indiscriminately. True love of God is grounded not in necessity but in goodness.

Spinoza says (*On the Improvement of the Intellect* p. 388) that there is no knowledge [*scientia*] of particular things, that is, of things "whose existence has no connection with their essence, and which are thus not eternal truths"; for them there is only experience.[373] This contradicts what he had said elsewhere, that everything is necessary and everything flows necessarily from the divine essence. In the same way he opposes those who say that the nature of God relates to [*spectare*] the essence of created things (*Ethics* part 2, scholium to prop. 10),[374] and yet elsewhere he had claimed that things neither are nor are conceived without God, and arise from him necessarily.[375] He contends, for that reason (*Ethics* part 1 prop. 21), that finite and temporal things cannot immediately be produced by an infinite cause, but are produced by other particular and finite things. ([*Ethics* part 1] prop. 28). But how, in the end, do they arise from God? For they don't arise mediately from him in this way, since we will never come to things which did not similarly arise through another finite thing. Therefore, it cannot be said that God acts by means of secondary causes, unless he produces these secondary causes. Consequently, it must, rather, be said that God produces substances, but not their actions, with which he only concurs.

Two Sects of Naturalists (1677–80)[376]

T HERE ARE TWO SECTS of naturalists fashionable today which have their source in antiquity; the one revives the opinions of Epicurus and the other is, in fact, composed of Stoics. The former believes that any substance, including the soul and God himself, is corporeal, that is to say, composed of extended matter or mass.[377] From this it follows that there cannot be an all-powerful and all-knowing God, for how could a body act on everything

---

372. Leibniz follows Wachter's incorrect reference here. The intellectual love of God is introduced in E 5 P 32 C, and discussed in the following propositions.

373. Cf. Geb II 36–37; a near quote from 36 ll. 28–29, followed by a paraphrase of 37 ll. 21–27.

374. Geb II 93 ll. 25–28; Spinoza uses "*pertinere*" rather than "*spectare*." Wachter follows Spinoza.

375. E 1 P 15 and P 16. Cf. also E 2 P 10S: Geb II 93 ll. 21–22.

376. Editors' title. VE I 212–15; G VII, 332–36. French.

377. Leibniz originally began this sentence as follows: "The former deny providence in explicit terms."

without being affected by everything and without being destroyed? This is what somebody named Vorstius recognized; he refused his God all of the grand attributes that other men ordinarily give to theirs.[378] Some have believed that the sun, which, judging by the senses, is undeniably the most powerful of all visible things, is God; but they did not know that the fixed stars are suns as well, and that consequently, one sun alone cannot see everything nor do everything. All bodies are heavy and very active if they are large, and weak if they are small, but if they have a great power in spite of their smallness (as in the case of gunpowder), then they destroy themselves by acting. This is why a body cannot be God. Moreover, Epicurus in times past, and Hobbes today, who hold all things to be corporeal, have given enough evidence to show that, on their view, there is no providence.

The sect of the new Stoics believes that there are incorporeal substances, that human souls are not bodies, and that God is the soul of the world, or, if you wish, the primary power of the world, that he is the cause of matter itself, if you wish, but that a blind necessity determines him to act; for this reason, he will be to the world what the spring or the weight is to a clock. They further believe that there is a mechanical necessity in all things, that things really act because of his power and not due to a rational choice of this divinity, since, properly speaking, God has neither understanding nor will, which are attributes of men. They believe that all possible things happen one after the other, following all the variations of which matter is capable; that we must not seek final causes; that we are not sure of the immortality of the soul or of future life; that there is no justice or benevolence with respect to God, that he determines what constitutes benevolence and justice, and that, consequently, he would have done nothing contrary to justice by making the innocent always miserable. This is why these gentlemen admit providence in name only. And as for what is of consequence and what concerns the conduct of our lives, everything reduces to the opinions of the Epicureans, that is, to the view that there is no happiness other than the tranquility of a life here below content with its own lot, since it is madness to oppose the torrent of things and to be discontented with what is immutable. If they knew that all things are ordered for the general good and for the particular welfare of those who know how to make use of them, they would not identify happiness with simple patience. I know that their phrases are very different from some of the ones I have just presented, but anyone fathoming their views would agree with what I have just stated. In fact, these are Spinoza's views, and there are many people to whom Descartes appears to be of the same opinion. Certainly, he made himself very suspect by rejecting the search for final causes, by maintaining that there is no justice nor benevolence, nor even truth, except because God has determined them in an absolute way, and finally, by letting slip (though in passing) that all the possible variations of matter happen successively, one after another.[379]

---

378. C. von dem Vorst, *Tractatus theologicus de Deo*, (Steinfurt, 1610).

379. The views of Spinoza to which Leibniz is referring are found in the appendix to *Ethics* I. Descartes rejects the search for final causes in Meditation IV (AT VII 55), *Reply to Objections*

If these two sects of Epicureans and Stoics are dangerous to piety, the sect of Socrates and Plato, which (I believe) comes partly from Pythagoras, is so much the more suitable for it. One need only read Plato's admirable dialogue on the immortality of the soul to discover some opinions that are completely opposed to those of our new Stoics.[380] In it, Socrates speaks on the very day of his death, a bit before receiving the deadly cup. He chases sadness from the minds of his friends, substituting wonder in them through marvelous arguments, and it appears that he leaves this life only to enjoy in another the happiness prepared for lofty souls. I believe, he says, that in departing I will find better men than those here; but, at very least, I am certain that I will find the gods there. He maintains that final causes are the principles in physics and that we must seek them in order to account for things. And it seems that he is mocking our new physicists when he mocks Anaxagoras. What he says about him deserves to be heard.

I heard one day (he said) someone reading in a book of Anaxagoras, in which it was said *that an intelligent being was the cause of all things and that he had disposed and arranged them.* That pleased me greatly, for I believed that if the world were the effect of an intelligence, everything would be done in the most perfect manner possible. That is why I believed that anyone who wanted to account for why things are produced or perish, or why they subsist, must look for what would be appropriate to the perfection of any given thing. And so, a man would need to consider in himself or in something else only that which would be the best or the most perfect. One who knows the most perfect could easily judge what is imperfect from this, for knowing the one amounts to knowing the other.[381]

Considering all this, I rejoiced in having found a teacher who could teach the reasons for things—for example, whether the earth is round rather than flat, and why it was better that it be this way rather than otherwise. Moreover, I expected that when saying that the earth is at the center of the universe, or that it is not, he would explain to me why it was most appropriate for it to be this way, and I expected he would tell me as much about the sun, moon, stars and their motions. And finally, after having shown what was most suitable for each thing in particular, he would have shown what was best in general. Filled with this hope, I quickly got hold of the books of Anaxagoras and ran through them with great haste. But I found myself far from my expectation, for I was surprised to see that he did not make use of the governing intelligence that he had first posited, that he no longer spoke of the arrangement nor of the perfection of things, and that he introduced certain ethereal matters that are hardly probable. In this he seemed like someone who, having said that Socrates does things through intelligence, and then going on to explain in

---

V (AT VII375), and *Principles of Philosophy* I 28. For Descartes's account of how God determines what is good, see *Replies to Objections* III (AT VII 432). On how matter assumes all possible forms, see *Principles of Philosophy* III 47 and Descartes to Mersenne, 9 January 1639 (AT II 485).

380. Leibniz is here referring to Plato's *Phaedo.*

381. Literally: "there is only a single science for both the one and the other."

particular the causes of his actions, says that he is seated here because he has a body composed of bones, flesh and sinews, that his bones are hard, but that they are separated by intervals or junctures, that the sinews can be tightened or relaxed, and that this is why the body is flexible and finally why I am seated here. Or, if, wishing to account for this present discourse, he were to refer to the air, to the organs of voice and hearing, and the like, forgetting, however, the true causes, namely that the Athenians believed that it would be better to condemn me rather than to absolve me, and that I believed that it was better to sit here rather than to flee. For, by my faith, without this, these sinews and bones would long have been among the Boeotians and Megarians, if I hadn't thought it more just and more honorable [*honneste*] of me to suffer the penalty imposed by my native land rather than to live elsewhere as a wanderer and an exile. That is why it is unreasonable to call these bones and sinews and their motion causes. It is true that whoever would say that I could not do all this without bones and sinew would be right. But something else is the true cause, and they constitute only a condition without which the cause could not be a cause. Those who only say, for example, that motions of bodies around the earth keep it here, where it is, forget that divine power disposes everything in the finest way, and do not understand that it is the good and the beautiful that join, form, and maintain the world. Until now this has been Socrates, for that which follows on ideas or forms in Plato is a bit more difficult, though no less excellent.

Locke

From a Letter to Thomas Burnett, on the Occasion of Rereading Locke (3 December 1703)[382]

I THANK YOU, sir, for what you wrote me concerning the learned men of Geneva, who are already known to me by reputation. The *Annals* of the late Father Pagi are worthy of being published. I have Ray's *Wisdom of God* and Grew's *Cosmotheorie*. These are good books, for they enter into the details of nature and are not satisfied with general reasons, which I do not take too seriously when they are not written up in a demonstrative manner. Locke's book has been translated into French. That caused me to reread it, especially since I only had the English in the old edition; and to tell the truth, I see many things in it with which I do not agree. I am for innate ideas, and against

---

382. G III 291–92. French.

his *tabula rasa*. In our mind there is not only a faculty, but also a disposition to knowledge, from which innate knowledge can be derived. For all necessary truths derive their proof from this internal light, and not from the experiences of the senses, which merely give us the occasion for thinking of these necessary truths and can never prove a universal necessity, giving us only inductive knowledge from some examples and probability in others yet untried. Locke does not sufficiently understand the nature of demonstrations; I also notice that he speaks in a cavalier fashion about substance because he has not sufficiently fathomed just what it is, and he does not sufficiently disentangle true and false ideas. He says some good things about freedom, but he does not, however, explain it sufficiently, and what he says about identity—as if it consisted only in self-consciousness—is not completely right. Above all, I would prefer that he had not held that it is only through grace, that is to say, by miracle, that the soul is immortal, for this view does not have good consequences. Finally there are a great many things which I would have expressed in an entirely different way than Locke did. I often find his reflections a little too superficial and his philosophy a little too accommodating to the taste of certain persons who do not make it their business to inquire after truth and who believe in finding vanity everywhere, and thereby degrade themselves. However, one must also admit that there are a great many fine thoughts in Locke's work and that when he defends true opinions, he illuminates them beautifully, so that it is, without doubt, one of the best philosophical books of this time. I say this on the occasion of Locke's Apology, about which you have spoken to me, but which I have not seen.[383] Since I haven't learned the contrary, I imagine that he is still in good health.

From the Letters to Thomas Burnett, on Substance (1699)[384]

*****

20/30 January 1699

. . . AS FOR THE DISPUTE between [Edward Stillingfleet,] the Bishop of Worcester and Locke, and what I thought of the Bishop's *Vindication* and Locke's letter to the Bishop and the Bishop's reply to that letter, I believe that persons of such great merit cannot be as far apart as first appears, and that very often they differ only in the way they express themselves. The misuse that the bold author of *Christianity Not Mysterious*[385] had made of some of the thoughts from the *Essay Concerning Understanding* had alarmed that

---

383. The reference is probably to *Mr. Locke's Reply to the Right Rev. The Lord Bishop of Worcester's Answer to his Second Letter* (1699), Locke's last contribution to the exchange of pamphlets that passed between him and Edward Stillingfleet, Bishop of Worcester. It can be found in vol. Ill of the *Works*, pp. 191–498.

384. G III 245–49, 259–61. French.

385. *Christianity Not Mysterious,* published anonymously in 1696. The author was John Toland; see G III 229.

prelate, who thought himself obliged to respond to them, though acknowledging Locke's good intentions. The latter declares that he does not reject substance, and that he does not claim to reject terms for which we do not have
a clear and distinct notion. And in this way he sufficiently demonstrates that
he does not approve of the use that the anonymous author made of his book.
He hopes that someone might provide him with a more distinct notion of
substance than the one that says simply that it is a *substratum*. I believe that I
have provided something that can contribute to this in some small discourses
published in the *Acta Eruditorum* of Leipzig, for in fact, I consider the notion
of substance to be one of the keys to the true philosophy. Whether it is true
that our simple ideas come to us from the senses and reflection, and in what
sense this might be so, these are things I do not wish to examine here; I would
much rather say that they are only awakened in us by these means, as I have
explained in a paper I sent to you on another occasion. If Locke had indicated to you where he found any obscurity in this, I would have attempted to
clarify it, but that does not enter into the present dispute. It seems also that
the two able antagonists basically agree that there are ideas for which we are
not exclusively indebted to the comparison of these simple ideas, or to their
simple combination, and that, in order to form the idea of substance, we need
something other than the assemblage of accidents attributed to it. It is true
that Locke's expressions, asserting that having put together this assemblage
and having given it a name, we later speak of it *inadvertently* as if it were a
simple idea and *accustom* ourselves to assume a *substratum*, these expressions, I say, joined with ingenious jests about the tortoise of the Indian philosopher that supports the earth, that supports houses, which support us, led
Worcester to believe that the author of the *Essay* entirely rejected the notion
of substance as based on inadvertence and custom. But Locke explains that
the custom is based on reason and that the inadvertence and the tortoise of
the Indian philosopher should be applied only to those who satisfy themselves
with the word, and who believe that they have said a great deal when they
speak of this I-know-not-what we call *subject* or *substratum*. On this question
Locke says quite rightly in his letter that our judgment on this is like that of
a baby in the arms of his mother who recognizes that what supports him is
supported by something I-know-not-what, whereas, a more distinct knowledge would make us similar to a knowledgeable person who knows what the
foundations of houses are, whether they are built on rocks, gravel, or on trees,
things used to make the earth firmer. However, Worcester also has a strong
remark in his reply, that when philosophers say that substance supports accidents, they add that it subsists by itself, that is, that nothing supports it, or,
in a word, that it is the ultimate support. For in fact, there are accidents that
support other accidents. It is true that this is not yet sufficient to give us a
distinct notion of these supports or inherences [*inhesions*]. But it is also the
case that Worcester had no need of these for his aim, which was to show us
that we admit many things in philosophy, and with reason, even though we
do not have any distinct ideas of them, and that, consequently, we should not
reject the mysteries under the pretext that we do not have any such ideas.

This is not against Locke, but against the anonymous author. Worcester also recognizes this; if he had stated it more strongly at first, he would have removed any fear Locke might have had of being confused with the anonymous author. However, when I consider that this precaution would have deprived us of both of their profound treatises, I find it difficult to prevent myself from including such a well-conducted dispute between those of whom one can say *strife is good for mortals*.

And so the disputes between them that remain are incidental, such as, for example, whether the idea of substance is as clear and distinct to us as the ideas of the senses are (*Letter*, p. 48). Now, if I dared to mix my thoughts in with the thoughts of these excellent men, I would distinguish between clear and distinct, as I did elsewhere in the *Acts* of Leipzig.[386] I call an idea clear when it is sufficient for recognizing a thing, as when I remember a color well enough to recognize it when it is brought to me; but I call an idea *distinct* when I conceive its conditions or requisites, in a word, when I have its definition, if it has one. Thus I do not have a distinct idea of all colors, being often required to say that it is a something-I-know-not-what that I sense very clearly, but cannot explain well. And similarly, I believe that we have a clear idea, but not a distinct idea, of substance, which arises, in my opinion, from the fact that we who are substances have an internal sensation [*sentiment*] of it in ourselves. When Newton publishes his book on colors we will understand them more distinctly. And I imagine that philosophers will one day know the notion of substance a bit better than they do now. Thus, when Worcester says on p. 238 of his *Vindication*, that the conception of substance we have in our mind is as clear and distinct as those we can derive from the senses, I agree that it is as clear. And when Locke replies on p. 49 of his letter that there is neither obscurity nor confusion in a sound one hears well, I agree that there is no obscurity, and I call that clear, but not distinct, in order to make a distinction between clear knowledge and distinct knowledge. However, everyone can understand the terms as it suits him, and it is true that it is commonly said, with Locke, that a sound is heard distinctly; I also believe, in this sense, that Worcester is right in saying that we know distinctly, that is, clearly, what substance is. In fact, we see that people know very well how to recognize it and distinguish it from an accident, even though they do not distinguish what it contains in its notion. It seems to me that my use of the terms clear and distinct does not depart from Descartes's, who is most responsible for making them fashionable. However, I confess that this noted author has misused ideas a little, and I am of the opinion of Worcester—with whom Locke seems to agree—that some of those who have made so much noise about ideas today misuse them even more. Whether one talks of ideas or notions, whether one talks of distinct ideas or definitions, it is all the same (at least when an idea is not absolutely primitive). And those who determine the implications [*pretensions*] of their ideas say nothing unless they explain

---

386. The reference is to the "Meditations on Knowledge, Truth, and Ideas" of 1684, translated above, pp. 23–27.

them, and unless they come to their reasoning in accordance with the rules of logic. I have attempted to give a mark appropriate for discerning true ideas from false ones in an essay inserted into the Acts of Leipzig several years ago, in which I also spoke of what is lacking in Descartes's argument derived from the idea of God, which he borrowed from your former Archbishop, known by the name of Saint Anselm; for I find that this argument is not sophistical, but imperfect, insofar as it assumes something that still needs demonstration.[387]

There is another incidental, but rather important question, namely, whether thought is absolutely incompatible with matter. Locke, in his *Essay on Understanding*, book 4, chap. 3 [sec. 6], admits that he does not perceive this incompatibility; moreover, he wishes, in his letter, p. 67, that someone give him this demonstration, and on p. 75, he even seems to believe that this demonstration cannot be derived from our ideas. However, in his *Essay*, book 2*, chap. 23, sec. 17, and elsewhere, he seems to have taken the nature of mind to be opposed to that of body (*contradistinguished*), placing the nature of the former in the faculty of thinking and moving the body through thought, and that of the latter in the fact that is an extended solid substance capable of communicating motion by impulsion. Worcester notes this apparent inconsistency in the *Essays* in his reply to the letter, pp. 50ff. I have not yet seen Locke's reply. But if, in sec. 15, he had not taken mind and immaterial substance to be the same thing, adding that we have as clear a perception of the one as of the other, one could reply in his name, that since on his view (sec. 30) the substance of body and the substance of mind are equally unknown to us (which comes to the same as my saying that we do not ordinarily have a sufficiently distinct idea of them), Locke does not deny that in their innermost nature [*dans l'intérieur*] the one might reduce to the other, though they might be distinct in appearance, just as someone insufficiently skilled in geometry, enumerating the sections of the cylinder and those of the cone, might at first oppose the oval of the cylinder to that of the cone, since he does not know that they are both the same ellipse, which can be drawn on a plane with the help of a string moved around two centers, something that is discovered after a more exact analysis. However, I believe, at bottom, that one can demonstrate that thinking substance has no parts, though I agree that extension alone does not constitute the essence of matter. Thus I agree with those who believe that souls are immortal by nature and not by grace. I would not dare to venture an opinion about the other incidental question of fact, whether there are nations knowing nothing of divinity, insofar as it is a question of fact. I remember that an able theologian of the Palatinate named Fabritius wrote an apologia for the human species against the accusation of atheism, in which he replies to the alleged examples. However, I am persuaded, furthermore, that the idea of the supreme being is innate with us, even though there may be people in whom it is not awakened through explicit reflections. In leaving this subject, I wish to say that I am alarmed by the

---

387. Again, the reference is to the "Meditations" of 1684.

news you have given me about the poor health of the Bishop of Worcester and Locke. Their preservation is very important for the public good and for the honor of your nation.

*****

Draft, 1699

I FOUND a remarkable passage in Locke's reply. Having seen how Newton explains many phenomena of nature so well by assuming gravity, that is, the attraction of matter to matter, Locke wishes to retract what he said in his *Essay on Understanding*, that matter has no motion except through the impulsion of another body.[388] Bentley in his *Sermons* also showed the merits of Newton's fine thought.[389] Since the issue is important, I am quite pleased to reflect upon it. The late Mr. Huygens was not of the same opinion, yet I am strongly inclined to believe that Newton's opinion is not to be disdained, and I myself am also of the opinion that elastic force is essential to matter and is found everywhere. And even though I believe that both gravity and elasticity are in matter only because of the structure of the system and can be explained mechanically or through impulsion, nevertheless, as I understand it, two things follow: (i) that the system of the universe is formed and maintained through metaphysical reasons of order; and (ii) that each corporeal substance acts only through its own force and never receives anything over and above it. As for the important question about which Worcester and Locke disputed, whether thought can be given to matter, I believe that some distinctions should be drawn. In bodies I distinguish corporeal substance from matter, and I distinguish primary from secondary matter. Secondary matter is an aggregate or composite of several corporeal substances, as a flock is composed of several animals. But each animal and each plant is also a corporeal substance, having in itself a principle of unity which makes it truly a substance and not an aggregate. And this principle of unity is that which one calls soul, or it is something analogous to soul. But, besides the principle of unity, corporeal substance has its mass or its secondary matter, which is, again, an aggregate of other smaller corporeal substances—and that goes to infinity. However, primitive matter, or matter taken in itself is what we conceive in bodies when we set aside all the principles of unity, that is, it is what is passive, from which arise two qualities: resistance, and tardiness or inertia [*resistentia et restitantia vel inertia*]. That is to say, a body gives way to another rather than allowing itself to be penetrated, but it does not give way

---

388. The passage to which Leibniz is referring here is found in his reply to Stillingfleet's second letter (1699), in *Works* 467–68. There he admits that "Mr. Newton's incomparable book," the *Principia*, influenced him to give up the idea that matter could only act on matter by contact. See also *Essay* 2.8.11, which was altered in the 4th edition (1700) to allow for the possibility of action at a distance. Leibniz brings this observation up in the Preface to the *New Essays* below, pp. 291–306.

389. See Richard Bentley, *Eight Sermons against Atheism* (London, 1693). See Newton, *Papers and Letters*, pp. 271–394.

without difficulty and without weakening the total motion of the body pushing it. Thus one can say that matter in itself, besides extension, contains a primitive, passive power. But the principle of unity contains the primitive active power, or the primitive force, which can never be destroyed and always persists in the exact order of its internal modifications, which represent those outside it. As a result, that which is essentially passive cannot receive the modification of thought without receiving, at the same time, some substantial active principle which would be joined to it; and, consequently, matter considered apart cannot think, but nothing prevents active principles or principles of unity, which are found everywhere in matter, and which already essentially contain a kind of perception, from being elevated to the degree of perception that we call thought. Thus even though matter in itself cannot think, nothing prevents corporeal substance from thinking.

From a Letter to Lady Masham, on Thinking Matter (30 June 1704)[390]

. . . THE PREFERENCE one must give to the natural over the miraculous in the ordinary course of nature is something, I think, all philosophers down to now agree on, except for some near-fanatics like Fludd in his Mosaic philosophy. I say that this preference is also the reason why I hold that it is not matter that thinks, but a being, simple and apart by itself, that is, independent but joined to matter. It is true that the illustrious Locke maintained in his excellent *Essay* and in his writings against the late Bishop of Worcester that God can give matter the power [force] of thinking, because he can make everything we can conceive happen. But then matter would think only by a perpetual miracle, since there is nothing in matter in itself, that is, in extension and impenetrability, from which thought could be deduced, or upon which it could be based. We can therefore say that the *natural immortality of the soul* is demonstrated and that we can affirm its destruction only by affirming a miracle, either by attributing the power [force] of thinking to matter, a power which is *received and maintained* miraculously (in which case the soul could perish through the cessation of the miracle), or by holding that the thinking substance, which is distinct from the body, is annihilated, which would also be miraculous, but a new miracle. Now I say that God, in the case of thinking matter, must not only give matter the capacity to think, but he must also *maintain* it continually by the same miracle, since this capacity has no root [racine], unless God gives matter a new nature. But if one says that God gives matter this new nature or the radical power [force] to think, which is afterwards maintained by itself, he would simply have given it a thinking soul, or else something that differs from a thinking soul only by name. And since this radical power is not properly a modification of matter (for

---

390. G III 355–56. French.

modifications are explicable by the natures they modify and this power is not so explicable), it would be independent of matter.

Preface to the New Essays (1703–05)[391]

Leibniz became acquainted with the outline of John Locke's Essay Concerning Human Understanding *before it was actually published, through an abstract of the book, written by Locke, translated into French, and published in Le Clerc's* Bibliothèque Universelle *(1688). When the* Essay *was published in 1690, Leibniz read it in English and sent some criticisms of it to Locke through Thomas Burnet (ca. 1635–1715) and Lady Masham (1658–1708). When, in 1700, Pierre Coste's French translation of the* Essay *was published, Leibniz was able to make a thorough study of it; he planned to publish his critique under the title* New Essays on the Understanding. *When Locke died in 1704, Leibniz abandoned his project to publish the work.*

SINCE THE *Essays on the Understanding*, published by an illustrious Englishman, is one of the finest and most esteemed works of our age, I resolved to comment on it, insofar as I had given sufficient thought for some time to the same subject and to most of the matters touched upon there; I thought that this would be a good opportunity to publish something entitled *New Essays on the Understanding* and to procure a more favorable reception for my thoughts by putting them in such good company. I further thought that I might profit from someone else's work, not only to make my task easier (since, in fact, it is easier to follow the thread of a good author than to work out everything anew), but also to add something to what he has given us, which is always easier than starting from the beginning. It is true that I often hold an opinion different from his, but far from denying on that account the merit of this famous writer, I bear witness to it by showing in what and why, I differ from his view, when I deem it necessary to prevent his authority from prevailing against reason on some important points.

In fact, although the author of the *Essay* says a thousand fine things of which I approve, our systems are very different. His bears more relation to Aristotle's and mine to Plato's, although we both differ in many ways from the doctrines of these two ancients. He is more popular while I am forced at times to be a little more esoteric and abstract, which is not an advantage to me, especially when writing in a living language. However, I believe that by making two characters speak, one of whom presents the views of the author of the *Essay*, while the other adds my observations, the parallel will be more to the liking of the reader than some dry remarks, whose reading would have to be interrupted at every moment by the necessity of having to return to the author's book in order to understand mine. Nevertheless, it would be good

391. A VI, 6, 43–68; G V 41–61. French.

to compare our writings from time to time, and to judge his views by his work alone, even though I have usually retained his expressions. It is true that the constraint of having to follow the thread of someone else's discourse in making my remarks has meant that I could not think of capturing the charm of which the dialogue is capable, but I hope that the content will make up for the defect in style.

Our differences are about subjects of some importance. There is the question about whether the soul in itself is completely empty like tablets upon which nothing has been written (*tabula rasa*), as Aristotle and the author of the *Essay* maintain, and whether everything inscribed on it comes solely from the senses and from experience, or whether the soul contains from the beginning the source [*principe*] of several notions and doctrines, which external objects awaken only on certain occasions, as I believe with Plato and even with the Schoolmen, and with all those who find this meaning in the passage of St. Paul (Romans 2:15) where he states that the law of God is written in our hearts. The Stoics call these principles *Prolepses*, that is, fundamental assumptions, or what is taken as agreed in advance. Mathematicians call them *common notions*, (*koinai ennoiai*). Modern philosophers give them other fine names, and Julius Scaliger in particular called them the seeds of eternity, and also *zopyra*, meaning living fires, or flashes of light hidden inside us but made to appear through the contact of the senses, like sparks that can be struck from a steel. And it is not unreasonable to believe that these flashes reveal something divine and eternal, something that especially appears in necessary truths. This raises another question, namely, whether all truths depend upon experience, that is, upon induction and instances, or whether some of them have another foundation. For if some occurrences can be foreseen before they have been tested, it is obvious that we contribute something of our own here. Although the senses are necessary for all our actual knowledge, they are not sufficient to give us all of it, since the senses never give us anything but instances, that is, particular or individual truths. Now all the instances confirming a general truth, however numerous they may be, are not sufficient to establish the universal necessity of that same truth, for it does not follow that what has happened before will always happen in the same way. For example, the Greeks, Romans, and all other people of the earth have always observed that before the passage of twenty-four hours, day changes into night and night into day. But they would have been mistaken if they had believed that the same rule is observed everywhere, since the contrary was observed during a visit to Nova Zembla. And anyone who believed that this is a necessary and eternal truth, at least in our climate, would also be mistaken, since we must recognize that the earth and even the sun do not exist necessarily, and that there may be a time when this beautiful star will no longer exist, at least in its present form, and neither will its whole system. As a result it appears that necessary truths, such as we find in pure mathematics and particularly in arithmetic and geometry, must have principles whose proof does not depend on instances nor, consequently, on the testimony of the senses, although without the senses it would never occur to us to think of them. This is a distinction that should be noted carefully, and it is one Euclid understood so well that he proves by reason things that are sufficiently evident through experience and sensible images. Logic, together with metaphysics and morals, of which the one shapes natural theology and the other natural jurisprudence, are full of such truths, and consequently, their proof can only arise from internal principles, which are called innate. It is true that we must not imagine that we can read these eternal laws of reason in the soul from an open book, as the edict of the praetor can be read from his tablet without effort and scrutiny. But it is enough that they can be discovered in us by dint of attention; the senses furnish occasions for this, and the success of experiments also serves to confirm reason, a bit like empirical trials help us avoid errors of calculation in arithmetic when the reasoning is long. Also, it is in this respect that human knowledge differs from that of beasts. Beasts are purely empirical and are guided solely by instances, for, as far as we are able to judge, they never manage to form necessary propositions, whereas man is capable of demonstrative knowledge [*sciences demonstratives.*] In this, the faculty beasts have for drawing consequences is inferior to the reason humans have. The consequences beasts draw are just like those of simple empirics, who claim that what has happened will happen again in a case where what strikes them is similar, without being able to determine whether the same reasons are at work. This is what makes it so easy for men to capture beasts, and so easy for simple empirics to make mistakes. Not even people made skillful by age and experience are exempt from this when they rely too much on their past experiences. This has happened to several people in civil and military affairs, since they do not take sufficiently into consideration the fact that the world changes and that men have become more skillful in finding thousands of new tricks, unlike the stags and hares of today, who have not become any more clever than those of yesterday. The consequences beasts draw are only a shadow of reasoning, that is, they are only connections of imagination, transitions from one image to another; for, when a new situation appears similar to the preceding one, they expect to find again what was previously joined to it, as though things were linked in fact, just because their images are linked in the memory. It is, indeed, true that reason ordinarily counsels us to expect that we will find in the future that which conforms to our long experience of the past; but this is not, on that account, a necessary and infallible truth, and it can fail us when we least expect it, when the reasons which have maintained it change. This is why the wisest people do not rely on it to such an extent that they do not try to probe into the reason for what happens (if that is possible), so as to judge when exceptions must be made. For only reason is capable of establishing sure rules and of providing what uncertain rules lack by formulating exceptions to them, and lastly, capable of finding connections that are certain in the compulsion [*force*] of necessary consequences. This often provides a way of foreseeing an occurrence without having to experience the sensible links between images, which the beasts are reduced to doing. Thus what justifies the internal principles of necessary truths also distinguishes humans from beasts.

Perhaps our able author will not entirely disagree with my opinion. For after having devoted his whole first book to rejecting innate illumination, understood in a certain way, he admits, however, at the beginning of the second book and in what follows, that the ideas which do not originate in sensation come from reflection. Now, reflection is nothing other than attention to what is within us, and the senses do not give us what we already bring with us. Given this, can anyone deny that there is a great deal innate in our mind, since we are innate to ourselves, so to speak, and since we have within ourselves being, unity, substance, duration, change, action, perception, pleasure, and a thousand other objects of our intellectual ideas? And since these objects are immediate and always present to our understanding (though they may not always be perceived consciously [aperçus] on account of our distractions and our needs), why should it be surprising that we say that these ideas, and everything that depends upon them, are innate in us? I have also used the comparison with a block of veined marble, rather than a completely uniform block of marble, or an empty tablet, that is, what the philosophers call a *tabula rasa*. For if the soul were like these empty tablets, truths would be in us as the shape of Hercules is in a block of marble, when the marble is completely indifferent to receiving this shape or another. But if the stone had veins which marked out the shape of Hercules rather than other shapes, then that block would be more determined with respect to that shape and Hercules would be as though innate in it in some sense, even though some labor would be required for these veins to be exposed and polished into clarity by the removal of everything that prevents them from appearing. This is how ideas and truths are innate in us, as natural inclinations, dispositions, habits, or potentialities [*virtualités*] are, and not as actions are, although these potentialities are always accompanied by some corresponding, though often insensible, actions.

Our able author seems to claim that there is nothing *potential* [*virtuel*] in us, and even nothing that we are not always actually conscious of perceiving [appercevions]. But he cannot hold this in all strictness; otherwise his position would be too paradoxical, since, again, acquired habits and the contents of our memory are not always consciously perceived [aperçues] and do not even always come to our aid when needed, though often we easily recall them to mind when some trivial occasion reminds us of them, as when we need only the beginning of a song to make us remember the rest. He also limits his thesis in other places, saying that there is nothing in us that we did not at least previously perceive consciously [aperçu]. But no one can guarantee by reason alone how far back our past and perhaps forgotten apperceptions can go, especially in view of the Platonists' doctrine of reminiscence, which, fabulous though it is, is not at all incompatible with pure reason. Furthermore, why must it be that everything is acquired by apperceptions of external things and that nothing can be unearthed from within ourselves? Is our soul in itself so empty that, without images borrowed from the outside, it is nothing? This is not, I am convinced, a view our judicious author could approve. Where could one find some tablets which do not have a certain amount of variety in themselves? Will we ever see a perfectly homogeneous and uniform surface?

Then why could we not also provide ourselves some object of thought from our own depths, when we are willing to dig there? Thus I am led to believe that, fundamentally, his view on this point is no different from mine, or rather from the common view, insofar as he recognizes two sources of our knowledge, the senses and reflection.

I do not know whether it will be as easy to reconcile him with me and with the Cartesians when he maintains that the mind does not always think, and in particular, that it is without perception during dreamless sleep, and when he objects that since bodies can be without motion, souls can just as well be without thought. But here I reply somewhat differently from what is customary. For I maintain that a substance cannot naturally be without action, and that there is never even any body without motion. Experience already supports me, and to be convinced of this, one need only consult the book of the illustrious Mr. Boyle against absolute rest.[392] But I believe that reason also supports this, and it is one of the proofs I use for refuting atoms. Moreover, there are a thousand indications that allow us to judge that at every moment there is an infinity of perceptions in us, but without apperception and without reflection—that is, changes in the soul itself, which we do not consciously perceive [*appercevons*], because these impressions are either too small or too numerous, or too homogeneous, in the sense that they have nothing sufficiently distinct in themselves; but combined with others, they do have their effect and make themselves felt in the assemblage, at least confusedly. It is in this way that custom makes us ignore the motion of a mill or of a waterfall, after we have lived nearby for some time. It is not that this motion ceases to strike our organs and that there is nothing corresponding to it in the soul, on account of the harmony of the soul and the body, but that the impressions in the soul and in the body, lacking the appeal of novelty, are not sufficiently strong to attract our attention and memory, which are applied only to more demanding objects. All attention requires memory, and when we are not alerted, so to speak, to pay heed to some of our own present perceptions, we let them pass without reflection and without even noticing them. But if someone alerts us to them right away and makes us take note, for example, of some noise we have just heard, we remember it, and we consciously perceive that we just had some sensation of it. Thus there were perceptions that we did not consciously perceive right away, the apperception in this case arising only after an interval, however brief. In order better to recognize [*juger*] these tiny perceptions [*petites perceptions*] that cannot be distinguished in a crowd, I usually make use of the example of the roar or noise of the sea that strikes us when we are at the shore. In order to hear this noise as we do, we must hear the parts that make up this whole, that is, we must hear the noise of each wave, even though each of these small noises is known only in the confused assemblage of all the others, and would not be noticed if the wave making it were the only one. For we must be slightly affected by the motion of this wave, and we must have some perception of each of these noises, however

---

392. Robert Boyle, *Discourse about the Absolute Rest in Bodies* (1669).

small they may be, otherwise we would not have the noise of a hundred thousand waves, since a hundred thousand nothings cannot make something. Moreover, we never sleep so soundly that we do not have some weak and confused sensation, and we would never be awakened by the greatest noise in the world if we did not have some perception of its beginning, small as it might be, just as we could never break a rope by the greatest effort in the world, unless it were stretched and strained slightly by the least efforts, even though the slight extension they produce is not apparent.

These tiny perceptions are therefore more effectual than one thinks. They make up this I-know-not-what, those flavors, those images of the sensory qualities, clear in the aggregate but confused in their parts; they make up those impressions the surrounding bodies make on us, which involve the infinite, and this connection that each being has with the rest of the universe. It can even be said that as a result of these tiny perceptions, the present is filled with the future and laden with the past, that everything conspires together (*sympnoia panta*, as Hippocrates said), and that eyes as piercing as those of God could read the whole sequence of the universe in the smallest of substances.

The things that are, the things that have been, and the things that will soon be brought in by the future.[393]

These insensible perceptions also indicate and constitute the individual, which is individuated [*caractérise*] by the traces which these perceptions preserve of its previous states, connecting it up with his present state. They can be known by a superior mind, even when the individual himself does not sense them, that is, when he no longer has an explicit memory of them. But these perceptions even provide a way of recovering the memory, as needed, through periodic unfoldings which may occur one day. That is why death might only be a state of sleep, and might not even remain one, insofar as the perceptions merely cease to be sufficiently distinct and, in animals, are reduced to a state of confusion which suspends apperception, but which cannot last forever; I shall not speak here of man, who ought to have great prerogatives in this matter in order to retain his personality.

It is also by means of these insensible perceptions that I explain the marvelous pre-established harmony between the soul and the body, and also between all the monads or simple substances, which takes the place of that untenable influence of the one on the others, and which, in the judgment of the author of the finest of dictionaries,[394] raises the greatness of divine perfections beyond anything ever conceived before. After this I would add little if I said that it is these tiny perceptions which determine us in many situations without our thinking of them, and which deceive the common people by giving the appearance of an *indifference of equilibrium*, as if it made no difference to us, for example, whether we turned right or left. Nor is it necessary for me to

---

393. Virgil, *Georgics* IV 393.

394. Pierre Bayle. The reference is to Bayle's discussion of Leibniz in notes H and L to the article "Rorarius" in his *Dictionary*. Bayle's point is that Leibniz's pre-established harmony puts implausibly severe demands on God's power.

point out here, as I've done in the book itself,[395] that they cause this uneasiness, which I show to consist in something that differs from pain only as the small differs from the great, and yet which often brings about our desire and even our pleasure by giving it a kind of spice. The insensible parts of our sensible perceptions also bring about a relation between those perceptions of color, heat, and other sensible qualities, and the motions in bodies that correspond to them. But the Cartesians and our author, penetrating though he is, think of the perceptions we have of these qualities as arbitrary, that is, as if God had given them to the soul according to his good pleasure without having regard to any essential relation between perceptions and their objects, a view which surprises me and seems to me unworthy of the wisdom of the author of things, who does nothing without harmony and reason.

In short, *insensible perceptions* have as much use in philosophy of mind [*Pneumatique*] as corpuscles do in physics; and it is equally unreasonable to reject the one as the other under the pretext that they are beyond the reach of the senses. Nothing takes place all at once, and it is one of the greatest and best verified maxims that nature never makes leaps; this is what I called *the law of continuity* when I once spoke about this in the *Nouvelles de la république des lettres*,[396] and this law is of considerable use in physics. It entails that one always passes from the small to the large and back again through what lies between, both in degrees and in parts, and that a motion never arises immediately from rest nor is it reduced to rest except through a lesser motion, just as we never manage to pass through any line or length before having passed through a shorter one. But until now, those who have given the laws of motion have not observed this law, believing that a body can instantaneously receive a motion opposite to the previous motion. All this can allow us to judge that noticeable perceptions arise by degrees from ones too small to be noticed. To judge otherwise is to know little of the immense subtlety of things, which always and everywhere involves an actual infinity.

I have also noticed that because of insensible variations, two individual things cannot be perfectly alike and must always differ in something over and above number. This puts an end to the empty tablets of the soul, a soul without thought, a substance without action, void space, atoms, and even particles in matter not actually divided, complete uniformity in a part of time, place, or matter, the perfect globes of the second element that derive from the perfect original cubes, and a thousand other fictions of philosophers which arise from their incomplete notions. These are things that the nature of things does not allow, things that are allowed to pass because of our ignorance and lack of attention; they cannot be tolerated unless we limit them to being abstractions of the mind, which protests that it does not deny the things it sets aside, but only judges that they need not enter into consideration at present. If we thought in earnest that things we do not consciously perceive

---

395. In the *New Essays* II.23.
396. The reference is to "A Letter of Mr. Leibniz on a General Principle Useful in explaining the Laws of Nature..." which appeared in the July 1687 issue of the *Nouvelles*, and is translated in L 351–53.

[*s'apperçoit*] are not in the soul or in the body, we would fail in philosophy as in politics, by neglecting the mikron, imperceptible changes. But an abstraction is not an error, provided we know that what we are ignoring is really there. This is similar to what mathematicians do when they talk about the perfect lines they propose to us, uniform motions and other regular effects, although *matter* (that is, the mixture of the effects of the surrounding infinity) always provides some exception. We proceed in this way in order to distinguish various considerations and, as far as is possible, to reduce effects to their reasons, and foresee some of their consequences. For the more careful we are not to neglect any consideration we can subject to rules [*reguler*], the more closely practice corresponds to theory. But only the supreme reason, which nothing escapes, can distinctly understand the whole infinite, all the reasons, and all the consequences. With respect to infinities, we can only know them confusedly, but at least we can distinctly know that they exist, otherwise we would be very poor judges of the beauty and greatness of the universe, just as we would also be unable to develop a good physics which explains the nature of things in general, and still less a good philosophy of mind [*Pneumatique*], which includes the knowledge of God, of souls, and of simple substances in general.

This knowledge of insensible perceptions also serves to explain why and how two souls of the same species, whether human or otherwise, never leave the hands of the creator perfectly alike, and why and how each of them always has its original relation to the point of view it will have in the universe. But this already follows from what I pointed out previously about two individuals, namely that the *difference* between them is always *more than numerical*. There is another significant point on which I must differ, not only from the opinion of our author, but also from those of most of the moderns. I hold with most of the ancients that all spiritual beings [*génies*], all souls, all simple created substances, are always joined to a body, and that souls are never completely separated from bodies. I have *a priori* reasons for this, but this doctrine will be found to have the further advantage that it resolves all the philosophical difficulties about the state of souls, their perpetual conservation, their immortality, and their operation. Since the difference between one of their states and another is never, nor has it ever been anything but the difference between the more and the less sensible, between the more and the less perfect (or the other way around), the past or future state of souls is just as explicable as their present one. The slightest reflection is sufficient to show that this is reasonable, and that a leap from one state to an infinitely different one cannot be natural. I am surprised that the schools, by needlessly abandoning nature, have been willing to readily plunge into enormous difficulties, and thus to give free thinkers [*esprits forts*] an opportunity for their apparent triumphs. The arguments of the free thinkers collapse all at once with this explanation of things, in which it is no more difficult to conceive the preservation of souls (or rather, on my view, of the animal), than it is to conceive the change from caterpillar to butterfly and the preservation of thought in sleep, to which Jesus

Christ has divinely compared death.[397] Also, I have already said that no sleep can last forever; but it will have less duration or almost no duration at all in the case of rational souls, which are always destined to remain the persons [*personnage*] they were in the city of God, and consequently, to retain their memory, so that they can be better able to receive rewards and punishments. I further add that, in general, no disordering of its visible organs is capable of bringing things in the animal to the point of complete confusion, or to destroy all its organs, and to deprive the soul of the whole of its organic body and of the ineradicable remains of all its preceding traces. But the ease with which people have abandoned the ancient doctrine that angels have subtle bodies (a doctrine which has been confused with the corporality of angels), the introduction of the allegedly separated intelligences among created things (to which the intelligences that rotated Aristotle's heavens have contributed much), and finally the poorly understood opinion some have held that we cannot retain the souls of beasts without falling into metempsychosis, all these in my opinion have resulted in the neglect of the natural way of explaining the preservation of the soul. This has done great harm to natural religion, and has led many to believe that our immortality is nothing but a miraculous grace of God. Our celebrated author speaks with some doubt about this, as I will soon point out. But I wish that all who are of this opinion discussed it as wisely and as sincerely as he does. For it is to be feared that several who speak of immortality through grace merely do so in order to preserve appearances, and are at bottom not very far from those Averroists and certain pernicious Quietists who imagine an absorption and reunion of the soul with the ocean of divinity, a notion whose impossibility is clearly shown by my system alone, perhaps.

It seems, moreover, that we also disagree about matter, insofar as the author judges that the void is necessary for motion, since he believes that the small parts of matter are rigid. I admit that if matter were composed of such parts, motion in a plenum would be impossible; it would be as if a room were filled with a quantity of little pebbles without containing the least empty place. But I cannot grant this assumption, for which there seems to be no reason, even though this able author goes so far as to believe that the rigidity or the cohesion of the small parts constitutes the essence of bodies. Rather, we should conceive of space as filled with matter that was originally fluid, matter capable of any division, and indeed, actually subjected to division and subdivision to infinity, but with this difference, however, that it is unequally divisible and unequally divided in different places because of the motions there, motions which are already more or less harmonious. This brings it about that it has rigidity as well as fluidity everywhere, and that no body is hard or fluid to the ultimate degree, that is, that no atom has insuperable hardness, nor is any mass entirely indifferent to division. The order of nature, and particularly the law of continuity, also destroys both alternatives equally well.

I have also shown that *cohesion*, which is not itself an effect of impulsion or

---

397. John 11:11.

motion, would cause traction, properly speaking. For if there were an originally rigid body, an Epicurean atom, for example, which had a part projecting in the form of a hook (since we can imagine atoms in all sorts of shapes), this hook when pushed would pull with it the rest of the atom, that is to say, the part not pushed and not falling within the line of the impulse. However, our able author is himself opposed to those philosophic tractions, like the ones formerly attributed to the fear of the void, and he reduces them to impulses, maintaining with the moderns that one part of matter operates on another only by pushing against it from close by. I think that they are right about this, because otherwise the operation would not be intelligible at all.

I must not, however, conceal the fact that I have noticed a kind of retraction on this point on the part of our excellent author, and I cannot refrain from praising his modest sincerity about it, just as I have admired his penetrating insight on other occasions. His retraction occurs on page 408 of the reply to the second letter of the late Bishop of Worcester, printed in 1699. There, in order to justify the view he maintained against this learned prelate, namely that matter is capable of thought, he says among other things: *It is true, I say "that bodies operate by impulse and nothing else"* (*Essay*, II, chap. 8, sec. 11). *And so I thought when I writ it, and can yet conceive no other way of their operation. But I am since convinced by the judicious Mr. Newton's incomparable book, that it is too bold a presumption to limit God's power, [in this point], by our narrow conceptions. The gravitation of matter towards matter, by ways inconceivable to me, is not only a demonstration that God can, if he pleases, put into bodies powers and ways of operation, above what can be derived from our idea of body or can be explained by what we know of matter, but also an unquestionable [and everywhere visible] instance, that he has actually done so. And therefore, in the next edition of my book I shall take care to have that passage rectified.*[398] I find in the French version of this book, which was no doubt taken from the latest editions, that sec. 11 reads thus: *It is manifest, at least insofar as we can conceive it, that it is by impulse and nothing else that bodies operate one upon another, it being impossible to conceive that body should operate on what it does not touch, which is all one to imagine that it can operate where it is not.*[399]

I can only praise the modest piety of our famous author, who recognizes that God can do what goes beyond our understanding, and thus, that there may be inconceivable mysteries in the articles of faith. But I would not want us to be obliged to appeal to miracles in the ordinary course of nature, and to admit absolutely inexplicable powers and operations there. Otherwise, on the strength of what God can do, we would grant too much license to bad philosophers, allowing them those *centripetal virtues* or those *immediate attrac-*

---

398. *Works* III, 467–68. The two passages in the brackets were omitted in Leibniz's French translation of Locke's text. In addition, Locke talks of "my narrow conceptions" rather than "our narrow conceptions."

399. Leibniz is referring here to Pierre Coste's translation, *Essai Philosophique Concernant l'Entendement Humain*. Published in 1700, the same year as the important 4th edition of the *Essay*, it represents an intermediate stage between the 3rd and 4th editions. See *Essay*, ed. Nidditch, pp. xxxiv–xxxvi.

tions at a distance, without it being possible to make them intelligible; I do not see what would prevent our Scholastics from saying that everything happens simply through faculties and from maintaining their intentional species, which go from objects to us and find a way of entering our souls. If this is acceptable,

> *What I said could not be will now happen.*[400]

So it seems to me that our author, judicious as he is, is here going rather too much from one extreme to the other. He raises difficulties about the operations of *souls*, when it is merely a matter of admitting what is not *sensible*, while here he grants *bodies* what is not even *intelligible*, allowing them powers and actions beyond everything which, in my opinion, a created mind could do or understand; for he grants them attraction, even at great distances, without limitation to any sphere of activity, and he does so in order to maintain a view which is no less inexplicable, namely the possibility of matter thinking in the natural order of things.[401]

The question he is discussing with the noted prelate who had attacked him is whether *matter can think*. Since this is an important point, and an important point for the present work as well, I cannot avoid going into it a bit, and taking account of their debate. I shall represent the substance of their dispute and take the liberty of saying what I think of it. The late Bishop of Worcester, fearing (but without great cause, in my opinion) that the author's doctrine of ideas was subject to some abuses prejudicial to the Christian faith, undertook to examine some aspects of it in his *Vindication of the Doctrine of the Trinity*. He first gives this excellent writer his due, by recognizing that the writer judges that the existence of the mind is as certain as that of the body, even though as regards these substances, the one is as little known as the other. He then asks (pages 241 seqq.) how reflection could assure us of the existence of the mind if God can give matter the faculty of thinking, as our author believes (Book IV, chap. 3, [sec. 6]) since, as a consequence, the way of ideas, which should serve to discriminate what can belong to the soul or to the body, would become useless. However, it was said in Book II of the *Essay on the Understanding* (chap. 23, sec. 15, 27, 28), that the operations of the soul provide us with the idea of the mind, and that the understanding, together with the will, makes this idea as intelligible to us as the nature of body is made intelligible by solidity and impulse. Here is how our author replies to this in his *First Letter* (pp. 65 seqq.): [[*I think that I have proved that there is a spiritual substance in us. For*]] *we experiment in ourselves thinking. The idea of this action, or mode of thinking, is inconsistent with the idea of self-subsistence, and therefore has a necessary connection with a support or subject of inhesion: the idea of that support is what we call substance. . . . The general idea of substance*

---

400. Ovid, *Tristia*, I.7.7.

401. In his notes for the preface, Leibniz wrote: "The philosophy of the author destroys what appears to me to be the most important thing, that the soul is imperishable, whereas on his view there must be a miracle for it to endure. This is directly opposed to the Platonic philosophy joined to that of Democritus and Aristotle, such as mine is." (A VI, 6, 48)

being the same everywhere, the modification of thinking, or the power of thinking, joined to it, makes it a spirit, without considering what other modification it has, as whether it has the modification of solidity or not. As, on the other side, substance, that has the modification of solidity, is matter, whether it has the modification of thinking or no. And therefore, if your lordship means by a spiritual, an immaterial substance, I grant I have not proved, nor upon my principles, can it be proved [. . .] that there is an immaterial substance in us [. . . .] Though I presume, what I have said about the supposition of a system of matter [. . .] (Book IV, chap 10, sec. 16) *(which there demonstrates that God is immaterial) will prove it in the highest degree probable, that the thinking substance in us is immaterial. . . .* [[*Yet I have shown* (adds the author, p. 68)]] *that all the great ends of religion and morality are secured . . .by the immortality of the soul, without a necessary supposition that the soul is immaterial.*[402]

In his *Reply* to this letter, to show that our author was of another opinion when he wrote Book II of the *Essay*, the learned Bishop quotes (p. 51) the following passage (Book II, chap. 23, sec. 15), where it is said that *by the simple ideas we have taken from those operations of our own minds* [. . .] *we are able to frame the complex idea of spirit. And thus, by putting together the ideas of thinking, perceiving, liberty, and power of moving our bodies, we have as clear a* [. . .] *notion of immaterial substances as we have of material.*[403] He further cites other passages to show that the author opposed mind to body. He says (p. 54) that the end of religion and morality is better secured by proving that the soul is immortal by its very nature, that is, immaterial. He further cites this passage (p. 70), that *all the ideas we have of particular, distinct sorts of substances are nothing but several combinations of simple ideas*[404] and that, consequently, the author believed that the idea of thinking and willing results in a substance different from that given by the idea of solidity and impulse. And he says that in sec. 17 the author remarks that the latter ideas constitute the body as opposed to the mind.

The Bishop of Worcester could have added that from the fact that the *general idea* of substance is in body and in mind, it does not follow that their differences are *modifications* of a single thing, as our author just said in the passage I cited from his *First Letter.* We must distinguish between modifications and attributes. The faculties of having perception and of acting, as well as extension, and solidity, are attributes, or perpetual and principal predicates; but thought, impetuosity, shapes, and motions are modifications of these attributes. Moreover, we must distinguish between the physical (or real) genus and logical (or ideal) genus. The things of the same physical genus, or those which are *homogeneous*, are of the same matter, so to speak, and can often be changed from one into another by changing their modifications, like circles and squares. But two heterogeneous things can have a common logical genus, and then their *differences* are neither simple accidental modifications

---

402. *Works* III 33-34. Passages in double brackets are transitional phrases added by Leibniz.
403. . In Locke, it was "themselves" rather than "our bodies." In later editions Leibniz added "immaterial" to spirit.
404. *Essay*, II.23.6.

of a single subject, nor of a single metaphysical or physical matter. Thus time and space are quite heterogeneous things, and we would be wrong to imagine some common real subject I-know-not-what which had only continuous quantity in general and whose modifications resulted in time or space. Yet their common logical genus is continuous quantity. Someone might perhaps make fun of these philosophical distinctions between two genera, the one only logical and the other real, and between two matters, the one physical—that of bodies—and the other only metaphysical or general, as if someone were to say that two parts of space are of the same matter or that two hours are also of the same matter as one another. Yet these distinctions concern not only terms, but also things themselves, and seem to be particularly relevant here, where their confusion has given rise to a false conclusion. These two genera have a common notion, and the notion of real genus is common to both sets of matters, so that their genealogy would be as follows:

GENUS
- the merely *logical*, distinguished by simple *differences*
- the *real*, that is, MATTER, where differences are *modifications*
  - the merely *metaphysical*, in which there is homogeneity
  - the *physical*, in which there is a solid, homogeneous mass

I have not seen the author's *Second Letter* to the bishop; the *Reply* that the prelate makes to it hardly touches the point about the thinking of matter. But our author's *Reply* to this *Second Reply* returns to it. God (he says, nearly in these words, page 397) *adds the qualities and perfections that please him to the essence of matter; to some parts [he adds] simple motion, to plants vegetation, and to animals sensation. Those who agree with me so far exclaim against me as soon as I go a step further and say that God may give to matter thought, reason, and volition—as if this would destroy the essence of matter. But to prove this assertion they advance that thought or reason is not included in the essence of matter; this proves nothing since motion and life are not included in it either. They also advance that we cannot conceive that matter can think; but our conception is not the measure of God's power.*[405] After this he quotes the example of the attraction of matter (p. 99, but especially p. 408), in which he speaks of the gravitation of matter toward matter, attributed to Mr. Newton, in the words I quoted above, admitting that we can never conceive how this happens. This is, in fact, a return to occult qualities or, what is more, to inexplicable qualities. He adds (p. 401) that nothing is more apt to favor the skeptics than denying what we

---

405. This is a paraphrase of *Works* III 460-61.

don't understand, and (p. 402) that we do not even conceive how the soul thinks. He holds (p. 403) that since the two substances, material and immaterial, can be conceived in their bare essence without any activity, it is up to God to give the power of thinking to the one or to the other. And he wants to take advantage of his adversary's view, which grants sensation to beasts, but does not grant them any immaterial substance. He claims that freedom, self-consciousness (p. 408), and the power of making abstractions can be given to matter, not as matter, but as enriched by divine power. Finally he reports (p. 434) the observation of a traveller as eminent and judicious as Mr. de la Loubere that the pagans of the East know of the immortality of the soul without being able to understand its immateriality.

With regard to all this I will note, before coming to the explanation of my opinion, that it is certain that matter is as little capable of producing sensation mechanically as it is of producing reason, as our author agrees. Furthermore, I note, indeed, that I recognize that we are not allowed to deny what we do not understand, though I add that we have the right to deny (at least in the order of nature) what is absolutely unintelligible and inexplicable. I also maintain that substances (material or immaterial) cannot be conceived in their bare essence without activity, and that activity is of the essence of substance in general. And finally, I maintain that the conception of creatures is not the measure of God's power, but that their conceptivity, or ability [force] to conceive, is the measure of nature's power; everything in conformity with the natural order can be conceived or understood by some creature.

Those who understand my system will judge that I will not be in complete agreement with either of these two excellent authors, whose dispute, however, is very instructive. But to explain myself distinctly, one must above all take into account that the modifications which can come naturally or without miracle to a single subject must come to it from the limitations or variations of a real genus or of an original nature, constant and absolute. For this is how in philosophy we distinguish the modes of an absolute being from the being itself; for example, we know that magnitude, shape, and motion are obviously limitations and variations of corporeal nature. For it is clear how a limitation of extension produces shapes, and that the change which takes place there is nothing but motion. And every time we find some quality in a subject, we ought to think that, if we understood the nature of this subject and of this quality, we would understand how this quality could result from that nature. Thus in the order of nature (setting miracles aside) God does not arbitrarily give these or those qualities indifferently to substances; he never gives them any but those which are natural to them, that is to say, those that can be derived from their nature as explicable modifications. Thus we can judge that matter does not naturally have the attraction mentioned above, and does not of itself move on a curved path, because it is not possible to conceive how this takes place, that is to say, it is not possible to explain it mechanically, whereas that which is natural should be capable of becoming distinctly conceivable, if we were admitted into the secrets of things. This distinction between what is natural and explicable and what is inexplicable and miraculous removes all the difficulties: if we were to reject it, we would uphold something worse than occult qualities, and in doing so we would renounce philosophy and reason, and throw open refuges for ignorance and idleness through a hollow system, a system which admits not only that there are qualities we do not understand (of which there are only too many) but also that there are some qualities that the greatest mind could not understand, even if God provided him with every possible advantage, that is, qualities that would be either miraculous or without rhyme or reason. And it would indeed be without rhyme or reason that God should ordinarily perform miracles, so that this do-nothing hypothesis would equally destroy philosophy, which searches for reasons, and the divine wisdom, which provides them.

As for the question of thinking, it is certain—and our author recognizes in more than one place—that thinking cannot be an intelligible modification of matter, that is, that a sensing or thinking being is not a mechanical thing like a watch or a windmill, in the sense that we could conceive of magnitudes, shapes and motions whose mechanical conjunction could produce something thinking, and even sensing, in a mass in which there was nothing of the kind, that would likewise cease to be if the mechanism got out of order. Thus it is not natural for matter to sense and to think, and there are only two ways in which it could do so. One of these would be for God to join to it a substance to which thought is natural, and the other would be for God to endow it with thought miraculously. In this, then, I agree entirely with the Cartesians, except that I extend the view to beasts as well, and believe that they have sensation and souls which are, properly speaking, immaterial and as imperishable as the atoms of Democritus or Gassendi. But the Cartesians, who are confused about the souls of beasts, and do not know what to do with them if they are preserved (since it did not occur to them that the animal might be preserved in a reduced form), have been forced to deny them even sensation, contrary to all appearances, and contrary to the judgment of mankind. But if someone said that God, at very least, can add this faculty of thinking to a mechanism properly prepared, I would answer that if this occurred, and if God added this faculty to matter without at the same time endowing it with a substance that was the subject in which this same faculty inhered (as I conceive it), that is, without adding an immaterial soul there, then matter would have to be raised miraculously so as to be capable of receiving a power of which it is not capable naturally, just as some Scholastics claim that God raises fire to the point of giving it the power directly to burn minds separated from matter, which would be a miracle, pure and simple. It is enough that we can maintain that matter thinks only if we attribute to it either an imperishable soul, or else a miracle, and thus, that the immortality of our souls follows from what is natural, since we could then hold that they are destroyed only by miracle, whether by exalting matter or by annihilating the soul. For we know, of course, that the power of God could make our souls mortal, even though they may be immaterial (or immortal by nature alone), since he is capable of annihilating them.

Now the truth of the immateriality of the soul is undoubtedly important.

For it is infinitely more useful to religion and morality, especially in our days (when many people have scant respect for revelation by itself or for miracles), to show that souls are naturally immortal, and that it would be a miracle if they were not, than it would be to maintain that our souls must naturally die, and that it is due to a miraculous grace, based solely on God's promise, that they do not die. Moreover, we have known for a long time that those who wished to destroy natural religion, and reduce everything to revelation, as if reason taught us nothing about it, have been held suspect, and not always without reason. But our author is not of their number. He maintains a demonstration of God's existence and he attributes to the immateriality of the soul *a probability of the highest degree*, which may consequently pass for a *moral certainty*, so that I imagine that, having as much sincerity as penetration, he might quite well come to agree with the doctrine I have just expounded, a doctrine fundamental in every reasonable philosophy. For otherwise, I do not see how we can prevent ourselves from falling back into a fanatical philosophy, such as the *Mosaic philosophy* of Fludd, which saves all phenomena by attributing them immediately and miraculously to God, or into a barbaric philosophy, like that of certain philosophers and physicians of former days, who still savored of the barbarism of their own age, and who today are justly despised. They saved the appearances by explicitly fabricating suitable occult qualities or faculties, which were thought to be like little demons or spirits able to do what was required of them without any fuss, just as if pocket watches told time by some faculty of clockness without the need of wheels, or mills crushed grain by a fractive faculty without the need of anything like millstones. As for the difficulty many people have had in conceiving an immaterial substance, it soon ceases (at least in large part) when one no longer requires substances separated from matter; I hold, in fact, that such substances have never existed naturally among created things.

Berkeley

From a Letter to Des Bosses
(5 March 1715)[406]

T HE ONE in Ireland who attacks the reality of bodies does not seem to bring forward suitable reasons, nor does he explain himself sufficiently. I suspect that he is one of that sort of men who wants to be known for his paradoxes.

---

406. G II 492; W 636. Latin.

Remarks on Berkeley's Principles
(Winter 1714–15)

THERE IS MUCH here that is correct and close to my own view. But it is expressed paradoxically. For it is not necessary to say that matter is nothing, but it is sufficient to say that it is a phenomenon, like the rainbow; and that it is not a substance, but the resultant of substances, and that space is no more real than time, that is, that space is nothing but the order of coexistents, just as time is the order of things that have existed before [*subexistentia*]. True substances are monads, that is, perceivers. But the author should have gone further, to the infinity of monads, constituting everything, and to their pre-established harmony. Badly, or at least in vain, he rejects abstract ideas, restricts ideas to imaginations, and condemns the subtleties of arithmetic and geometry. The worst thing is that he rejects the division of extension to infinity, even if he might rightly reject infinitesimal quantities.[407]

Newton

Absolute and Relative Motion,
From Letters to Huygens (1694)[408]

In the scholium following the definitions in book I of the Mathematical Principles of Natural Philosophy, *his* Principia, *Newton attempted to distinguish between motion in an absolute, nonrelativistic sense, and rest. Appealing to his famous bucket experiment, Newton attempted to show how, from its effects, we can know when a body is really in motion. If a vessel, hung by a long cord, is so often turned about that the cord is strongly twisted, then filled with water, . . . [and] is whirled about the contrary way . . . the surface of the water will at first be plane; but after that, . . . [the water will] recede by l ittle and little from the middle, and ascend to the sides of the vessel, forming itself into a concave figure. . . . This ascent of the water shows its endeavor to recede from the axis of its motion; and the true and absolute circular motion of the water, which is directly contrary to the relative, becomes known, and may be measured by this endeavor. [Newton,* Mathematical Principles, *p. 10.] In these letters to Huygens, Leibniz expresses his rejection of this important aspect of Newton's physics, and argues that all motion is relative to the extent that one can never say, strictly speaking, that a given body is really in motion or at rest.*

---

407. This remark was written in Leibniz's hand on the last page of his copy of George Berkeley, *A Treatise Concerning the Principles of Human Knowledge* (Dublin, 1710).
408. GM II 184–85, 199. French.

12/22 June 1694

AS FOR the difference between absolute and relative motion, I believe that if motion, or rather the motive force of bodies, is something real, as it seems we must acknowledge, it would need to have a *subject* [*subjectum*]. For, if *a* and *b* approach each other, I assert that all phenomena would be the same, no matter which of them is assumed to be in motion or at rest; and if there were 1,000 bodies, I agree that the phenomena could not furnish us (nor even the angels) with infallible grounds [*raison*] for determining the subject of motion or its degree, and that each separately could be conceived as being at rest. I believe that this is all you asked of me. But you would not deny (I think) that it is true that each of them has a certain degree of motion, or, if you wish, a certain degree of force, notwithstanding the equivalence of hypotheses. It is true that I derive from this the consequence that there is something more in nature than what is determined by geometry. And this is not among the least important of the several reasons I use to prove that, other than extension and its variations, which are purely geometric things, we must acknowledge something higher, namely, force. Newton recognized the equivalence of hypotheses in the case of rectilinear motions; but he believes, with respect to circular motions, that the effort circulating bodies exert to move away from the center or from the axis of circulation allows us to recognize their absolute motion. But I have reasons that lead me to believe that there are no exceptions to the general law of equivalence. It seems to me, however, that you once were of Newton's opinion concerning circular motion.

* * *

4/14 September 1694

... YOUR EXPLANATION of gravity [*pésanteur*] seems to be the most plausible one so far. The only thing that remains to be desired is an account of why the gravity that appears in the heavens is inversely proportional to the squares of the distances. When I told you one day in Paris that the true subject of motion is difficult to recognize, you replied that this can be done by means of circular motion. That stopped me for a while; and I remembered reading almost the same thing in Newton's book. But that was when I thought that I had already seen that circular motion has no advantage in this. And I see that you now agree with me.[409] I hold, of course, that all hypotheses are equivalent, and when I assign certain motions to bodies, I do not and cannot have any reason other than the simplicity of the hypothesis, since I believe that one can hold the simplest hypothesis (everything considered) as the true one. Thus, having no other criterion, I believe that the difference between us is only in our manner of speech. I attempt as much as possible to accommodate common usage, *salva veritate*. I am not even very distant from yours, and I have adapted myself to it in a small paper I communicated to Mr. Viviani, a

---

409. See GM II, 192.

paper which, it seemed to me, was capable of persuading those at Rome to allow the opinion of Copernicus.[410] Yet if you are in agreement with these views concerning the reality of motion, I imagine that you should have some opinions about the nature of bodies that are different from the common ones. My opinions on that are curious enough, and they seem to me to have been demonstrated. I hope one day to learn about your reflections on my *Remarks concerning Descartes* and on what I have written against atoms and the void, reflections you have led me to hope for.

Planetary Theory, from a Letter to Huygens (1690)[411]

In his Principia, *Newton proposed the law of universal gravitation, in accordance with which every body attracts every other body with a force directly proportional to the masses and inversely proportional to the square of the distances. In this way, Newton offered an explanation for why the planets move about the sun in the particular path they follow. But, for a mechanist like Leibniz, this was not enough. What one needs is an account of what causes the gravitational pull between sun and earth, say, an account that can be cashed out in terms of the communication of motion from one body to another body by collision, the only way it can be done, for a mechanist. Furthermore, Leibniz claims that Newton's theory cannot explain everything it should, such as why the planets orbit in the same plane. Leibniz attempted a mechanical explanation of the phenomena by way of a vortex theory of planetary motion. According to such a theory, popularized by Descartes earlier in the century in part III of his* Principles, *the planets are carried around the sun in a huge whirlpool of subtle matter. Leibniz uses two such vortices to account for the astronomical observations upon which Newton based his theory.*

AFTER HAVING CONSIDERED Newton's book, which I read in Rome for the first time, I naturally admired many fine things he put in it. However, I do not understand how he conceives gravity, that is, attraction. It seems that, according to him, it is only a certain incorporeal and inexplicable power [*vertu*], whereas you explained it very plausibly by the laws of mechanics. When I worked out my arguments about harmonic circulation, that is to say, [circulatory motion in which speed is] inversely proportional to distances, and encountered Kepler's rule (of times proportional to areas), I perceived the excellent advantage of this kind of circulation: it alone is able to conserve itself in a medium that also circulates, and to bring into lasting accord the motion of a solid body and that of the ambient fluid. This was the physical

---

410. See "On Copernicanism and the Relativity of Motion": Loemker suggests that the letter in question may be GM VI 145–47.
411. GM VI 189–193. French.

explanation which I once claimed to give for this circulation, bodies having been determined in this way the better to be harmonized with one another. For harmonic circulation alone has the property that the body circulating in this way keeps exactly the force of its direction or previous impression as if it moved in a vacuum merely by its own impetuosity together with [*jointe à*] gravity. And the same body also moves in the ether as if it swam peacefully without having any impetuosity of its own, nor any remaining previous impressions, and (paracentric motion aside), as if it absolutely obeyed the ether surrounding it. [. . .] However, I did not venture to reject the action of the surrounding ether, as Newton did. And even now I am not persuaded that it is superfluous. For although Newton is satisfactory when one considers only a single planet or satellite, nevertheless, he cannot account for why all the planets of the same system move over approximately the same path, and why they move in the same direction, using only impetuosity [*trajection*] together with gravity. That is what we observe, not only for the sun's planets, but also for those of Jupiter and those of Saturn. This is good evidence for there being a common reason that determines them to behave in this way; and what other more probable reason can be brought to bear than that some kind of vortex or common matter carries them around? For to have recourse to the decision of the author of nature is not sufficiently philosophical when there is a way of assigning proximate causes; and it is even less reasonable to attribute this agreement among the planets of the same system to good luck, given that the agreement is found in all three systems, that is, in all the systems known to us. It also surprises me that Newton did not think to give some explanation of the law of gravitation, to which I was also led by elliptical motion. You rightly state, on p. 161, that it is worth looking for such an explanation.[412] I would like to have your judgment on my thoughts on this matter, which I had kept for another occasion when I published my first thoughts in the *Acts*, as I stated at the end of the piece.[413] Here are two ways; you may judge which one seems best to you and whether they can be reconciled. Let us think of gravity as an attractive force with rays like light. It happens that this attraction keeps exactly the same proportion as illumination does. For others have demonstrated that the illumination of objects is inversely proportional to the squares of the distances from the luminous point, and that the illumination in each portion of the spherical surfaces is inversely proportional to the said spherical surfaces through which the same quantity of light passes. Now, spherical surfaces are proportional to the squares of distances. You may judge whether one can think of these rays as arising from the effort of matter trying to get farther from the center. I thought of another way which succeeds just as well, and which seems to be more closely related to your explanation of gravity by the centrifugal force of the circulation of the ether, which always seemed very plausible to me.[414] I make use of a hypothesis which appears

---

412. The reference is actually to p. 160 of Huygens's *Discours de la cause de la pésanteur* (Leiden, 1690).
413. See GM VI, 161.
414. Here Leibniz is referring to Huygens's account of *terrestrial* gravity.

extremely reasonable to me, that there is the same amount of power
[*puissance*] in each orbit or concentric circular circumference of this circulating matter. This also means that they counterbalance each other best and that
each orbit conserves its own power. Now, I measure power or force by the
quantity of its effect. For example, the force needed to raise a pound one foot
is one fourth the force capable of raising one pound four feet, for which only
twice the speed is required. Whence it follows that absolute [*absolue*] forces
are proportional to the squares of speeds. Let us consider, for example, two
orbits or concentric circumferences. Since the circumferences are proportional
to the rays or distances from the center, the quantities of matter in each fluid orbit are also proportional. Now, if the powers of the two orbits are equal,
the squares of their velocities must be inversely proportional to their quantity
of matter, and consequently to their distances. Or, in other words, the velocities of the orbits should be inversely proportional to the square roots of the
distances from the center. From this, two important corollaries follow, both
verified by observation. The first is that the squares of periodic times are proportional to the cubes of distances. For periodic times are directly proportional to the orbits or distances and inversely proportional to the velocities;
and velocities are inversely proportional to the distances and to the square
roots of the distances; therefore, periodic times are jointly proportional to
the distance and to the square root of the distance, which is to say that the
squares of periodic times are as the cubes of distances. And that is what Kepler
observed about the sun's planets, and what the discoveries of the satellites of
Jupiter and Saturn have so marvelously confirmed, given what I have read of
Cassini's observations. The other corollary is the one we need about gravity,
namely, that centrifugal tendencies are inversely proportional to the square
of the distances. For the centrifugal tendencies of circulations are jointly proportional to the velocity squared and to the reciprocal of the rays or
distances. Now here, velocity squared is also inversely proportional to the
distances; therefore, the centrifugal tendencies are inversely proportional
to the square of the distances, just as gravity should be. That is almost all of
what I set aside for a separate discussion when I presented my essays to the
public;[415] but there is an advantage to giving you my thoughts since it is a way
to have them corrected. That is why I am asking you for your judgment of
them. Given these fortunate agreements, you should not be surprised that
I have a penchant for retaining vortices—perhaps they are not as flawed as
Newton claims. And given my way of thinking of them, even bodies carried
around [*trajections*] serve to confirm the fluid orbits carrying them. Perhaps
you might say, at first, that the hypothesis of inverse proportionality of speed
squared and distance is inconsistent with harmonic circulation. But the reply
is easy: harmonic circulation is found in each body taken individually, comparing its different distances, but virtual harmonic circulation (in which velocities squared are inversely proportional to distances) is found when comparing different bodies, whether they describe a circular line, or whether we take

---

415. The discourse in question was never published; see p. 526n of Huygens, *Works*, vol. IX.

their average motion (that is, in brief, the result equivalent to the composite of motions in the different distances) for the circular orbit they describe. However, I distinguish between the ether that causes gravity (and perhaps also the direction or parallelism of the axes) and the one that carries along the planets, which is much more coarse.[416]

Against Barbaric Physics:

Toward a Philosophy of What There Actually Is and Against the Revival of the Qualities of the Scholastics and Chimerical Intelligences (1710–16?)[417]

In this essay, Leibniz continued his attack against Newton's theory of universal gravitation, comparing it with the occult qualities of the Scholastics, so roundly criticized by his mechanist contemporaries. Though undated, it is certainly from Leibniz's later years. In theme it resembles the attacks on gravity in the Theodicy *of 1710 (sec. 19 of the* Preliminary Discourse*) and in letters from that period (G III 517–24). But in tone it is very close, indeed, to sec. 114 of Leibniz's Fifth Paper (1716) in the Leibniz-Clarke letters [see below, p. 344]. The title, "Anti-barbarus physicus," translates literally as "The Antibarbaric Physicist," unfortunately a barbarism in English. The title may be a borrowing from Marius Nizolius, whose* Anti-barbarus, seu de veris principiis . . . *was edited by Leibniz in 1670.*

IT IS, UNFORTUNATELY, our destiny that, because of a certain aversion toward light, people love to be returned to darkness. We see this today, where the great ease for acquiring learning has brought forth contempt for the doctrines taught, and an abundance of truths of the highest clarity has led to a love for difficult nonsense. Clever people have such a lust for variety that, in the midst of an abundance of fruits, it seems they want to revert to acorns. That physics which explains everything in the nature of body through number, measure, weight, or size, shape and motion, which teaches that nothing is moved naturally except through contact and motion, and so teaches that, in physics, everything happens mechanically, that is, intelligibly, this physics seems excessively clear and easy. We must return to chimeras, to Archae, to certain plastic *intelligences* that attend to the formation of the fetus, and afterwards, to the care of the animal, intelligences that are sometimes lively and bold, sometimes timid and gentle, and despairing, at the end, like people, having lost control. It has often been observed that feelings [*affectus*]

---

416. Both Leibniz and Huygens seem to be using '*pésanteur*' throughout as Newton uses '*gravitas*,' not for weight, strictly speaking, but for the force that holds the planets and moons in their orbits. For more details concerning Leibniz's planetary theory, see E. J. Aiton, *The Vortex Theory of Planetary Motions* (London, 1972), chap. 6.

417. G VII, 337–44. Latin.

in the mind [*animus*] lead to illness, but this is not astonishing, since pleasant motions always accompany joyful feelings, and great motions always accompany vehement feelings. However, this has given some people an excuse for imagining in animals certain inner guardians [*praeses*], which are stimulated, calmed, excited, or dulled as circumstances arise, some of which are general guardians for the governing of the whole body, some of which are particular supervisors of certain limbs or internal organs, cardiosupervisors, gastrosupervisors, and others of that kind. And it is surprising that they don't teach that these spirits can be summoned with magic words, as a certain monk, seeking the philosopher's stone summoned the Spirit of Mercury. They would do . well to recognize a more divine mechanism in the body of animals. But they believe that nothing is quite divine enough unless it is opposed to reason, and they think that what happens in [animate] bodies is so elevated that not even divine skill could make such machines.[418] These barely skilled judges think that divine works are necessary, and so they think that God everywhere uses little vice-deities (lest God himself always have to act miraculously), just like those who once attributed the motions of the stars to their own special intelligences.

It pleases others to return to *occult qualities* or to *Scholastic faculties*, but since those crude philosophers and physicians [see that] those [terms are] in bad repute, changing the name, they call them forces.[419] But true corporeal forces are only of one kind, namely, those arising through the impression of impetus (as for example, when a body is flung forward), which even have a role to play in insensible motions. But these persons imagine specific forces, and vary them as the need arises. They bring forth attractive, retentive, repulsive, directive, expansive, and contractive faculties. This can be forgiven in Gilbert and Cabaeus, and even quite recently in Honoratus Fabri, since the clear foundation [*ratio*] for philosophizing either had not yet become known, or had not yet been sufficiently appreciated. But what person of understanding would now bring forward these chimerical qualities, which have been repeatedly offered up as the ultimate principles of things? It is permissible to recognize magnetic, elastic, and other sorts of forces, but only insofar as we understand that they are not primitive or incapable of being explained, but arise from motions and shapes. However, the new patrons of such things don't want this. It has been observed in our own times that there is a truth in the suggestion of earlier thinkers who maintained that the planets gravitate and tend toward one another. It pleased them to make the immediate inference that all matter essentially has a God-given and inherent attractive power and, as it were, mutual love, as if matter had senses, or as if a certain intelligence were given to each part of matter by whose means each part could perceive and desire even the most remote thing. [They argue] as if there were no room for mechanical explanations by which the effort [*conatus*] gross [*crassus*] bodies make in striving toward the great bodies of the cosmos could be accounted for through the

---

418. Gerhardt's text has a lacuna; the word in brackets is a conjecture.
419. Again, Gerhardt's text has a lacuna; the words in brackets are conjectures.

motion of smaller pervading bodies. These same people threaten to give us other occult qualities of this sort, and thus, in the end, they may lead us back to the kingdom of darkness.

First the ancients, and on their example, many more recent people have rightly used intermediate principles for explaining the nature of things, principles that are, indeed, insufficiently explained, but principles which could be explained and which we could hope to reduce to prior and simpler principles, and, in the end, to first principles. I think that this is praiseworthy as long as composite things are reduced to simpler things. For in nature, things must proceed by steps, and one cannot go immediately to the first causes. Therefore, those who have shown that the astronomical laws can be explained by assuming the mutual gravitation of the planets have done something very worthwhile, even if they may not have given the reason for this gravitation. But if certain people, abusing this beautiful discovery, think that the explanation [ratio] given is so satisfactory that there is nothing left to explain, and if they think that gravity is a thing essential to matter, then they slip back into *barbarism in physics* and into the *occult qualities of the Scholastics*. They even fabricate what they cannot prove through the phenomena, for so far, except for the force by which sensible bodies move toward the center of the earth, they have not been able to bring forward any trace of the general attraction of matter in our region. Consequently, we must be careful not to proceed from a few instances to everything, as Gilbert sees a magnet everywhere, and the chemists smell salt, sulphur, and mercury everywhere. Such explanations are usually considered insufficient, and sometimes we derive not only things of uncertain existence from assuming such explanations, but also false and impossible things, like that general striving [nisus] of matter for matter.

Now physicists have taken either things or qualities as causes. Some have assumed things as elements, like Thales' water, or Heraclitus' fire, others, the four elements, fire, air, water, and earth. Some unknown contriver of the greatest antiquity convinced even the common people of this latter view, and the author of the book *On Generation and Corruption*, the author of the book *On the Universe*, attributed to Ocellus Lucanus, and Galen have followed the common opinion on the matter (Aristotle seems to have added to this a fifth stellar element). Later, the older chemists brought forward sulphur and mercury, and the more recent chemists brought forward salt, sulphur and mercury, and added the passive matters phlegm and *terre damnata* to these primary active matters. Boyle examined these in his *Sceptical Chemist*. The most recent chemists have introduced alkali and acid as active things. Bohnius has written about the insufficiency of this. There were also those, such as Anaxagoras, inventor of the idea of homoeomeria, who set up innumerable principles, and those who gave things their own seeds, not only to animals and plants, but also to metals, jewels, and other things of this kind.

Also, there is no lack of people who have advocated certain incorporeal substances operating in bodies, like the Soul of the World [*Anima Mundi*], or like particular souls that belong to each and every thing. Similar are those who attributed sense to everything, as Campanella advanced in his book on sensation in things and on magic, and as Henry More did with his hylarchic principle, which corresponds to the Soul of the World, and against which Sturm wrote. The ancients had already spoken of a certain wise Nature, acting for ends, doing nothing in vain, something worthy of praise if it is understood as applying to God or to some artifice God placed in things from the beginning, but otherwise empty. Certain persons place in things various Archae, like so many souls or spirits, indeed, like little gods, wonderfully intelligent plastic substances, which order and regulate organic bodies. And finally, there were those who summoned God or gods *ex machina* in the way that the pagans imagined that Jupiter rains or thunders and that he has filled the woods and waters with gods or near gods. Certain ancient Christians, and in our age, Fludd, author of the *Mosaic Philosophy* (elegantly refuted by Gassendi), and more recently the authors and advocates of the system of occasional causes, all believed that God acts immediately on natural things through perpetual miracle.

These people, indeed, have used substances as causes. But some people have added qualities which they have also called faculties, virtues, and most recently, *forces*. Such were the sympathy or antipathy, or strife and friendship of Empedocles; such were heat, cold, moistness, and dryness, the four *primary qualities* of the Peripatetics and followers of Galen; such were the *sensible and intentional species* of the Scholastics, and also the expulsive, retentive, and change-causing *faculties* of the physicians who taught in barbaric times. More recently, Telesio has tried to set many things straight with operant heat, and some chemists, especially the followers of [J.B.] van Helmont and Marcus Marci, have introduced certain *effective ideas* [*ideas operatrices*]. Most recently in England, some have tried to bring back *attractive and repulsive forces*, about which we shall soon have more to say. We also ought to add those who imagine motion to be like an incorporeal substance or Pythagorean soul, transmigrating from body to body. And many who use substances as principles attribute unexplained qualities to them. And so, for example, they attribute to the elements those four often mentioned qualities,[420] and they attribute to chemical principles their strife and friendship, and forces for fermenting, dissolving, coagulating, and precipitating; they attribute to *Archae* their *effective ideas*, and their *plastic* powers. Bayle has recently begun to attack these things. The author of the book on ancient medicine, attributed to Hippocrates, long ago opposed the four qualities as sufficient principles. Sennert also added diseases independent of these four qualities, which he attributed to the substance as a whole.

Some of these people can be excused, indeed, they ought to be praised, since they tried to explain more composite things through certain simpler bodies or qualities. Thus many things have been explained, and not badly, through fire, air, water, and earth, and then through salts soluble in water, oils or sulphurs soluble in fire, and finally through limes or earth, that persist in fire, and spirits or waters that evaporate in fire. Indeed, in this way, sensible

---

420. Heat, cold, moistness, and dryness.

effects have been explained by causes which fall within the senses, something most conducive to practical applications and to imitating and improving upon nature, whose customs, so to speak, are best observed in the realm of plants and animals, especially with regard to propagation, growth, and diminishment. It will also be useful for us to observe that things separated from one another by force, or things akin to them, promptly join with one another, even after setting other things into motion, and that many bodies in the realm of minerals are true products of the chemical laboratory of nature, produced by real fire, either now by subterranean fire, or long ago by fire contained in the whole crust of the earth, vitrifying some of them, and expelling others that are capable of evaporation. From this we have shown how to explain the sea, sand, shores, stones, earths, and many qualities observed in them.[421]

But many sensible effects remain which we have not been able to reduce to sensible causes, like the workings of the magnet, or like the particular powers [vires] that belong to simple things, no trace of which is found in the parts derived from them through chemical analysis, as, for example, appears to be the case with poisonous or medicinal plants. Here we sometimes turn to analogy, and we are not doing badly if we can explain many things on the example and likeness of few. Thus having observed the attraction and repulsion of certain things, such as magnets and things made of amber, it seemed that one could establish the forces that are at work there and also found in other things. And so Gilbert, who was the first to write about the magnet with care, and not without good results, conjectured that magnetism also lay hidden in many other things. In this, however, he was repeatedly mistaken, as was Kepler—in other respects a most excellent man—who devised certain attracting or repelling magnetic fibres among the planets. It was also in this way that the common philosophers invented a certain 'avoidance of vacuum' from a few experiments with pumps and bellows, until Galileo showed that the power [potentia] of aspirating pumps, as they call them, or the power of those things into whose place air cannot come, a resistance to separation which they attributed to that avoidance of vacuum, can be overcome.[422] Torricelli, in the end, reduced it to the weight of the air above us, a palpable cause existing in nature. Nor was there any reason why they should have attributed a quality of abhorring a vacuum to Nature. For us to know that a vacuum cannot be created with any amount of force, it is sufficient for us to know that everything is, once and for all, full, and that the matter exactly filling a place cannot be squeezed into a smaller space. The sensible vacuum, which we create by machines and which nature was long believed to abhor and refuse, does not exclude subtler bodies. And so, learned men often imagined things that don't exist, and they extended too far what they did observe in certain cases. However, we should praise them because they gave us conjectures that should not be scorned, conjectures which were successful in certain respects, at least.

---

421. Leibniz is here referring to the *Protogaea*, a work on geology from the early 1690s that was published only after his death.
422. See Galileo, *Two New Sciences*, pp. 19–26. The reference is to the inseparability of two polished marble slabs.

Furthermore, we shouldn't criticize these men because they tried to put certain subordinate principles in place so that they might, step by step, advance toward their causes.*

But we should criticize those who hold these subordinate principles as primitive and inexplicable, as, for example, those who fabricated miracles, or those who fabricated incorporeal ideas [*sententia*] that produce, regulate, and govern bodies, those who put forward the four elements or the four primary qualities as if they contain the ultimate explanation of things, or those who, uninterested in understanding the particular force by which we evacuate with pumps, the force which we find to resist our opening a bellows lacking an aperture, set up in nature which abhors, as it were, the vacuum a primitive, essential, and insuperable quality. And whoever isn't, with us, eager to know qualities hitherto hidden, that is, unknown, has invented qualities of eternal obscurity, mysterious, inexplicable, which not even the greatest genius can know or render intelligible.

Such are those who, induced by the successful discovery that the great bodies of this planetary system have an attraction for one another and for their sensible parts, imagine that every body whatsoever is attracted by every other by virtue of a force in matter itself, whether it is as if a thing takes pleasure in another similar thing, and senses it even from a distance, or whether it is brought about by God, who takes care of this through perpetual miracle, so that bodies seek one another, as if they sensed each other. However it might be, these people cannot, at any rate, reduce this attraction to impulse or to intelligible reasons (as Plato already did in the *Timaeus*), nor do they want to. The seeds of this view are apparent in Roberval's *Aristarchus*, elegantly criticized by Descartes in a certain letter to Mersenne, though Roberval, perhaps, had not excluded mechanical causes.[423] But it is astonishing that there are those who now, in the great light of our age, hope to persuade the world of a doctrine so foreign to reason. John Locke, in the first edition of his *Essay Concerning Human Understanding*, judged that it is appropriate that no body is moved except through the impulse of a body touching it, as did Hobbes and Boyle, distinguished countrymen of his, and, following them, many others who strengthened mechanistic physics.* But afterwards, having followed the authority of his friends, I think, more than his judgment, he retracted this opinion and believed that I know not what wonderful things can lie hidden in the essence of matter. It is just as if someone believed that there are occult qualities hidden in number, in time, in space, in motion considered in and of themselves, that is, it is just as if someone were to look for a knot on a bullrush[424] and wanted to force the clear to be obscure.[425]

Robert Boyle once refuted such views quite nicely when he rejected the thread [*funiculus*] binding matter together proposed by Franciscus Linus and Thomas White, because, of course, it assumed something imaginary and

---

423. See AT IV 397–403, especially assumptions 3 and 4 on p. 399.
424. I.e., a difficulty where there is none.
425. See the "Preface to the *New Essays*," above, pp. 291–306.

inexplicable which binds the very thread together.[426] But, at least, this thread was corporeal and more intelligible (indeed, intelligible in something contiguous) than the new and incorporeal attractive force,* working at any distance whatsoever without any medium or means. We can scarcely imagine anything more foolish than this in nature! And nevertheless, these people seem to have thought that they said something worthy of admiration. And now they go further and find fault with the idea that the flow of the light of the stars is instantaneously diffused through the medium, by which means the Scholastics once tried to render more intelligible the operation on distant things. What might Descartes or Boyle now say if they came back? What refutations would suffice for them to bury this new and revived chimera? And once assumed, they are forced by this view of the essential attraction of matter to defend the vacuum, since the attraction of everything for everything else would be pointless if everything were full. But in the true philosophy, the vacuum is rejected for other reasons. Indeed, I myself, when young, tried in a little book of physical hypotheses to reduce all phenomena to three operative qualities, namely to gravity, elastic force, and magnetic force.[427] However, I did not deny, in fact, I explicitly judged, that they ought to be explained through the simplest and most truly primitive things, that is, through size, shape, and motion.

As is well known, Democritus, together with Leucippus, was the first to try to cleanse physics of mysterious qualities, and said that qualities exist only by convention [ex opinione], that they are appearances, not true things.[428] However, one mysterious quality remained, the insuperable hardness of his atoms, or at least, the insuperable hardness he imagined to be in his atoms, and since errors are fertile soil for bringing forth further errors, from this he was also led to defend the vacuum. Epicurus added two further fictions, the heaviness [gravitas] of atoms, and their deflection without cause, which Cicero elegantly ridiculed. In his Physics, Aristotle proceeded most correctly from the report of those views, and quite clearly had already set out the position against the vacuum and atoms that Descartes and Hobbes later revived. Other works in which Aristotle seems to have philosophized more crudely are either not his, or were written exoterically. Gassendi also maintained atoms and the vacuum (two things both mysterious and absurd). Kenelm Digby[429] (together with Thomas White), who otherwise didn't philosophize badly in his main

---

426. *New Experiments physico-mechanical Touching the Spring of Air and its Effects Whereunto is added A defence of the authors explication of the experiments, against the objections of Franciscus Linus, and Thomas Hobbes* (1662), in Boyle, *Works*, vol. I. Linus, in response to Boyle's air-pump experiments, elaborated a theory in accordance with which it is tiny threads, funiculi, that pull one's finger down at the top of an evacuated tube. This theory to explain air-pump phenomena was extended to a general theory of the make-up of body. See his *Tractatus de corporum inseparabilitate* ... (1661).

427. The reference is to the *Hypothesis Physica Nova* (1671). For a more extended discussion of this book, see "A Specimen of Dynamics" above, pp. 117–38.

428. Cf. Diogenes Laertius, *Lives of the Eminent Philosophers* IX 45.

429. See Digby, Two Treatises (1644) and *A late Discourse Made in a Solemne Assembly* . . . *touching the Cure of Wounds by the Powder of Sympathy* (1658).

work (for I won't linger over the incredible passages of his little book on sympathies), retained an absolute condensation and rarefaction, as did Honoratus Fabri, who consequently also assumed elastic force as something primitive, over and above heaviness [*gravitas*], Galileo Galilei, Joachim Jungius, René Descartes, and Thomas Hobbes, to whom one can add Gassendi and his followers, setting aside atoms and the vacuum, have quite clearly purged inexplicable chimeras from physics, and having revived Archimedes's use of mathematics in physics, they have quite clearly purged inexplicable chimeras from philosophy and taught that everything in corporeal nature should be explained mechanically. But (not to mention, for the moment, the insufficiently trustworthy mechanical hypotheses, to which they were excessively addicted) they have not sufficiently recognized the true metaphysical principles or the explanations of motion and laws of nature that derive from them.

Therefore, I tried to fill this gap, and have at last shown that *everything happens mechanically in nature, but that the principles of mechanism are metaphysical*, and that the laws of motion and nature have been established, not with absolute necessity, but from the will of a wise cause, not from a pure exercise of will, but from the fitness [*convenientia*] of things. I have shown that force must be added to mass [*massa*], but that force is exercised only through an impressed impetus. Instead of Archae, intelligences or plastic faculties, instincts, anti-sympathies or similar qualities, the artifice of divine mechanism is sufficient for explaining how things work, especially in the organic bodies of plants and animals, keeping only the perception and appetite of the soul, having eliminated all physical influx of body into soul or of soul into body. But even if not all bodies are organic, nevertheless organic bodies lie hidden in everything, even in inorganic bodies, so that all mass [*massa*], either unordered [*rudis*] or completely uniform in appearance, is within itself not uniform but diversified, however, ordered, not confused in its diversity. And so, I have shown that organisms are everywhere, and nowhere is there chaos unworthy of wisdom, and that *all organic bodies in Nature are animated, but neither souls nor bodies change one another's laws*. I have shown that everything in bodies takes place through shape and motion, everything in souls through perception and appetite; that in the latter there is a kingdom of final causes, in the former a kingdom of efficient causes, which *two kingdoms are virtually independent of one another, but nevertheless are harmonious*; that God (the common final and efficient cause of things) accommodates everything to his ends through intermediaries that act through themselves [*per media spontanea*], and that *souls and bodies*, though infallibly following their own laws, *agree nevertheless through a harmony pre-established by God, without any physical influx between one another*, and that in this a new and most beautiful proof of divinity lies hidden.

Finally, I showed that bodies are only aggregates that constitute a unity accidentally [*per accidens*], or by extrinsic denomination and, to that extent, are well-founded phenomena; that only monads (among which the best are souls, and among souls, the best are minds) are substances, and from this I showed that the indestructibility of all souls (which in minds is also the true immortality of the person) can be settled beyond controversy. And so, I showed that a more elevated metaphysics and ethics, that is, a more elevated natural theology and an eternal and divine jurisprudence can be established, and that from the known causes of things is derived a knowledge of true happiness.

From the Letters to Clarke (1715–16)[430]

The rivalry between Leibniz and Newton is celebrated. Yet Leibniz never managed to start a genuine and extended exchange of views with the great English physicist; the correspondence with Samuel Clarke, Newton's friend and the translator into Latin of his Opticks, *was as close as Leibniz got. The correspondence began in November 1715, with a letter to Caroline, Princess of Wales, whom Leibniz had known in Hanover. Caroline showed the letter to Clarke, and the exchange of letters began. The letters continued until Leibniz's death, Leibniz and Clarke each contributing five papers. While Newton was not officially involved in the exchange, he almost certainly had a hand in preparing some of Clarke's replies. The entire exchange was published in English, with French on facing pages, by Clarke in 1717, shortly after Leibniz's death. The translation below is a slightly updated version of the translation Clarke published. Leibniz's first four papers are given in their entirety; the fifth is abridged.*

I. Leibniz's First Paper, Being an Extract of a Letter (November 1715)

1. NATURAL RELIGION itself seems to decay [in England] very much. Many will have human souls to be material; others make God himself a corporeal being.

2. Mr. Locke and his followers are uncertain, at least, whether the soul is not material and naturally perishable.

3. Sir Isaac Newton says that space is an organ which God makes use of to perceive things by. But if God stands in need of an organ to perceive things by, it will follow that they do not depend altogether on him, nor were produced by him.

4. Sir Isaac Newton and his followers also have a very odd opinion concerning the work of God. According to them, God Almighty needs to wind up his watch from time to time,[431] otherwise it would cease to move. He had not, it seems, sufficient foresight to make it a perpetual motion. No, the machine of God's making is so imperfect, according to these gentlemen, that he is obliged

---

430. G VII 352, 357–59, 363–66, 371–78, 393–406, 415–20; ALC; RLC.

431. Leibniz here calls attention to a passage in Newton's *Opticks*, p. 402, in which Newton intimates that there are regularities in planetary motions caused by the (gravitational) interaction of the planets with one another, and that these irregularities will increase "till this system wants a reformation."

to clean it now and then by an extraordinary concourse, and even to mend it, as a clockmaker mends his work, who must consequently be so much the more unskillful a workman as he is more often obliged to mend his work and to set it right. According to my opinion, the same force and vigor remains always in the world and only passes from one part of matter to another agreeably to the laws of nature and the beautiful pre-established order. And I hold that when God works miracles, he does not do it in order to supply the wants of nature, but those of grace. Whoever thinks otherwise must needs have a very mean notion of the wisdom and power of God.

II. Leibniz's Second Letter

1. IT IS RIGHTLY observed in the paper delivered to the Princess of Wales, which Her Royal Highness has been pleased to communicate to me, that next to corruption of manners, the principles of the materialists do very much contribute to keep up impiety. But I believe that one has no reason to add that the mathematical principles of philosophy are opposite to those of the materialists. On the contrary, they are the same, only with this difference—that the materialists, in imitation of Democritus, Epicurus, and Hobbes, confine themselves altogether to mathematical principles and admit only bodies, whereas the Christian mathematicians admit also immaterial substances. Wherefore, not mathematical principles (according to the usual sense of that word) but *metaphysical principles* ought to be opposed to those of the materialists. Pythagoras, Plato, and Aristotle in some measure had a knowledge of these principles, but I claim to have established them demonstratively in my *Theodicy*, though I have done it in a popular manner. The great foundation of mathematics is the *principle of contradiction or identity*, that is, that a proposition cannot be true and false at the same time, and that therefore A is A and cannot be not A. This single principle is sufficient to demonstrate every part of arithmetic and geometry, that is, all mathematical principles. But in order to proceed from mathematics to natural philosophy, another principle is required, as I have observed in my *Theodicy*; I mean the *principle of sufficient reason*, namely, that nothing happens without a reason why it should be so rather than otherwise. And therefore Archimedes, being desirous to proceed from mathematics to natural philosophy, in his book *De aequilibro*, was obliged to make use of a particular case of the great principle of sufficient reason. He takes it for granted that if there is a balance in which everything is alike on both sides, and if equal weights are hung on the two ends of that balance, the whole will be at rest. That is because no reason can be given why one side should weigh down rather than the other.[432] Now by that single principle, namely, that there ought to be a sufficient reason why things should be so and not otherwise, one may demonstrate the being of God and all the other parts of metaphysics or natural theology and even, in some measure,

---

432. See Archimedes, *On the Equilibrium of Planes*, book I, postulate 1, in Heath, *The Works of Archimedes*, p. 189.

those principles of natural philosophy that are independent of mathematics; I mean the dynamic principles or the principles of force.

2. The author proceeds and says that according to the *mathematical principles*, that is, according to Sir Isaac Newton's philosophy (for *mathematical principles* determine nothing in the present case), matter is the most inconsiderable part of the universe. The reason is because he admits empty space besides matter and because, according to his notions, matter fills up a very small part of space. But Democritus and Epicurus maintained the same thing; they differed from Sir Isaac Newton only as to the quantity of matter, and perhaps they believed there was more matter in the world than Sir Isaac Newton will allow; wherein I think their opinion ought to be preferred, for the more matter there is, the more God has occasion to exercise his wisdom and power. This is one reason, among others, why I maintain that there is no void at all.

3. I find, in express words in the Appendix to Sir Isaac Newton's *Opticks*, that space is the sensorium of God.[433] But the word 'sensorium' has always signified the organ of sensation. He and his friends may now, if they think fit, explain themselves quite otherwise; I shall not be against it.

4. The author supposes that the presence of the soul is sufficient to make it consciously perceive what passes in the brain. But this is the very thing which Father Malebranche and all the Cartesians deny; and they rightly deny it.[434] More is required besides bare presence to enable one thing to represent what passes in another. Some communication that may be explained, some sort of influence, or a common source [*cause*] is requisite for this purpose. Space, according to Sir Isaac Newton, is intimately present to the body contained in it and commensurate with it. Does it follow from thence that space perceives consciously what passes in a body and remembers it when that body is gone away? Besides, the soul being indivisible, its immediate presence, which may be imagined in the body, would only be in one point. How then could it perceive consciously what happens out of that point? I claim to be the first who has shown how the soul perceives consciously what passes in the body.

5. The reason why God perceives everything consciously is not his bare presence, but also his operation. It is because he preserves things by an action which continually produces whatever is good and perfect in them. But the soul having no immediate influence over the body, nor the body over the soul, their mutual correspondence cannot be explained by their being present to each other.

6. The true and principal reason why we commend a machine is rather taken from the effects of the machine than from its cause. We don't inquire so much about the power of the artist as we do about his skill in his workmanship. And therefore, the reason alleged by the author for extolling God's machine, that he made it entirely, without borrowing any materials from outside—that

---

433. See the *Opticks*, p. 403.

434. Malebranche and other later Cartesians argued that brain events do not cause sensations in the mind, strictly speaking. Rather, the claim is that it is God who causes sensations in minds *on the occasion of* certain brain events. This is one feature of the so-called doctrine of occasionalism. See, e.g., Malebranche, *Search after Truth*, pp. 446–52.

reason, I say, is not sufficient. It is a mere shift the author has been forced to have recourse to, and the reason why God exceeds any other artisan is not only because he makes the whole, whereas all other artisans must have matter to work upon. This excellency in God would only be on the account of power. But God's excellency also arises from another cause, namely, wisdom, whereby his machine lasts longer and moves more regularly than those of any other artisan whatsoever. He who buys a watch does not mind whether the workman made every part of it himself, or whether he got the several parts made by others and only put them together—provided the watch goes right. And if the workman had received from God even the gift of creating the matter of the wheels, yet the buyer of the watch would not be satisfied unless the workman had also received the gift of putting them well together. In like manner, he who will be pleased with God's work cannot be so without some other reason than that which the author has here alleged.

7. Thus the skill of God must not be inferior to that of a workman; no, it must go infinitely beyond it. The bare production of everything would indeed show the power of God, but it would not sufficiently show his wisdom. They who maintain the contrary will fall exactly into the error of the materialists and of Spinoza, from whom they profess to differ. They would, in such case, acknowledge power but not sufficient wisdom in the principle or cause of things.

8. I do not say the material world is a machine or watch that goes without God's interposition, and I have sufficiently insisted that creatures need his continual influence. But I maintain it to be a watch that goes without needing to be mended by him; otherwise we must say that God revises himself. No, God has foreseen everything. He has provided a remedy for everything beforehand. There is in his works a harmony, a beauty, already pre-established.

9. This opinion does not exclude God's providence or his government of the world; on the contrary, it makes it perfect. A true providence of God requires a perfect foresight. But then it requires, moreover, not only that he should have foreseen everything but also that he should have provided for everything beforehand with proper remedies; otherwise he must either want wisdom to foresee things or power to provide for them. He will be like the God of the Socinians who lives only from day to day, as Mr. Jurieu says. Indeed, God, according to the Socinians, does not so much as foresee inconveniences, whereas the gentlemen I am arguing with, who oblige him to mend his work, say only that he does not provide against them.[435] But this seems to me to still be a very great imperfection. According to this doctrine, God must either want power or good will.

10. I don't think I can be rightly blamed for saying that God is *intelligentia*

---

435. Socinianism was a rationalistic movement in theology, a forerunner of unitarianism, founded by Laelius Socinus (1525-62) and his nephew Faustus Socinius (1539-1604). Socinius held a variety of heterodox views on the Trinity, the divinity of Christ, and the immortality of the soul. By the later seventeenth century, the term was used quite broadly to cover a multitude of unorthodoxies.

supramundana. Will they say that he is *intelligentia mundana*, that is, the soul of the world? I hope not. However, they will do well to take care not to fall into that notion unawares.

11. The comparison of a king under whose reign everything should go on without his interposition is by no means to the present purpose, since God continually preserves everything and nothing can subsist without him. His kingdom therefore is not a nominal one. It is just as if one should say that a king who should originally have taken care to have his subjects so well raised, and should, by his care in providing for their subsistence, preserve them so well in their fitness for their several stations and in their good affection toward him, as that he should have no occasion ever to be amending anything among them, would be only a nominal king.

12. To conclude. If God is obliged to mend the course of nature from time to time, it must either be done supernaturally or naturally. If it is done supernaturally, we must have recourse to miracles in order to explain natural things, which is reducing a hypothesis *ad absurdum*, for everything may easily be accounted for by miracles. But if it is done naturally, then God will not be *intelligentia supramundana*; he will be comprehended under the nature of things, that is, he will be the soul of the world.

1. III. Leibniz's Third Paper

1. ACCORDING TO the usual way of speaking, *mathematical principles* concern only pure mathematics, namely, numbers, figures, arithmetic, geometry. But *metaphysical principles* concern more general notions, such as cause and effect.

2. The author grants me this important principle, that nothing happens without a sufficient reason why it should be so rather than otherwise. But he grants it only in words and in reality denies it. This shows that he does not fully perceive the strength of it. And therefore, he makes use of an instance, which exactly falls in with one of my demonstrations against real absolute space, the idol of some modern Englishmen. I call it an idol, not in a theological sense, but in a philosophical one, as Chancellor Bacon says that there are idols of the tribe and idols of the cave.[436]

3. These gentlemen maintain, therefore, that space is a real absolute being. But this involves them in great difficulties, for it appears that such a being must be eternal and infinite. Hence some have believed it to be God himself, or one of his attributes, his immensity. But since space consists of parts, it is not a thing which can belong to God.

4. As for my own opinion, I have said more than once that I hold space to be something merely relative, as time is, that I hold it to be an order of coexistences, as time is an order of successions. For space denotes, in terms of possibility, an order of things which exist at the same time, considered as existing together, without entering into their particular manners of existing.

---

436. See Bacon, *New Organon*, book I, aphorisms 41–42.

And when many things are seen together, one perceives this order of things among themselves.

5. I have many demonstrations to confute the fancy of those who take space to be a substance, or, at least, an absolute being. But I shall only use, at present, one demonstration, which the author here gives me occasion to insist upon. I say, then, that if space were an absolute being, something would happen for which it would be impossible that there should be a sufficient reason—which is against my axiom. And I can prove it thus. Space is something absolutely uniform, and without the things placed in it, one point of space absolutely does not differ in anything from another point of space. Now, from hence it follows (supposing space to be something in itself, besides the order of bodies among themselves) that is impossible there should be a reason why God, preserving the same situations of bodies among themselves, should have placed them in space after one certain particular manner and not otherwise—why everything was not placed the quite contrary way, for instance, by changing east into west. But if space is nothing else but this order or relation, and is nothing at all without bodies but the possibility of placing them, then those two states, the one such as it is now, the other supposed to be the quite contrary way, would not at all differ from one another. Their difference therefore is only to be found in our chimerical supposition of the reality of space in itself. But in truth, the one would exactly be the same thing as the other, they being absolutely indiscernible, and consequently there is no room to inquire after a reason for the preference of the one to the other.

6. The case is the same with respect to time. Supposing anyone should ask why God did not create everything a year sooner, and the same person should infer from this that God has done something concerning which it is not possible that there should be a reason why he did it so and not otherwise; the answer is that his inference would be right if time was anything distinct from things existing in time. For it would be impossible that there should be any reason why things should be applied to such particular instants rather than to others, their succession continuing the same. But then the same argument proves that instants, considered without the things, are nothing at all and that they consist only in the successive order of things; this order remaining the same, one of the two states, namely, that of a supposed anticipation, would not at all differ, nor could be discerned from the other which now is.

7. It appears from what I have said that my axiom has not been well understood and that the author denies it, though he seems to grant it. It is true, says he, that there is nothing without a sufficient reason why it is, and why it is thus rather than otherwise, but he adds that this sufficient reason is often the simple or mere will of God—as when it is asked why matter was not placed otherwise in space, the same situations of bodies among themselves being preserved. But this is plainly to maintain that God wills something without any sufficient reason for his will, against the axiom or the general rule of whatever happens. This is falling back into the loose indifference which I have amply refuted and showed to be absolutely chimerical, even in creatures, and contrary to the wisdom of God, as if he could operate without acting by reason.

8. The author objects against me that, if we don't admit this simple and mere will, we take away from God the power of choosing and bring in a fatality. But quite the contrary is true. I maintain that God has the power of choosing, since I ground that power upon the reason of a choice agreeable to his wisdom. And it is not this fatality (which is only the wisest order of providence) but a blind fatality or necessity void of all wisdom and choice which we ought to avoid.

9. I had observed that by lessening the quantity of matter, the quantity of objects upon which God may exercise his goodness will be lessened. The author answers that instead of matter there are other things in the void on which God exercises his goodness. Be it so, though I don't grant it, for I hold that every created substance is attended with matter. However, let it be so. I answer that more matter was consistent with those same things, and consequently the said objects will still be lessened. The instance of a greater number of men or animals is not to the purpose, for they would fill up place in exclusion of other things.

10. It will be difficult to make me believe that sensorium does not, in its usual meaning, signify an organ of sensation. See the words of Rudolphus Goclenius in his *Dictionarium philosophicum* under *sensiterium*. "Barbarum Scholasticorum," says he, "qui interdum sunt simae Graecorum. Hi dicunt *aitheterion*. Ex quo illi fecerunt *sensiterium* pro sensorio, id est, organo sensationis."[437]

11. The mere presence of a substance, even an animated one, is not sufficient for perception. A blind man, and even someone distracted, does not see. The author must explain how the soul perceives what is outside itself.

12. God is not present to things by situation but by essence; his presence is manifest by his immediate operation. The presence of the soul is quite of another nature. To say that it is diffused all over the body is to make it extended and divisible. To say it is, the whole of it, in every part of the body is to make it divisible of itself. To fix it to a point, to diffuse it all over many points, are only abusive expressions, idols of the tribe.[438]

13. If active force should diminish in the universe by the natural laws which God has established, so that there should be need for him to give a new impression in order to restore that force, like an artisan's mending the imperfections of his machine, the disorder would not only be with respect to us but also with respect to God himself. He might have prevented it and taken better measures to avoid such an inconvenience, and therefore, indeed, he has actually done it.

14. When I said that God has provided remedies beforehand against such disorders, I did not say that God suffers disorders to happen and then finds

---

437. Goclenius, *Lexicon Philosophicum* (1613). Goclenius was a standard reference work for seventeenth-century school philosophers, an alphabetical compendium of standard definitions and distinctions. The passage translates: "[Sensiterium is] a barbarism due to the Schoolmen, who sometimes aped the Greeks. The Greeks said 'aitheterion,' from which the Schoolmen made up 'sensiterium,' in place of 'sensorium,' that is, the organ of sensation."
438. See Bacon, *New Organon*, book I, aphorism 41.

remedies for them, but that he has found a way beforehand to prevent any disorders happening.

15. The author strives in vain to criticize my expression that God is *intelligentia supramundana*. To say that God is above the world is not denying that he is in the world.

16. I never gave any occasion to doubt but that God's conservation is an actual preservation and continuation of the beings, powers, orders, dispositions, and motions [of all things], and I think I have perhaps explained it better than many others. But, says the author, this is all I contended for. To this I answer, your humble servant for that, Sir. Our dispute consists in many other things. The question is whether God does not act in the most regular and most perfect manner; whether his machine is liable to disorder, which he is obliged to mend by extraordinary means; whether the will of God can act without reason; whether space is an absolute being; also concerning the nature of miracles; and many such things, which make a wide difference between us.

17. Theologians will not grant the author's position against me, namely, that there is no difference, with respect to God, between natural and supernatural; and it will be still less approved by most philosophers. There is an infinite difference between these two things, but it plainly appears that it has not been duly considered. The supernatural exceeds all the powers of creatures. I shall give an instance which I have often made use of with good success. If God wanted to cause a body to move free in the aether round about a certain fixed center, without any other creature acting upon it, I say it could not be done without a miracle, since it cannot be explained by the nature of bodies. For a free body naturally recedes from a curve in the tangent. And therefore, I maintain that the attraction of bodies, properly so called, is a miraculous thing, since it cannot be explained by the nature of bodies.

1. *IV. Leibniz's Fourth Letter*

• IN THINGS absolutely indifferent there is no foundation for choice,[439] and consequently no election or will, since choice must be founded on some reason or principle.

2. A mere will without any motive is a fiction, not only contrary to God's perfection, but also chimerical and contradictory, inconsistent with the definition of the will, and sufficiently confuted in my *Theodicy*.

3. It is an indifferent thing to place three bodies, equal and perfectly alike, in any order whatsoever, and consequently they will never be placed in any order by him who does nothing without wisdom. But then, he being the author of things, no such things will be produced by him at all, and consequently, there are no such things in nature.

4. There is no such thing as two individuals indiscernible from each other. An ingenious gentleman of my acquaintance, discoursing with me in the presence of Her Electoral Highness, the Princess Sophia, in the garden of

---

439. In Leibniz's original, the claim is that "there is no choice at all."

Herrenhausen, thought he could find two leaves perfectly alike. The princess defied him to do it, and he ran all over the garden a long time to look for some; but it was to no purpose. Two drops of water or milk, viewed with a microscope, will appear distinguishable from each other. This is an argument against atoms, which are confuted, as well as the void, by the principles of true metaphysics.

5. Those great principles of sufficient reason and of the identity of indiscernibles change the state of metaphysics. That science becomes real and demonstrative by means of these principles, whereas before it did generally consist in empty words.

6. To suppose two things indiscernible is to suppose the same thing under two names. And therefore the hypothesis that the universe could have had at first another position of time and place than that which it actually had, and yet that all the parts of the universe should have had the same situation among themselves as that which they actually had—such a supposition, I say, is an impossible fiction.

7. The same reason which shows that extramundane space is imaginary proves that all empty space is an imaginary thing, for they differ only as greater and less.

8. If space is a property or attribute, it must be the property of some substance. But of what substance will that bounded empty space be an affection or property, which the persons I am arguing with suppose to be between two bodies?

9. If infinite space is immensity, finite space will be the opposite to immensity, that is, it will be mensurability, or limited extension. Now extension must be the affection of something extended. But if that space is empty, it will be an attribute without a subject, an extension without anything extended. Wherefore, by making space a property, the author falls in with my opinion, which makes it an order of things and not anything absolute.

10. If space is an absolute reality, far from being a property or an accident opposed to substance, it will have a greater reality than substances themselves. God cannot destroy it, nor even change it in any respect. It will be not only immense in the whole but also immutable and eternal in every part. There will be an infinite number of eternal things besides God.

11. To say that infinite space has no parts is to say that it is not composed of finite spaces, and that infinite space might subsist though all finite space should be reduced to nothing. It would be as if one should say, in accordance with the Cartesian supposition of a material extended unlimited world, that such a world might subsist, though all the bodies of which it consists should be reduced to nothing.

12. The author attributes parts to space, on page 19 of the third edition of his *Defense of the Argument against Mr. Dodwell*, and makes them inseparable one from another. But on page 30 of his *Second Defense* he says they are parts improperly so called—which may be understood in a good sense.

13. To say that God can cause the whole universe to move forward in a right line or in any other line, without otherwise making any alteration in it, is

another chimerical supposition. For two states indiscernible from each other are the same state, and consequently, it is a change without any change. Besides, there is neither rhyme nor reason in it. But God does nothing without reason, and it is impossible that there should be any here. Besides, it would be *agendo nihil agere*, as I have just now said, because of the indiscernibility.

14. These are idols of the tribe, mere chimeras, and superficial imaginations. All this is only grounded upon the supposition that imaginary space is real.[440]

15. It is a like fiction, (that is) an impossible one, to suppose that God might have created the world some millions of years sooner. They who run into such kind of fictions can give no answer to those who would argue for the eternity of the world. For since God does nothing without reason, and no reason can be given why he did not create the world sooner, it will follow either that he has created nothing at all, or that he created the world before any assignable time, which is to say that the world is eternal. But when once it has been shown that the beginning, whenever it was, is always the same thing, the question why it was not otherwise becomes needless and insignificant.

16. If space and time were anything absolute, that is, if they were anything else besides certain orders of things, then indeed my assertion would be a contradiction. But since it is not so, the hypothesis (that space and time are anything absolute)[441] is contradictory, that is, it is an impossible fiction.

17. And the case is the same as in geometry, where by the very supposition that a figure is greater than it really is, we sometimes prove that it is not greater. This indeed is a contradiction, but it lies in the hypothesis, which appears to be false for that very reason.[442]

18. Space being uniform, there can neither be any external nor internal reason by which to distinguish its parts and to make any choice among them. For any external reason to discern between them can only be grounded upon some internal one. Otherwise we should discern what is indiscernible or choose without discerning. A will without reason would be the chance of the Epicureans. A God who should act by such a will would be a God only in name. The cause of these errors proceeds from want of care to avoid what derogates from the divine perfections.

19. When two incompatible things are equally good, and neither in themselves, nor by their combination with other things, has the one any advantage over the other, God will produce neither of them.

20. God is never determined by external things but always by what is in himself, that is, by his knowledge, before anything exists outside himself.

21. There is no possible reason that can limit the quantity of matter, and therefore, such limitation can have no place.

22. And supposing this arbitrary limitation of the quantity of matter, something might always be added to it without derogating from the perfection of the things which do already exist, and consequently, something must always

---

440. See Bacon, *New Organon*, book I, aphorism 41.
441. The parenthetical remark is Clarke's addition.
442. Leibniz's text reads: ". . . which is found to be false for that reason."

be added, in order to act according to the principle of the perfection of the divine operations.

23. And therefore, it cannot be said that the present quantity of matter is the fittest for the present constitution of things. And even supposing it is, it would follow that this present constitution of things would not be the fittest absolutely, if it hinders God from using more matter. It is therefore better to choose another constitution of things, capable of something more.

24. I should be glad to see a passage of any philosopher who takes *sensorium* in any other sense than Goclenius does.

25. If Scapula says that *sensorium* is the place in which the understanding resides, he means by it the organ of internal sensation. And therefore, he does not differ from Goclenius.[443]

26. *Sensorium* has always signified the organ of sensation. The pineal gland would be, according to Descartes, the *sensorium* in the above-mentioned sense of Scapula.

27. There is hardly any less appropriate expression on this subject than that which makes God to have a sensorium. It seems to make God the soul of the world. And it will be a hard matter to put a justifiable sense upon this word, according to the use Sir Isaac Newton makes of it.

28. Though the question is about the sense put upon that word by Sir Isaac Newton, and not by Goclenius, yet I am not to blame for quoting the Philosophical Dictionary of that author, because the design of dictionaries is to show the use of words.

29. God perceives things in himself. Space is the place of things and not the place of God's ideas, unless we look upon space as something that makes the union between God and things in imitation of the imagined union between the soul and the body, which would still make God the soul of the world.

30. And indeed, the author is much in the wrong when he compares God's knowledge and operation with the knowledge and operation of souls. The soul knows things because God has put into it a principle representative of things without. But God knows things because he continually produces them.

31. The soul does not act upon things, according to my opinion, any otherwise than because the body adapts itself to the desires of the soul, by virtue of the harmony which God has pre-established between them.

32. But they who fancy that the soul can give a new force to the body, and that God does the same in the world to mend the imperfections of his machine, make God too much like the soul by ascribing too much to the soul and too little to God.

33. For none but God can give a new force to nature, and he does it only supernaturally. If there was need for him to do it in the natural course of things, he would have made a very imperfect work. At that rate, he would

---

443. Scapula, *Lexicon Graeco-Latinum* (1639). Clarke had attempted to counter Gloclenius with Scapula.

be, with respect to the world, what the soul, in the vulgar notion, is with respect to the body.

34. Those who undertake to defend the vulgar opinion concerning the soul's influence over the body by instancing God's operating on things external, still make God too much like the soul of the world. The author's affecting to find fault with the words *intelligentia supramundana* seems also to incline that way.

35. The images with which the soul is immediately affected are within itself, but they correspond to those of the body. The presence of the soul is imperfect and can only be explained by that correspondence. But the presence of God is perfect and manifested by his operation.

36. The author wrongly supposes against me that the presence of the soul is connected with its influence over the body, for he knows I reject that influence.

37. The soul's being diffused through the brain is no less inexplicable than its being diffused through the whole body. The difference is only in more and less.

38. They who fancy that active forces decrease of themselves in the world do not well understand the principal laws of nature and the beauty of the works of God.

39. How will they be able to prove that this defect is a consequence of the dependence of things?

40. The imperfection of our machines, which is the reason why they need to be mended, proceeds from this very thing, that they do not sufficiently depend upon the workman. And therefore, the dependence of nature upon God, far from being the cause of such an imperfection, is rather the reason why there is no such imperfection in nature, because nature is so dependent upon an artist too perfect to make a work that needs to be mended. It is true that every particular machine of nature is in some measure liable to be disordered, but not the entire universe, which cannot diminish in perfection.

41. The author contends that space does not depend upon the situation of bodies. I answer: It is true, it does not depend upon such or such a situation of bodies, but it is that order which renders bodies capable of being situated, and by which they have a situation among themselves when they exist together, as time is that order with respect to their successive position. But if there were no creatures, space and time would only be in the ideas of God.

42. The author seems to acknowledge here that his notion of a miracle is not the same as that which theologians and philosophers usually have. It is therefore sufficient for my purpose that my adversaries are obliged to have recourse to what is commonly called a miracle, which one attempts to avoid in philosophy.

43. I am afraid the author, by altering the sense commonly put upon the word 'miracle', will fall into an inconvenient opinion. The nature of a miracle does not at all consist in usualness or unusualness, for then monsters would be miracles.

44. There are miracles of an inferior sort which an angel can work. He can, for instance, make a man walk upon the water without sinking. But there are

miracles which none but God can work, they exceeding all natural powers. Of this kind are creating and annihilating.

45. It is also a supernatural thing that bodies should attract one another at a distance without any intermediate means, and that a body should move around without receding in the tangent, though nothing hinders it from so receding. For these effects cannot be explained by the nature of things.

46. Why should it be impossible to explain the motion of animals by natural forces? Though, indeed, the beginning of animals is no less inexplicable by natural forces than the beginning of the world.

P.S. All those who maintain a vacuum are more influenced by imagination than by reason. When I was a young man, I also gave in to the notion of the void and atoms, but reason brought me into the right way. It was a pleasing imagination. Men carry their inquiries no further than those two things: they (as it were) nail down their thoughts to them; they fancy they have found out the first elements of things, a *non plus ultra*. We would have nature to go no further, and to be finite as our minds are; but this is being ignorant of the greatness and majesty of the author of things. The least corpuscle is actually subdivided *in infinitum* and contains a world of other creatures which would be wanting in the universe if that corpuscle were an atom, that is, a body of one entire piece without subdivision. In like manner, to admit the void in nature is ascribing to God a very imperfect work; it is violating the grand principle of the necessity of a sufficient reason, which many have talked of without understanding its true meaning; as I have lately shown in proving, by that principle, that space is only an order of things, as time also is, and not at all an absolute being. To omit many other arguments against the void and atoms, I shall here mention those which I ground upon God's perfection and upon the necessity of a sufficient reason. I lay it down as a principle that every perfection which God could impart to things, without derogating from their other perfections, has actually been imparted to them. Now let us fancy a space wholly empty. God could have placed some matter in it without derogating, in any respect, from all other things; therefore, he has actually placed some matter in that space; therefore, there is no space wholly empty; therefore, all is full. The same argument proves that there is no corpuscle but what is subdivided. I shall add another argument grounded upon the necessity of a sufficient reason. It is impossible there should be any principle to determine what proportion of matter there ought to be, out of all the possible degrees from a plenum to a void, or from a void to a plenum. Perhaps it will be said that the one should be equal to the other, but, because matter is more perfect than the void, reason requires that a geometrical proportion should be observed and that there should be as much more matter than void, as the former deserves to be preferred. But then, there must be no void at all, for the perfection of matter is to that of the void as something to nothing. And the case is the same with atoms: what reason can anyone assign for confining nature in the progression of subdivision? These are fictions, merely arbitrary and unworthy of true philosophy. The reasons alleged for the void are mere sophisms.

V. Leibniz's Fifth Paper (excerpts)

* * * * *

To SECTIONS 3 and 4:

21. It must be confessed that though this great principle has been acknowledged, yet it has not been sufficiently made use of. This is in great measure the reason why the *prima philosophia*[444] has not hitherto been so fruitful and demonstrative as it should have been. I infer from that principle, among other consequences, that there are not in nature two real, absolute beings, indiscernible from each other, because, if there were, God and nature would act without reason in treating the one otherwise than the other, and that therefore, God does not produce two pieces of matter perfectly equal and alike. The author answers this conclusion without confuting the reason of it, and he answers with a very weak objection. "That argument," says he, "if it was good, would prove that it would be impossible for God to create any matter at all. For the perfectly solid parts of matter, if we take them of equal figure and dimensions (which is always possible in supposition), would be exactly alike." But it is a manifest begging of that question to suppose that perfect likeness, which, according to me, cannot be admitted. This supposition of two indiscernibles, such as two pieces of matter perfectly alike, indeed seems to be possible in abstract terms, but it is not consistent with the order of things, nor with the divine wisdom by which nothing is admitted without reason. The vulgar fancy such things because they content themselves with incomplete notions. And this is one of the faults of the atomists.

22. Besides, I don't admit in matter parts perfectly solid, or that are the same throughout without any variety or particular motion in their parts, as the pretended atoms are imagined to be. To suppose such bodies is another ill-grounded popular opinion. According to my demonstrations, every part of matter is actually subdivided into parts differently moved, and no one of them is perfectly like another.

23. I said that in sensible things two that are indiscernible can never be found, that, for instance, two leaves in a garden or two drops of water perfectly alike are not to be found. The author acknowledges it as to leaves and perhaps as to drops of water. But he might have admitted it without any hesitation, without a 'perhaps' (an Italian would say *senza forse*), as to drops of water likewise.

24. I believe that these general observations in things sensible also hold in proportion in things insensible, and that one may say in this respect what Harlequin says in the *Emperor of the Moon*: it is there just as it is here. And it is a great objection against indiscernibles that no instance of them is to be found. But the author opposes this consequence, because (says he) sensible bodies are composed, whereas he maintains there are insensible bodies which are simple. I answer again that I don't admit simple bodies. There is nothing simple, in my opinion, but true monads, which have neither parts nor exten-

---

444. *Prima philosophia*, literally 'first philosophy,' or metaphysics.

sion. Simple bodies, and even perfectly similar ones, are a consequence of the false hypothesis of the void and of atoms, or of lazy philosophy, which does not sufficiently carry on the analysis of things and fancies it can attain to the first material elements of nature, because our imagination would be therewith satisfied.

25. When I deny that there are two drops of water perfectly alike, or any two other bodies indiscernible from each other, I don't say it is absolutely impossible to suppose them, but that it is a thing contrary to the divine wisdom, and which consequently does not exist.

To Sections 5 and 6:

26. I own that if two things perfectly indiscernible from each other did exist they would be two; but that supposition is false and contrary to the grand principle of reason. The vulgar philosophers were mistaken when they believed that there are two things different in number alone, or only because they are two, and from this error have arisen their perplexities about what they called the *principle of individuation*. Metaphysics has generally been handled like a science of mere words, like a philosophical dictionary, without entering into the discussion of things. *Superficial philosophy*, such as is that of the atomists and vacuists, forges things which superior reasons do not admit. I hope my demonstrations will change the face of philosophy, notwithstanding such weak objections as the author raises here against me.

27. The parts of time and place, considered in themselves, are ideal things, and therefore they perfectly resemble one another like two abstract units. But it is not so with two concrete ones, or with two real times, or two spaces filled up, that is, truly actual.

28. I don't say that two points of space are one and the same point, nor that two instants of time are one and the same instant, as the author seems to impute to me. But a man may fancy, for want of knowledge, that there are two different instants where there is but one; in like manner, as I observed in the seventeenth paragraph of the foregoing answer, that frequently in geometry we suppose two, in order to represent the error of a gainsayer, and only find one. If any man should suppose that a right line cuts another in two points, it will be found, after all, that these two pretended points must coincide and make but one point.

29. I have demonstrated that space is nothing else but an order of the existence of things observed as existing together, and therefore the fiction of a material finite universe moving forward in an infinite empty space cannot be admitted. It is altogether unreasonable and impracticable. For besides the fact that there is no real space out of the material universe, such an action would be without any design in it; it would be working without doing anything, in acting nothing would be done by the action. There would happen no change which could be observed by any person whatsoever. These are the imaginations of philosophers who have incomplete notions, who make space an absolute reality. Mere mathematicians who are only taken up with the conceits of imagination are apt to forge such notions, but they are destroyed by superior reasons.

30. Absolutely speaking, it appears that God can make the material universe finite in extension, but the contrary appears more agreeable to his wisdom.

31. I don't grant that every finite is movable. According to the hypothesis of my adversaries themselves, a part of space, though finite, is not movable. What is movable must be capable of changing its situation with respect to something else, and to be in a new state discernible from the first; otherwise the change is but a fiction. A movable finite must therefore make part of another finite, that any change may happen which can be observed.

32. Descartes maintains that matter is unlimited, and I don't think he has been sufficiently confuted. And though this be granted him, yet it does not follow that matter would be necessary, nor that it would have existed from eternity, since that unlimited diffusion of matter would only be an effect of God's choice judging that to be the better.

To Section 7:

33. Since space in itself is an ideal thing like time, space out of the world must be imaginary, as the Schoolmen themselves have recognized. The case is the same with empty space within the world, which I take also to be imaginary, for the reasons before alleged.

34. The author objects against me the vacuum discovered by Mr. Guericke of Magdeburg, which is made by pumping the air out of a receiver, and he claims that there truly is a perfect vacuum or a space without matter (at least in part) in that receiver. The Aristotelians and Cartesians, who do not admit a true vacuum, have said in answer to that experiment of Mr. Guericke, as well as to that of Torricelli of Florence (who emptied the air out of a glass tube by the help of quicksilver), that there is no vacuum at all in the tube or in the receiver, since glass has small pores which the beams of light, the effluvia of the lodestone, and other very thin fluids may go through. I am of their opinion, and I think the receiver may be compared to a box full of holes in the water, having fish or other gross bodies shut up in it, which, being taken out, their place would nevertheless be filled up with water. There is only this difference—that though water is fluid and more yielding than those gross bodies, yet it is as heavy and massive, if not more, than they, whereas the matter which gets into the receiver in the room of the air is much more subtle. The new partisans of a vacuum allege in answer to this instance that it is not the grossness of matter but its mere quantity that makes resistance, and consequently that there is of necessity more vacuum where there is less resistance. They add that the subtleness of matter has nothing to do here and that the particles of quicksilver are as subtle and fine as those of water, and yet that quicksilver resists above ten times more. To this I reply that it is not so much the quantity of matter, as its difficulty of giving place, that makes resistance. For instance, floating timber contains less of heavy matter than an equal bulk of water does, and yet it makes more resistance to a boat than the water does.

35. And as for quicksilver, it is true, it contains about fourteen times more of heavy matter than an equal bulk of water does, but it does not follow that

it contains fourteen times more matter absolutely. On the contrary, water contains as much matter, if we include both its own matter, which is heavy, and the extraneous matter void of heaviness which passes through its pores. For both quicksilver and water are masses of heavy matter, full of pores, through which there passes a great deal of matter void of heaviness (and which makes no sensible resistance), such as is probably that of the rays of light and other insensible fluids, and especially that which is itself the cause of the gravity of gross bodies, by receding from the center toward which it drives those bodies. For it is a strange fiction to make all matter gravitate, and that toward all other matter, as if each body did equally attract every other body according to their masses and distances—and this by an attraction properly so called, which is not derived from an occult impulse of bodies, whereas the gravity of sensible bodies toward the center of the earth ought to be produced by the motion of some fluid. And the case must be the same with other gravities, such as is that of the planets toward the sun or toward each other. (A body is never moved naturally except by another body which touches it and pushes it; after that it continues until it is prevented by another body which touches it. Any other kind of operation on bodies is either miraculous or imaginary.)[445]

To Sections 8 and 9:

36. I objected that space, taken for something real and absolute without bodies, would be a thing eternal, unchangeable, and not dependent upon God. The author endeavors to elude this difficulty by saying that space is a property of God. In answer to this I have said, in my foregoing paper, that the property of God is immensity but that space (which is often commensurate with bodies) and God's immensity are not the same thing.

37. I objected further that if space is a property, and infinite space is the immensity of God, finite space will be the extension or mensurability of something finite. And therefore the space taken up by a body will be the extension of that body. This is an absurdity, since a body can change space but cannot leave its extension.

38. I asked also, if space is a property, of what thing will an empty, limited space (such as that which my adversary imagines in an exhausted receiver) be the property? It does not appear reasonable to say that this empty space, either round or square, is a property of God. Will it then perhaps be the property of some immaterial, extended, imaginary substances which the author seems to fancy in the imaginary spaces?

39. If space is the property or affection of the substance which is in space, the same space will sometimes be the affection of one body, sometimes of another body, sometimes of an immaterial substance, and sometimes perhaps of God himself, when it is void of all other substance, material or immaterial. But this is a strange property or affection, which passes from one subject to another. Thus subjects will leave off their accidents like clothes, that other

---

445. Clarke gives this last parenthetical remark as a note, though it is in the main text of Leibniz's letter.

subjects may put them on. At this rate how shall we distinguish accidents and substances?

40. And if limited spaces are the affections of limited substances which are in them, and infinite space is a property of God, a property of God must (which is very strange) be made up of the affections of creatures, for all finite spaces taken together make up infinite space.

41. But if the author denies that limited space is an affection of limited things, it will not be reasonable either, that infinite space should be the affection or property of an infinite thing. I have suggested all these difficulties in my foregoing paper, but it does not appear that the author has endeavored to answer them.

42. I have still other reasons against this strange imagination that space is a property of God. If it is so, space belongs to the essence of God. But space has parts; therefore, there would be parts in the essence of God. *Spectatum admissi!*[446]

43. Moreover, spaces are sometimes empty and sometimes filled up. Therefore, there will be in the essence of God parts sometimes empty and sometimes full and consequently liable to a perpetual change. Bodies filling up space would fill up part of God's essence and would be commensurate with it; and in the supposition of a vacuum, part of God's essence will be within the receiver. Such a *God having parts* will very much resemble the Stoics' god, which was the whole universe considered as a divine animal.

44. If infinite space is God's immensity, infinite time will be God's eternity; and therefore, we must say that what is in space is in God's immensity and consequently in his essence, and that what is in time is also in the essence of God. Strange expressions, which plainly show that the author makes a wrong use of terms.

45. I shall give another instance of this. God's immensity actually makes him present in all spaces. But now if God is in space, how can it be said that space is in God or that it is a property of God? We have often heard that a property is in its subject, but we never heard that a subject is in its property. In like manner, God exists in all time. How then can time be in God, and how can it be a property of God? These are perpetual *alloglossies*.[447]

46. It appears that the author confounds immensity, or the extension of things, with the space according to which that extension is taken. Infinite space is not the immensity of God; finite space is not the extension of bodies, as time is not their duration. Things keep their extension, but they do not always keep their space. Everything has its own extension, its own duration, but it has not its own time and does not keep its own space.

47. I will here show how men come to form to themselves the notion of space. They consider that many things exist at once, and they observe in them a

---

446. This is a reference to Horace, the first words of a line that reads: "admitted to such and such a sight [*spectatum admissi*], could you restrain your laughter, friends?" [*De Arte Poetica*, 1.5].

447. Literally, this corresponds to the Greek for 'foreign'; Leibniz probably has in mind here the associated meaning of its Latin counterpart, '*barbarus*', barbaric.

certain order of coexistence, according to which the relation of one thing to
another is more or less simple. This order is their situation or distance. When
it happens that one of those coexistent things changes its relation to a multitude of others which do not change their relations among themselves, and
that another thing, newly come, acquires the same relation to the others as
the former had, we then say it is come into the place of the former; and this
change we call a *motion* in that body wherein is the immediate cause of the
change. And though many, or even all, the coexistent things should change
according to certain known rules of direction and swiftness, yet one may always determine the relation of situation which every coexistent acquires with
respect to every other coexistent, and even that relation which any other coexistent would have to this, or which this would have to any other, if it had
not changed or if it had changed any otherwise. And supposing or feigning
that among those coexistents there is a sufficient number of them which have
undergone no change, then we may say that those which have such a relation
to those fixed existents as others had to them before, have now the same *place*
which those others had. And that which comprehends all those places is called
space. This shows that, in order to have an idea of place, and consequently of
space, it is sufficient to consider these relations and the rules of their changes,
without needing to fancy any absolute reality beyond the things whose situation we consider. And to give a kind of definition, *place* is that which we say
is the same to A and to B, when the relation of the coexistence of B with C,
E, F, G, etc., agrees perfectly with the relation of the coexistence which
A had with the same C, E, F, G, etc., supposing there has been no cause of
change in C, E, F, G, etc. It may also be said, without entering into any further particularity, that place is that which is the same in different moments
to different existent things when their relations of coexistence with certain
other existents which are supposed to continue fixed from one of those moments to the other agree entirely together. And *fixed existents* are those in
which there has been no cause of any change of the order of their coexistence
with others, or (which is the same thing) in which there has been no motion.
Lastly, *space* is that which results from places taken together. And here it may
not be amiss to consider the difference between place and the relation of situation of the body that fills up the place. For the place of A and B is the same,
whereas the relation of A to fixed bodies is not precisely and individually the
same as the relation which B (that comes into its place) will have to the same
fixed bodies; but these relations only agree. For two different subjects, as A
and B, cannot have precisely the same individual affection, it being impossible that the same individual accident should be in two subjects or pass from
one subject to another. But the mind, not contented with an agreement, looks
for an identity, for something that should be truly the same, and conceives
it as being extrinsic to these subjects; and this is what we here call *place* and
space. But this can only be an ideal thing, containing a certain order, wherein
the mind conceives the application of relations. In like manner, as the mind
can fancy to itself an order made up of genealogical lines whose size would
consist only in the number of generations, wherein every person would have

his place; and if to this one should add the fiction of a metemphyschosis and bring in the same human souls again, the persons in those lines might change place; he who was a father or a grandfather might become a son or a grandson, etc. And yet, those genealogical places, lines, and spaces, though they should express real truths, would only be ideal things. I shall allege another example to show how the mind uses, upon occasion of accidents which are in subjects, to fancy to itself something answerable to those accidents outside of the subjects. The ratio or proportion between two lines L and M may be conceived three ways: as a ratio of the greater L to the lesser M, as a ratio of the lesser M to the greater L, and lastly, as something abstracted from both, that is, the ratio between L and M without considering which is the antecedent or which the consequent, which the subject and which the object. And thus it is that proportions are considered in music. In the first way of considering them, L the greater, in the second, M the lesser, is the subject of that accident which philosophers call 'relation'. But which of them will be the subject in the third way of considering them? It cannot be said that both of them, L and M together, are the subject of such an accident; for, if so, we should have an accident in two subjects, with one leg in one and the other in the other, which is contrary to the notion of accidents. Therefore, we must say that this relation, in this third way of considering it, is indeed out of the subjects; but being neither a substance nor an accident, it must be a mere ideal thing, the consideration of which is nevertheless useful. To conclude, I have here done much like Euclid, who, not being able to make his readers understand well what *ratio* is, absolutely, in the sense of geometricians, defines what are the *same ratios*. Thus, in like manner, in order to explain what *place* is, I have been content to define what is the *same place*. Lastly, I observe that the traces of movable bodies, which they sometimes leave upon the immovable ones on which they exercise their movement, have given men occasion to form in their imagination this idea, as if some trace did still remain, even when there is nothing unmoved. But this is a mere ideal thing and imports only that *if there were any unmoved thing there, the trace might be marked out upon it.* And it is this analogy which makes men fancy places, traces, and spaces, though these things consist only in the truth of relations, and not at all in any absolute reality.

48. To conclude, if the space (which the author fancies) void of all bodies is not altogether empty, what is it then full of? Is it full of extended spirits perhaps, or immaterial substances capable of extending and contracting themselves, which move therein and penetrate each other without any inconveniency, as the shadows of two bodies penetrate one another upon the surface of a wall? I think I see the revival of the odd imaginations of Dr. Henry More, otherwise a learned and well-meaning man, and of some others who fancied that those spirits can make themselves impenetrable whenever they please. Some have even fancied that man in the state of innocency had also the gift of penetration, and that he became solid, opaque, and impenetrable by his fall. Is it not overthrowing our notions of things to make God have parts, to make spirits have extension? The principle of the want of a sufficient reason

does alone drive away all these specters of imagination. Men easily run into fictions for want of making a right use of that great principle.

To Section 10:

49. It cannot be said that a certain duration is eternal but that things, which continue always, are eternal, gaining always new duration. Whatever exists of time and of duration, being successive, perishes continually,[448] and how can a thing exist eternally which (to speak exactly) does not exist at all? For how can a thing exist of which no part does ever exist? Nothing of time does ever exist but instants, and an instant is not even itself a part of time. Whoever considers these observations will easily apprehend that time can only be an ideal thing. And the analogy between time and space will easily make it appear that the one is as merely ideal as the other. (But if in saying that the duration of a thing is eternal, it only meant that the thing endures eternally, I have nothing to say against it.)

50. If the reality of space and time is necessary to the immensity and eternity of God, if God must be in space, if being in space is a property of God, he will in some measure depend upon time and space and stand in need of them. For I have already prevented that subterfuge—that space and time are in God and like properties of God. (Could one maintain the opinion that bodies move about in the parts of the divine essence?)[449]

To Sections 11 and 12:

51. I objected that space cannot be in God because it has parts. Hereupon the author seeks another subterfuge by departing from the received sense of words, maintaining that space has no parts because its parts are not separable and cannot be removed from one another by plucking them out. But it is sufficient that space has parts, whether those parts be separable or not, and they may be assigned in space, either by the bodies that are in it or by lines and surfaces that may be drawn and described in it.

To Section 13:

52. In order to prove that space without bodies is an absolute reality, the author objected that a finite material universe might move about in space. I answered, it does not appear reasonable that the material universe should be finite, and though we should suppose it to be finite, yet it is unreasonable it should have any motion otherwise than as its parts change their situation among themselves, because such a motion would produce no change that could be observed, and would be without design. It is another thing when its parts change their situation among themselves, for then one would recognize a motion in space, but it consists in the order of relations which are changed. The author replies now that the reality of motion does not depend upon being observed and that a ship may go forward, and yet a man who is in the ship may not perceive it. I answer, motion indeed does not depend upon being observed, but it does depend upon being possible to be observed. There is no motion when there is no change that can be observed. And when there is no

---

448. This paragraph, up to this point, is in a note in Clarke, though it is in Leibniz's text.

449. This parenthetical remark is a note in Clarke's edition, though it is in Leibniz's text.

change that can be observed, there is no change at all. The contrary opinion is grounded upon the supposition of a real absolute space, which I have demonstratively confuted by the principle of the want of a sufficient reason.

53. I find nothing in the eighth definition of the *Mathematical Principles of Nature*, nor in the scholium belonging to it, that proves or can prove the reality of space in itself.[450] However, I grant there is a difference between an absolute true motion of a body and a mere relative change of its situation with respect to another body. For when the immediate cause of the change is in the body, that body is truly in motion, and then the situation of other bodies with respect to it will be changed consequently, though the cause of that change is not in them. It is true that, exactly speaking, there is not any one body that is perfectly and entirely at rest, but we frame an abstract notion of rest by considering the thing mathematically. Thus have I left nothing unanswered of what has been alleged for the absolute reality of space. And I have demonstrated the falsehood of that reality by a fundamental principle, one of the most certain both in reason and experience, against which no exception or instance can be alleged. Upon the whole, one may judge from what has been said that I ought not to admit a movable universe, nor any place out of the material universe.

To Section 14:

54. I am not sensible of any objection but what I think I have sufficiently answered. As for the objection that space and time are quantities, or rather things endowed with quantity, and that situation and order are not so, I answer that order also has its quantity; there is in it that which goes before and that which follows; there is distance or interval. Relative things have their quantity as well as absolute ones. For instance, ratios or proportions in mathematics have their quantity and are measured by logarithms, and yet they are relations. And therefore, though time and space consist in relations, yet they have their quantity.

To Section 15:

55. As to the question whether God could have created the world sooner, it is necessary here to understand each other rightly. Since I have demonstrated that time, without things, is nothing else but a mere ideal possibility, it is manifest that if anyone should say that this same world which has been actually created might have been created sooner without any other change, he would say nothing that is intelligible. For there is no mark or difference whereby it would be possible to know that this world was created sooner. And, therefore (as I have already said), to suppose that God created the same world sooner is supposing a chimerical thing. It is making time a thing absolute, independent upon God, whereas time must coexist with creatures and is only conceived by the order and quantity of their changes.

56. But yet, absolutely speaking, one may conceive that a universe began sooner than it actually did. Let us suppose our universe or any other to be represented by the figure AF and that the ordinate AB represents its first

450. See Newton, *Mathematical Principles* . . . vol. I, pp. 4–12.

state, and the ordinates CD and EF its following states; I say one may conceive that such a world began sooner by conceiving the figure prolonged backward and by adding to it SRABS. For thus, things being increased, time will also be increased. But whether such an augmentation is reasonable and agreeable to God's wisdom is another question, to which we answer in the negative; otherwise God would have made such an augmentation. It would be like as

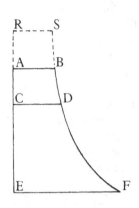

Figure 15

> Humano capiti cervicem pictor equinam
> Jungere si velit.[451]

The case is the same with respect to the duration of the universe. As one might conceive something added to the beginning, so one might also conceive something taken off toward the end. But such a retrenching from it would also be unreasonable.

57. Thus it appears how we are to understand that God created things at what time he pleased, for this depends upon the things which he resolved to create. But things being once resolved upon, together with their relations, there no longer remains any choice about the time and the place, which of themselves have nothing in them real, nothing that can distinguish them, nothing that is at all discernible.

58. One cannot therefore say, as the author does here, that the wisdom of God may have good reasons to create this world at such or such a particular time, that particular time considered without the things being an impossible fiction, and good reasons for a choice being not to be found where everything is indiscernible.

59. When I speak of this world, I mean the whole universe of material and immaterial creatures taken together, from the beginning of things. But if anyone mean only the beginning of the material world, and suppose immaterial creatures before it, he would have somewhat more reason for his supposition. For time then being marked by things that existed already, it would no longer be indifferent, and there might be room for choice. And yet, indeed, this would only be putting off the difficulty. For supposing the whole universe of immaterial and material creatures together to have a beginning, there is no longer any choice about the time in which God would place that beginning.

60. And therefore, one must not say as the author does here, that God created things in what particular space and at what particular time he pleased. For all time and all spaces being in themselves perfectly uniform and indiscernible from each other, one of them cannot please more than another.

61. I shall not enlarge here upon my opinion explained elsewhere, that there

---

451. These are the opening words of Horace's *De Arte Poetica*: "If a painter wished to join a horse's neck to a human head." The sentence in Horace ends with the quotation alluded to above in sec. 42 of this letter.

are no created substances wholly destitute of matter. For I hold with the ancients, and according to reason, that angels or intelligences, and souls separated from a gross body, have always subtle bodies, though they themselves are incorporeal. The vulgar philosophy easily admits all sorts of fictions; mine is more strict.

62. I don't say that matter and space are the same thing. I only say there is no space where there is no matter and that space in itself is not an absolute reality. Space and matter differ as time and motion. However, these things, though different, are inseparable.

63. But it does not at all follow that matter is eternal and necessary, unless we suppose space to be eternal and necessary—a supposition ill grounded in all respects.

To Sections 16 and 17:

64. I think I have answered everything, and I have particularly replied to that objection that space and time have quantity and that order has none. See above, No. 54.

65. I have clearly shown that the contradiction lies in the hypothesis of the opposite opinion, which looks for a difference where there is none. And it would be a manifest iniquity to infer from this that I have acknowledged a contradiction in my own opinion.

* * * * *

To Section 42:

107. I maintained that an operation of God by which he should mend the machine of the material world, tending in its nature, as this author claims, to lose all its motion, would be a miracle. His answer was that it would not be a miraculous operation because it would be usual and must frequently happen. I replied that it is not usualness or unusualness that makes a miracle properly so called, or a miracle of the highest sort, but its surpassing the powers of creatures, and that this is the general opinion of theologians and philosophers; and that therefore, the author acknowledges at least that the thing he introduces and I disallow is, according to the received notion, a miracle of the highest sort, that is, one which surpasses all created powers, and that this is the very thing which all men endeavor to avoid in philosophy. He answers now that this is appealing from reason to vulgar opinion. But I reply again that this vulgar opinion, according to which we ought in philosophy to avoid as much as possible what surpasses the natures of creatures, is a very reasonable opinion. Otherwise nothing will be easier than to account for anything by bringing in the deity, *deum ex machina*, without minding the natures of things.

108. Besides, the common opinion of theologians ought not to be looked upon merely as vulgar opinion. A man should have weighty reasons before he ventures to contradict it, and I see no such reasons here.

109. The author seems to depart from his own notion, according to which miracle ought to be unusual, when in Section 31, he objects to me—though without any ground—that the pre-established harmony would be a perpetual miracle. Here I say, he seems to depart from his own notion, unless he had a mind to argue against me *ad hominem*.

To Section 43:

110. If a miracle differs from what is natural only in appearance and with respect to us, so that we call that only a miracle which we seldom see, there will be no internal real difference between a miracle and what is natural, and at the bottom everything will either be equally natural or equally miraculous. Will theologians accommodate themselves to the former, or philosophers to the latter?

111. Will not this doctrine, moreover, tend to make God the soul of the world, if all his operations are natural like those of our souls upon our bodies? And so, God will be a part of nature.

112. In good philosophy and sound theology we ought to distinguish between what is explicable by the natures and powers of creatures and what is explicable only by the powers of the infinite substance. We ought to make an infinite difference between the operation of God, which goes beyond the extent of natural powers, and the operations of things that follow the laws which God has given them, and which he has enabled them to follow by their natural powers, though not without his assistance.

113. This overthrows attractions, properly so called, and other operations inexplicable by the natural powers of creatures, which kinds of operations the assertors of them must suppose to be effected by miracle, or else have recourse to absurdities, that is, to the occult qualities of the Schools, which some men begin to revive under the specious name of forces, but they bring us back again into the kingdom of darkness. This is *inventa fruge, glandibus vesci.*[452]

114. In the time of Mr. Boyle and other excellent men who flourished in England under Charles the Second, in the early part of his reign, nobody would have ventured to publish such chimerical notions. *I hope that happy time will return under so good a government as the present* [and that minds a little too much distracted by the misfortune of the times will return to cultivate sound knowledge better].[453] Mr. Boyle made it his chief business to inculcate that everything was done mechanically in natural philosophy. But it is men's misfortune to become disgusted with reason itself and to be weary of light. Chimeras begin to appear again, and they are pleasing because they have something in them that is wonderful. What has happened in poetry also happens in the philosophical world. People are grown weary of rational romances such as were the French *Clélie* or the German *Aramene*, and they are become fond again of the *tales of fairies.*

115. As for motions of the celestial bodies, and even the formation of plants and animals, there is nothing in them that looks like a miracle except their beginning. The organism of animals is a mechanism which supposes a divine preformation. What follows upon it is purely natural and entirely mechanical.

116. Whatever is performed in the body of man and of every animal is no less mechanical than what is performed in a watch. The difference is only such

---

452. "To feed on acorns when corn has been discovered."
453. The passage in brackets was in the notes in Clarke's edition.

as ought to be between a machine of divine invention and the workmanship of such a limited artist as man is.

To Section 44:

117. There is no difficulty among theologians about the miracles of angels. The question is only about the use of that word. It may be said that angels work miracles, but less properly so called, or of an inferior order. To dispute about this would be a mere question about a word. It may be said that the angel who carried Habakkuk through the air, and he who troubled the water of the pool of Bethesda, worked a miracle. But it was not a miracle of the highest order, for it may be explained by the natural powers of angels, which surpass those of man.

To Section 45:

118. I objected that an attraction properly so called, or in the Scholastic sense, would be an operation at a distance without any means intervening. The author answers here that an attraction without any means intervening would indeed be a contradiction. Very well. But then, what does he mean when he will have the sun to attract the globe of the earth through an empty space? Is it God himself that performs it? But this would be a miracle if ever there was any. This would surely exceed the powers of creatures.

119. Or perhaps, are some immaterial substances or some spiritual rays, or some accidents without a substance, or some kind of *species intentionalis*, or some other I-know-not-what, the means by which this is claimed to be performed? Of which sort of things the author seems to have still a good stock in his head, without explaining himself sufficiently.

120. That means of communication, says he, is invisible, intangible, not mechanical. He might as well have added inexplicable, unintelligible, precarious, groundless, and unprecedented.

121. But it is regular, says the author; it is constant and consequently natural. I answer, it cannot be regular without being reasonable, nor natural unless it can be explained by the natures of creatures.

122. If the means which causes an attraction, properly so called, are constant and at the same time inexplicable by the powers of creators, and yet are true, it must be a perpetual miracle, and if it is not miraculous, it is false. It is a chimerical thing, a Scholastic occult quality.

123. The case would be the same as in a body going round without receding in the tangent, though nothing that can be explained hindered it from receding. This is an instance I have already alleged, and the author has not thought fit to answer it because it shows too clearly the difference between what is truly natural, on the one side, and a chimerical occult quality of the Schools, on the other.

To Section 46:

124. All the natural forces of bodies are subject to mechanical laws, and all the natural powers of spirits are subject to moral laws. The former follow the order of efficient causes, and the latter follow the order of final causes. The former operate without liberty, like a watch; the latter operate with liberty,

though they exactly agree with that machine which another cause, free and superior, has adapted to them beforehand. I have already spoken of this above, No. 92.

125. I shall conclude with what the author objected against me at the beginning of this fourth reply, to which I have already given an answer above, Nos. 18, 19, 20. But I have deferred speaking more fully upon that head to the conclusion of this paper. He claimed that I have been guilty of a *petitio principii*. But of what principle, I beseech you? Would to God less clear principles had never been laid down. The principle in question is the principle of the want of a sufficient reason for a thing to exist, for an event to happen, for any truth's obtaining. Is this a principle that wants to be proved? The author granted it or pretended to grant it, No. 2 of his third paper, possibly because the denial of it would have appeared too unreasonable. But either he has done it only in words, or he contradicts himself or retracts his concession.

126. I dare say that without this great principle one cannot prove the existence of God, nor account for many other important truths.

127. Has not everybody made use of this principle upon a thousand occasions? It is true, it has been neglected out of carelessness on many occasions, but that neglect has been the true cause of chimeras such as are, for instance, an absolute real time or space, a void, atoms, attraction in the Scholastic sense, a physical influence of the soul over the body, and a thousand other fictions, either derived from erroneous opinions of the ancients, or lately invented by modern philosophers.

128. Was it not upon account of Epicurus' violating this great principle that the ancients derided his groundless declination of atoms? And I dare say the Scholastic attraction, revived in our days and no less derided about thirty years ago, is not at all more reasonable.[454]

129. I have often defied people to allege an instance against that great principle, to bring any one uncontested example wherein it fails. But they have never done it, nor ever will. It is certain there is an infinite number of instances wherein it succeeds, or rather it succeeds in all the known cases in which it has been made use of. From whence one may reasonably judge that it will succeed also in unknown cases, or in such cases as can only by its means become known, according to the method of experimental philosophy which proceeds *a posteriori*, even if the principle were not otherwise justified by pure reason, or *a priori*.

130. To deny this great principle is to do as Epicurus did, who was reduced to deny that other great principle, namely, the principle of contradiction, which is that every intelligible enunciation must either be true or false. Chrysippus undertook to prove that principle against Epicurus, but I think I need not imitate him. I have already said what is sufficient to justify mine, and I might say something more upon it, but perhaps it would be too abstruse for this present dispute. And I believe reasonable and impartial men will grant me that having forced an adversary to deny that principle is reducing him *ad absurdum*.

---

454. Newton's *Mathematical Principles* was published in 1687, 29 years before this letter.

Appendixes

The following are textual notes, by page and line numbers; their positions are indicated by asterisks (*) in the texts.

Preface to a Universal Characteristic

p. 6, l. 30: Reading '*cerebro*' for '*crebro*'.

Samples of the Numerical Characteristic

p. 14, l. 25: Reading '5' for '11'.
p. 16, l. note 26: Reading '*omnis*' for '*omnia*'.

On Freedom and Possibility

p. 21, l. 37: Reading '*aequales*' for '*majus*'.

On Contingency

p. 29, l. 41: Reading '*aliquando*' for '*aliquanto*'.

Primary Truths

p. 34, l. 5: Reading '*sortiatur*' for '*sortiantur*'.

Discourse on Metaphysics

p. 48, l. 28: Reading '*perfection*' for '*perception*' in LD.

From the Letters to Arnauld

p. 76, l. 23: Reading '*ses*' for '*ces*'.
p. 78, l. 37: Reading '*les ames des brutes*,' for '*les ames brutes*', following R-L.
p. 81, l. 6: Reading '*l'atome*' for '*l'Homme*', following R-L.
p. 81, l. 11: Reading '*marques*' for '*effets*', following R-L.
p. 85, l. 4: Reading '*suite*' for '*sorte*', following R-L.
p. 86, l. 35: Reading '*formes*' for '*termes*', following R-L.
p. 87, l. 25: Reading '*représentative*' for '*représentation*', following R-L.
p. 87, l. 31: Reading '*entrepretent*' for '*entrepriment*', following R-L.
p. 88, l. 16: Reading '*monde de petites*' for '*monde et de petites*', following R-L.
p. 90, l. 17: Reading '*parélies*' for '*parties*', following R-L.

On Freedom

p. 95, l. 23: Reading *'intricari'* for *'inextricari'*, following Descartes, *Principles* I 40.
p. 96, l. 20: Reading *'seu'* for *'sen.'*
p. 97, l. 2: Grammatical number altered in this sentence for consistency.
p. 97, l. 33: Reading *'proportiones'* for *'propositions'*.
p. 97, l. 43: Reading *'accedente'* for *'accidente'*.

Preface to the Dynamics

p. 108, l. 12: Reading '$_1$B' for 'B.'
p. 109, l. 6: Reading '$_3$BM' for '$_3$BN.'
p. 109, l. 36: Reading '$_1$C$_1$G' for '$_1$C$_1$B.'.
p. 109, l. 39: Reading '$_3$C3A' for '$_3$B$_3$A.'
p. 110, l. 5: Reading *'major'* for *'minor'*.

Dialogue on Human Freedom and the Origin of Evil

p. 115, l. 34: Reading *'exprimer'* for *'expliquer'*.
p. 116, l. 34: Reading *'tirer'* for *'dire.'*

A Specimen of Dynamics

p. 123, l. 19: Reading *'quod nobis constat'* for *'quod constat'*, following the ms.
p. 129, l. 24: Reading '$_2$C' for 'C'
p. 137, l. 24: Reading *'excusso'* for *'excussa'*.

On the Ultimate Origination of Things

p. 150, l. 3: Reading *'contraria implicet contradictionem'* for *'contraria implicet'*.
p. 150, l. 28: Reading *'existentiam'* for *'essentiam'*.

On Nature Itself

p. 156, l. 33: Reading *'propius'* for *'proprius'*, following the original publication.
p. 159, l. 16: Reading *'consequentur'*, for *'consequenter'*, following the original publication.
p. 166, l. 6: Reading *'suspicor'* for *'suspicer'*.

From the Letters to de Volder

p. 176, l. 22: Reading *'primitiva'* for *'primitivis'*.

To Queen Sophie Charlotte of Prussia, On What Is Independent of Sense and Matter

p. 188, l. 41: Reading 'exempte' for 'exemple'.

From the Letters to Des Bosses

p. 200, l. 32: Reading *'solet'* for *'solent'*.
p. 201, l. 30: Reading *'a loco'* for *'loco'*.
p. 204, l. 20: Reading *'composita'* for *'composisti'*.
p. 204, l. 27: Reading *'adest'* for *'abest'*.
p. 205, l. 22: Reading *'nunc'* for *'tunc'*.

Letter to Samuel Masson, on Body

p. 228, l. 27: Reading *'continuité'* for *'continuation.'*
p. 229, l. 9: Reading *'la'* for *'sa'*.

From the Letters to Wolff

p. 232, l. 37: Reading *'quam'* for *'quae'*.

On the Nature of Body and the Laws of Motion

p. 248, l. 3: Reading '$_1A_2A$' for '$_1A_2B$'
p. 249, l. 6: Reading 'habent' for 'babent'.

On Body and Force, Against the Cartesians

p. 253, l. 14: Reading *'obnoxias'* for *'obnoxia'*.
p. 256, l. 29: Reading *'limitis'* for *'limitatis'*.

Comments on Spinoza's Philosophy

p. 279, l. 1: Reading *'dicto loco'* for 'd. 1.'
p. 279, l. 9: Reading *'idem'* for *'idea'*.

From the Letters to Thomas Burnett, on Substance

p. 288, l. 15: Reading '2' for '4'.

Against Barbaric Physics

p. 317, l. 3: Reading *'causas'* for *'causis'*.
p. 317, l. 34: Reading *'qui stabiliverant'* for *'stabiliverant'*.
p. 318, l. 3: Reading *'attractivis'* for *'attractive'*.

Brief Biographies of Some
Contemporaries of Leibniz

ARNAULD, Antoine (1612–94), was a philosopher and mathematician, though primarily a theologian (associated with the Jansenist movement). He was first a critic of Cartesian philosophy, writing the "Fourth Set of Objections" to Descartes's *Meditations* (1641), but later he became one of its proponents. He carried on a significant philosophical correspondence with most of the principal thinkers of the seventeenth century. His main works include the Port-Royal *Logique* (with Pierre Nicole—1662) and *Des vraies et des fausses idées* (1683), a work dealing with Malebranche's thought, which set off a lengthy and important controversy.

AVERROISTS were followers of Averroes (Ibn Ruschd, 1126–98), who held that the active intellect in each individual human soul is part of a single active intellect to which one is reunited in death.

BARBARUS, Hermolaeus (1454–93), was an Italian scholar who attempted, through retranslations of Aristotle, to recover Aristotle's original doctrine from under the layers of Scholastic interpretations. His works include popular compendia of ethics and natural philosophy, drawn from the writings of Aristotle.

BARON, Vincent (1607–74), was a theologian who wrote a book on the Augustinian and Thomist doctrines on divine and free will, *Sanctorum Augustini et Thomae vera et una mens de libertate humana* (Paris, 1666), also published as vol. 3 of his *Theologia Moralis, adversus laxioress probabilistas* (Paris, 1665–66).

BASNAGE DE BEAUVAL, Henri (1656–1710), was the editor of the *Histoire des Ouvrages des Sçavans* (1687–1709); he also published some tracts on religious tolerance.

BAYLE, Pierre (1647–1706), was the editor and founder of the *Nouvelles de la République des Lettres*, a review of new books, in which frequent reference to Leibniz's works could be found. In 1695–96, he published the *Dictionaire Historique et Critique*, a precursor to the encyclopaedist movement of the eighteenth century. The *Dictionary* was extremely influential.

BEAUNE, Florimond de (1601–52), was a mathematician and correspondent of Descartes; his *De aequationum natura* . . . was published posthumously in 1659.

BENTLEY, Richard (1662–1742), was a classicist and theologian, and one of the early appreciators of Locke and Newton. He was the author of *Matter and Motion Cannot Think* (1692), and *A Confutation of Atheism* (1693), delivered as one of the Boyle lectures.

BERKELEY, George (1685–1753), was a philosopher and critic of seventeenth-century science and mathematics. He published one of his most important works, *A Treatise Concerning the Principles of Human Knowledge*, while a young man, in 1710. Also significant are *An Essay Toward a New Theory of Vision* (1709) and *Three Dialogues Between Hylas and Philonous* (1713).

BERNOULLI, Johann (1667–1748), was a mathematician and physicist. He published little during his lifetime but maintained an extensive correspondence with many scholars; both he and his brother Jakob (1654–1705) corresponded with Leibniz.

BÖHME, Jacob (1575–1624), was a German mystical theologian and philosopher.

BONARTES, Thomas (fl. 1665), was a natural philosopher and theologian, the author of *Concordia scientia cum fide* . . . (1665).

BORELLI, Giovanni Alphonso (1608–79), was an astronomer, mathematician, and physiologist. He was a prolific writer, publishing many tracts, among which were *Theoricae mediceorum planetarum ex causis physicis deductae* (1666), *De vi percussionis liber* (1667), and a posthumous *De motu animalium*, 2 vols. (1680–81).

BOYLE, Robert (1627–91), was a physicist and chemist, a prolific author whose main contributions were researches on the elasticity of the air and the air pump. Moreover, he was instrumental in the popularization of experimental science and the corpuscular theory, against the natural philosophy of Aristotle and Scholasticism. Among his works were *New experiments physico-mechanical, touching the spring of air* . . . (1660), *The Sceptical Chymist* (1661), and *The origine of forms and qualities* . . . (1666).

BRAHE, Tycho de (1546–1601), an observational astronomer who proposed a hybrid geocentric astronomical system, as a solution to problems connected with the ancient geocentric systems. His main works were the *De mundi aetheri recentionibus phaenomenis* . . . (1588); his collected letters, . . . *Epistolarum astronomicum libri* (1596); and the *Astronomiae instauratae progymnasmata* (1588).

BURNETT, Thomas (1656–1729), Scottish lawyer, known as Burnett of Kemnay. He was well received in intellectual circles both in England and on the Continent, and thus was in an ideal position to act as an intermediary between Leibniz and Locke.

CAMPANELLA, Thommaso (1568–1639), was a natural philosopher, an advocate of powers or active principles in nature. He was the author of several works, including *De sensu Rerum et Magia libros quattuor* (1620) and an . . . *Apologia pro Galileo, mathematico Florentino* (1622).

CASSINI, Gian Domenico (1625–1712), was a experimental astronomer. His *Découverte de deux nouvelles planetes autour de Saturne* was published in 1673. Many of his publications were collected in *Recueil d'observations* . . . (1693).

CHALES, Claudius de (1621–1678), was a physicist, technologist, and mathematician. He published his *Traitté du mouvement local, et du ressort* . . . in 1682. He also published some works on the arts of fortification and navigation, and a textbook on Euclid's *Elements*.

CLARKE, Samuel (1675–1729), was a friend and disciple of Newton's. He is best known for his exchange of letters with Leibniz, which he translated into

English and published in 1717. He also translated a number of scientific works into Latin—Newton's *Opticks* (1706), among others.

CLAVIUS, Christoph (1537–1612), was a Jesuit mathematician and Professor at the Collegio Romano. He is known for his reform of the Jesuit curriculum, arguing for the importance of mathematics. He wrote a commentary on the *Sphere* of Sacro Bosco (1570) and an *Algebra* (1609).

CLERSELIER, Claude (1614–84), was the editor of Descartes's literary remains; he published the *Lettres de Descartes*, 3 vols. (1657–67).

CORDEMOY, Géraud de (d. 1684), was a Cartesian and occasionalist who adopted an atomic theory; his most important philosophical work, *Le discernement de l' âme et du corps*, was published in 1666.

COSTE, Pierre (1668–1747), was the French translator of English philosophical works, including John Locke's *Essay* in 1700. He corresponded with Leibniz and acted as a channel between Leibniz and Locke.

DES BOSSES, Bartholomaeus (1668–1728), was a Jesuit theologian and mathematician, one of Leibniz's correspondents; he published a collection of his letters in 1716.

DESCARTES, René (1596–1650). It would be difficult to overstate the importance of Descartes's work for any aspect of seventeenth-century intellectual life: for mathematics and optics—the *Geometry, Optics,* and *Meteorology,* the essays appended to his *Discourse on Method* (1637); for natural philosophy, biology, and geology—the *Principles of Philosophy,* Parts II, III, and IV (1644); for metaphysics, epistemology, and philosophical psychology—the aforementioned *Discourse,* the *Meditations on First Philosophy* (1641), and the *Passions of the Soul* (1648).

DIGBY, Kenelm (1603–65), was a natural philosopher, the author of *Two treatises. In the one of which, the nature of bodies; in the other, the nature of mans soule . . .* (1644). Some of his experimental work was published posthumously as *Choice and Experimental Receipts in Physick and Chirurgery* (1668) and *A choice collection of rare chymical secrets and experiments in philosophy* (1682).

FABRI, Honoratus (1607–88), was a Jesuit natural philosopher and mathematician. Among his physical works were a *tractatus physicus de motu locali . . .* (1646) and a *physica* (1669).

FERMAT, Pierre de (1601–65), was a mathematician. He did not write for publication, but he maintained an extensive correspondence with friends to whom he would send manuscripts. Probably his most important unpublished manuscript was the "Ad locos pianos et solidos isagoge" of 1636, in which he developed analytic geometry.

FLUDD, Robert (1574–1637), was a follower of Paracelsus who maintained, in his *Philosophica Mosaica* (1638), that the true philosophy has been revealed by Moses and could be extracted from the Old Testament, especially the Pentateuch.

FONTENELLE, Bernard de (1657–1757), was secretary of the Paris Académie des Sciences, from 1699 to 1741; he published the *Conversations on the Plurality of Worlds* in 1686.

FOUCHER, Simon (1644–97), was a philosophical skeptic who tried to restore the teachings of the later Academics. His principal work was a critique of Malebranche, the *Critique de la Recherche de la Vérité* (1675). Leibniz corresponded with Foucher between 1675 and 1695.

GALILEI, Galileo (1564–1642), was one of the great natural philosophers of the seventeenth century. His principal works were the *Starry Messenger* (1610), the *Dialogue Concerning the Two Chief World Systems* (1632), and the *Two New Sciences* (1638).

GASSENDI, Pierre (1592–1655), was a philosopher, astronomer, and humanist. He defended the atomistic doctrines of Epicurus and attempted to adapt them to modern (and Christian) thought. His most important work was the voluminous *Syntagma philosophicum*, volumes I and II of the *Opera Omnia* of 1658, which was best known through François Bernier's *Abrégé de la philosophie de Mr Gassendi* (1684).

GILBERT, William (1544–1603), was an English physician and experimentalist whose investigation of magnetic phenomena, *De Magnete . . .* , was published in 1600.

GREW, Nehemiah (1641–1712), was a naturalist who wrote a number of treatises in plant morphology and plant anatomy. However, his most important treatise was the religious and philosophical *Cosmologia sacra: or a discourse of the universe as it is the creature and kingdom of God* (1701).

GUERICKE, Otto von (1602–86), was an experimental physicist, the inventor of the air pump; he published an account of his experiments, *Expérimenta nova (ut vocantur) magdeburgica de vacuo spatio*, in 1672.

HARTSOEKER, Nicholas (1656–1725), was an early microscopist and correspondent of Leibniz's. He published an *Essai de dioptrique* in 1694, in which he developed an atomic theory. His physical work included the *Principes de physique* (1696), *Conjectures physiques* (1708), and *Eclaircissements sur les conjectures physiques* (1710).

HARVEY, William (1578–1657), was the discoverer of the circulation of the blood. He published the *Exercitatio anatomica de motu cordis et sanguinis in animalibus* in 1628 and its English translation, the *Two anatomical exercitations concerning the circulation of the blood*, in 1653. Also significant (and translated into English in 1653) were the *Exercitatio anatomica de circulatione sanguinis* (1649) and the *Exercitationes de generatione animalium* (1651).

HELMONT, Francis Mercurius von (1614–98), was an alchemist who believed in the transmigration of souls. He was the son of Johannes von Helmont (1579–1644), whose work he edited—*Ortus medicinae* (1648). He became known through his collaboration with Knorr von Rosenroth on the *Kabbala denudata* (1677–84). In 1697, with Leibniz's help, he published two volumes, including some essays on various religious topics to which Leibniz himself may have contributed.

HOBBES, Thomas (1588–1679), was an English philosopher and mathematician. By Leibniz's own account, Hobbes was a great influence on him in his early years. Hobbes's most important works are the *Leviathan* (1651) and the *De corpore* (1655).

HUYGENS, Christiaan (1629–95), was a mathematician, physicist, and astronomer, who corresponded with Leibniz. Of his numerous works, the most important is the *Traité de la lumière* . . . (1690); also significant are *Horologium oscillatorium* . . . (1673) and the *De terris coelestibus* . . . (1698).

JUNGIUS, Joachim (1587–1657), was a physicist, astronomer, logician, and mathematician. Much of his work has been lost, including treatises on arithmetic and geometry (for example, *Geometria numerosa* and *Mathemasis specialis*) and physics (*Phoranomica*). Some of the more important works he published during his lifetime include . . . *Dialectica* . . . (1613), *Geometrica empirica* (1627), and *Logica Hamburgensis* (1638).

JURIEU, Pierre (1637–1713), was a Protestant theologian. In 1683 he published his *Abrégé de l' histoire du Concile de Trente* . . . , appended to which was a discourse arguing that Protestants are not required to follow the Council of Trent.

KEPLER, Johann (1571–1630), was an experimental astronomer and optical theorist. Kepler was a defender of the Copernican heliocentric system; his most important works are the *Mysterium Cosmographicum* (1596), *Astronomia nova* (1609), and *Harmonice mundi* (1619).

LEEUWENHOEK, Antoni van (1632–1723), was an early microscopist and maker of instruments. He published the *Arcana naturae* . . . (1695) and *Continuatio Arcanorum naturae detectorum* . . . (1697).

LINUS, Franciscus (1595–1675), was an Aristotelian natural philosopher. His *Tractatus de corporum inseparabilitate* . . . (1661) was directed against Robert Boyle's experimental work on the air pump.

LOCKE, John (1632–1704), was an English philosopher whose fame rests mainly on his *Essay Concerning Human Understanding* (1690) and *Two Treatises on Government* (1690). The *Essay* underwent numerous stages: early manuscripts are dated 1671; the manuscript seems to have reached final form by 1686; Locke published a summary of it in France in 1688; there were editions with substantial revisions in 1690, 1694, 1695, 1700, and posthumously in 1706. Coste's French translation was published in 1700, and a Latin translation, in 1701.

LOUBÈRE, Simon de la (1642–1729), was sent to Siam in order to establish diplomatic and commercial relations with France; as a result of his stay, he published an account of the history, institutions, and customs of Siam, *Du Royaume de Siam* (1691).

MALEBRANCHE, Nicholas (1638–1715), the great Cartesian and exponent of occasionalism, is best known for his *Search after Truth*, published in 1674; also significant are the *Traité de la nature et de la grace* (1680), *Méditations chrétiennes* (1683), *Dialogues on Metaphysics* (1688), and *Traité des lois de la communication des mouvements* (1692).

MALPIGHI, Marcello (1628–94), was an early microscopist. Among his works is an *Anatomes plantarum* (1675–79).

MARCI, Marcus (1595–1667), was an advocate of powers or active principles in nature, author of *Philosophia vetus restituta* (1662).

MARIOTTE, Edmé (ca. 1620–84), was an experimental physicist and mathematician. Among his numerous works are a *Traité de la percussion ou choc des corps* (1673) and a *Traité du mouvement des eaux et des autres corps fluides* (1686).

MASHAM, Lady Damaris (1658–1708), was a correspondent of Leibniz's. She maintained an important circle of philosophers, scientists, and theologians. Locke lived at her house during the final years of his life. Coste was her son's tutor.

MERSENNE, Marin (1588–1648), a Minim Friar, was an important intellectual figure in the first half of the seventeenth century. He published many works, . . . *Cogitata physico mathematica* (1644), for example, and translated two volumes of Galileo from Italian into French, but he is best known for the extensive correspondence he conducted with most of the main figures of the day, especially with Descartes.

MOLINA, Louis de (1535–1600). Molina was a Spanish Jesuit who is best known for his views on human freedom and grace. Molina argued that, though God has perfect foreknowledge, humans are nonetheless capable of free action, that God's foreknowledge of what we do freely is simply knowledge of what we will do, not knowledge of what God himself willed to create. Molina's principal work is his *Liberi arbitrii cum gratiae donis, divina praescientia, providentia, praedestinatione et reprobatione concordia* (Lisbon, 1588), known as the *Concordia*. The debate between Molina and his followers and the Thomists, who argued that God foreknows what free actions we will perform by simply knowing what he willed to create, continued long after Molina's death.

MOLYNEUX, William (1656–98), was a philosopher and physicist. He was a friend of John Locke's and the English translator of Descartes's *Meditations*; his *Dioptrica nova* (1692) summarized and commended Leibniz's theory of the refraction of light.

MORE, Henry (1614–87), was a philosopher and theologian—a Cambridge Platonist—who corresponded with Descartes. He published *Immortality of the Soul* in 1659 and *Enchiridion Metaphysicum* in 1671.

NEWTON, Isaac (1642–1727), was probably the greatest natural philosopher of his age. His most important works were the *Mathematical Principles of Natural Philosophy* (1687) and the *Opticks* (1704).

OLDENBURG, Henry (ca. 1620–77), was a founding member of the Royal Society and one of its two secretaries; he founded and edited the Royal Society's *Philosophical Transactions*. He maintained a voluminous correspondence with scholars and scientists throughout Europe, playing a role in London similar to that Mersenne played in Paris.

PAPIN, Denis (1647–1712), was a technologist. He constructed an air pump and performed experiments under the direction of Christiaan Huygens— published as *Nouvelles experiences du vuide* (1674).

PARDIES, Ignatius Baptista (1636–73), was a Jesuit natural philosopher and mathematician. He published his most important work, the *Discours de la connoisance des Bestes*, in 1672.

PASCAL, Blaise, Blaise (1623–62), was a philosopher and theologian. During his brief life he published a number of mathematical and physical treatises, but he is best known for his posthumously published philosophical and religious *Pensées*.

QUIETISTS were followers of Miguel de Molinos (ca. 1640–97) and others who stressed passive contemplation and complete resignation to the will of God.

RAY, John (1627–1705), was a naturalistic theologian who wrote *The wisdom of God manifested in the works of creation* (1691), also *Historia plantarum . . .* (1686–1704).

RÉGIS, Pierre Sylvain (1656–1726), was a Cartesian physicist, the author of *Cours entier de philosophie ou système général d'après les principes de Descartes* (1691).

ROBERVAL, Gilles Personne de (1602–75), was a mathematician who published little during his lifetime but who was very influential in the seventeenth century, in part because of his extensive correspondence.

SCALIGER, Julius Caesar (1484–1558), was a Renaissance scholar, a translator of Greek and Latin works, and the author of a Latin grammar.

SCHELHAMMER, Günther Christopher (1649–1716), was a natural philosopher and physician, the author of *Natura sibi et medicis vindicata sive de natura liber bipartitus* (1697).

SENNERT, Daniel (1572–1637), was a chemist and physician. His main work was *Epitome naturalis scientae* (1618).

SNELL, Willebrord (1581–1626), was a naturalist, physicist, and optical theorist who published . . . *De re nummaria liber singularis* (1613), a work on money, and . . . *Tiphus batavus, sive histiodromice, de navium cursibus, et re navali* (1624), some lessons on navigation. His best-known discovery, of the laws of the refraction of light, was probably formulated in 1621 and described in a now lost manuscript.

SPINOZA, Baruch (1632–77), was a philosopher. He published little during his lifetime, but his posthumously published *Ethics* was extremely important and provocative.

STENO, Nicholas (1638–86), was a naturalist and geologist whose main work was the influential *De solido intra solidum naturaliter contento dissertationis prodromus* (1669), translated into English as the *Prodromus* (1671).

STEVIN, Simon (1548–1620), was a Dutch thinker who wrote widely in mathematics, mechanics, astronomy, engineering, and many other areas. His works were posthumously translated into French and were widely available as *Oeuvres mathematiques* (1634).

STILLINGFLEET, Edward (1635–99), Bishop of Worcester, attacked Locke's *Essay*, in his *Discourse on the Vindication of the Trinity* (1696); Locke defended himself in a *Letter* (1697), eliciting a reply from Stillingfleet (1697), thereby eliciting a further defense from Locke—*Reply to Worcester's Answer . . . to His Letter* (1697)—these were followed by another reply from Stillingfleet (1698) and Locke's *Reply to . . . Worcester's Answer to His Second Letter* (1699).

STURM, Johann Christopher (1635–1703), was a natural philosopher who published numerous tracts on natural phenomena, such as the nature of comets and tides. His works prompted Leibniz to consider the concept of nature. He published *Idolum naturae . . . sive naturae agentis . . . conceptibus dissertatio* (1692), *Physica electiva sive hypothetica* (1697), and *Physica eclectica* (1698).

SWAMMERDAM, John (1637–80), was an early microscopist. He published *Historia insectorum generalis . . .* (1669).

TELESIO, Bernadino (1509–88), was a natural philosopher. An anti-Aristotelian, he published the *De rerum natura iuxta propria principia* (1565).

TOLAND, John (1670–1722), was an English freethinker and pamphleteer, the author of the very controversial *Christianity Not Mysterious* (1696). Toland visited the court of Hanover in 1701, where he met Leibniz and Queen Sophie Charlotte, with whom he maintained contact.

TORRICELLI, Evangelista (1608–47), was a student of Galileo's and the inventor of the barometer. He published his *Opera geometrica* in 1644. His most important work was the *Lezione accademiche* (1715?).

VIÈTE, François (1540–1603), was a lawyer and mathematician, the author of an *Algebra* (1636) and the rediscoverer of much ancient mathematics.

VOLDER, Burchardus de (1643–1709), was a natural philosopher and physician, one of Leibniz's correspondents. He wrote a number of minor tracts on respiration, the motion of the earth, and the weight of air.

WORSTIUS, Conrad von dem (1559–1622), was a natural philosopher, the author of *Tractatus theologicus de Deo* (1610).

WACHTER, Johann Georg (1673–1757), was a Spinozist; he wrote the *Elucidarius cabalisticus, sive Reconditae Hebraeorum succincta recensio* (Rome, 1706). He also wrote *Der Spinozismus im Jüdenthumb . . .* (1699).

WALLIS, John (1616–1703), was a physicist and mathematician. He published *A discourse of gravity and gravitation . . .* (1675), *A treatise of algebra . . .* (1685), and *. . . Opera Mathematica . . .* (1693–99).

WHITE, Thomas (1593–1676), was a natural philosopher and theologian, the author of the *De mundo dialogi tres* (1643).

WREN, Christopher (1632–1723), was a mathematician and architect. He published some essays in the *Philosophical Transactions of the Royal Society*.

This index is largely limited to Leibniz's text. It was prepared with the help of Rachana Kamtekar.